Comparative and International Criminal Justice Systems

Second Edition

Comparative and International Criminal Justice Systems: Policing, Judiciary, and Corrections

Second Edition

by

Obi N. Ignatius Ebbe

Butterworth–Heinemann
Boston Oxford Auckland Johannesburg Melbourne New Delhi

Library of Congress Cataloging-in-Publication Data

Comparative and international criminal justice systems : policing, judiciary, and corrections / edited by Obi N. Ignatius Ebbe.

     p. cm.
  Includes bibliographical references and index.
  ISBN 0-7506-7197-1 (alk. paper)
     1. Criminal justice, Administration of I. Ebbe, Obi N. Ignatius.

HV7419.C65 2000
364—dc21   99-049840

British Library Cataloging-in-Publication Data
A catalogue record for this book is available from the British Library.

The publisher offers special discounts on bulk orders of this book.
For information, please contact:
Manager of Special Sales
Butterworth–Heinemann
225 Wildwood Avenue
Woburn, MA 01801–2041
Tel: 781-904-2500
Fax: 781-904-2620

For information on all Butterworth-Heinemann publications available, contact our World Wide Web home page at:
http://www.bh.com

10 9 8 7 6 5 4 3 2 1

Printed in the United States of America

Dedicated to my mother, Virginia Uduola Ebbe
and my daughter, Nneka Ndidiamaka Ijeoma Ebbe

Contents

CHAPTER 6 / THE CRIMINAL JUSTICE SYSTEM OF SIERRA LEONE   91

Bankole Thompson

CHAPTER 7 / AN OVERVIEW OF THE CRIMINAL JUSTICE SYSTEM IN HONG KONG   113

T. Wing Lo

CHAPTER 10 / POLICING AND PUBLIC DISORDER IN THE UNITED KINGDOM   157

Michael Bullock

CHAPTER 11 / THE POLICE SYSTEM IN THE PEOPLE'S REPUBLIC OF CHINA   171

Zheng Wang

Contributors

Obi N. I. Ebbe, Ph.D.
Department of Criminal Justice
State University of New York
College at Brockport
Brockport, NY 14420

Mary Clifford, Ph.D.
Department of Criminal Justice
St. Cloud State University
720 4th Avenue South
St. Cloud, MN 56301-4498

Ian K. McKenzie, Ph.D.
University of Portsmouth
Institute of Police and Criminological
  Studies
2 Kings Terrace
Southsea
Portsmouth, U.K.

Michael Bullock
Gloucestershire Constabulary
6 Wessex Drive Cheltenham
Gloucestershire GL 5 25 AU, U.K.

Zelma W. Henriques, PhD.
Law, Police Science and Criminal Jus-
  tice
John Jay College of Criminal Justice
The City University of New York
899 Tenth Avenue
New York, NY 10019

John A. Arthur, Ph.D.
Department of Sociology and Anthropol-
  ogy
University of Minnesota
Duluth, MN 55811

Paul Douglas O'Mahony, Ph.D.
Department of Psychology

University of Dublin
Trinity College
Dublin, Republic of Ireland

Ruben G. Ruiz de Olano, Esq.
Criminal Law Researcher
Cordoba National University
Cordoba, Argentina

Maria R. Haberfeld, Ph.D.
Department of Law, Police Science and
  Criminal Justice Administration
John Jay College of Criminal Justice
The City University of New York
899 Tenth Avenue
New York, NY 10019

Sergio Herzog, Ph.D.
The Hebrew University
Faculty of Law, Institute of Criminology
Mt. Scopus, Jerusalem
Israel

Bankole Thompson, Ph.D.
Department of Police Studies
Eastern Kentucky University
Richmond, KY 40475

Yingyi Situ, Ph.D.
Criminal Justice Program
Richard Stockton College of New Jersey
Pomona, NJ 08240

Weizheng Liu, Ph.D.
Criminal Justice Department
Monmouth College
West Long Branch, NJ 07764

Robert Davidson, Ph.D.
Northern Michigan University
Criminal Justice Department

Greis Hall
Marquette, MI 49855

John Z. Wang, Ph.D.
Department of Criminal Justice
California State University—Long Beach
1250 Bellflower Blvd.
Long Beach, CA 90840

Elmer H. Johnson, Ph.D.
Distinguished Professor Emeritus

Southern Illinois University at Carbondale
Carbondale, IL 62901

T. Wing Lo, Ph.D.
Department of Applied Social Studies
City University of Hong Kong
Tat Chee Avenue
Kowtoon, Hong Kong

Preface to Second Edition

Spanning the globe of continents and nations from the West to the East, observing the policing, judicial, and penological models of different countries, the tourist is amazed by the ingenious dynamics in the construction and execution of criminal justice among nations. This second edition of Comparative and International Criminal Justice Systems takes you on this amazing journey.

This edition has more comparative and contrasting features than the first edition. The first edition covered eight countries and one region; this second edition covers twelve countries and one region. The four countries added are Ireland (Europe), Israel (Middle East), Hong Kong (Asia), and Argentina (South America). These four countries are added because of their historical evolution, which affected their present criminal justice systems. Such evolutionary histories have much to tell scholars and students about the nature of law and justice. Additionally, the enormous interest in the study of comparative criminal justice systems in recent years calls for expansion of the first edition by including more comparative and contrasting systems. Furthermore, in this edition, we have developed more comprehensive review questions at the end of each chapter, than the first edition.

The structure of this edition is different from the first. This edition is topically organized and not by continents as in the first edition. This is done to help professors and students to easily find the topic they are looking for in the book.

This edition is divided into six parts. Part I is "Comparative and International Criminal Justice." This part answers the question, "Why do we have to study the criminal justice systems of other countries or cultures?" Part II is "Overview of Criminal Justice Systems and Policy." This part presents seven chapters involving the criminal justice systems of the United States of America, Ireland, Israel, Argentina, Sierra Leone, Hong Kong, and China, in that order. The United States system of criminal justice is presented ahead of others because it is the point of comparison. The other countries follow in a comparative and contrasting order. Part III is "Comparative Policing." In this part we have policing in the United Kingdom and China. There are two chapters on policing in the United Kingdom. Part IV is "Comparative Judicial Systems." This part presents the judiciary and criminal procedure in Nigeria and the court system in China. Part V is "Comparative Corrections." In this part we have corrections in Japan (Chapters 14 and 15), West African regions (Chapter 16), and treatment of offenders in Denmark and Brazil (Chapter 17). The last part, Part VI, is "Synthesis of the Criminal Justice Systems." This chapter makes an in-depth critique of the whole criminal justice systems in the light of criminal justice system in the United States.

This second edition is by far stronger and better than the first edition, because this edition studies more countries, adds more chapters (including the synthesizing chapter), and is more topically structured than the first edition.

This book is intended for both undergraduate and graduate students in criminal justice, criminology, law, political science, and sociology. Students will see similarities and dissimilarities in the criminal justice systems among nations and can observe how their own country's system of justice compares and contrasts with other systems. Although there are many disturbing operating approaches in the policing, judiciary, and correctional sectors of various nations, there are many good systems of justice to be copied from among the nations.

Preface to the
First Edition

Comparisons, an adage has it, are odious; but this is not the case in Comparative Criminal Justice Systems. Reading this book, you will find that in the criminal justice system of some nations, normative standards and punitive measures emanate from traditional religions. However, in the process of time, industrialized and nonindustrialized nations in their march to civilization learned various aspects of criminal justice from each other. The following scholarly essays describe diverse justice systems that provoke tears of pain and smiles of joy.

Socio-cultural philosophies of a society set the tone for its reaction to the deviant. Whether you approve or disapprove of a justice system of a country, do not forget the cultural significance of the system to the people involved. The American social philosophy says, "Do your own thing and go your own way." The intolerance for social control in this individualistic philosophy has weakened the reintegration model of corrections in the American criminal justice system. One might weigh the American social philosophy against the Japanese, which says: "Find your own group and belong to it. You and your group will rise or sink together. Without belonging you will be lost in the wilderness. Apart from dependence there is no human happiness" (Ozaki, 1978:183 cited in Elmer H. Johnson, Chapter 14: "Guided Change in Japan: Correctional Association Prison Industrial Cooperative [CAPIC] and Prison Industry"). The humane Japanese approach to policing and correction reflects Japanese social philosophy. Certainly, such philosophy influences a society's attitudes toward offenders; this is evident in all of the eight countries and regions studied in this text.

Every topical study presented in this book is in its original form. The scholarly analyses and the comparative structure of the text will be particularly useful for courses in comparative and international criminal justice and criminology. Only in this book are criminal justice systems of all major continents (Africa, Asia, Europe, and the Americas) represented. Policing, judiciary, and corrections in industrialized and nonindustrialized countries are presented side by side, giving faculty, students, and practitioners diverse perspectives from which to compare and contrast the characteristics and changes in criminal justice systems today.

This text can be useful to undergraduate and graduate students in criminal justice and criminology, enabling them to compare and contrast their own systems of justice with those of other countries. It will also help clarify why some countries copied the policing and correctional methods of others. It can be used as the major text in comparative criminal justice courses, or as a supplement to other texts.

There are four sections in this book. Section I deals with the nature of comparative and international criminal justice. Section II treats America and Europe, Section III Africa, and Section IV Asia. Countries studied include Brazil, China, Denmark, Japan, Nigeria, Sierra Leone, the United Kingdom, and the United States. There is a regional chapter on West Africa.

The first section includes an essay on "The Purpose of Comparative and International Criminal Justice Systems," provided in order to answer an important question: given differences in customs, traditions, standards, values, and criminal law across cultures, why should we study comparative criminal justice systems? It is hoped that this essay will provide a convincing answer, and also arm the student and the instructor with knowledge to comprehend the diverse systems presented in subsequent sections.

After justifying the need for the study of comparative and international criminal justice systems in Section I, American and European criminal justice are analyzed in Section II, thus forming grounds for comparing them to the criminal justice systems of African and Asian countries, described in Sections III and IV, respectively. The criminal justice system of the United States is the first presented in this section and in this book, because most of the students and instructors using this book will be in the United States. Starting from the known and proceeding to the unknown will make comparisons and contrasts flow more smoothly.

Europe and America are presented in the same section because of the profound affinity between European laws and American laws; indeed, English law formed the basis of American law.

Section III, on Africa, is presented just after America and Europe, because the laws of the African countries studied are also based on English law, as the countries are former British colonies. The United States, Great Britain, and the African countries studied belong to the English common law tradition.

The last section, on Asia, is presented after Africa because African and Asian countries have many common cultural beliefs and standards. Both the African and the Asian countries presented in this book use village councils and lay judges in their criminal justice systems; both also hold entire communities or villages responsible for the crimes committed within a community or by village members; and both have dual systems of criminal justice—formal and informal.

The chapters have been arranged in a logical order, with those dealing with a complete criminal justice system preceding those dealing with an agency of the system at issue. Chapters dealing with policing, therefore, come before chapters on courts, and chapters on courts before chapters on correction.

I have developed discussion and revision questions at the end of each chapter to help both student and instructor in their readings. Also, at the end of the text, I have developed a glossary of terms used in various chapters, including foreign terms. Teachers have additional recourse to the accompanying instructor's manual and test bank, which I developed based on my thorough study of the chapters.

This is the first book of readings ever published in comparative and international criminal justice systems. My profound regards to the late Harold Smith, of the OICJ at the University of Illinois at Chicago, who encouraged me, in 1988 during the Academy of Criminal Justice Sciences (ACJS) annual meeting in San Francisco, California, to compose a book of this nature. Also, my thanks to all the international contributors who submitted articles (both those whose papers fit and those whose papers did not fit the focus of this book), for without their interest, getting a book of this nature together would have been a wild goose chase. I am also highly indebted to the following reviewers whose suggestions helped enormously: Robert McCormack, Trenton State College, Gregg Barak, Eastern Michigan University, and Liqun Cao, Eastern Michigan University.

I am also very much obliged to Laurel DeWolf and her associates at Butterworth-Heinemann Publishers for their interest in this topic. Finally, I say gracia to the Director of Document Preparation at the State

University of New York at Brockport, Jeanne Saraceni and her team of keyboard specialists.

While every contributor is responsible for the facts and figures presented in each chapter, I am entirely responsible for any editorial inadequacies.

Obi N. I. Ebbe, Ph.D.
State University of New York,
College at Brockport
May 1995

Acknowledgments

This book would not have taken the shape it has without the contributors. I am very much obliged to them. My thanks also go to the following reviewers whose suggestions gave this edition its wonderful structure: Debra Heath-Thornton of Roberts Wesleyan College, Rochester, New York, Barbara Lavin of Marist College, Roger McNally of the State University of New York College at Brockport, and Bob Walsh of the University of Houston-Downtown.

Last, but not the least, my profound thanks to Distinguished Professor Emeritus Don MacNamara of John Jay College of Criminal Justice, who wrote me in April 1996 after seeing the first edition of this book at the ACJS meeting in Las Vegas, and requested to write on Israel, Ireland, and Singapore for the second edition. But when his health did not permit him to write on those countries, he recommended scholars that I should contact to write on Ireland and Israel. I doff my hat to him.

Obi N. Ignatius Ebbe, Ph.D.
State University of New York
College at Brockport
June 11, 1999

Part I

The Purpose of Comparative and International Criminal Justice Systems

Obi N. I. Ebbe

To understand criminal justice one must study the criminal law and constitutional law of a country or state, the agencies of the justice system, and what happens to the accused from the time of his/her arrest to disposal of the case. Comparative criminal justice studies build on such knowledge, investigating similarities and dissimilarities in the structure and operation of the criminal justice agencies of various nations or states. The factors which make two different countries have similar or dissimilar methods of handling offenders are religious belief; custom and tradition; historical experiences such as civil war, international war, ethnic or racial conflicts; economic structure; and political organization.

Studies of international criminal justice, on the other hand, focus on one country's criminal law, criminal procedure, and penology when the accused is a foreigner, and when the criminal law and penology of the home country of the accused differs from the criminal law and penology of the country in which the crime was committed. For example, the United States and Singapore do not agree on the appropriate punishment for vandalism. When Michael Fay vandalized a car in Singapore with graffiti in 1994, Singapore prescribed 90 days in jail and twenty-four lashes, whereas the United States would have disposed of such an offense with probation, warning, or reparation.

International criminal justice also addresses the attempts of two countries to resolve a crime incident where citizens of one country victimize those of another—as when Singapore and the United States debated over Michael Fay. Such situations may be resolved by deporting the offender and allowing the trial to take place in the offender's country, or by getting the victim's country to reduce the severity of the crime's penalty.

International criminal justice also includes the administration of extradition agreements between nations, and criminal laws and court procedures in communities of nations who have agreed that legal violations by citizens will all be treated in a certain way.

This part of the book descriptively analyzes systems of comparative and international criminal justice, highlighting important features of comparative criminal justice. It is intended to arm the student and the instructor with the ability to understand and consider various ways of handling offenders in different countries, and assumes the perspective of one who has basic knowledge of the American system of criminal justice.

1

Introduction
The Purpose of Comparative and International Criminal Justice Systems

Obi N. I. Ebbe

Introduction

This chapter answers the question, "Why do we study comparative and international criminal justice systems?" Some scholars have wondered why some countries have very low crime rates, while others have very high rates. Some studies have shown that procedures and mechanisms for handling offenders may contribute to high crime and delinquency rates (Ebbe, 1988 and 1989). While some mechanisms for handling offenders in a given culture are very effective, others are criminogenic.

It is expedient that there be a text that provides students and scholars an opportunity to know how criminal justice systems vary across cultures, and the good reasons for engaging in comparative studies of criminal justice systems. Study of comparative and international criminal justice systems goes beyond controversy, sharpening our awareness of the ubiquitous operational dynamics in criminal law and of the variety of cultural concepts, which brought different criminal justice systems into being.

In the process of studying the ways social order is achieved and maintained across nations, we learn how to modify our own society, bearing in mind that what works for one country may not work for another. Cultural values define behavior as good or bad and also determine the mechanisms for offender disposal. However, cultural values can change through international or inter-ethnic relations. For example, persons found guilty of crimes of "abomination" (such as incest or murder of a kinsman) in pre-colonial Southern Nigeria were dedicated to the gods as outcasts or untouchables.[1] This mechanism of offender disposal, however, became obsolete when English laws and cultural values overtook most of Nigerian society and condemned the outcast disposal mechanism. Presently, the Holy Shrines to which the outcasts were dedicated are still in existence, but they are no longer used as offender disposal mechanisms.

Furthermore, the use of halfway houses in the United States to reintegrate an offender who has spent some years in prison and has one year or less before final release was borrowed from European correctional methods, particularly from Scandinavia (Sweden, Norway, Denmark) and the Netherlands. The interdependency of countries today enables them to learn from each other's way of life, and this includes their social control methods.

I postulate here seven motivating approaches to studies in comparative and international criminal justice systems: the varied political history of nations; the international character of the modern crime scene; the usefulness of "varied social control mechanisms and learning from others' experiences" (Fairchild, 1993); the philosophical and utilitarian ideals that propel the criminal justice goals of various nations; the provision of bases for research and comparisons; acquaintance with the nature and dynamics of the criminal law of nations; and the provision of a source of governmental policy modifications in criminal procedures, law enforcement, and corrections.

Varied Political History of Nations

Criminal justice systems reflect a nation's government (unitary, federal, or confederate) and its politics (democratic, socialist, or communist), and therefore reflect a nation's political history. Consequently, criminal justice systems vary, both within continents and between continents.

Given the changes, which have occurred in governments in Africa, Asia, the Middle East, and South America, the criminal justice systems of countries in those parts of the world clearly will reflect their political evolution. The dynamics in the various criminal justice systems of African and Asian countries may issue in developments useful to both industrialized and non-industrialized countries' systems of criminal justice. The historical backgrounds of various criminal justice systems enable us to pose and answer two important questions: Do countries with similar historical experiences have similar systems of justice? If not, why not?

In the historical dimension, we must note that political system, economic system, religious belief, tradition, and custom determine the criminal justice system of a country and its unique position in international criminal justice.

International Character of the Modern Crime Scene

Criminal victimization has taken on an international character. We have seen this especially in the areas of terrorism, money laundering, and narcotics trafficking (Stewart, 1989; Bossard, 1990). The exist-

ence of the International Police (INTERPOL) for many decades now shows the international nature of some crimes since the "Age of Discovery" (A.D. 1400–1700), when people began to trespass into others' territories.

Because crime has become a worldwide social problem, the need for research in comparative and international criminal justice systems is more pressing today than ever before. There are crimes perpetrated today in both Western and non-Western countries which have foreign origins, including acts of terrorism, industrial burglary to steal manufacturing secrets, industrial sabotage, organized crime, counterfeit currency trafficking, narcotics drug trafficking, money-laundering, and computer fraud (Stewart, 1989; Grassi, 1989; David and Brierly, 1989; Kube, 1989; Bossard, 1990; Martin and Romano, 1992). Criminals have found international crime to be a very lucrative enterprise (Chang, 1976). The rewarding nature of international crimes has even attracted officials of numerous governments, leading to wholesale official corruption such as the Iran–Contra affair in the United States, the Noriega drug hysteria in Panama, the illegal money-laundering in Great Britain by Umaru Diko of Nigeria, and the looting of the Ugandan and Philippine treasuries by Idi Amin and Ferdinand Marcos, respectively. The fabulous amount of money involved in narcotic drug trafficking and illegal arms trafficking has caused them to develop into "multinational systemic crimes" (Martin and Romano, 1992): even if the United Nations imposes economic sanctions against an offending country, there are multinational syndicated criminals who are ready to provide that country with the needed goods. These multinational syndicated criminals have formed a transnational criminal cartel (Rodriguez, 1989) to provide necessary information and other needs to their members in various continents.

Unless comparative and international criminal justice systems are studied, effective control of national and international crimes will continue to be insignificant: presently, very few attempts are being made to study international crimes. Comparative and international criminal justice studies will help identify the various crimes in each country, determine those that are international in execution, and suggest solutions for their control through international cooperation. The high human toll taken by international crimes and transnational crimes thoroughly justifies comparative criminal justice studies, which can be applied to shore up legitimate governments and fend off threats to the lives of innocent citizens.

Varied Social Control Mechanisms and Learning from Others' Experiences

Industrialized and non-industrialized nations around the world use various mechanisms of social control. While industrialized nations have very formalized social control systems, the non-industrialized nations often depend on informal control mechanisms.

Non-industrialized countries generally have lower crime rates than industrialized nations (Adler, 1983; Archer and Gartner, 1984). These lower crime rates may result from the non-industrialized countries' frequent use of informal criminal justice. If this is true, one should ask in what ways the industrialized nations can apply both formal and informal methods of criminal justice, as in civil cases in the State of New York and other parts of the United States. In New York, a state court is allowed to submit a civil case such as a divorce to a third-party mediator, who meets with the parties in an informal setting. Most divorce cases in the State of New York are settled in this manner; and in most of the non-industrialized world, this is how most criminal cases are settled. The third party could be an individual (an elder), a chief,

a council of chiefs, or a council of elders. This is typical of African and Asian societies in both property and personal crimes. Third-party mediation in criminal matters in the State of New York certainly would eliminate the use of incarceration for some minor property and personal crimes. One of the advantages of using informal control mechanisms in the criminal justice systems of industrialized countries would be the reduction of prison overcrowding.

Philosophical and Utilitarian Ideals That Propel the Criminal Justice Goals of Various Nations

Whenever there is a unique system of social control, there must be some philosophical and functional thrust behind it. If such a unique social control mechanism is effective, such as the "Maxi Trials" or "Bunker Courts" in Italy (Grassi, 1989), other nations may learn from those philosophies and ideals.

I strongly agree with Pope Clement VI that any punishment which makes the offender not commit a crime again is worth administering; and that a punishment which does not correct should not be given (Schafer, 1976).

Comparative and international criminal justice studies therefore should evaluate various cultures' offender disposal mechanisms for their effectiveness and for worthwhile philosophies which may lie behind their use.

Provision of Bases for Research and Comparisons

Studies of the criminal justice systems of other nations have the potential for stimulating similar studies in other countries. In the process of accumulation of criminal justice data, interest in international comparison is aroused. For example, a study of "the crime rate in Tokyo, Japan and the number of police officers per 100,000 population" can trigger similar studies in large cities of other industrialized countries. When "special tribunals" are used in Nigeria for the trials of persons accused of armed robbery, narcotics drug possession and trafficking, and counterfeit currency trafficking, a foreigner may ask how these tribunals work, how they differ from the regular criminal courts, and why the government uses special tribunals. Such questions are grounds for empirical research. Non-participant observation of a Maxi Trial or a special tribunal trial of an armed robber can be very beneficial to comparative criminal justice.

Acquaintance with the Nature and Dynamics of the Criminal Law of Nations

By studying the criminal justice systems of various countries we come to know the nature of their laws. Also we may come to know why certain forms of behavior are criminal in one country but not in another.

Criminal law, belonging as it does to the social sciences, is dynamic rather than static. As a nation grows and becomes more complex through urbanization and industrialization, new laws are created to meet the exigencies of that difficult period. Also under the heterogeneous social conditions of urban areas, values may change as time passes, rendering old laws obsolete. Comparative criminal justice therefore amounts, in many cases, to studying how criminal laws of nations change.

Part of the study of comparative criminal justice includes the study of criminal codes and penal codes of countries (Stewart, 1989; Bossard, 1990). Such studies emphasize the diverse features of those codes and the similarities and dissimilarities between Western and non-Western criminal codes: the distinctive features of codes in countries where common law, Roman law, or Islamic law prevail.

The development of nations' criminal law has always paralleled their political history and development; therefore, such developments vary from society to society (Gutteridge, 1949). Among the factors that influence the development of criminal law are war, coup d'etat, technological innovations, migration and immigration, urbanization, industrialization, religious conflict, national economic disaster (e.g., depression), colonization, international trade and transportation, inter-ethnic conflict, multi-ethnicity, and increase or decrease in political power. Among these factors we can trace the ones that played a part in the enactment of various laws in a country. Generally, countries with similar political experiences have come under the same groups of laws, as we see in the similar historical backgrounds of the common law countries, Roman law countries, and Islamic law countries.

Study of the criminal codes or penal codes of nations is very much essential, because different codes often mandate different penalties for the same offenses. The criminal code is very much determined by substantive criminal law—the law of crimes and penalties (Day, 1964). For instance, the Netherlands' permissive policies toward use of cannabis "contributed to the emergence of Amsterdam as an important transit place for narcotic drugs in the 1970s" (Bossard, 1990). Furthermore, one must keep in mind that a criminal code does not contain all of the criminal laws of a country. Students of comparative and international criminal justice must also study statutory law, applicable "judge-made laws" (stare decisis), and law reports and arguments of university legal scholars which are accepted by courts in some countries such as France and Nigeria as sources of law (Day, 1964). To understand criminal justice, one must comprehend and compare systems of criminal law in all their complexity. Transnational crimes influence legislation, and very often contemporary criminal court judges are confronted with situations covered neither by the criminal code nor by statutory law. In these cases, judges effectively create new laws through their own discretionary power, basing their decisions on the circumstances of the case, and on other exigencies of the situation.

Provision of a Source for Governmental Policy Modifications in Criminal Procedures, Law Enforcement, and Corrections

There is no aspect of the criminal justice system of any country more volatile than criminal procedure, law enforcement, and correctional mechanisms. Almost all of the industrialized and non-industrialized nations are uncomfortable with these three aspects of the criminal justice system. Global increase in crime rates, resulting from global increase in population and urbanization, has rendered inadequate some old methods of offender disposal. Consequently, many countries are initiating as experiments new methods of handling offenders.

The United States, for instance, is one of the non-European countries that has copied the practices of halfway houses, day fines, and prison structures from Sweden and the Netherlands. Governments are eager to copy what works in other countries for social control.

Of course, there are some pitfalls in comparative studies that should be guarded against, such as ethnocentrism in gathering and interpretation of foreign-based data, and the effects of governmental corruption on the reliability of official data from developing countries.

Also, comparing arrest, prosecution, conviction, and incarceration rates across cultures may yield little or no reliable evidence, because many developing countries such as India, Nigeria, Ghana, and Kenya have resorted to static law enforcement systems in which the police do not routinely patrol the neighborhoods watching for law breakers, but rely instead on victims and concerned citizens reporting crimes to their nearest police station. Not every victim and not every concerned citizen will report crime to the police; and, even if reporting were dependable, many developing countries have not adopted systematic record keeping of criminal justice data. In short, countries with a static law enforcement system may have lower arrest rates than countries routinely patrolling neighborhoods, but the comparison is not sound. Similarly, comparing prosecution, conviction, and incarceration rates is not wise, for perception of seriousness of criminal offenses varies from culture to culture (Ebbe, 1977).

Summary

Comparative and international criminal justice studies provide nations with an opportunity to know and learn from offender disposal mechanisms that are effective in other countries. By studying comparative and international criminal justice, we learn the varied political history of nations, the international character of the modern crime scene, the varied social control mechanisms of nations and the possibilities of learning from the experiences of others, and the philosophical and utilitarian ideals that propel the criminal justice goals of various countries; we are also able to provide bases for research and comparison of results, to get acquainted with the nature and dynamics in the criminal law of nations, and finally to provide a source for governmental policy modifications in all aspects of the criminal justice system.

Our study of the justice system of selected countries will start in the next section with the United States, followed by treatments of the United Kingdom and a contrast between Denmark and Brazil.

Notes

1. The Outcast or Untouchable institution was a status created in pre-colonial Southern Nigeria, prevalent among the Igbos, for disposing of offenders who committed an abomination such as incest, murder of a kinsman, or a son having sexual relations with one of his father's wives when his father was still alive. The individual was ostracized, dedicated to a god, and he became an untouchable ("osu"). The Holy Shrine grove, the home of his god, was his abode. His only companions were a few other untouchables. He was proscribed from shaving his hair or taking a bath (Achebe, 1959). He was dehumanized.

Worst of all, the status was inherited. In 1955, however, the Eastern Region Government of Dr. Nnamdi Azikiwe abolished the untouchable institution by a law. But the abolition did not stop discriminative attitudes towards the descendants of untouchables; and throughout Igboland, the descendants of untouchables are still not allowed to take the ozo title. (The ozo title is a cultural initiation taken only by the sons of nobles or aborigines of a town. Women do not take the title. Only when a man takes the title does his wife become an adjunct—a lolo-ozo—to the title.)

Now, why should anybody suffer the consequences of a crime committed by another, especially when the person who committed the crime died centuries ago? Yet the Nigerian government is doing nothing to remedy the situation, mainly because the descendants of untouchables do not want to go through the trouble of identifying themselves in order to solve the problems imposed on them by society.

Discussion and Review Questions

1. What factors determine the nature of the criminal justice system of a country?

2. What are the seven motivating approaches to the study of comparative and international criminal justice systems?

3. Give at least eight examples of international crime.

4. What is a "multinational systemic crime?" Give examples of such crimes.

5. What are the merits and demerits of the use of a third-party mediation or arbitration in a criminal case?

6. What did Pope Clement VI recommend regarding punishment?

7. Name at least three different classes of law in the Western world.

8. What factors lead to the development of criminal law?

9. What is substantive criminal law?

10. Can criminal court judges create crimes? If yes, how?

11. What are some of the pitfalls in comparative criminal justice studies?

12. What is a static law enforcement system?

13. What factors bring changes to the criminal justice system of a country?

14. Why are crime rates higher in industrialized nations than in non-industrialized nations?

15. What is the author's view about punishment vis-à-vis Pope Clement VI's postulation?

16. What is the place of INTERPOL in international criminal justice?

17. What are the advantages and disadvantages of the informal criminal justice system?

18. Why is the informal criminal justice system prevalent in less industrialized nations?

19. Explain the role of the following:
    (a) Special Tribunals in Nigeria.
    (b) Maxi Trial in Italy.

20. What is statutory law?

Part II

Overviews of Criminal Justice Systems and Policy

2

Criminal Justice System in the United States

General Overview

Mary Clifford

Brief History

The contemporary American system of criminal justice is a result of centuries of evolution and social change. American colonists settling in the new world brought the criminal procedures, courts, and crime definitions of the English common law tradition along with them (Henderson, 1985). This tradition originally did not define crimes or their remedies as public matters, but rather considered them private matters between the individual who was wronged and the wrongdoer (Siegel, 1992). Later, the concept of public crime developed, but it was confined to acts committed against the king, with individuals and their families left to resolve their own disputes. Church representatives handled those acts considered to be sinful, and local courts dealt with most secular violations. Because royal administrators were not constantly present in each community, a system developed for holding court sessions in each county several times a year. The royal administrator, or judge, used local customs and rules of conduct as a guide for determining an appropriate sentence for an offender (Siegel,

1992). The structure and content of this English system was modified to meet different community needs and geographic circumstances in the new world (Chapin, 1983).

Early in the development of the American system of justice, the framers of the United States Constitution (1787) gave Congress considerable latitude to "establish inferior courts, to define crimes and stipulate punishments, and to provide for modes of process and procedures to be used in the courts" (Henderson, 1985). According to the Constitution, Congress must "set up all tribunals (federal courts) inferior (lower in rank) to the Supreme Court . . ." and legislate "to decide which acts that take place at sea are piracies (thefts) or felonies (serious crimes such as murder), to make laws to punish these crimes, and crimes against international law . . ." (Cullop, 1984:4). Response to the original draft of the Constitution resulted in the passage of several amendments known as the Bill of Rights, adopted in 1791. The Bill of Rights includes ten amendments identifying personal liberties (individual rights) not listed in the

Constitution, but which people had come to believe were their rights as citizens of the United States (Cullop, 1984).

Several provisions within the Bill of Rights are of particular importance in the United States system of justice. The Fourth Amendment prohibits unreasonable search and seizures. The Fifth Amendment requires an indictment to be held on a capital offense; no double jeopardy (i.e., only one trial per offense); no compulsion to be a witness against one's self; and no deprivation of life, liberty, or property without due process. The Sixth Amendment assures that one accused of a crime will have a speedy trial, the right to confront adverse witnesses, and the assistance of counsel. The Seventh Amendment guarantees the right to a trial by jury. The Eighth Amendment prohibits both excessive bail and cruel and unusual punishment.

The Constitutional provisions, the adoption of the Bill of Rights, and the Crimes Act of 1790 formed the initial structure of the federal criminal justice system (Henderson, 1985). The Crimes Act of 1790 defined seventeen crimes ranging from obstruction of process to treason. Death by hanging was the penalty for six crimes: treason, murder, piracy, accessory to piracy, forgery, and rescue of a person found guilty of any capital crime. Henderson (1985) argues that the crimes listed in the Act of 1790 were consistent with the constitutional authority of Congress and reviews several additions which followed the initial provisions, including the Judiciary Act, the Neutrality Act, Sedition Act, and the Logan Act.

Legal System

The American legal system, reminiscent of the legal system the Puritans left behind in England, mandated courts similar to English courts (Stucky, 1986), which employed the "trial by adversary" process (Weston and Wells, 1987). In this process,

legal counsel represents both parties involved in a case. It is believed that such partisan advocacy develops the best possible arguments for the guilt or innocence of the parties involved.

Also significant in the American legal system is the concept of "due process." Due process assures the accused of basic individual rights and freedoms in the United States. The tenets of due process are outlined in the Fifth Amendment and more thoroughly described in the Fourteenth Amendment (Kolasa and Meyer, 1987). Due process of law assures the accused that he/she will receive a fair hearing, and that the provisions in the Constitution and the Fourth through Eighth Amendments will be followed. At all levels of justice proceedings, however, implementation of due process can be difficult. Social, economic, and political factors often influence outcomes of legal actions in this and other areas of the justice system (Kolasa and Meyer, 1987).

American law has developed along two lines: (1) a civil law system, and (2) a common law system. The operation of the judicial process is the primary difference between the two systems (Kolasa and Meyer, 1987). Adjudication under civil law is made by the judge, who follows an existing or an established set of laws. Common law, on the other hand, develops through the decisions of judges applying prior court decisions to the current case (Kolasa and Meyer, 1987).

Since the passage of the Constitution, Congress has made several changes to the structure and organization of various courts. The number of Supreme Court Justices has been changed, as have the number and forms of the lower courts (Vito and Holmes, 1994). Most states have created their own systems of specialized lower courts. Usually these courts hear civil cases, divorces, cases of property, and wills. Criminal courts address felonies and misdemeanors.

System of Government

The three branches of government outlined in the United States Constitution (the legislative, executive, and judicial powers) divide governing power into three segments capable of functioning together effectively (Weston and Wells, 1987). Article I of the Constitution establishes the legislative powers (Cullop, 1984), Article II establishes the executive powers, and Article III establishes the judicial branch of government. This structure provided a system of checks and balances, with each branch of government being allowed to operate independently but in relation to the other branches. While federal laws usually take precedence over state laws, states and local communities establish their own priorities in their own legislation, design the structure of their court system, and may identify specific acts as priorities at local community levels.

Crime

Classification of Crime

In the United States system of justice, before a crime is said to have been committed, there must be (1) a law that defines the crime, (2) an act or an omission by the accused, called actus reus, (3) a guilty state of mind, also called intent (mens rea), (4) a joining of the act and the intent to act, (5) harm that affects society or a person, (6) a causal relationship between the act or omission and the harm caused, and (7) a punishment as stated in the criminal code (Cole, 1981). English law classified crimes into three categories: treason, felonies, and misdemeanors, with emphasis on felonies and misdemeanors (Lindquist, 1988). Felonies were "common-law" crimes—that is, crimes that the people defined through traditional ways of living rather than through statute. Reid (1992) argues that there were very few common-law felonies: murder, manslaughter, sod-

omy, larceny, robbery, arson, and burglary. The misdemeanor classification developed much later than that of felony, emerging in the sixteenth century. Prior to that time individuals were fined, but their offenses were not considered crimes (Walsh, 1932). The misdemeanor category emerged from the notion of trespass (Lindquist, 1988) and was regarded primarily as a means of raising money for the Crown.

Felonies have been distinguished from misdemeanors using two traditional terms, mala in se (acts that are inherently wrong, i.e., felonies) and mala prohibita (acts that are wrong because they are prohibited by law, i.e., misdemeanors); this description, however, has been called into question by several scholars. Inciardi (1984) argues that "the felony–misdemeanor classification goes beyond the mala in se–mala prohibita distinction since a number of felonies fail to reflect moral turpitude." All such dispute is actually irrelevant in the United States, where all crimes are defined arbitrarily and conventionally by political apparatus (Michael and Adler, 1971).

Because state laws define felony and misdemeanor crimes, both vary from state to state (Lindquist, 1988). As a consequence, it is important to look at the statute in each state, not only to determine which acts are classified as misdemeanors or felonies, but also to understand how local law defines the terms. Length of sentence and where the sentence is served generally distinguish misdemeanors from felonious offenses. Generally, misdemeanors are defined as offenses punishable by no more than a year in a local jail, and/or a fine.

Sheley (1995) identifies four factors which can be used successfully to avoid being classified a criminal in the legal system: self-defense, action under duress, insanity, and age. In self-defense, the amount of force used must not exceed the amount of threatened harm. Furthermore, if one could have avoided the danger by flight, the defense cannot be used. Self-defense can be used only when no other avenue existed to protect one's self from deadly and imminent bodily harm. Another way to avoid criminal classification is the insanity defense. In the U.S. court system, "insanity" is a legal, not a medical, concept. One who uses the insanity defense argues that he/she could not avoid committing the crime in question because of a mental defect. Definitions of insanity vary by court systems. About a third of states use a formula based on the M'Naghten Rule, a definition of insanity established in England in 1843, for determining whether the accused may use the insanity defense at trial.

The duress defense against criminal classification is available when the defendant is forced by means of a deadly force to break the law or to help another break the law. For example, a criminal gang might enter a bank manager's house at night and enjoin him or her under gunpoint to go to the bank and open the bank vault. If the bank manager were to obey and later was accused as an accomplice, he or she could claim to have acted under duress.

The final defense against criminal classification is age of criminal responsibility. Juveniles who commit specific acts are treated differently from adults in the United States system of justice. "The term 'juvenile delinquency' or a 'delinquent act' is a non-criminal classification for acts done by juveniles (usually under age 17 or 18 depending on the state) that would otherwise be a violation of federal or state criminal law, or local ordinances. In about half the states, it should be noted, this terminology of delinquency extends to non-criminal offenses (status offenses) to include: unruly children, truancy, incorrigibles, and youngsters beyond the control of parents" (Weston and Wells, 1987).

Classification of Illegal Possession of Narcotic Drugs

The classification of illegal possession of narcotic drugs changed from misdemeanor

to felony during the twentieth century (Jones, Shainberg, and Byer, 1979). Siegel (1992) reviews several of the laws introduced to regulate drug use in the United States. The Pure Food and Drug Act (1906) required manufacturers to list the amounts of habit-forming drugs on the labels of products but did not restrict their use. In 1914, the Harrison Narcotics Act restricted the importation, manufacture, sale, and dispensing of narcotics. "Narcotics" were defined as any drug that produces sleep and relieves pain, such as heroin, morphine, and opium. In 1922 the act was revised to allow the importation of opium and coca leaves (cocaine) for qualified medical practitioners. The Marijuana Tax Act of 1937 required registration and tax payment from all persons who imported, sold, or manufactured marijuana. Because marijuana was classified as a narcotic, people who registered were subject to criminal penalty.

Many drug statutes include specific penalties for violating federal drug laws. The Boggs Act of 1951 provided mandatory sentences for violations of federal drug laws. The Durham–Humphrey Act of 1951 made it illegal to dispense barbiturates and amphetamines without a prescription. The Narcotics Control Act of 1956 increased penalties for drug offenders.

Drugs of Abuse (DEA, 1985), a Drug Enforcement Administration publication, references the Comprehensive Drug Abuse Prevention and Control Act of 1970, which regulates drugs at the federal level and classifies drugs into five schedules according to their abuse potential. Since 1970, a variety of federal laws have attempted to limit the manufacture and sale of new drugs. The Controlled Substances Act of 1984, the Anti-Drug Abuse Act of 1986, and the Anti-Drug Abuse Act of 1988 identify types of illegal drugs and penalties for violations of drug laws and set up programs for addressing the drug problem. For the most part state laws mirror federal statutes (Siegel, 1992).

The classification of drugs as legal or illegal is at present a rather tricky business. Alcohol, tobacco, and caffeine are currently legal drugs in the United States. These substances, however, have not always been legal (Brecher et al., 1972). At present, the legal status of marijuana varies by state. Between 1973 and 1978 eleven states decriminalized marijuana. One of these states, Alaska, has recriminalized marijuana, but the decision is under appeal and the law is not yet enforced (Sheley, 1995).

Crime Statistics

Two primary sources exist for the collection of statistics on crime in the United States: the Uniform Crime Reports (UCR) of the Federal Bureau of Investigation (FBI) and the National Crime Victimization Survey (NCVS) of the Bureau of Justice Statistics (BJS). More specific attention will be given to the NCVS below, in the section on victims. Because they differ in methodology and crime coverage, these two sources of data are not necessarily comparable; however, they can be used as complementary sources which together expand our understanding of the crime problem. The UCR program, it should be noted, is expanding to become a more comprehensive and detailed reporting system called the National Incident-Based Reporting System (NIBRS) which will provide detailed information about each criminal incident and an expanded category list of offenses (FBI, 1994:385).

Ever since 1929, the UCR has collected and reported information on all crimes reported to law enforcement agencies, whether or not there is further action on the case (Reid, 1994). The data are compiled from monthly law enforcement reports submitted directly to the FBI, and they reflect active law enforcement agencies from approximately 95% of the total U.S. population. Covered crimes include homicide, forcible rape, robbery, aggra-

vated assault, burglary, larceny–theft, motor vehicle theft, and arson—eight crimes known as Index Crimes or Part I Crimes. A crime is classified as an Index Crime based on a combination of three factors: high degree of seriousness of the offense; high degree of reportability of the offense; and high degree of occurrence of the offense. Serious offenses such as white collar crime, organized crime, and narcotics drug smuggling lack one or more of the three factors, and therefore are not included.

Various factors affect the volumes and types of crime from place to place, and from year to year. Factors identified in the Uniform Crime Reports include population density; urbanization; variations in population (particularly youth); stability of population; available modes of transportation; economic conditions; cultural factors; educational, recreational, and religious characteristics; family conditions; climate; strength of law enforcement; administrative and investigative emphasis of law enforcement; policies of other components of the criminal justice system; citizens' attitudes toward crime; and crime-reporting practices of the citizenry (FBI, 1994).

All of these factors must be taken into consideration as one reviews and analyzes the data reflected in the UCR. Here we will treat the UCR definitions and statistics for four crimes: murder, serious property offenses, forcible rape, and drug offenses.

For murder and non-negligent manslaughter, the definition is "the willful (non-negligent) killing of one human being by another" (FBI, 1994). The classification of this offense, and all other crimes in the UCR, is based solely on police investigation, not on the determination of a court, medical examiner, coroner, jury, or any other judicial body. The total number of murders in the United States during 1993 was estimated at 24,526, a 14% rise from murder counts in 1989. During the 10 years since 1984, the count rose by 31% (FBI, 1993:14).

The crime of robbery is a serious property offense defined by the UCR as "the taking or attempting to take anything of value from the care, custody, or control of a person or persons by force or threat of force of violence and/or by putting the victim in fear." The UCR estimated the volume of robberies in 1993 at 659,757 offenses. The national robbery rate in 1993 was 256 per 100,000 people, 3% lower than in 1992. (Again, this information reflects the number of reports to the police.)

Forcible rape is defined as "carnal knowledge of a female forcibly and against her will. Assaults or attempts to commit rape by force or threat of force are also included; however, statutory rape (without force) and other sex offenses are excluded." In 1993 an estimated 104,806 forcible rapes were reported to law enforcement agencies in the United States. This figure was down 4% from the 1992 volume and showed the first decline in forcible rape since 1987.

Drug abuse violations are state and local offenses relating to "the unlawful possession, sale, use, growing, and manufacturing of narcotic drugs" (FBI, 1994). They can include any of the following categories of drugs: opium or cocaine and their derivatives (morphine, heroin, codeine), marijuana, synthetic narcotics, manufactured narcotics that can cause true addiction (meperidine, methadone), and dangerous non-narcotic drugs (barbiturates, amphetamines). In 1993, drug abuse violation arrests were up 4% from the 1992 level; they were 14% lower than in 1989, but 56% higher than in 1984. Of total drug arrests in 1993, 29.7% were for sale/manufacture, and 70.3% were for possession (FBI, 1994:216).

In addition to drug abuse violations, drug abuse has often been associated with involvement in other serious crimes. The *Sourcebook* (BJS, 1991:457) reports that 67% of arrested men and 66% of arrested women tested positive for some type of drug abuse.

Crime Regions

For the purposes of FBI statistics, the United States is divided into regions, divisions, and states. Further breakdowns are based on population figures, and proximity to metropolitan areas—i.e., community type (FBI, 1994:382). There are four regions: Northeastern States, Midwestern States, Southern States, and Western States. These four state-based regions are further divided into nine divisions within each region.

The UCR data are presented in aggregations representing three types of communities: (1) Metropolitan Statistical Areas (MSAs), (2) cities outside MSAs, and (3) rural counties outside MSAs. Each MSA includes a central city of at least 50,000, suburban cities, and suburban counties. Non-MSA areas include cities outside metropolitan areas, and rural communities. As a general rule, sheriffs, county police, and state police report crimes committed within the limits of the counties, excluding the city limits, while the local police report crimes committed within the city limits.

Victims

The second primary resource for reviewing crime statistics in the United States is the National Crime Victimization Survey (NCVS). Beginning in 1973, the NCVS has collected information from the victim's point of view on the frequency and nature of the crimes of rape, personal robbery, aggravated and simple assault, household burglary, personal and household theft, and motor vehicle theft. It does not measure murder, kidnapping, and "victimless" crimes (public drunkenness, prostitution, drug abuse) (BJS, 1994e). Because the NCVS gathers data directly from crime victims, it can provide information on both reported and unreported crimes. When an act of victimization is reported, the most severe act is classified; for example, if a victim is raped and robbed, the rape is recorded. The NCVS documents crime data according to four regions defined by the Census Bureau: Midwest, Northeast, South, and West.

According to the Department of Justice statistics, 20% of all of the crimes committed in 1992 were violent crimes (BJS, 1994e). These include rape, robbery, and assault and are considered the most serious offenses by the NCVS. Personal/household larceny made up 60% of offenses in 1992. Household burglary and motor vehicle theft accounted for the last 20% of victimizations. The level of violent crime did not differ from 1981, which was a peak year for violent offenses. This breaks down into 6.6 million violent victimizations, 12.2 million personal thefts, and 14.8 million American households victimized (BJS, 1994e:10).

Blacks are more likely to be victims of violent crime than whites. People under the age of 25 have a higher victimization rate than older persons. Households with lower incomes are more likely to be violent crime victims than households with higher incomes. The statistically overrepresented victims of street crimes are male, young, poor, and black (Sheley, 1995:122).

Historically, the victim of a criminal act was not represented in the adversarial process. Victims would sign the complaint, which set the justice process in motion, and were brought into courtrooms to serve as "evidence" and to testify for the prosecution (Sheley, 1995:161). In 1982, Congress enacted standards for the fair treatment of victims and witnesses, and throughout the 1980s states granted to victims greater opportunities to participate in decision-making within the criminal justice process. But there is no penalty against a state that fails to allow victim participation in decision-making in the criminal justice process (BJS, 1991).

The National Victim Center of the victim's rights movement has outlined a model amendment for state constitutions that reads, "The victim of crime or his or her representative shall have the right to be informed of, to be present at, and to be heard at all criminal justice proceedings at which the defendant has such rights, subject to the same rules which govern defendants rights." See Austern (1987:23–27) for a listing of Victim/Witness assistance units by state.

Police

Administration

The American system of policing was modeled after the London Metropolitan Police, formed in 1829 by Sir Robert Peel (Reid, 1994:505). According to the FBI, the public law enforcement community services a population of over 224 million and employs 553,773 officers and 212,353 civilians (FBI, 1994:288). Unlike such countries as Kenya, Nigeria, and China, the system of policing in the United States is decentralized, having separate systems at the local, state, and federal levels of government. An additional police agency which is becoming more popular, but which does not have full police power, is called the private or special-purpose police (Langworthy and Travis, 1994:118).

Police agencies are organized bureaucratically (Reiss, 1992:69). Municipal police organizations are structured in several different ways, but the accepted model in the United States is the bureaucratic pyramid, with the chief of police at the top, management (reflecting specializations within the department) in the middle, and patrol officers at the bottom (Langworthy and Travis, 1994:143). Historically, metropolitan police organization was borrowed from the military model as outlined initially by Sir Robert Peel in England in 1829 (Skolnick and Fyfe, 1993:117). Using the military model helped to combat traditional British mistrust of official authority and made it easier to convince the skeptical British public that a new sort of official was needed to address social disorder and crime. In 1838, Boston, Massachusetts, introduced the London Metropolitan System of policing to help the night watchmen of Boston, and New York City followed in 1845.

Rural, county, and municipal police agencies are found at the municipal or local level (Reid, 1994). Local police agencies are relatively small organizations, and little is known about municipal operations (Langworthy and Travis, 1994). State and federal police agencies emerged as a response to a perceived lack of effectiveness in local police, with state-based policing developing as a hybrid between the federal and local experiences. All states except Hawaii have a statewide police or highway patrol. Policing at the state level is divided into state police and state patrol officers, with patrol officers responsible for traffic control, and state police enforcing certain regulations (Reid, 1994). Today, American police are predominantly associated with local government (Sheley, 1995). Most crimes committed in the United States are state crimes, but the FBI may, when requested, assist state and local enforcement agencies in solving a state crime, in addition to attending to federal crimes such as bank robbery, explosive trafficking, bombing of public buildings, and counterfeiting currency.

At least sixty-three distinct federal agencies exercise police powers or serve police functions (Langworthy and Travis, 1994:99). Four commonly known agencies are the Federal Bureau of Investigation; the U.S. Marshals; Alcohol, Tobacco and Firearms Bureau (ATF); and the Drug Enforcement Administration. Their primary functions as federal police agencies are specific and clearly defined, with detection and investigation being their primary responsibilities.

Resources

According to a 1993 Bureau of Justice Statistics study of state and local law enforce-

ment units, state and local governments funded 17,358 police and sheriff's departments, including 12,502 general-purpose local police departments, 3,086 sheriff's departments, 49 primary state police departments, and 1,721 special police agencies. These agencies employed approximately 604,000 full-time sworn officers with general arrest powers and 237,000 non-sworn civilian personnel (1993). The U.S. Department of Justice (BJS, 1991) reports that $60,980,334,000 was spent at all levels of government in the criminal justice system. At the federal level, the expenditures were $7,794,136,000. At the state levels of government, the total expenditures were $19,279,179,000. Local expenditures were $33,907,019,000, including municipal expenditures of $19,533,908,000 and county expenditures of $14,373,111,000.

For police, these expenditures included $27,955,660,000 for all levels of government. This breaks down to $3,555,248,000 at the federal level for police, and $4,513,297,000 at the state level; for rural, county, and municipal police the expenditures for police protection are $10,332,148,000, $4,015,310,000, and $5,539,657,000, respectively (BJS, 1991:2).

Police jurisdictions differ across the country. In addition to the 49 primary state police departments, the 1993 study included 12,502 general-purpose local police departments. County governments operated 59 of these local departments and municipalities. The study reflected 3,086 sheriff's departments operated by counties and independent cities, and 1,721 special police agencies. Included in the latter category were 751 county constable offices in Texas and 970 state and local agencies with special jurisdictions or specific enforcement responsibilities.

Sheley (1995) argues that policing has been dominated by white males who have modest amounts of formal education and training. In addition, certain ethnic and racial groups have not been well represented in policing, particularly African-

Americans, Asians, and Hispanics. Women are clearly underrepresented in the American police forces. According to the 1993 UCR information, males made up 91% of all sworn employees both nationally and in cities, 93% of those in rural counties, and 88% of those in suburban counties.

Technology

Police have implemented innovative technology at various levels. Computer-aided dispatch, computerized record-keeping procedures, and radio communication have become standard features in modern police departments; in some jurisdictions, video technology and computer terminals are used in patrol cars. Computers now allow information to be exchanged between dispatch and the police officer on patrol without tipping off the criminal (Newcombe, 1993). Technologies such as fingerprinting, DNA testing, and voice identification technologies are being used and perfected (Jasanoff, 1989) to aid in investigations (Sessions, 1992) and convictions.

Although police and other criminal justice officials have found innovative technologies useful throughout the adjudication process, such innovations have also provoked significant public attention and intense debate. In New Hampshire, police have been criticized for using high-tech thermal imaging devices to find marijuana growing operations (West, 1992). Stephens (1990) argues that police surveillance (audio and video) technology devalues individual rights.

The capture on video of the brutal arrest of Rodney King in Los Angeles in 1991 resulted in a highly public denunciation of the police and the arrest process (Skolnick and Fyfe, 1993). This negative publicity has prompted police to employ "less than lethal force" (Edwards, 1995), subduing offenders with technologies such as foams and pepper sprays.

In order to better understand how technologies can be used by the police in enforcing the law, the National Institute of Justice is developing the National Law Enforcement Technology Center (NLETC) and regional law enforcement technology centers (NIJ, 1995). Some technologies explored at the Technology Center are geared toward ensuring police officer protection: for example, the development and use of soft body armor, and videotaped interrogations (Geller, 1992). Standards for use and manufacture of soft body armor, vehicle tracking, security systems, pistols, and other innovative technologies continue to be examined at the Technology Center (NIJ, 1995).

Training and Qualifications

Few police departments require a college education to enter the force or to be advanced within the ranks, although college education can be important in promotion decisions (Carter, Sapp, and Stephens, 1989). Since 1967, most states have mandated minimum entry-level training standards, and many departments require much higher levels (Ostrom, Parks, and Whitaker, 1978). This trend toward professionalism in policing has resulted in departments requiring more formal training and education from their personnel. Reid (1994) cites the President's Commission on Law Enforcement and Administration of Justice report (1967) which identified "intelligence, education, tact, sound judgment, physical courage, emotional stability, impartiality, and honesty" as important qualities in a police officer; she also finds psychological factors such as ability to handle racial tension an important factor. Because earlier research findings reported police to be emotionally maladjusted, extremely cynical and authoritarian, and impulsive risk takers, she argues that temperament and personality should be important in qualifying to be a police officer (Reid, 1994:514).

Discretion

Police are expected to detect crime, to investigate how a particular criminal act happened, and then to make arrests when necessary. But because circumstances can vary in the arrest process, no aspect of police function is entirely predictable. Ultimately, individual officers must decide whether to arrest or to release a suspect. Studies of officer training and officer action are focusing increasingly on these discretionary powers.

Sworn police officers have the authority to make an arrest. In most cases the arresting officer will have a warrant. Officers are required to give an individual being arrested "adequate notice," which includes outlining the intention to arrest, the cause of the arrest, and the authority to make the arrest (Weston and Wells, 1987:25). A law enforcement officer also has the right to stop and frisk a suspect "when she/he observes unusual conduct which leads the officer to reasonably conclude, in the light of . . . experience, that a criminal activity may be in progress, and that the person involved may be armed and presently dangerous; when, in the course of investigating this behavior, she/he is identified as a police officer and makes reasonable inquiries; and when nothing in the initial stages of the encounter serves to dispel reasonable fear for the officer's or others' safety" (Kolasa and Meyer, 1987).

Although police are trained to use no more force than necessary, encounters with alleged law violators can result in the most extreme use of force—deadly force. The use of deadly force is governed by the criminal laws of individual states, which authorize officers to resort to this level of coercion in the imminent defense of their own lives or the lives of others (Skolnick and Fyfe, 1993). Because language permitting the use of deadly force can be vague in criminal law, well-run police departments generally supplement these laws with administrative guidelines and policies.

Brown v. Mississippi was a landmark case concerning the actions of police in securing a confession from an accused offender (Skolnick and Fyfe, 1993). In *Brown v. Mississippi* (1936), the issue was whether convictions which rest solely upon confessions shown to have been extorted by officers of the State by brutality and violence are consistent with due process of law required by the Fourth Amendment of the Constitution of the United States. The Federal Court of Appeals reversed the Mississippi Court conviction (Perkins and Boyce, 1984). Many court cases have since considered what actions are appropriate or acceptable in police interrogations. In many cases, misrepresentation of information by the police in an interrogation has been considered acceptable.

Manning (1989) identifies several issues associated with police decision-making: uncertainty, mutual dependence, autonomy, and authority. Police are confronted with many issues which are not openly expressed. Further, they are constantly relying on other officers to help them fend off physical, emotional, and career threats. Police officers treasure their ability to exercise judgment independently, and they consider this privilege essential.

Although scholars have given little attention to how police officers exercise their discretion, several note that departments give substantial leeway when they determine whether certain police actions are required or unnecessary. This would imply that the issue of police discretion and accountability needs increased attention.

Accountability

Reiss (1992) identifies a number of institutions intended to influence police practice and to limit the authority of the departmental hierarchy. These external bodies to which police are accountable include mayors, city managers, civil service boards, civilian review boards, police unions, prosecutors, the judiciary, labor relations boards, and a variety of other federal and state regulatory agencies. Lobbyists or other community groups can also affect how police are held accountable for their actions on the job.

Because of concern about the rights of individuals arrested by police, the Supreme Court ruled in *Miranda v. Arizona* (1966) that procedural safeguards should be in effect to inform an accused person of his/her right of silence. The Miranda warning states that the individual has the right to remain silent, and that any statement made can be used as evidence against him or her in a court of law. The accused is also informed of his or her right to an attorney, either retained by the accused or appointed by the court (Reid, 1994:473). This Supreme Court decision has proven to be extremely controversial and has resulted in extensive litigation.

Reid (1994) identified several methods to control police discretion. The exclusionary rule says that if police violate the rights of individuals accused of committing a crime by illegally seizing evidence, the evidence so obtained cannot be used at trial. This rule is not found in the systems of criminal justice of Nigeria, Sierra Leone, China, or Japan; particularly in Japan, society's rights take precedence over individual rights. Police officer misconduct can also be controlled by holding individuals accountable for their actions (traditionally, the police department has been held accountable for a police officer's action). Civil suits brought by individuals who argue that they have been harmed by a police officer's action are becoming more common, and some have succeeded. In contrast, bringing a court action against a police officer in African and Asian countries is rare, and the few actions attempted have failed.

Prosecutorial and Judicial Process

Rights of the Accused

According to Nagel (1972), the specific rights of someone who has been accused of committing a crime can be divided into four segments: rights prior to the first court appearance, rights from first court appearance to trial, rights during the trial stage, and post-trial rights of the defendant. Prior to the first court appearance, a suspect can be arrested or searched only if there is a probable cause, and the suspect is protected against self-incrimination or giving involuntary confessions. Once the accused has made his or her first court appearance, he or she is assured release pending a speedy trial, the right to hire or be provided with counsel, and a formal notice of the charges against him or her. Once at trial, the defendant is guaranteed an impartial jury and the right to cross-examine and subpoena witnesses. After the trial, the defendant can neither be subjected to excessive fines or punishment, nor be denied the right to appeal, and he or she can not be placed in double jeopardy—i.e., tried again for the same allegations.

Criminal Procedures

The standard processing of an accused offender through the system includes the officer making an investigation prior to an arrest, which includes (among other things) interviewing witnesses and checking for evidence. The arrest is followed by the "booking" of the accused, which includes logging the name of the suspect and the location, time, and purpose of the arrest. The accused may then have an initial appearance and preliminary hearing where all of the evidence against him or her is considered. The suspect will then be presented for "information" or before a grand jury to determine whether there is enough evidence to warrant a hearing. At the arraignment, the defendant is formally presented with the charges, and he/she may enter a plea. It is at this time that plea bargaining might be arranged. If there is no agreement, the defendant then appears at trial. If found guilty, he or she will be sentenced (Reid, 1994).

Being arrested and charged with a crime does not make it certain that one will appear in court. Because of the large number of initiated cases, certain informal measures have been taken which are not included in the formal court process. One of these efforts to reduce court overload is plea bargaining, where a prosecutor accepts a plea of guilty from the accused in exchange for a lesser sentence. By providing this "deal" to the accused, both the prosecution and the defense are saved the time and expense of a formal court proceeding (Kolasa and Meyer, 1987). In minor criminal cases, plea bargaining is the preferred outcome. In more serious cases, negotiations take much longer: the more serious the case, the fewer concessions will be offered by the prosecution; and the weaker the case, the more concessions will be offered (Sheley, 1995).

Another common practice to reduce the burden of the courts is to "funnel the offender away from the criminal justice system" (Reid, 1994:649) by placing the offender in a diversion program. This may include an acceptable program for rehabilitation such as supervised probation (Kolasa and Meyer, 1987). Much of the decision to pursue a specific case at this point depends on the prosecutor's determination of the likelihood of conviction at trial. In more recent years, the use of arbitration, mediation, and other forms of alternative dispute resolution has been accepted as standard practice for first offenders or minor offenses (Fox and Stinchcomb, 1994).

Pre-trial Incarceration

Most people assume that all people in jails are convicted, but this is not necessarily true. Fox and Stinchcomb (1994) argue that only 49% of the total jail population have actually been convicted of wrongdoing. The other 51% are awaiting trials. While the primary justification for detaining the accused is to ensure his/her presence at trial (Weston and Wells, 1987), about 63% of all felony defendants were released (on bond or otherwise) before court disposition, and some did commit crimes while on pre-trial release. Among those defendants already on pre-trial release when arrested, 56% were released once again (BJS, 1994a). About 1 in 12 defendants released by state courts absconded before their trials and were still missing a year later (BJS, 1994a).

Efforts have been made to reduce the number of people being detained prior to trial by using diversion programs (Fox and Stinchcomb, 1994). In these, persons awaiting trial are kept apart from convicted and sentenced offenders; this helps the detainees to reconstruct events for use at their trial (Weston and Wells, 1987). The rights of pre-trial detainees are controversial because the individual being detained has yet to be convicted and is presumed innocent until proven guilty. Most of the court decisions dealing with rights of detainees have ruled that any restrictions on individual rights are for jail security and not intended to punish the detainee (Weston and Wells, 1987: 53).

Bail may be granted to an accused offender for release prior to trial, except in the case of crimes punishable by death, where bail is at the discretion of the court. The institution of bail derives from the basic presumption of innocence upon which our system of criminal justice is founded. While release on bail is a right at the federal level, it is not delineated as a right at the state level (Weston and Wells, 1987).

Judicial System

Administration

Court proceedings for federal cases start at federal district courts. In larger states, there may be more than one federal district court in the state. Appeals from federal district court decisions go to the U.S. Court of Appeals, and appeals from decisions of the U.S. Court of Appeals go to the U.S. Supreme Court (Kolasa and Meyer, 1987). The United States is divided into eleven federal judicial circuits. Each has a Court of Appeals known as the U.S. Court of Appeals for that circuit. The U.S. Courts of Appeals are intermediate appellate courts created by Congress in 1891; they were known until 1948 as U.S. Circuit Courts of Appeals (Black, 1979).

At the state level, cases begin at the trial court of limited jurisdiction. This court handles less serious criminal cases and misdemeanors, such as traffic or prostitution law violations. The next level of state courts is the trial court of general jurisdiction where felony cases or major civil disputes (e.g., domestic violence, wills) are adjudicated. The next level of courts found in about half the states is the intermediate appellate court. The highest state court is the appellate court of last resort or the state supreme court. Cases appealed from the state appellate courts of last resort or the state supreme court may be heard by the U.S. Supreme Court.

Special Courts

The U.S. system of justice includes several specialized federal courts. Below the Supreme Court are the U.S. Courts of Federal Claims, U.S. Court of International Trade, Special Court Regional Rail Reorganization Act of 1973, a Judicial Panel on Multidistrict Litigation, the U.S. Court of Appeals for the Armed Forces, the U.S. Tax Court, and the U.S. Court of Veterans Appeals (Brownson, 1994).

Judges

The function of the judiciary in the judicial process is responsible supervision. They oversee the work of the police, the prosecution, the opposing counsel, and the jurors, and they preserve due process of law throughout the procedures (Weston and Wells, 1987). At the federal level, judges are chosen by the President of the United States with the advice and consent of the Senate. At the state level, many systems choose judges through bipartisan nominations and special bar association advisory committees, whereas in some states they are elected. In 1989 the number of federal judges was 1,035 (BJS, 1991). At the state level, the number of judges varies, depending on the number of courts and the population of the state.

Penalties and Sentencing

Sentencing Process

For the purpose of sentencing, all crimes are classified into categories reflecting substantial differences in the gravity of the offense. Sentencing is a two-step decision process. The first decision is whether to release a convicted offender to a community correctional program, and the second is determining the length of probation or imprisonment to be imposed (Weston and Wells, 1987). The judge, in most situations, has wide discretionary power over the severity of sentence to be imposed (Kolasa and Meyer, 1987). In some jurisdictions, the judge will delay sentencing until he/she receives advice from a behavioral clinic or similar group of professional evaluators of behavior, if there is some doubt about the kind of sentence that will best achieve the goals of the criminal justice system.

Terms of sentence vary from state to state and may be determinate or indeterminate. Determinate sentences send a convicted offender to prison for a specific number of years. In indeterminate sentences the offender receives minimum and maximum terms of imprisonment. At a later date, the case is reviewed to determine the convict's parole worthiness and a final release date. Mandatory sentences call for the sentencing judge to impose certain terms of imprisonment, as they have been outlined by the legislature (Weston and Wells, 1987).

Types of Penalties

Penalties for commission of a criminal offense vary dramatically depending on the type of crime committed. Sentencing alternatives include fines, probation with or without supervision—which reserves decision on a sentence until a time when (if) the offender is arrested and prosecuted again—commitment to a local jail for a short term, commitment to a state prison for a more lengthy term, and in some states, the death penalty (Weston and Wells, 1987).

This issue of capital punishment remains a constant controversy in the U.S. criminal justice systems. It is used in some states, but only for the most serious crimes. BJS Bulletin (1994d) states that 10 states executed 38 prisoners in 1993, and a total of 2,716 prisoners are on death row in various states. Only six prisoners in federal custody are on death row (1994d). In 1991, 10,354 inmates in federal and state facilities were sentenced to life in prison (BJS, 1991:625).

Prison

Description

According to the 1990 BJS Census of State and Federal Correctional Facilities (1992b), of the 1,207 state and 80 federal correctional facilities, 234 were maximum security, 403 were medium security, and 650 were minimum security. Maximum and medium security facilities are the most secure prison structures, typically surrounded by high walls or fences, secured with razor wire, and watched by armed correctional officers in observations towers (Reid, 1994:610). Minimum security facilities are surrounded by fences with barbed wire, but may or may not have armed correctional officers present. The total number of prisoners under the jurisdiction of the federal or state correctional authorities at the end of 1993 reached a record high of 948,881, with the states holding 859,295, and the federal jurisdiction holding 89,586 (BJS, 1994a).

The most recent information out of the U.S. Department of Justice identifies males as 92% of the federal prisons population, with females comprising 8% of the population (BJS, 1994a). For federal prison inmates, the median age is 36; 38% are white, 30% black, 28% Hispanic, and 4% other races; 38% are married, 30% are divorced or separated, and 33% have never been married; 77% have at least a high school education; and 18% are foreign nationals.

At the state level, males comprise 95% and females 5% of the prison population. Median age for state inmates is 30; 35% are white, 46% are black, 17% are Hispanic, and 2% are other races; 18% are married, 27% are widowed, divorced, or separated, and 55% have never been married; and only 4% are citizens of other countries.

The average daily population of jail inmates in 1990 was 408,075. This breaks down to 368,091 adult males, 37,844 adult females, and 2,140 juveniles (BJS, 1991). The ethnic breakdown of jail inmates in 1990 included 46% white males, 5% white females, 43% black males, 4% black females, and 2 % male and 1% female others (Native Americans, Aleuts, Asians, and Pacific Islanders).

When considering the types of crimes committed which resulted in the individual's incarceration, BJS (1994a) reports that 17% committed violent offenses,

10% property offenses, 58% drug offenses, 12% public order offenses, and 2% other offenses. BJS studies show that 47% of state inmates are incarcerated for violent offenses, 25% for property offenses, 21% for drug offenses, 7% for public order offenses, and 0.4% for other offenses.

Administration

Each correctional institution within a state is headed by an administrator, whose title is typically a chief warden or a superintendent. Their responsibilities are coordination of administrative divisions; establishment of institutional policies and procedures; personnel decision-making; preparation of the facility's budget; and development of external relationships with civic groups, professional associations, and the like (Fox and Stinchcomb, 1994).

Expenditures for a correctional facility depend on such factors as where the prison is located, the number of inmates, the number of personnel needed to staff the facility, the level of security, and the number of programs, and the number of inmates who received medical treatments. Because the state level of government is responsible for the majority of prison operations in the United States, the states bear the primary financial responsibility. Fox and Stinchcomb (1994) state that about 28.6 cents of every "justice dollar is spent on corrections," and break this total down: the federal government spends 1.5 cents or 5%, the state government spends 17.7 cents or 62%, and local governments spend 9.4 cents or 33% of overall corrections funding.

Using Bureau of Justice Statistics, Fox and Stinchcomb (1994) reviewed construction costs for new facilities ranging from: over $70,000 per bed for maximum security state prisons, to just under $30,000 per bed for minimum security facilities, to approximately $26,000 per bed for juvenile institutions. Operating costs vary from almost $6,000 to over $23,000 per inmate. Fox and Stinchcomb observed in their review that the cost of keeping someone in prison has increased to $14,000, but other studies placed the range much higher at $30,000 to $60,000.

Correction officer training has come a long way, and it had a very dubious beginning. Lombardo (1989) suggests that early prison training programs were run by the inmates. Because experienced officers were reluctant to instruct new correctional officers, new officers had to turn to the inmates they were supervising for advice. At present, the American Correctional Association's training standards for officers call for a minimum of 40 hours of orientation prior to job assignment, followed by 120 hours within the first year of employment (along with an additional 40 hours each year thereafter).

According to the *BJS Sourcebook* (1991), state correctional personnel in adult systems includes 160,115 white men and 58,814 white women; 36,117 black men and 19,526 black women; and 10,953 Hispanic men and 3,720 Hispanic women; all other races comprise 7,302 men and 3,131 women. At the federal level, correctional personnel includes 10,128 white men and 3,136 white women; 2,270 black men and 1,125 black women; and 1,030 Hispanic men and 247 Hispanic women; with all other races including 272 men and 76 women.

Conditions

The "crisis in corrections" has been synonymous with conditions of overcrowding. Gottfredson and McConville (1987) suggest that in addition to overcrowding, many prisons and jails are old and rotting; they are often inadequately staffed, lacking in medical care, and cannot adequately protect inmates from physical abuse. Although not as bad as Brazilian and Sierra Leonian prisons (see Chapters 6 and 17), conditions in prisons in the United States have been controversial. As indicated above, overcrowding has remained a constant problem. In 1993, according to the BJS report, thirteen states reported they were operating at 99% of their highest capacity. Federal prisons were estimated to be operating at 36% above their capacity. At the state level, 22 jurisdictions reported that a total of 50,966 state prisoners were held in local jails or other facilities because of overcrowding in state facilities.

Overcrowded conditions have caused some prisons to resort to early release programs. Some argue that early release programs are related to the rehabilitative functions of the prison systems. Prisoners can "earn" reduced sentences for "good time" (Thomas, 1987). However, many argue that the inmate should serve the time sentenced. This ongoing debate among criminal justice officials is commonly referred to as "truth in sentencing."

Inmates are often allowed to work within the prison system. Institutional programs for inmates include basic education, computer instruction, college education courses, vocational training, library services, and recreation. Unfortunately, the prison industry of the Chinese, Danish, and Japanese corrections (see Chapters 8, 14, and 17) is not used currently in America.

The seven areas of inmate complaints which have been most frequently litigated by the courts in recent years are the use of force, mail and visitation rights, isolated confinement ("keep-locked"), disciplinary proceedings, religious rights, legal services, and parole issues (Palmer, 1973). Three additional issues which have caused controversy are the right to treatment (see *Holt v. Sarver, Jones v. Wittenberg,* and *Rouse v. Cameron),* the right to medical aid, and the right to life (see *Furman v. Georgia)* (Palmer, 1973:126–131).

In recent years, the Texas prison system has been regarded as an example of how bad prison conditions have become in the United States. Martin and Ekland-Olson (1985) submitted that the Texas system had allowed "an agency with conglomerate business, agricultural, medical, and educational activities to escape accountability for its fiscal mismanagement, illegal operations, and the dehumanization of persons under its control." In what became the largest prisoner's rights lawsuit in the history of American jurisprudence, David Ruiz filed a prisoner petition in June 1972 claiming that the Texas prison system was oppressive, brutal, and in violation of the Eighth Amendment (prohibition against cruel and unusual punishments). An agreement was reached in 1985 by a court order, but the Texas Department of Corrections (TDC) failed to comply. Consequently, on December 31, 1985, the Texas Department of Corrections was held in contempt of court order and threatened with fines as high as $24 million per month if it did not comply with the 1985 settlement agreement.

While the actions of the Texas prison system are not representative of all state and federal prison systems, many express concern over the deterioration of prisons and jails in the United States. Recent years have witnessed unprecedented prison population growth and acute violence among inmates (Sheley, 1995). Prison populations are soaring, while budgets are being reduced (Reid, 1994). Reid argues that some difficult decisions need to be made by the public and by legislators to determine what we want our prisons to do for inmates.

Discussion

The U.S. Criminal Justice System has been organized around the notion of protecting the rights of the accused, while preserving the welfare of the public. This can often prove to be a difficult and delicate balance. Because this system fundamentally presumes that the accused is "innocent until proven guilty," it has been argued that the adjudication process should consider the rights of the accused before the rights of the victim(s). More and more provisions, therefore, protect the rights of criminals, yet the public is confronted with rising crime rates, drug abuse, and violence. Sometimes it can seem that this system of justice benefits criminals rather than the non-criminal public.

The system of justice in the United States can at times be a long, drawn out, tedious process. China allows a maximum of three days for an appeal, and Nigeria, Ghana, and Sierra Leone require that an appeal be filed within 30 days. In the United States, however, filing an appeal can take 6 months or longer. This aspect of the criminal justice system in the United States places an unacceptable burden on the overall working of the system. Efforts to protect individual rights, one might argue, have resulted in a system of justice that is at best inefficient, and at worst ineffective.

The American system of criminal justice has also been targeted by a debate over the role that wealth and positions of power can play in securing one's defense or innocence. Sometimes the rich and famous prove to be beyond incrimination. Critics argue that large sums of money can buy enough "reasonable doubt" to result in an acquittal. If one has the funds to secure the most powerful legal minds or the best team of investigators, it may be practically impossible to convict you. On the other hand, if you lack sufficient funds and are accused of a crime that you did not commit, you may be found guilty despite your court-appointed defense attorney because of inadequate legal support.

Some have also said that the present criminal justice system was designed to combat "street criminals" and does not adequately address other types of crime. The public fears street crime, and the criminal justice system has attempted to respond to this increasing concern. It has not, however, responded effectively to several new and possibly more destructive criminal enterprises of the privileged class, such as white collar crimes, corporate crimes, computer crimes, and environmental crimes. Although some legal scholars identify such actions as criminal, "legal loopholes" presently allow individuals (when and if arrested) to escape conviction. Furthermore, when one of the privileged class is actually convicted, punishment is usually quite lenient when compared to that meted out to "street criminals."

The American people are concerned about protecting themselves from criminals. They are disturbed by early release programs and other actions taken to address prison overcrowding problems, and they have grown skeptical of the system's ability to protect the public. This concern, in conjunction with the prevalence of drug abuse and misuse and the availability of guns to every sort of person in the society, poses a significant problem for the entire criminal justice system and the American public.

Innovative programs have been established in an effort to address these and other concerns about the criminal justice system in the United States. The revised data collection process of the Federal Bureau of Investigation provides one good example of such efforts. Better information on criminal acts, victimization, the role of drugs, and other related factors will aid the attempts at all levels of the criminal justice system to determine how to address criminal actions effectively. Focusing public attention on problems caused by crimes of all types—both those committed on and those committed off the street—will provide a context for public reexamination of "victim's rights" and increase popular awareness of how one can avoid being a victim of crime and of how to prevent crime in high places.

Finally, it must be admitted that defense lawyers and the U.S. criminal justice system have focused their attention on preserving the rights of the offender to the detriment of the safety and interests of the masses. Until our social control agencies make the safety and interests of the public central in their adjudication and disposal of offenders, our criminal justice system will continue to be a toothless bulldog.

Notes

1. This chapter follows an outline for writing criminal justice systems developed by Professor Graeme Newman of the State University of New York at Albany.

Discussion and Review Questions

1. What are the provisions of the following in the U.S. Constitution?
    (a) The Fourth Amendment
    (b) The Fifth Amendment
    (c) The Sixth Amendment
    (d) The Seventh Amendment
    (e) The Eighth Amendment

2. What were the provisions of the Crime Act of 1790?

3. What is meant by the English common law tradition?

4. What is "due process of law?"

5. What is the adversarial system of criminal justice?

6. What do you understand by mala in se offenses and mala prohibita offenses?

7. How did misdemeanor crimes come about?

8. Briefly explain the following:
    (a) Mens rea
    (b) Actus reus
    (c) Offense committed under duress
    (d) M'Naghten Rule
    (e) UCR and NCVS (NCS)
    (f) Miranda rule
    (g) Exclusionary rule
    (h) Double jeopardy
    (i) Determinate and indeterminate sentences
    (j) Death row

9. What is a mandatory sentence?

10. Which are the two states in the United States where the Court of Appeals is the highest appellate court for criminal matters?

11. What is "double jeopardy" in the United States criminal justice system?

12. In the United States system of criminal justice, what are the seven determining factors that a crime has been committed?

13. Differentiate between "statutory law" and "common law."

14. In the American system of criminal justice, what four factors could exculpate an accused person from criminal liability?

15. What are the provisions of the following Acts?
    (a) The Harrison Narcotics Act of 1914.
    (b) The Pure Food and Drug Act of 1906.
    c) The Marijuana Tax Act of 1937.
    (d) The Narcotics Control Act of 1956.
    (e) The Boggs Act of 1951.

16. What factors are identified in the UCR?

17. Compare and contrast the UCR and NCVS.

18. Why was Sir Robert Peel an important figure in the 19th century American system of policing?

19. What was the issue in *Brown v. Mississippi* (1936)?

20. What was the U.S. Supreme Court ruling in *Miranda v. Arizona* (1966)?

3

The Criminal Justice System of Ireland

Paul Douglas O'Mahony

Introduction

Ireland is a small island of about 5.2 million people with an area of 32,000 square miles situated on the Atlantic seaboard of northwestern Europe, just to the west of the island of Britain. Since 1922, the island has been divided into two separate jurisdictions. One was originally termed the Irish Free State, but, since the introduction of the 1937 Constitution of Ireland, has become known officially as Ireland (or "Eire" in the Irish language). The other, Northern Ireland, is a constituent part of the United Kingdom of Great Britain and Northern Ireland. This division was, at the time, thought necessary in some quarters, especially the Westminster government, because a substantial majority of the people of Ulster, the northeastern province of Ireland, who were largely Protestants, fervently desired to remain under British rule.

The partition of Ireland in 1922 has immense consequences for Irish political, social, and economic life down to the present day. The signing of the Anglo–Irish Treaty, establishing partition, provoked a short, but bloody and bitter, civil war within the Irish Free State between those who accepted and those who rejected the Treaty (Department of Foreign Affairs, 1995). Even today the two main political parties in Ireland trace their roots to the opposing sides in that war.

Since 1969, there has been a violent terrorist campaign in Northern Ireland waged by nationalist organizations, such as the IRA, seeking the reunification of Ireland. This in turn has led to a counter movement of violence by loyalist terrorists, seeking to maintain the links with the British Crown and Westminster. In the last few years, there has been a concerted effort on the part of both the British and Irish governments to broker a lasting peace agreement between Dublin and London and the unionist and nationalist communities in Northern Ireland. With considerable assistance from the U.S. administration by way of mediation, these efforts have resulted in the Good Friday agreement of 1998, a very hopeful step that has created new structures of local self-government for Northern Ireland, with intrinsic mechanisms for power-sharing across the sectarian and unionist/nationalist divide. A very significant aspect of this process has been the willingness of the Irish government and people (by way of a referendum) to amend the constitutional claim to the territory of the whole island. This formerly absolute claim has now been made subject to the democratic will of the people of Northern Ireland. Progress in the peace process has not completely eliminated civil strife and violence in Northern Ireland but has led to their substantial diminution.

This chapter will focus on the criminal justice system of the state known as Ireland, although it is necessary to acknowledge the continuing influence of the partition of the island even on the internal workings of the criminal justice system of Ireland. Ireland, then, is an independent state with a population of almost 3.8 million, occupying 26,000 square miles, or 26 of the total 32 administrative counties of the island of Ireland (Department of Foreign Affairs, 1995). Dublin, a city of about 1 million people, is the capital. It is the political, administrative, legal, and economic hub of the country and the only large city. The next largest city, Cork, has a population of about 200,000. The centrality of Dublin is indicated by the fact that it has about 60% of all reported crime occurring in the country.

Ireland is a relatively young, modern, independent state, founded in 1922, but it is also an ancient nation with a long and troubled history, which for the past 800 years has been inextricably interwoven with the history of the neighboring island. Contemporary Ireland can only be understood against the background of its history, namely, (a) the struggle over centuries for independence; (b) the experience by the majority of the population for most of that time of almost total exclusion from the processes of government; and (c) the savage trauma of the terrible famines of the 1840s. Over just a few years, famine led to the loss, through starvation, disease, and emigration, of a quarter of the then population of over 8 million. The population has never recovered its prefamine level. Indeed, even after independence, Ireland was a country noted for its exportation of people. For most of this century the Irish economy has been based mostly on agriculture and has experienced low levels of growth that have totally failed to provide sufficient employment. Several million people born in Ireland now live and work in Britain, the United States, Australia, and elsewhere. Until recently, Ireland has tended to be a conservative and inward-looking country in social and political matters, which state of affairs has been linked to the powerful position of the Roman Catholic Church in Irish society (Lee, 1989).

In recent years the political and social influence of the church has greatly declined. There has also been remarkable growth in the economy, leading to the provision of 250,000 new jobs in the mid-1990s, and a newfound dynamism in almost all areas of Irish life. There has been an associated rapid development of the national infrastructure, in terms of roads, buildings, telecommunications, etc. Much of this economic progress is linked to membership of the European Community since 1973, which has been very beneficial for Ireland in terms of economic support and increased opportunity for development. In the late 1990s, the pattern of migration has even been reversed for the first time since the Famine. Presently more immigrate into the country than emigrate from it.

Rapid economic development has entailed rapid and momentous social change. Indeed, Ireland's experience of industrialization and urbanization and its opening up to the powerful influence of global media, international market forces, and the values of consumerism, individualism, and materialism have been particularly intense and concentrated. This is very obvious in the criminal justice area, where the past few decades have seen rapid growth in crime rates and the emergence of certain types of crime, and related problems such as drug abuse, which were formerly almost unknown in Ireland.

Recent years have, therefore, been an especially challenging period for Irish criminal justice institutions and traditions. Many of these have been found to be wanting and in need of modernization (O'Mahony, 1996). For most of this century, perhaps reflecting the stagnant state of the economy, the high level of emigration of young people, and the highly conservative social milieu, crime was not a serious problem in Ireland. This meant that the criminal law and institutions, such as the courts and the prisons, changed very little. They tended to be backward-looking and inflexible and so ill-equipped to deal with the very much greater and more complex demands suddenly placed on them in the last quarter of the twentieth century.

The Irish System of Government

Ireland is a parliamentary democracy with a written constitution, a president as head of state, and a bicameral Parliament (Chubb, 1970). The constitution establishes, on the model of the United States, the doctrine of separation of powers as between the executive, the legislature, and the judiciary. The national Parliament, which is commonly known, both in English and in Irish discourse, by its Irish name—Oireachtas—consists of the president (in Irish an tUachtarán) and two houses: a House of Representatives (Dáil Éireann) and a Senate (Seanad Éireann).

The president, whose term of office is 7 years, is a figurehead, because he/she does not have executive powers. The president is elected by the direct vote of the people and may be reelected for a second term for up to a maximum period of office of 14 years. On the nomination of Dáil Éireann, the president appoints the Taoiseach, i.e., the head of government (prime minister). On the advice of the Taoiseach and with the prior approval of Dáil Éireann, the president appoints the members of the government. The president also appoints judges, on the advice of the government.

The president is not merely a ceremonial head of state and titular supreme commander of the defense forces, but has certain limited but significant powers that in effect make him or her the guardian of the Irish constitution. Before a bill can become a law, it must be signed by the president. However, the president also has the discretionary power, after consultation with the Council of State, an advisory body to the president, to refer any bill to the Supreme Court for a ruling as to whether it contains anything repugnant to the constitution. The president also has the option to accede to a petition from a majority of the Seanad and no less than a third of the Dáil to refuse to sign a bill, because it involves matters of such national importance that it should be subject to the direct democratic will of the people by means of a referendum. Finally, the president has the absolute discretion to refuse to dissolve the Dáil on the advice of a Taoiseach despite the fact that the Taoiseach no longer retains the support of a majority in the Dáil.

Representatives, who are titled Teachtaí Dála but almost invariably referred to as TDs, are directly elected by the people. The country is divided into forty-one multiseat constituencies, which return three, four, or five members depending on their population. Elections to the Dáil take place at least every 5 years. Resident citizens over 18 years of age are entitled to vote, as are British citizens living in Ireland. Voting is by secret ballot. The electoral system is proportional representation by means of a single transferable vote. The voter in effect rank orders the candidates, placing the numeral "1" against the name of his or her first choice candidate, "2" against the second choice candidate, and so on.

The second chamber, the Seanad, has 60 members. Eleven of these are nominated directly by the Taoiseach (the prime minister) of an incoming government; three are elected by the graduates of the National University of Ireland, and three by the graduates of the University of Dublin. The remaining 43 members are elected from five panels of persons with specialized knowledge and experience representing various social, cultural, and economic interests.

The sole power of making laws for the State is vested in the Oireachtas. Government policy and administration may be critically examined in both the Dáil and the Seanad, but according to the constitution, the government is responsible and accountable to the Dáil alone (Doolan, 1991). The Dáil also has superior powers in respect of lawmaking and indeed the amendment or repeal of a past legislation. An ordinary bill passed by the Dáil is sent on to the Seanad, which has 90 days to consider it (the role of the Seanad in money bills is more restricted). The Seanad may suggest amendments or even reject a bill, but if, after a period of 180 days, the Dáil wishes to proceed with the bill in its original form, it may resolve to do so and declare the bill to have passed both houses of the Oireachtas. In this event, if a majority of the Seanad and a third of the Dáil agree that a matter of national importance is at issue, they may petition the president not to sign the bill and to refer the matter to the people by way of referendum. The Seanad has in fact never exercised this power. The constitution is the basic law of the country. It may only be amended by means of a referendum, that is, by a majority vote in favor of amendment by the people of Ireland. Bills to amend the constitution can only be initiated in the Dáil.

A Brief History of the Irish Criminal Justice System

The history of the Irish criminal justice system is, like Irish political history, intimately linked with that of Britain. The current Irish system is the direct successor to the English legal system, which from 1169, the date of the Anglo–Norman invasion led by "Strongbow," the Earl of Pembroke, began to be imposed on the then prevailing native system of law known as Brehon law. The Brehon system was based on custom and is named after the traveling justices of the Celtic Christian period, who were called Brehons (Byrne and McCutcheon, 1996). The Brehons are thought to have evolved from, and to have undertaken a similar social role to, the pre-Christian Celtic druids. Brehon law was a quite extensive, well-developed, and so-

phisticated body of law, which, as far back as the seventh and eighth centuries, was carefully documented in the Irish language. There has been a recent publication, in six annotated volumes (Binchy, 1978), of all the extant Brehon laws.

Within the island, there was a long period of coexistence, but not commingling, of English and Brehon law. This period began at the King's Council of 1171 at Waterford, when the feudal Anglo–Norman King, Henry II, asserted his overlordship over the territory of Ireland and proclaimed that "the laws of England were by all freely received and confirmed." However, it was more than 400 years before this over-optimistic claim became a reality. Brehon law persisted in many areas and was active and influential, particularly in the North and West, until the early seventeenth century, when it was finally supplanted by English law throughout the land. The extension of the writ of English law and its ultimate dominance mirror the development of the English colony in Ireland. The original wave of Anglo–Norman invaders never established their dominion over the whole island and in fact, over the course of a few generations, began to be assimilated into the native Irish culture. Some of them adopted the Irish language and local customs, including in some cases Brehon law. In this way and through intermarriage with the native Irish noble families, they became, in a famous phrase, "more Irish than the Irish themselves."

Poyning's Law, which dates from 1494, was clearly designed to address the growing tendency for colonists and native Irish alike to assert more and more autonomy from the English Crown by means of legislation at local Irish parliaments. Poyning's Law curtailed the powers of Irish parliaments, in effect establishing the precedence of English legislation over Irish legislation and affirming the supremacy of English law in Ireland (Byrne and McCutcheon, 1996). Even then English law only held sway within the Pale, the eastern part of the country, and scattered areas of the South and Midlands, which were all under close control of the English. Elsewhere, Brehon law was still predominant. This situation prevailed until the Tudor monarchs finally extended and consolidated English hegemony over the whole island.

Henry VIII was the first English monarch to declare himself King of Ireland in 1541, but it was not until the 1800 Act of Union that Ireland was fully absorbed into the Westminster political system under the British Crown and became an integral part of the United Kingdom of Great Britain and Ireland. Indeed, from 1783 to 1800 Ireland enjoyed an unprecedented period of autonomy, prosperity, and rapid development under what is known as Grattan's Parliament. For this period, Poyning's Law was repealed, in effect meaning that Westminster renounced its claim to legislate for Ireland. Ireland's own House of Commons and House of Lords sat in Dublin.

However, this form of parliamentary independence, though beneficial in its effects for the country as a whole, was extremely limited in respect of its representation of the population at large. It was a parliament of and for the Protestant minority, and in particular the members of the established Church of Ireland. It essentially excluded the interests of the large Roman Catholic majority and the smaller but substantial group of dissenting Protestants concentrated in Ulster, the northeastern province. Indeed, legislation known as the penal laws, which discriminated against Roman Catholics and limited their civil and religious rights, was in force throughout this period and was only slowly modified and abolished throughout the nineteenth century (Cullen, 1976).

The rebellion of the United Irishmen in 1798, which resulted in the loss of more than thirty thousand lives, along with, for the British government, the fearsome examples of the American and French revolutions, led to a change of attitude on the part of Westminster toward a possibly too

successful Irish Parliament. With the Act of Union, the Dublin Parliament was dissolved and Westminster became the sole legislative authority for Ireland.

Until 1922, then, Ireland was an integral part of the United Kingdom, sending its own representatives to Westminster. The Irish criminal justice system was therefore, in this period, no more than a regional branch of the general British system. The court and legal systems were largely similar to those of the English, with some local modifications that reflected the political and social realities on the ground. For example, it was considered useful to have a corps of salaried professional judges called "resident magistrates" in the lower courts in Ireland rather than to rely on the English system of nonprofessional local magistrates. Policing, however, was more distinctive. There was a separate police authority for Dublin, but otherwise a national armed police force called the Royal Irish Constabulary. As Rob Reiner (1994), a leading British authority on policing, tells us, the concept of the unarmed, courteous English policeman was born out of the need to persuade and appease British voters, who were none too sure that they required to be policed at all, while "a more militaristic and coercive model was from the outset exported to the colonial situation, including John Bull's other island (i.e., Ireland)." Indeed, as Brogden (1987) has pointed out, the Royal Irish Constabulary was the explicit model for most of the colonial police forces of the British Empire.

By and large, exactly the same laws applied in Ireland and England, and consequently Ireland did benefit to a degree from the important improvements to the general legal framework for the protection of the rights of the individual introduced in this period in the United Kingdom. Most notable of these advances, perhaps, was the adoption by the Westminster government of a new, more enlightened approach to prisons. The 1842 prison rules, promulgated for the new penitentiary at

Pentonville in London, for the first time placed explicit legal constraints on prison authorities as well as on prisoners. These rules, which substantially advanced the human rights of prisoners (Ignatief, 1978), were also applied in Ireland.

The English philanthropist John Howard was the outstanding penal reformer of the era that led to the radical improvements in the conditions of imprisonment. Howard was mainly responsible for raising public awareness of the appallingly harsh, chaotic, and disease-ridden conditions in the prisons of his time. Howard played a very significant role in Ireland, visiting and publishing reports on almost every prison establishment in Ireland. Doorley (1987) reports that Howard described even the newly constructed Newgate Prison in Dublin in 1781 as "the reverse of every idea that I can form of a perfect and well-regulated prison." It was also Howard who publicized the fact that, in 1783, fifteen prisoners in Newgate and sixteen in Kilmainham (both prisons in the Dublin area) were being held indefinitely by the chief warder for nonpayment of various fees, sometimes including a special release fee, even though they had been acquitted at trial of all the crimes with which they had been charged (Anonymous, 1856). The growing awareness of these kinds of injustices provided a powerful impetus for reform.

The first Director of Irish Convict Prisons, Sir Walter Crofton, was appointed in the 1850s and proved to be a progressive and innovative thinker. He introduced the intermediate prison system, which has become Ireland's chief claim to fame in the annals of penal methods. According to the *Encyclopedia Britannica*, many features of what became known as the "Irish system" were adopted by reformatories in the United States in the late nineteenth century, and the Irish system and the subsequent U.S. modifications to it "had great impact on European correctional practices."

The system was essentially a matter of progressive stages in imprisonment, involving decreasing levels of control (O'Mahony, 1994). The convict was held in the penitentiary for the first 9 months of his sentence in the kind of solitary confinement prescribed by the "silent and separate system." The second stage saw the convict, while still housed in the penitentiary, involved by day in hard labor, usually on major public building and engineering works outside prison. This stage was of variable length and permitted a degree of association between prisoners. Finally, in the months running up to release the convict was held at an "intermediate prison" at a rural location. Here the prisoners worked on land reclamation and slept in specially erected iron huts. There were no walls and the guards were unarmed. Prisoners were, it was claimed, given sufficient freedom and responsibility to test their fitness to be released. A contemporary description (Anonymous, 1858) tells us that "as the convict's moral progress advances, his state of duress becomes less vile; and at last he is treated as a man and trusted as such."

In general, following the course of development in Britain, the criminal justice system in Ireland in the nineteenth century and the early twentieth century evolved slowly without dramatic or sudden change. On the other hand, more and more specific legislation was passed by Westminster defining and setting out penalties for criminal behavior, and thus limiting the scope of the common law. However, it is important to remember that in Ireland there was considerable additional tension within and pressure on the criminal justice system, because the system was very frequently used to suppress nationalist activists, landless peasant agitators, and the victims of famine and extreme poverty. The courts, the police, and the penal system continued to be perceived by large sectors of the population as the coercive arm of an alien colonial power.

The present criminal justice system, described below, has evolved over the years since independence. By and large, there has been a remarkable continuity with the British era in Ireland, and although distinctive structures and legal frameworks have emerged, there is still a strong similarity to the British system. Many of the innovations introduced in Ireland—for example, the penalty of a community service order—have been modeled on similar initiatives previously undertaken in Britain. One interesting historical note is that during the War of Independence, between 1920 and 1922, the revolutionary government set up its own courts, called the Dáil courts. This led to a brief, partial revival of Brehon law, because in a highly symbolic gesture, clearly signaling an ardent desire to reject everything associated with the colonial past and the imperial masters, English law textbooks were not to be cited in the Dáil courts. Brehon and European Civil Law decisions, on the other hand, could be used as persuasive precedents. However, this experimental attempt to resurrect the ancient native Irish system of law was short-lived. After the Treaty of 1922, establishing the Irish Free State, the Dáil courts were abolished and the court system reverted to its previous form. Brehon precepts and rules have no place in the contemporary Irish legal system. Indeed, it is one of the ironies of the modern, independent state of Ireland that some Westminster legislation of the last century is still law, although the same legislation has long ago been repealed or revised in England and Wales.

The Legal System in Ireland

The Irish legal system is firmly rooted in the English common law tradition, and many statutes passed by the British Parliament before 1921 continue to have the force of law, because they have not been repealed by the Irish Parliament. Nonethe-

less, the current Irish legal system has been termed by Rottman and Tormey (1985) "a hybrid, combining basic features of both the American and the British models as well as some distinctive native innovations."

The common law as the source of law has been described by Byrne and McCutcheon (1996) as "consisting of the hundreds of thousands of decisions which have been delivered by the courts over the centuries and which, by virtue of the demands of the doctrine of precedent, enjoy binding force of law. . . . To this day significant areas of Irish law are governed by common law rules unaffected by rules derived from other sources." The principal, further sources of Irish Law are legislation and the constitution of 1937, and these take precedence over common law. Indeed, the provisions of the constitution supersede both the common law and legislative rules. It is with respect to the central role of the constitution that the Irish system can be described as having a strong affinity to the American model. Since the function of interpreting the provisions of the constitution, which is the basic law of the country, is entrusted by the constitution itself to the courts, the judiciary have come to play a major role in defining the actual operation of the criminal justice system (Doolan, 1991).

There is a growing body of Irish criminal law legislation and an accumulation of constitutional law rulings by the Supreme Court that have given a distinctive shape both to the criminal law and the courts, police, and penal procedures. The Irish legal system, then, can be seen to be growing ever more distinct from the British system despite the shared legacy of common law.

There is one major source of Irish law that, in its quite circumscribed area of competence, takes precedence over the common law—that is, Irish legislation and even the Irish Constitution. This is European Community law. The Court of Justice of the European Communities, sitting in Luxembourg, presides over this legal system and takes precedence over national law both as a matter of Community law and national law. On Ireland's accession to the membership of the European Community in 1973, an amendment to the Irish Constitution acknowledged this precedence. The European Court of Justice is mainly active in the economic and social areas—for example, in the establishment of a free market within the European Union (EU) and of sexual equality in matters of pay and social welfare. The European Court of Human Rights, sitting in Strasbourg under the aegis of the Council of Europe, has heard a number of significant Irish cases and has, arguably, had a profound, liberalizing effect on Irish social life and attitudes. For example, rulings of the European Court of Human Rights have led to decriminalization of homosexuality and the provision of free legal aid in civil and matrimonial matters.

Since the criminal law creates both the crime and the criminal, we are now going to look at the nature and incidence of crime in Ireland.

The Nature of Crime in Ireland

There is little by way of a criminological tradition in Ireland, as is clear from the lack of a department of criminology at any of the Irish universities and of either public sector or independent institutes for criminological research. Although scattered scholars and researchers from a variety of disciplines have begun to build a body of useful texts and research findings over recent decades, there remain numerous gaps in our knowledge and understanding of crime in Ireland.

The most reliable source of information on the nature and extent of crime is the Annual Crime Report of the Garda Síochana. This report gives a statistical accounting of indictable, more serious crimes, broken down into the following categories: offenses against the person,

such as murder, rape, and assault; offenses against property with violence, such as arson, robbery, and burglary; offenses against property without violence, such as petty larceny, embezzlement, and forgery; and a fourth catch-all category, covering miscellaneous offenses such as indecent exposure, misuse of drugs, and poaching. The Crime Report chronicles, in less detail, nonindictable, summary offenses, which normally number about 500,000 in a year. These offenses are police defined, in the sense that they are only recorded if a culprit is caught and proceeded against. The majority of summary offenses are Traffic Acts Offenses, such as speeding, drunken driving, and driving an automobile without insurance. However, the category also covers a large variety of criminal offenses such as minor assaults, taking a car for the purpose of joy-riding, and public order offenses.

In 1947, when the Annual Garda Report on Crime was first published, crime was at a very low level. In that year, there were a total of 15,000 indictable crimes recorded (429 crimes per 100,000 population). By 1970, this figure doubled to a total of 30,000 indictable crimes and the following decades have seen an even more rapid increase in crime. The figures for 1983 were more than three times greater than those for 1970. Indeed, the increase in indictable crimes in the one year from 1980 to 1981 was greater than the total figure of 15,000 for 1947. In 1995, indictable crimes reached an historic peak of 102,000 (2,684 per 100,000 of population), but have declined in both 1996 and 1997.

However, even the peak figures for Ireland suggest that it is, comparatively speaking, a low-crime country. The Irish crime rate is about half of that for the United States (5,060 per 100,000; FBI, 1992) and a third of that for both England and Wales (9,620 per 100,000; Home Office, 1995) and Denmark, a similarly sized Northern European country (9,960 per 100,000; Danish Statistical Abstract, 1995). However, there are inevitably definitional and equivalence problems with such comparisons.

Indictable crimes in Ireland are, furthermore, overwhelmingly dominated by property crimes. The largest single category is burglary, which normally accounts for about 30% of all crimes. Larceny accounts for a further 55% of all indictable crimes, with larceny from unattended vehicles the single largest category in this group (17,000 in 1996). Robbery is also a relatively common crime, accounting for about 3% of the total, but armed robbery and armed aggravated burglary are relatively rare, numbering about 550 in 1996.

The most serious crimes are offenses against the person, and these are also relatively rare. In 1996, there were 1,500 such crimes, but this figure included almost 500 less serious assaults. In 1996 there were 46 homicides, which is a rate of about 12 per million. This represents a recent increase from a fairly constant average of about 9 per million over the previous 20 years. Thus, the Irish homicide rate is currently at about the same level as that in England and Wales (Home Office, 1995) and can be regarded as very low by international norms. By comparison, the Italian rate is close to 30 per million (Dooley, 1995) and the U.S. rate is about 98 per million (FBI, 1992).

One area that has seen dramatic increases in the level of reported crime is that of rape and other serious sex assaults (Department of Justice, 1997). In the 1980s there were an average of about 60 reports of rape per annum and an average of about 160 other serious sex assaults. In 1996, the figures were 180 for rape and 620 for other serious sex assaults (47 and 166 per million, respectively). This marked increase is thought to be mainly due to changing attitudes and a greater willingness to report such crime. However, according to evidence from rape crisis centers, even now, as few as 20 to 30% of rape victims report the crime to the police (*Report of the Conference on the Safety of Women*, 1993). The current Irish figures for reported

sex crime are, nonetheless, still low by international comparison. For example, in the United States, there are annually more than 400 reported rapes per million of population (FBI, 1992) and in England and Wales more than 100 per million (Home Office, 1995).

A very significant development in Irish criminal justice in the past 10 years is the exposure of a hitherto unacknowledged level of child sexual abuse by people in positions of trust, such as parents, clergy, sports coaches, and care workers. Revelations in this area, often relating to offenses dating back several decades, have led to many trials, convictions, and long prison sentences. Public, institutional, and criminal justice attitudes have been profoundly influenced by these revelations.

Current Irish crime rates are not high by international comparison; however, the Irish public's perception of the crime problem does not by any means reflect this relatively favorable position. In 1983, American criminologist Freda Adler included Ireland in her study of ten nations around the world with particularly low crime rates. She called this study *Nations Not Obsessed with Crime* (Adler, 1983). This title now appears ironic since, in recent years, the Irish media and general public have become greatly preoccupied with what they believe to be a severely deteriorating crime situation. The political response to crime, driven by public perceptions of crime, has arguably been overheated and disproportionate. For instance, the 1997 general election campaign made crime the number one issue, and the victorious political parties in that election are thought to have gained a considerable advantage at the polls by promising to introduce a "zero tolerance" policy on crime and to almost double available prison places. Many of the recent reforms and much new legislation in the criminal justice area has been inspired by a hard-line, "get tough" ideology.

The fear of crime is somewhat exaggerated in Ireland and has itself become a social problem (McCullagh, 1996). There are, nonetheless, a number of reasonable grounds for the intensified public concern about crime. Understandably, Irish attitudes and expectations are shaped mainly by consideration of internal social change rather than by statistical comparison with other countries. In this regard, the past 20 or 30 years have seen a very dramatic decline in the average Irish person's sense of personal security and interpersonal trust, related to the greatly increased crime rate.

Another factor is that there is controversy about the reliability of official statistics. Indeed, there have been studies (McCullagh, 1996) indicating that a large amount of crime goes unreported and a sizeable amount goes reported but unrecorded. However, much of the intense public concern is driven less by statistical data than by the conviction that the quality of crime has worsened and, in particular, that crime is now more vicious and more frequently accompanied by excessive, gratuitous violence.

The recent exposure of previously hidden crime, such as child sex abuse, rape, and white collar crime, at all levels in society has certainly had a deleterious effect and fueled public disquiet. But another major influence has been the role of drug abuse in crime. Heroin and other hard drug use was almost unknown in Ireland before 1979. However, there are now about ten thousand heroin addicts in the socially deprived areas of Dublin, and a recent study (Keogh, 1997) indicated that heroin addicts are responsible for about two-thirds of all indictable crime in Dublin.

The advent of serious levels of drug abuse have affected the nature of crime in various ways. Individual addicts, who finance their habit through crime, tend to be reckless, desperate, and indifferent to victims. This has translated into a growth in violence of crime and in the breaking of previously well-established taboos against victimizing the vulnerable. Old people and women have been targeted to an unprecedented degree, including cases of torture

and murder of old people in isolated rural areas. Another new phenomenon is robbery using a syringe as a weapon. This involves the direct threat of infection with AIDS or hepatitis, which are rife among the drug-using population. In 1996 there were 1,100 such robberies in Dublin (and these were, incidentally, not categorized as offenses against the person).

The involvement of organized criminal gangs in the importation and distribution of drugs has also had a major negative effect. These gangs have made huge illegal profits and introduced a climate of violence and intimidation new to the Irish crime scene. In June 1996, one such gang organized the murder of a well-known investigative journalist, Veronica Guerin, who was working to expose their operations. There was a huge public outcry at this killing and it led directly to a period of more resolute policing and intense legislative activity. By 1998, most of those involved in the killing had been identified and arrested. However, in the year before Guerin's murder, there were twelve gangland assassinations of criminally involved victims. None of these cases has been solved.

Finally, although recent changes in the Irish crime scene do justify public concern, it can be argued that the small size of the Irish community and its still considerable level of interconnectedness play a powerful role in amplifying the climate of fear about crime. Saturation coverage in the media of gruesome murder cases or ghastly sex crimes resonates throughout Irish society and often provokes an enormous amount of interest and intense emotional reaction in the general public. The fearmongering tone and selective emphasis of the media on crime issues is undoubtedly influential. The media are centered in Dublin, the one large city, which has about 60% of all indictable crime in the country. The understandable focus of the media on Dublin means that the whole country is very familiar with the situation in the most crime-ridden area and tends to take this situation to be the norm—despite the fact that in some areas the crime rates are one-sixth or less of the Dublin rates.

Next, we discuss how the police in Ireland respond to crime problems.

The Police in Ireland

Administration and Organization

The Garda Síochana is the national police force, dating from the foundation of the state in 1922. There are no separate police forces, whether local or auxiliary, with the exception of very small groups of airport and harbor police, who exercise limited powers. A commissioner, who is appointed by the government and reports to the minister for justice, has responsibility for the general direction and the day-to-day management of the police. The Garda Síochana is (apart from a number of specialized units) an unarmed police force and aspires, in the words of its first commissioner, to succeed "not by force of arms or numbers, but by their moral authority as servants of the people." For most of their history they have been a highly respected force, enjoying the broad support of the population and operating within a relatively crime-free environment that has been termed a "policeman's paradise" (Brady, 1974).

Rapid social change and the growth of lawlessness and drug abuse in socially deprived urban areas have challenged this happy position in recent decades. There is currently considerable tension between the police and some sectors of the population and a clear need for more proactive community policing and bridge-building with certain alienated, socially deprived groups in Irish society. A special challenge has been liaison with local community groups in drug-infested areas, who in the mid-1990s engaged widely in vigilante-type actions that threatened to usurp the role of the police.

At the close of 1996 the strength of the Garda Síochana was 10,817, just over 6% of whom were women. In addition, the force employed 1,576 civilian ancillary staff. This is a rather small civilian support staff by comparison with other jurisdictions—for example, in Britain, civilian staff working for police forces make up about 40% of the numbers of policemen.

Recent years have been a time of rapid development for (Garda Síochana) the force. An international advisory group has examined the efficiency and effectiveness of the force and made recommendations for change, and a strategic management initiative is ongoing to oversee the restructuring and reform process There have been many positive developments both at the level of organizational structure and in the introduction of new technologies, training methods, and operational systems. Management has been regionalized, in order to enhance operational effectiveness, with the country divided into six regions each headed by an assistant commissioner.

At the same time, a number of centralized, specialized bureaus and units have been set up to handle specific areas of crime. The National Bureau of Criminal Investigation, set up in 1997, assists local police in the investigation of all serious crimes, such as murder. They put their specialist forensic skills at the disposal of the local force, manage and control incident room procedures, and prepare files for the director of public prosecutions. Other new units include the National Drugs Unit, the National Crime Prevention Unit, and the National Bureau of Fraud Investigation. The last, which was initiated in 1995, has had a significant impact and, in 1996, had a caseload of 1,344 major cases of money-laundering, commercial fraud, and check and computer fraud. The National Drugs Unit has also had considerable success in intercepting and seizing consignments of illegal drugs valued at hundreds of millions of pounds.

The Garda Síochana also have a responsibility for national security. In this regard, there is a Special Detective Unit dedicated to national security duties and, in particular, to antiterrorist measures. There is also an Emergency Response Unit, which is highly trained and effectively armed in order to "resolve any situation where armed resistance is known or anticipated." In the 1970s and 1980s especially, a great deal of police resources were committed to antiterrorist activity. In this period, there were many politically motivated armed robberies and a considerable number of outrages, involving explosions, kidnappings, and murders.

Perhaps the most noteworthy new development in policing is the Criminal Assets Bureau, which was set up in October 1996. This bureau is a significant innovation in Irish terms, not only because it identifies and then proceeds to freeze or confiscate the criminally derived assets of offenders, most especially drug dealers, but also because it involves a multiagency approach. It is staffed by gardaí and officers and officials from the Department of Social Welfare and the revenue commissioners (both taxation and customs and excise wings). This bureau has already had some notable successes and confiscated well over 10 million pounds worth of assets. It is credited with the disruption of a number of major criminal gangs and the flight from the country of leading criminal figures.

Resources, Technology, and Training of Personnel

There has also, in recent years, been major investment in new technology for the Garda Síochana. A new computerized information and records system is being developed, which will provide access to a comprehensive national database for all garda stations in Dublin and all divisional and district headquarters throughout the country. Other initiatives in the area of new technology include a new radio communications system; the expansion of CCTV systems in urban areas; a new computerized national database for fingerprints with a much improved automated system for fingerprint identification; the introduction of high-tech computer and photographic equipment to tackle speeding offenses; and a new air support unit with both a fixed-wing aircraft and a helicopter.

The Training College at Templemore has been put on a new, highly professional footing as a third-level institution, providing a 2-year course for recruits that covers such subjects as social science, communication, law, and police studies interspersed with on-the-job, apprenticeship-style training. The college also offers a wide variety of in-service training for gardaí at various stages of their careers. A newly established Garda Research Unit is based at the college. Two distinctive features of the Irish system are that recruitment into the force is under the control of the Civil Service Commission rather than the police themselves, and that all higher ranks up to and including that of commissioner are filled only by people who have risen through the ranks.

Garda Síochana and Community Relations

Notwithstanding the many positive developments in Irish policing and, since 1996, several years of declining crime rates and improving detection rates, the Garda Síochana face their share of serious problems. The need to develop more successful and vigorous community policing and partnership approaches has already been mentioned. There are large, socioeconomically deprived and, often, drug-infested areas of the cities, where much of the population, especially the youth, are disaffected and harbor antagonistic attitudes toward the police. The police have begun a process of consultation with local community representatives and have initiated youth diversion programs and other crime-preventive schemes, but much work still needs to be done in this area. The gathering strength of the victim support movement has also meant that the Garda Síochana are required to show more awareness of the plight of victims and more sensitivity in their dealings with them.

The 1990s have seen a series of incidents, mainly arising from rank and file policemen's concerns about pay and conditions, that have indicated a serious problem with morale and seriously damaged the Garda Síochana's previously very positive public image. The most obvious problem was a highly acrimonious split within the Garda Representative Association, the body that represents ordinary level gardaí. At one stage there were three bitterly opposed organizations claiming to represent the gardaí, and the minister for justice had to threaten legislation to restore order. These bodies had by 1998 reunited, but then began pressing for increased pay with a campaign of unprecedented boldness. The Garda Síochana are forbidden by law to strike, but in 1998 they instituted a new form of protest in which many thousands of them telephoned in, on a specific day, to say they were sick. This form of protest became known popularly as "the blue flu" after the color of the police uniform. The government soon settled the pay claims of the gardaí, but not before considerable damage was done to the public reputation of the force.

Another vitally important area on which the Garda Síochana are open to severe criticism is their handling of civil liberties and basic human rights. In particular, there appear to be problems surrounding methods of interrogation, the holding of suspects, and the management of prosecutions and evidence. Uncorroborated confessions can lead to a conviction in Ireland, and in recent years a number of cases have been exposed in which the police have been shown to have extracted confessions from innocent people. The most notorious of these was the Kerry Babies Case (O'Mahony, 1992), in which a whole ordinary farming family falsely confessed in considerable detail to the murder of a baby. Despite recommendations to do so from a public commission, the Garda Síochana have yet to introduce automatic video and audio recording of interrogations.

An international body, the Committee for the Prevention of Torture and Inhuman or Degrading Treatment or Punishment (CPT, 1995), published a report on an investigatory visit to Ireland, in which they raised serious questions about detention in Garda custody. The CPT was led, "in the light of all the information at its disposal," to the extremely uncomfortable conclusion that "persons held in certain police establishments in Ireland—and more particularly in Dublin—run a not inconsiderable risk of being physically ill-treated." The CPT go on to emphasize the important role of police culture and attitudes in this area and they state that "the best possible guarantee against ill-treatment is for its use to be unequivocally rejected by police officers." Consequently, the CPT turned its attention to the nominally independent Garda Complaints Board and were clearly somewhat disquieted by the rarity of disciplinary action against gardaí accused of mistreating arrestees, since they saw fit to comment that the presence of serving police officers on the Complaints Board is capable of "damaging public confidence in the capacity of the complaints system to deal objectively with complaints about police conduct." They believed that the present system was unlikely to be considered impartial by either complainants or police officers. A fully effective system "must be, and be seen to be, independent and impartial." As it happens, and underlining the need for reform in this area, complaints to the Garda Complaints Board about abuse of power by the gardaí have been increasing rapidly over recent years, especially in Dublin.

The Courts, the Judiciary, and the Legal Profession

The Courts

Administration and Organization

In accordance with the constitution of 1937, justice in Ireland is administered in public in courts established by law. In serious criminal matters, there is, with a few notable exceptions, a constitutional right to trial by jury. Judges are appointed by the president on the advice of the government and are invariably senior practicing members of the legal profession. Under the constitutional doctrine of the separation of powers, the judiciary is guaranteed independence in the exercise of its functions. A judge can only be removed from office for misbehavior or incapacity, and removal can only be achieved by resolution of both houses of the Oireachtas (i.e., the Dáil and the Seanad).

There are four levels of ordinary courts, including, in order of importance, three courts of first instance—the district court, the circuit court, and the high court—and one court of final appeal—the Supreme Court. The high court has original and full jurisdiction in criminal and civil matters, and also has the power to rule on the constitutionality of legal rules. The high and circuit courts hear appeals from lower courts. The Supreme Court does not have original jurisdiction but exercises appellate and consultative jurisdiction, most significantly on constitutional matters. The high and Supreme Courts, therefore, play an immensely important role in shaping the legal framework of Irish life and in particular in deciding criminal justice principles and procedures.

With respect to criminal jurisdiction, there are currently five separate courts in operation (Byrne and McCutcheon, 1996)—the district court, the circuit court, the central criminal court (by which name the high court is known when dealing with criminal cases), the court of criminal appeal, and the special criminal court.

The lowest court in the system and the court of summary jurisdiction is the district court. There are 50 judges of the district court including the president of the district court, and these judges serve in 23 different districts, covering more than 200 different district courts. A district court judge presides alone without a jury both to arrive at a verdict and to hand down sentence. However, the district court is severely restricted both in the cases over which it can exercise jurisdiction and in its sentencing powers.

The district court tries all minor, summary, criminal offenses with regard to which the accused does not have a right to jury trial. However, some accused charged with indictable offenses, which do confer a right to a jury trial, may waive that right and opt for trial before the district court. This decision is not the sole prerogative of the accused, as the district judge has the discretion to refuse to hear the case and return it for trial to the circuit court on the grounds that it is not minor. The director for public prosecutions has a similar discretion. The district court also undertakes a preliminary examination of a case that is being returned to a higher court and in this respect has substituted for grand juries, which no longer exist in the Irish system. There are currently proposals by government to abolish this function of the district court.

The district court has powers to impose fines of up to one thousand pounds or prison sentences up to a maximum of 2 years, or both. The district court also handles minor civil cases and family law cases and occasionally sits as a children's court dealing with criminal and child protection matters. The district court, in fact, handles the huge bulk of criminal offenses, and the majority of these involve guilty pleas.

The next higher court is the circuit court. There are twenty-five circuit court judges, who operate in the eight different circuits into which the country is divided. In criminal matters, the circuit judge sits with a jury of twelve ordinary citizens, who are the sole arbiters of fact and arrive at a verdict. Sentencing is the prerogative of the judge. In recent years the law has been changed to allow majority jury verdicts. Those convicted at the district court have an absolute right of appeal to the circuit court, and when the appeal is of conviction rather than of severity of sentence solely, there is a full rehearing of the case by the circuit court.

The circuit court can try all more serious criminal cases except murder, treason, piracy, genocide, and a small number of other offenses, which are regarded as the most serious of offenses and are reserved for trial by the central criminal court (the high court). There are twenty-two high court judges, but very few of them would be involved in criminal cases at any one time. Like the circuit court, the central criminal court is presided over by a single judge sitting with a jury of twelve ordinary citizens.

The court of criminal appeal sits to hear certain appeals of both sentence and conviction from the circuit court, the central criminal court, and the special criminal court. There is no full rehearing of the case, and the appeal is based on the transcript of the evidence given at the trial (Doolan, 1991). The court is composed of one Supreme Court judge and two high court judges. A majority of the judges decides the issue, and only one judgment is given. There are currently proposals by government to abolish the court of criminal appeal and have its functions undertaken instead by the Supreme Court.

Special Courts

The special criminal court is a rather anomalous court in the context of the Irish Constitution and is quite controversial. The special criminal court is contentious because it is a nonjury court that tries serious criminal cases despite the general provision in the constitution that accused should have the right to trial by jury.

The special criminal court was set up in 1972 by proclamation of the government, invoking the Offences Against the State Act of 1939 and as envisaged by the constitution at Article 38.3.1, which allows for the establishment of nonjury special criminal courts whenever the government deems that the "ordinary courts are inadequate to secure the effective administration of justice, and the preservation of public peace and order." The relatively serious political terrorist problem in 1972, which spilled over from Northern Ireland, was the spur for the establishment of the special criminal court. Defendants charged with offenses scheduled under the Offences Against the State Act (including membership of illegal organizations, handling of explosives, and possession of firearms) were to be tried by a nonjury court composed of three judges, one each from the District, Circuit, and high courts. However, there is also provision for the director of public prosecutions to have accused persons tried before the special criminal court on charges relating to nonscheduled offenses, i.e., ordinary, nonpolitical criminal offenses. In recent years, this has resulted in the use of the special criminal court to try a number of defendants charged with involvement in organized crime, especially drug-related crime. Some critics of the system (O'Mahony, 1998) consider that the current level of political unrest and terrorist danger no longer justify the continuation of a special criminal court and that accused persons are unnecessarily being deprived of their constitutional right to a jury trial. The main argument for continuation of the special criminal court and its extension to cover nonterrorist cases centers on the serious danger of intimidation and subornation of witnesses and jury members in cases involving organized criminal gangs.

The Offences Against the State Act is part of permanent legislation and has been referred to the Supreme Court and found by them to be consistent with the constitution. It is, therefore, highly significant as well as providing an instrument for the setting up of the special criminal court. It provides for the suspension of certain normal legal safeguards in the area of police detention and admissible evidence.

The high court has struck down as unconstitutional one section of the Act, which provided that anyone convicted before the special criminal court could be barred from public service employment for a 7-year period. However, Section 52 of the Offences Against the State Act, which requires persons to account for their movements and so is a clear infringement on the right to silence, and Section 12, which permits possession of a pro-IRA poster to be used along with the word of a senior police officer to convict a person of IRA membership and so breaches the normal precepts of admissible evidence, have both received the seal of approval of the Supreme Court. Challenges to the constitutionality of the special criminal court itself and of the powers of the director of public prosecutions to refer nonsubversive offenders to it have failed.

If the involvement of the judiciary in the special criminal court is the most controversial aspect of their activities, in general it can be said that the judiciary is widely respected in Ireland for its independence, professionalism, and genuine concern for the protection of civil rights. Indeed, the high and Supreme Courts, in exercising their interpretative powers, have fleshed out the constitution, which is not particularly expressive or detailed in the area of criminal justice procedures. The judiciary has "read into" the constitution a whole set of safeguards, which come close to the American Bill of Rights in content and comprehensiveness.

Judicial interpretation and argument, leaning on and elaborating articles of the constitution, have led to the doctrine of unenumerated rights through which certain rights, such as of access to the courts, to privacy, to bail, to legal counsel, and to fair procedures in decision-making, have been granted constitutional status (Forde,

1987). In this way the framework of constitutional safeguards has been extended and reinforced to an extent that might make the scant provisions in the actual constitution appear irrelevant.

The Judiciary and the Legal Profession

The Irish judiciary is an appointed body of men and, increasingly, women, who all have a background in professional law. There is no lay magistracy as in England and Wales, and there is no form of election to the judiciary as in parts of the United States. Judges are appointed by the government, but, since 1995, this is done on the advice of a Judicial Appointments Board, which is chaired by the chief justice and has representatives from the judiciary, the legal professions, and the lay public. This new procedure, which even entails newspaper advertisements for judicial positions, including membership of the Supreme Court, was prompted by a newfound concern in Irish society for transparency and accountability. Previously, judicial appointments were highly politicized. As one commentator, drawing attention to the dangers of the old system, put it, "alliance with a particular political party can almost certainly bring political favor, possibly resulting in a judicial appointment" (Houlihan, 1986). The current system is not immune to political favoritism, but it introduces a strong component of peer review and extends the scope of scrutiny over the appointment process. Generally, it can be said that the judiciary, although overwhelmingly middle-class and often from a legal family background, have tended to include strong representation of minorities. For example, the present Supreme Court includes Jewish and Protestant members, though the country is, nominally at least, 95% Catholic.

The legal profession from which the judiciary is recruited is dual in nature, being divided into solicitors and barristers.

Solicitors deal with noncontentious legal issues such as the conveyancing of property and with the preparation of cases for court. Barristers deal with the preparation of cases for court but are also specialists in advocacy before the courts. Barristers have no direct contact with the public and are hired by a solicitor on behalf of his or her client.

The Law Society of Ireland and the Honorable Society of King's Inns, respectively, control the systems of professional education and internal discipline for solicitors and barristers. These institutions, which are housed in historic buildings in Dublin, have overseen a huge increase in the size of their professions in recent decades, with solicitors increasing from 1,300 in 1960 to more than 4,000 in 1995, and with barristers increasing from about 200 in 1968 to more than 900 in 1996 (Byrne and McCutcheon, 1996). As in Britain, senior barristers may "take silk," that is, rise to the rank of senior counsel, the equivalent of the British Queen's counsel. The two professions are steeped in tradition and tend to be conservative in outlook. Barristers, when attending court, still wear gowns, wing-collared shirts, tabs, and often wigs, although the last are no longer obligatory. Trainee barristers must still attend the King's Inns for dinner on ten occasions in each of their 2 years of study. Barristers are not organized in chambers, as in Britain, but all belong to the Law Library, which has a strongly collegiate ethos. The Law Library is based at the Four Courts, Ireland's main legal center.

The dual nature of the legal profession in Ireland has come under attack in recent years, and there have been important reforms arising from the *Report into Restrictive Practices in the Legal Profession* (1990). However, the report did not recommend a unified profession, as in the United States, but was content to recommend increased rights of audience before the courts for solicitors and the opening up of judgeships at the circuit court to them.

Indeed, in recent years, the whole court system has been examined with a view to radical overhaul of the way the system is managed. In the early 1990s, there was a growing concern among the judiciary, the public, and politicians alike that the physical and organizational structures and staffing and resource provision of the courts system were inadequate to deal with the greatly increased demands now being placed on them. In six reports to date, the Denham Commission on the Courts (1996–1998) has produced an incisive and thorough critical analysis of the problems of the system. A political commitment has been made to the setting up of a properly resourced Independent Courts Service, which for the first time would take control of the courts out of the hands of the Department of Justice. The Denham Commission reports have delineated the problems of the system, such as dilapidated court buildings, lengthy delays to trial, and lack of information technology and a comprehensive database. They have also put in place a rational and credible framework for remedying some of these problems. The Denham Commission has recently (1998) recommended the establishment of Drugs Courts in Ireland along the model of those in Dade County, Florida. If this recommendation is implemented, it will mean that minor property offenders who are drug addicts can be sentenced directly to treatment rather than correctional custody. This would be a major innovation in the Irish context.

Prosecutorial and Judicial Process

The Legal Aspects of Offender Prosecution

The prosecutorial process starts with the police arrest of the offender. Under the common law, a Garda (policeman or woman) may arrest a person on a reasonable suspicion that the person has committed a felony. A private citizen has similar rights of arrest, but such an arrest is lawful only when the felony has actually been committed. Generally, in other circumstances, the Garda must have a warrant of arrest issued by a judge, although a number of statutes grant specific rights of arrest without a warrant. The person effecting a lawful arrest may use reasonable force, but excessive force is unlawful.

The common law does not permit detention without a charge, e.g., for questioning or for helping the police with their inquiries. But statutory law provides some exceptions to this rule. The Offenses Against the State Act of 1939 permits detention for up to 48 hours on suspicion of having committed a range of specified offenses, particularly offenses involving firearms or explosives or paramilitary activity. The Criminal Justice Act of 1984 permits detention for up to 12 hours of persons suspected of having committed an offense that carries a sentence of 5 years' imprisonment or more.

Rights of the Accused

The Garda must inform an arrested person, without delay and in an ordinary language, of the charge against him/her. He/she has the right to consult a solicitor (lawyer) and the right to have a person, reasonably named by him/her, informed of his/her arrest. The charged person must be brought before a court as soon as is practicable.

Article 38 of the Irish Constitution provides that no person should be tried on a criminal charge except "in due process of law." In practice this basic constitutional principle has translated into a set of procedural and evidential rules aimed at the protection of individuals charged with criminal offenses (Forde, 1987). For example, the accused must be furnished in advance of the trial with the evidence to be used by the prosecution—in form of what is called the Book of Evidence. The accused also have the right to cross-examine prosecution witnesses, call their own witnesses, give evidence themselves, and address the court. Since 1976, there has been recognition for the right of an impecunious defendant to free legal representation, funded by the state.

Until recently, the right to bail, that is, the right to liberty in the period awaiting trial, has been recognized. The Supreme Court had consistently vindicated this right, arguing that the basic test for granting bail is the probability of the accused evading justice by leaving the country or otherwise failing to appear for trial. Denying bail on the grounds that an accused might interfere with witnesses or commit another offense was rejected by the Supreme Court as "a form of preventive justice which has no place in our legal system."

In contemporary Ireland, it has become a commonplace assumption of political and public discourse that some aspects of the criminal law, especially those dealing with criminal justice procedures, are antiquated and inappropriate to modern circumstances. Dominant public and political attitudes today depict the legal system as burdened by the accumulation, over centuries, of a complex, unwieldy, and confusing set of legal rules, which have resulted in a system weighted in favor of defendants rather than crime victims or society at large. This view, which would probably not withstand a robust critical analysis, has nonetheless translated into pressure on the established tradition of legal procedures and principles such as the right to bail, which were often expressly designed to protect civil liberties, particularly the civil liberties of criminal defendants. The most obvious example of Irish public and political zeal for radical legal reform, usually repressive in tone, is the bail referendum of November 1996 in which an amendment to the constitution was passed by a three-to-one majority, allowing the refusal of bail on the grounds that there is reasonable suspicion that the suspect would commit an offense while free on bail. The referendum is a rare but interesting example of the people, at the initiative of the government, deciding to overrule the Supreme Court in its interpretation of the constitution. There have been other examples where politicians, in response to the perceived seriousness of the crime problem and public concern about it, have introduced relatively harsh legislative measures in the certainty of wide popular support. Recent innovations include the introduction of 7-day detention without charge for alleged drug dealers and the curtailment in certain circumstances of the "right to silence," also in the case of those suspected of drug-dealing.

Also reflecting more punitive attitudes, the right of the state to appeal the leniency of a sentence has been recognized and sentence lengths for certain offenses have been increased by legislation, including the introduction of life sentences for serious drug and sex offenders. Some legal commentators (Fennell, 1993), have held that this avalanche of populist legislative reform, aimed at the repression of criminals, has damaged due process, seriously eroded the role of the fundamental principle of the presumption of innocence in the Irish criminal legal system, and increased the likelihood of conviction of innocents.

Criminal Procedure

The actual business of prosecution is, in the case of jury trials and the special criminal court, the responsibility of the director of public prosecutions. This office dates from 1974 and was established primarily to protect the prosecution process from extralegal influences, particularly political interference. The office of the director of public prosecutions is independent and has absolute discretion to decide whether or not there is sufficient evidence to prosecute an indictable case. A notable feature of the Irish system is that at the level of summary offenses before the district court, prosecutions are handled by the Garda Síochana (in English, Guardians of the

Peace)—that is, by members of the national police force. However, in the event of such a case proceeding to a higher court, the director of public prosecutions, after consideration of the available evidence, has the discretion to enter a "nolle prosequi," thus terminating the prosecution on indictment that arrived from the district court at the initiative of the Garda Síochana or some other agent.

The office of the official state solicitor and local state solicitors assist the director of public prosecutions by implementing his or her instructions and by preparing the case for court, including the compilation of the Book of Evidence. Advocacy of a prosecution at trial is handled, on the other hand, by a barrister in private practice, hired for that purpose by the director of public prosecutions. Unlike in Britain and the United States, there is no corps of salaried lawyers in state employ dedicated to the prosecution process. There is in Ireland no explicit system of plea-bargaining, but analogous negotiation between the prosecutor and defendant does occur in an informal and limited way. This would usually involve a promise by the prosecution to drop certain charges in exchange for a guilty plea to another lesser charge.

The Irish trial process, as in all common-law jurisdictions, is based on an accusatory system. The prosecuting authority accuses the defendant and has an adversarial relationship with him or her. The district court judge or special criminal court judges assess, in a neutral fashion, the relative merits of the prosecution and defense cases and arrive at a verdict. At the circuit and central criminal court, the jury performs this role, but is instructed by the presiding judge, who oversees the fairness of procedures and rules on matters of law. As in the U.S. system, a guilty verdict should only be declared when proof is found to be "beyond a reasonable doubt." In every court, it is the judge or a panel of judges who decides on the appropriate penalty in the event of a conviction,

customarily after hearing pleas in mitigation and, when relevant, victim impact
statements and police information on the
past criminal conduct of the convicted
person.

The Constitution of Ireland created the
office of the attorney general. The attorney general is not a member of the government but attends cabinet meetings and acts
as the chief legal advisor to the government. The attorney general is appointed
by the president on the advice of the
Taoiseach (the prime minister) and must
resign with the Taoiseach.

The office of the Director of Public Prosecutions (DPP), created by statute in 1974,
has assumed most of the responsibilities
formerly held by the attorney general in
relation to criminal prosecutions. The attorney general, however, has a role in litigation, because he/she is the forensic representative of both the government and the
public. Today the role of the attorney general in criminal justice is in the area of law
reform such as advising the government
on the constitutionality of proposed
changes to the criminal law and in the
drafting of new statutes.

Finally, approximately, half a million
summary offenses are recorded each year,
and almost 90% of these arise under the
Road Traffic Acts. In the last few years,
between 90,000 and 100,000 indictable
crimes have been recorded per annum.
There are no statistics held on arrests, but
a study in the 1980s indicated that the
Garda made about 40,000 arrests each year.
Crime rates at that time were similar to the
present , so it is reasonable to suggest that
arrests are currently running at about
40,000 per annum.

At present, statistics focused on reported indictable crimes as the unit of
analysis rather than individual offenders.
Approximately one-third, or 30,000, of the
reported indictable offenses led to criminal proceedings. These, however, refer to
an estimated 18,000 different individuals
who are proceeded against for indictable

crimes. Most of these offenders (more than
90%) do not opt for their right to a jury
trial and are proceeded against at the district court level. About 500 indicted suspects go forward for a jury trial either because they opted for it or, in serious cases,
on the instruction of the director of public
prosecutions.

Nearly half of the half-million summary
offenses led to a conviction. In the vast
majority of these cases, the sanction is a
fine. The Garda claimed that 43% of the
90,000 indictable crimes were solved in
1997. Out of that number, only 16,000 offenders were convicted or had the charge
proved for indictable offenses.

Penalties

The sentencing process in Ireland is quite
complex, involving a wide range of options
(Law Reform Commission, 1993). The least
severe sentencing option, open only to the
district court, is a discharge under the 1907
Probation of Offenders Act. This in effect
is a decision not to impose a sanction and
not to record a conviction, although the
case against the accused is deemed to have
been proved.

A fine is by far the most common sanction, the punishment for the vast majority
of summary offenses. When provision for
a fine for a particular offense is laid down
by statute, there is always a related period
of imprisonment, which will be imposed
if the convicted person defaults on fine
payment. In recent years, up to 35% of
people committed to prison on conviction
have been fine-defaulters.

The 1907 Probation of Offenders Act
also allows for a system of probation
whereby a convicted person can be sentenced either to a period of probation under the supervision of a probation and
welfare officer or to a period of probation
under recognizance, when the offender
promises to abide by certain conditions
laid down by the court.

Since 1983 the courts have been empowered to impose a community service order as a direct alternative to imprisonment. Such orders can only be imposed on offenders over 16 years of age and for offenses that would normally be sanctioned by a prison sentence. The community service order entails the offender undertaking up to 240 hours of unpaid work under the supervision of a probation and welfare officer.

The courts quite frequently resort to both deferred sentences and adjourned sentencing. In the first case a custodial sentence is imposed but, at the judge's discretion, the warrant for its execution is not issued for a period. If the offender is of good behavior in this period and complies with the wishes of the court, for example, by undergoing treatment for drug abuse, then the sentence will be deemed to have been administered; otherwise, the court may proceed to enforce the custodial sentence. Adjourned sentencing is similar except that no sentence is imposed in advance of the testing period of supervised release. The eventual decision on sentencing will depend very much on a probation and welfare officer's report on the conduct of the offender in the testing period.

Another option available to a judge is the suspension of a custodial sentence or part thereof. The offender will be bound to keep the peace and be of good behavior for a period and may also be subject to further conditions such as a treatment program. Compliance with these conditions will ensure that the offender does not have to serve the suspended custodial sentence. A variant on this sentencing option, whereby the judge imposes a relatively long custodial sentence, but sets a date, usually after 3 years of custody, for judicial review of the sentence, has become quite popular with the judiciary in recent years. The remainder of the sentence will be suspended, if on review it is found that the offender has been of good behavior in prison and has made rehabilitative progress. This option is often used with

drug addict offenders to encourage them to undergo drug therapy and stay drug-free within prison.

Deprivation of Liberty is the most severe sanction available to the Irish courts. It is also very frequently the automatic sanction for failure to comply with the conditions of less severe sentences such as fines or community-based sanctions. Maximum prison sentence lengths are set by statute, but minimum and mandatory prison sentences are rare in the Irish system. There is, however, a minimum, mandatory life sentence for murder, and a minimum, mandatory sentence of 10 years has recently been introduced for certain drug-dealing offenses. The death penalty for murder was abolished in 1964 and for capital murder (the killing of a policeman, a prison officer, and such categories) in 1990. However, there has been no judicial execution in Ireland since 1958. The sentence for capital murder is a minimum "life sentence" of at least 40 years.

Life sentences in Ireland do not literally mean life, and in the 1980s were in fact averaging less than 10 years. The life sentence offender can be released "on licence," meaning that he can be recalled to prison on suspicion of misconduct without further judicial process. The average life sentence is presently a little longer than 10 years, although a few offenders serve very much longer terms. All prison sentences apart from a life sentence are subject to automatic remission of 25% of sentence length, in the case of males, and 33%, in the case of females.

The position of the insanity defense to murder has long been under examination in Ireland, but as yet the laws in this area have not been modernized (McAuley, 1993). A successful insanity defense leads to a verdict of "guilty but insane," which, despite the terminology, is regarded in law as an acquittal. It can, however, lead to an order that the accused be held in a secure psychiatric hospital at the pleasure of the government. This can be regarded as, in effect, an indeterminate sentence. There is, then, no concept of "diminished responsibility" due to mental illness in the Irish legal system, although there is considerable support for its introduction.

There are a number of other sanctions available to the judiciary in certain circumstances, which include a compensation order, which forces an offender to compensate a victim for personal injury or loss, and a confiscation order, which provides for the forfeiture of ill-gotten gains. Juveniles are a special case and, while the age of criminal responsibility is 7 and about to be raised to 10, it is not in law permitted to imprison anyone under the age of 15. Children, however, may be sent to a reformatory or an industrial school operated under the auspices of the Department of Education. It is also possible for a judge to commit a child offender to the care of a relative or other fit person or to levy a fine, costs, and damages from the parent of a young offender. Children of 15 may be sent to prison, though only if a court issues a certificate that the young person is "unruly or depraved"; this is a relatively rare event. There is one preprosecution diversion scheme in the Irish system, aimed specifically at juvenile offenders under 18 years of age. This is run by the Garda Síochana and involves a formal or informal caution and a period of supervision, but it is conditional on the offender admitting the offense and on a degree of cooperation from the offender's family. This scheme has grown greatly in recent years: in 1997 there were 12,000 cautions, up from about 3,000 in 1990.

The Prisons

At present, approximately, 6,000 persons are committed to prison on conviction each year. Another 4,000 convicted offenders receive a probation order, broken down into about 1,000 probation orders, 1,750 community service orders, and 1,250 Supervisions during Deferment of Penalty.

The remaining 6,000 offenders receive other sanctions such as a fine or a suspended sentence, or, in a number of cases (approximately 500), they have the charge proved but order made without conviction.

Description, Administration, and Organization

Like other sectors of the criminal justice system, the Irish prison system has experienced immense change in recent decades but, unlike other sectors, it still faces the need for major, fundamental reform. In 1961, the daily average number of prisoners in the country, including unconvicted remand prisoners, was only 447. In the following two decades, as a consequence of large increases both in the length of prison sentences, especially for drug and sex offenses, and in the numbers committed to prison, the Irish prison population more than quintupled. Ireland, among the Council of Europe countries, had the most rapid growth in its prison population in the 17-year period to 1987 (Tournier and Barre, 1990). The number of Irish prison cells increased by 156% compared to an increase of only 19.8% in the United Kingdom, which suffered even greater increases in crime over the relevant period.

This rate of numerical growth has not been matched by an equivalent growth in facilities, services, and regimes. Indeed, the current prison system still, in the main, relies on old Victorian prisons, which are grossly overcrowded, often unsanitary, and totally inadequate to fulfill the functions of a modern penal institution. Many hundreds of Irish prisoners are doubled up in single cells without sanitation. The custom of "slopping out" of night waste buckets is still a feature of some older prisons.

There is, however, a considerable range of different types of prison and regime. There are presently fifteen different institutions, including two medium-sized modern facilities with satisfactory facilities;

three small open prisons; a training prison with special work and training facilities; a prison for young offenders; a women's prison; a high-security prison, used to hold subversive or political terrorist prisoners; two long-stay prisons, which hold sex offenders and murderers and similar categories; and four older prisons, which in fact handle the majority of prisoners passing through the system and have by far the worst conditions.

In 1998, the total number of prisoners stood at about 2,500. However, the number of prisoners was set to increase dramatically, with the government committed to providing 2,000 extra prison cells by the year 2002. One planned prison of 400 cells is specifically for remand prisoners and is necessitated by the recent change in the bail laws allowing preventative detention. Principally, the building program is an effort to solve the problem of overcrowding and to end the policy of wholesale early release of prisoners, presently caused by lack of prison accommodation. At present many hundreds of prisoners are released early because of overcrowding. They, in effect, serve their sentences at liberty and without supervision. This highly undesirable situation not only undermines the deterrent effect of a prison sentence and brings the criminal justice system into disrepute, but also affects the morale of the prison system and creates difficulties for the planning and organization of rehabilitative services, since the turnover of prisoners is rapid and unpredictable.

In the larger Dublin prisons, most notably Mountjoy, the largest and most important committal prison in the country (750 prisoners), poor prison conditions are exacerbated by the fact that majority of the prisoners are heroin addicts, many of who maintain their addiction in prison. AIDS and hepatitis are common among drug-abusing prisoners. Idleness and long periods of lock-up are also features of these prisons, because there is a chronic lack of work, educational, and recreational facilities.

Throughout the system, there is a shortage of rehabilitative services. However, some progress has been made in this area in recent years. There is a substantial educational service, but it manages to affect only a minority of prisoners. A new sex offender treatment program is in place, but it processes less than 10% of the large group of sex offenders passing through the system. There is a new detoxification center for the treatment of addict prisoners, but this has only 12 cells. One prison of about 100 cells has recently been designated as a drug-free prison, but large numbers of inmates are returned to the mainstream prisons from this center after failing urine analysis tests.

In general, it can be said that the Irish prison population is highly homogeneous, with few foreign prisoners, and is characterized by a background of marked socioeconomic deprivation, educational failure, and lack of vocational training. It is overwhelmingly male and young (under 30 years) with only about 80 women prisoners (3% of the total prison population). In addition many prisoners have alcohol, addiction, or psychiatric problems, and a large number come from disturbed family backgrounds. In many of the larger prisons, medical, social work, and psychiatric services appear to be overwhelmed by the problems they face.

There are some interesting, highly distinctive features of the Irish prison system. For example, Ireland spends far more money than most other countries on prison officers. This is chiefly because of a very high prison officer to prisoner ratio (1.1 prison officer to every prisoner). Ireland also has, in European terms, a very high proportion of prisoners who are under 21 years of age. About a third of Irish prisoners are under 21, while many European countries have less than 10% of their prisoners in this age category. The recidivism rate among Irish prisoners is also extraordinarily high by international comparison. A recent survey of Mountjoy prisoners (O'Mahony, 1997) showed that the vast majority (almost 90%) had been in prison before and that, on average, they had been imprisoned following conviction on 10 separate occasions.

One of the most significant features of the Irish penal system is the fact that Ireland tends to send to prison a greater proportion of its citizens than any other country in the Council of Europe (Council of Europe, 1992), and about 75% of these have been convicted of nonviolent crimes. This is to say, when one focuses on the numbers sent to prison (the imprisonment rate) rather than on the numbers held in prison at any one time (the detention rate), the use of incarceration by the Irish courts is found to be extremely high. Looking at committals under conviction only, we find that the Irish imprisonment rate in 1992 was 174 per 100,000. This compared with only 34 per 100,000 in France, 24 in Italy, 12 in Portugal, and 90 in the Netherlands. These are remarkable differences and demonstrate a comparatively heavy use of the sanction of imprisonment by the Irish courts. The importance of this finding is underlined by the fact that the crime rate is considerably lower in Ireland than in most of the other European countries that use imprisonment far less. This anomaly has not received the attention it deserves, mainly because the Irish detention rate is quite low by European standards. There are several reasons why the detention rate does not fully reflect the very high imprisonment rate. Most importantly, the current policy of early release, to ease overcrowding, artificially lowers prison population numbers. However, it is also the case that an unusually large proportion of Irish sentences to prison are for very short periods. In particular, about 35% of committals to prison are for failure to pay a fine. Such prisoners, whose offenses were originally considered by the court not to merit imprisonment, spend only a short period in prison but extend the resources of the sys-

tem. The use of short sentences and of the early release mechanism also help explain the very high recidivism rates in Ireland.

The Irish imprisonment rate will inevitably rise when the planned new prison places are completed. This will provide an opportunity for deeper reflection on the use of imprisonment by the Irish courts. This may lead to more resources being devoted to the small Probation and Welfare Service, which supervises the alternative, community-based sanctions, such as probation and community service orders. At present, the Probation and Welfare Service, with a staff of about 150, supervises about 4,000 offenders per annum, but there is clearly great potential for the expansion of these alternative approaches.

An important new development in the penal system has been the commitment by government to the establishment of an Independent Prisons Board, along the lines of the Independent Courts Service. This will take the day-to-day running of the system out of the hands of politicians and the Department of Justice. It will also present a real opportunity for a more accountable system, characterized by goals and performance-driven management, and for the requisite renewal of reformist energy and resolution. An independent inspectorate of prisons, which would have an important role in informing the public about the realities of prison life, has also been proposed.

Discussion

Ireland is a good example of a small jurisdiction, which has faced, in the last quarter of the twentieth century, many new challenges and pressures for change across its whole criminal justice system. Chief among the challenges has been an ongoing campaign by political subversives seeking the reunification of Ireland by violent means, and a marked deterioration with respect to both the quantity and quality of ordinary crime. Among the important influences on the latter are increased affluence and urbanization, the spread of consumerist lifestyles, the decline of the extended family, the adoption of mores and moral standards from cinema and television and other global mass media, increased social competitiveness, rapid secularization, and the advent of a serious level of heroin abuse. The old restraining bonds of family, church, and community have weakened everywhere in Ireland, but in terms of crime, this is most obvious at the deprived margins of urban society, where a criminal subculture has always existed and epidemic levels of drug abuse now flourish.

The different parts of the Irish criminal justice system have responded to the new challenges with varying levels of speed, efficiency, and effectiveness. The Garda Síochana have readily grasped the opportunities provided by new technology, but still face major challenges in the area of community relations. Their formerly highly respected position in society and the model of consensus policing, while still in place in mainstream Irish society, are in some jeopardy in the marginalized communities that produce most of the visible crime. The prison system has been least effective in adjusting to new conditions, and, particularly with respect to unplanned early release, physical conditions, and lack of rehabilitative programs, can be described as inadequate and chaotic. A waiting list system for prison, as adopted in Denmark, would surely have been preferable to the Irish reliance on unsupervised early release, but it has never been seriously considered. The court system has also been under considerable strain, but this is currently being addressed with some hope of success. Although the political system has stood up well to the stresses of recent decades, legislators can be faulted for lack of vision in the area of criminal justice. There has been a rash of new legislation, but it has lacked cohesion and any sense of an informed, well-thought-through program. There has been

a dearth of research and analysis, and much new legislation seems to have been driven by a populist agenda and to have been concerned with symbolic gestures to convince the electorate that politicians are tough on crime, rather than with a serious engagement with the task of fundamental reform. As a consequence resources have been squandered in some areas, while other areas are starved of funds. Culturally inappropriate models from abroad, such as "zero tolerance," have been overly influential and, along with the crime-obsessed media, have helped obscure the basic fact that Ireland has a relatively moderate and manageable crime problem.

Many of the criminal justice problems faced in Ireland closely mirror those of other jurisdictions, large and small. Although Ireland can now be considered a relatively wealthy, developed nation, its process of social and economic progress has been compressed into a short period, and the price paid in increased criminality parallels that experienced in rapidly modernizing nations in the developing regions of Africa and Asia. The process of the differentiation and growing distinctiveness of the Irish legal system, within the common law tradition, also has parallels in developing nations, especially other former British colonies. Finally, similar to the situation in many other countries, such as Cyprus and Belgium, the presence of two opposed cultural identities on the island of Ireland continues to be a source of civic unrest and so a major influence on the criminal justice system both in Ireland and Northern Ireland, as well as a core and urgent challenge for political leaders.

Discussion and Review Questions

1. Discuss the similarities and differences between the role played by the British legal model in Ireland and in other former British colonies such as Nigeria and Sierra Leone.

2. In what ways do the Irish experiences since 1922 mirror American legal development within the English common law tradition?

3. Discuss the importance of a written constitution and the doctrine of separation of powers to the Irish criminal justice system.

4. Discuss, in the context of the fate of African customary systems of law, whether the attempt to reintroduce the traditional Brehon law system in Ireland in 1920–1922 had any realistic chance of success.

5. Compare the role of drug abuse in crime in the United States and Ireland.

6. How can Ireland be said to overuse imprisonment when its detention rate is only a small fraction of that in the United States?

7. Can the policy and practice of New York–style zero tolerance have any relevance to a small jurisdiction such as Ireland with its own distinctive pattern of crime problems?

8. Discuss how a relatively severe political terrorism problem can adversely affect the criminal justice system of a small but fundamentally stable nation such as Ireland.

9. How can economic progress and liberalizing social change lead to significant increases in crime?

10. Discuss the pernicious effects of unrealistic fear of crime and how such fear can be generated.

11. Why would it be a mistake for police forces to overemphasize the role of new technology and advanced equipment in the fight against crime?

12. Discuss the direct and indirect influences of the European Community on the criminal justice systems of small member states such as Denmark and Ireland.

13. Are the Irish judicial practices of adjourned sentencing and suspension of all or part of a prison sentence useful measures for combating crime?

14. Are there meaningful parallels between the overrepresentation of African-Americans in the U.S. prison system and that of socioeconomically deprived people in Irish prisons?

15. Ireland has a centrally organized, unarmed national police force. Is this model only suited to small jurisdictions?

16. Compare and contrast prison inmates' daily life in Ireland and Japan.

17. European Community Law takes precedence over national laws of member nations. Is national sovereignty sacrificed? Discuss.

18. Compare and contrast the structure and role of the following in criminal justice systems of their nations: the district attorney (DA), the director of public prosecutions (DPP), and the procuratorate general (PG).

19. The Irish president, like the contemporary British monarch, rules but does not reign. What do you understand by that statement? Discuss fully.

20. What is the difference between probation and community service orders in the Irish criminal justice system?

4

The Criminal Justice System in Israel

Maria R. Haberfeld and Sergio Herzog

Introduction

The state of Israel has been shaped by ancient and modern history, and so have its laws. The laws of modern Israel are derived from many diverse sources, including Israeli legislative acts, British mandate law, Ottomans, and religious laws. The nation's criminal justice institutions trace their origins to the period that preceded the establishment of the state. Israel proclaimed its independence on May 15, 1948.

This ended the British jurisdiction in Palestine, which originated with the defeat of the Ottoman Empire in World War I. Having conquered Palestine in 1918, Britain was granted a mandate by the League of Nations over Palestine in 1922. During the period of British hegemony and the official mandate (1918–1948), the foundations were laid for Israel's criminal justice institutions (Bensinger, 1998).

Today, Israel is a democratic republic with a parliamentary system of government. It has a strong cabinet, a multiparty system with two major parties (although this situation is changing because of the direct national election of the prime minister, since 1996), and a marked tendency toward political and administrative centralization. Israel does not have a formal written constitution. The foundation on which the system of government has been built is composed of legislation, administrative acts, and parliamentary practice. The Knesset, or Israeli national assembly, is a 120-member, single-chamber legislature whose members are elected every 4 years. The president, who is the head of state, is elected by the Knesset for a 5-year term, which can be renewed once. The president has neither executive nor veto powers. He exercises only ceremonial functions. The cabinet is the main policy-making body. The prime minister is the leading figure in the cabinet and in the government. The population of Israel in 1997 was estimated at 5,652,000 people residing in an area of 7,846 square miles, not including territory occupied in the June 1967 War (Encyclopaedia Britannica, 1998).

Since Israel has no constitution or bill of rights, Israeli law is derived from statutes passed by the Knesset, including the Judges Law (1953), the Rabbinical Court's Jurisdiction (marriage and divorce) Law (1953), the Courts Law (1957), the Criminal Code (1965), and the Penal Law (1977). The principle of separation of powers is maintained in Israel, with three branches of government: the legislative (the Knesset), the executive (the government of Israel), and the judiciary (Israeli courts do not have the power of judicial review). However, Israel's Supreme Court can suggest the desirability of legislative changes and can rule on constitutional and administrative matters. The criminal justice system is adversarial in nature; in criminal hearings the state is represented by district attorneys who work in the states attorney's office. In magistrate courts, the state is also represented by police prosecutors who normally do not prosecute felonies (Bensinger, 1998).

The Israeli Legal System

The only formal body entitled to pass any law in Israel is the Knesset (the Israeli Parliament). The Parliament consists of 120 members who are nationally elected every 4 years. There are two types of proposals (bills) that can be promulgated into the law of the country. The first is a private legislative bill that is introduced by a single member of the Parliament or a group of the members. The second type, called a governmental legislative bill, is introduced by the government or one or a group of the government ministers. Each proposal is brought for a preliminary reading before the Knesset, and a parliamentary discussion is conducted on the bill. A vote is taken either for or against the new law. If the majority of the members of the Parliament vote against the proposal, it is dismissed and for a period of time, at least 6 months, neither the original proposal nor one similar to it can be brought back for discussion. If the majority of the members vote for the proposed new legislation, it is transferred to one of the Knesset's subcommittees (one that is most relevant to the newly proposed law) to be formally defined as a new piece of legislation. Upon completion of the subcommittee's work, the newly defined bill is brought back to the Knesset for a second vote. The vote is accompanied by a discussion and possible amendments are recommended.

Finally, the proposed new legislation, together with any amendments, is brought to the Knesset for a third vote. If the majority of the members present in the Parliament vote for the new legislation, it becomes a new law of Israel. This new law becomes formalized when it is published by the Knesset in the Law Ordinance.

The Laws of Israel

Israeli law is based on English law. The definition of particular behavior or conduct as criminal is based on the principle of *nullum crimen, nulla poena, sine lege*, which means that not every act that appears to be repulsive or deviant is automatically defined as a crime; for an act or behavior to become a crime, it has to be specifically defined as such in the Israeli Criminal Code (of 1977). The Criminal Code clearly defines the prohibited behavior, and/or the circumstances under which such behavior is prohibited. Additionally, the Code specifies the punishment attached to the violations. Based on this principle, an act or behavior becomes a crime only when the judge or judges who have the jurisdictional authority to preside over the criminal trial decide that the behavior or act is indeed criminal. This decision must be based on the evidence and the testimony of witnesses presented to the judge or judges. The evidence and the testimony of witnesses must be sufficient to enable the judge to reach the decision, beyond a reasonable doubt, that the defendant engaged in a behavior or an act defined as criminal in the Israeli Criminal Code, and that the behavior or act was included in the original indictment submitted at the initial stage of the prosecution.

Crime and Deviance

Crimes in Israel are classified into three categories: crimes (equivalent to an American felony), *avonot* (equivalent to an American misdemeanor), and *chataim* (equivalent to an American administrative violation).

Types of Statistics

The major source of criminal statistics in Israel is the statistics branch at the Israeli

National Police (INP) Headquarters. The police compile the daily number of complaints registered (either by citizens or by various police stations) and transfer the data tapes to the Central Bureau of Statistics (CBS),which publishes them monthly. The data tapes are then kept at the CBS and are used for the calculation of the annual summaries.

These annual summaries are published regularly in the statistical abstracts and the statistical monthly. Every now and then, based on budgetary considerations, the CBS also publishes a special issue in the special series publications. So far these series include reports for most years since 1956. There are also special issues on juvenile delinquency, court statistics, and victimization surveys (Rahav, 1998a).

Drugs

The drug problem in Israel began after the Six-Day War of 1967, but heroin did not enter the Israeli drug market until the latter half of 1975. Prior to 1979 most of the heroin in Israel was either Mexican or Asian, but since 1980 the more potent Turkish heroin had been smuggled into the country, first from Turkey and since 1988 from Lebanon. Lebanon has become the major source of hashish and heroin smuggled into Israel. More recently, the INP has become more concerned about

drug trafficking across the border with Egypt (Bensinger, 1998). Table 4-1 presents the demographic distribution of drug offenders in 1996 (Israel National Police Annual Report, 1998).

Organized Crime

The roots of organized criminal activity in Israel can be traced to the establishment of the country in 1948. It was only in the 1960s, though, that organized criminality emerged as a serious problem. Mostly reported were robberies, burglaries, sale of stolen goods, and smuggling of highly taxable goods. It involved some persons known to the police, primarily groups of Israeli-born young men, or those whose parents immigrated to Israel, mainly from Muslim countries.

New immigrants from the Republic of Georgia, who arrived in Israel by the thousands in the mid-1970s, contributed to the birth of a new era in organized crime. In 1980–1982, it appeared repeatedly in the media and in police statements that among the Georgian Jews were found a "special" type of criminals, engaged in "big and serious" crimes. They specialized in large-scale theft of passengers' luggage at Ben Gurion International Airport, theft from warehouses, sophisticated frauds, theft of religious objects and diamonds, counterfeiting of money, large-scale fencing opera-

Table 4-1: Drug Offenders—Demographic Distribution by Age and Gender (1996)

Type of Offense	Total Number of Offenders	Age 12–17	Age 18–21	Age 22+	Males	Females
Drug use	7,108	479	1,700	4,929	6,287	821
Trafficking, import, and export	1,732	160	265	1,307	1,610	122
Growth, production, and distribution	184	10	27	147	162	22
Possession (not for personal use)	3,726	157	569	3,000	3,333	393

Source: INP Annual Reports 1998
*Each offender is represented only once per year, based on the most severe offense committed.

tions, and smuggling. A new phase in the existence of organized crime in Israel emerged with the arrival, between 1988 and 1993, of about 500,000 immigrants from Russia and other states of the former Soviet Union. Many arrived with forged documents that either falsified their Jewish status for the sake of receiving preferential treatment as Jewish immigrants, or forged certificates about professional status to qualify for high-skilled positions. The Russians formed organized gangs that are active in various areas of crime through the use of violence.

Some continue their criminal connections with their accomplices in Russia, or with those who immigrated to the United States. They brought with them their expertise in extortion, forgeries, and counterfeiting, group violence in the service of extortion, loan sharking, organized prostitution, and smuggling of women and contraband goods. Some groups enter the drug-dealing market in Israel and thus come in contact with "native" organized crime groups. The beginning of cooperation between them can already be seen in distribution of drugs and some joint ventures in grand theft and fraudulent schemes in Israel and in Russia, in unlawful gambling where the Russians serve as financiers, and in enforcement tasks. The tendency of the Russians to resort to violence added more acts of violence in cases of group competitions and rivalries (Amir, 1998). As of today, the INP does not have enough resources or manpower to pose any serious threat to the phenomenon of organized crime in Israel (Haberfeld et al., 1998).

Juvenile Delinquents

The Hebrew terminology does not distinguish among juvenile offenders, delinquents, or juvenile criminals. Status offenses hardly exist in Israel. Thus, juvenile delinquency is actually defined by the special institutions for handling young offenders: the juvenile court, the juvenile units of the police, the juvenile probation service, and to some extent, penal and treatment institutions for juveniles. Under the British mandatory government law of 1937 a person less than 9 years old is not legally responsible for his or her acts. Children between the ages of 9 and 12 could be held legally responsible, but the prosecution has to prove that the child could know that he or she should not have behaved as he or she did. Under the new Israeli law this situation changed; the minimum age was raised to 14, and then lowered again to 12. The maximum age under Israeli law was raised to 18 (from 16, under the British mandatory government law), first for females, and later on for males as well. The following changes, over the years, affect, necessarily, the delinquency rates: 9–16 [9–18 for girls] (1948–1977), 9–18 (1977–1978), 13–18 (1978–1984), and 12–18 (since 1984).

The critical age is the age at the day of prosecution. However, in some instances, when the act was committed before age 18, a case may be submitted to the youth probation service even if the case was prosecuted past this age (Rahav, 1998b). There are three main youth laws pertaining to juvenile delinquents. The first is the Youth Law 1960 (treatment and supervision), which deals mainly with nondelinquent minors who require protection. Underage (e.g., for legal responsibility) minor delinquents are handled by welfare officers and not by correctional officers.

The second is the Probation Ordinance 1969 (new version), which details the operating procedures and authority given to probation officers (Hassin and Horovitz, 1998); and the third is the Youth Law 1971 (trial, punishment, and modes of treatment), which deals solely with juvenile delinquents.

Table 4-2 presents the demographic distribution of offenders by age, sex, and religious affiliation (INP, Annual Report, 1998).

Table 4-2: Offenders: Demographic Distribution—Age, Sex, and Religious Affiliation

Year	Total	Juveniles*	Adults	Males	Females	Jews	Non-Jews
1991	64,659	6,163	58,496	56,153	8,506	46,292	18,367
1992	70,863	6,194	64,669	61,749	9,114	49,546	21,317
1993	74,598	6,225	68,373	65,064	9,534	51,306	23,292
1994	75,789	6,477	69,312	65,994	9,795	50,868	24,921
1995	82,683	6,514	76,169	72,314	10,369	52,952	29,731
1996	88,695	7,226	81,469	78,220	10,475	55,421	33,274

Source: INP Annual Reports 1998
*Juveniles between ages 12 and 17

Victims and Issues in Victimology

Israel has played quite a significant role in the development of victimology as an independent scientific field of inquiry. Today, victimology is taught in all major Israeli universities and a growing number of scholars devote their research efforts to this field.

Some unique features related to Israel's history and political situation (the Holocaust victims and the security tensions) are also reflected in the victimological research in this country (Landau and Sebba, 1998). In recent years, however, no victimization survey has been conducted in Israel (Landau, 1999).

So far, only four national victim surveys have been conducted in Israel, in 1979, 1981, 1986, and 1990. However, these surveys, which comprised representative samples of about 5,000 to 6,000 Jewish households each, cannot be seen as representing the total population, as they excluded the Israeli Arab population (within the pre-1967 borders). Approximately one-sixth of the Israeli population within the Green Line (excluding the administered territories) is Arab. There is no evidence of a high degree of criminal victimization on the part of this group, although there is little direct documentation of this, as the victimization surveys did not include the Arab population in their ambit. Agencies dealing with special categories of victims, such as battered women and sexually

abused children, report a relatively low representation of the Arab population, but this may be due, at least in part, to a reluctance to report such acts to the authorities (Landau and Sebba, 1998). Ethnic differences between Arabs and Jews with regard to the decision to close juvenile criminal files rather than to prosecute were recently studied by two Israeli sociologists (Mesch and Fishman, 1998), in an attempt to find patterns of differential outcomes in the criminal justice system.

The findings of their study provided evidence that different criteria are indeed applied to different ethnic groups in the decision-making process to close a file. Previous criminal involvement influences the decision to terminate a file for both Jews and Arabs. However, age and juvenile occupation are found to apply only to Jewish juveniles, resulting in a higher likelihood of closing files of Jews than of Arabs. The authors caution, however, that the findings are limited to less serious crimes only (property offenses). In an earlier study Fishman and Rattner (1997) examined the effect of legal and extralegal variables on record closing and convictions, focusing on differences in dispositions between Jews and Arabs. Their findings confirmed, at least partially, the hypothesis that Arabs have a greater chance of being discriminated against as their cases move along in the criminal justice system. However, the impact of nationality on record termination was very small. In the conviction phase, the proportion of records attributed to Arabs was higher; however, the information regarding previous convictions raised some statistical questions regarding the final interpretation of the data.

Two unique aspects of the victimological research in Israel focus on the victims of terrorism and the Holocaust. Research studies of survivors of major terrorist incidents found out the long-lasting experience of significant negative feelings and thoughts related to the hostage incident, some clearly experiencing posttraumatic stress disorder.

An extensive body of literature has developed on the traumatic effects of the Holocaust experience on survivors, including second and third generations of survivors. Many of the studies report long-range detrimental effects of the Holocaust on the survivors or on the second or third generations. Empirical evidence shows that children of Holocaust survivors tend to internalize feelings of anger and aggression and have problems in their ability for direct expression of these impulses (Landau and Sebba, 1998).

Friedmann (1998), in his discussion of Landau and Sebba's extensive research in the field of victimology, summarizes the three "profiles" of victimization in Israel, which include both research and political activism in the area. The first is "moral crusader," where research focuses on particularly sensitive topics such as the elderly, women, and children. The second, unique to Israel, is "national political," with the ethnic, religious, and community cleavages, terrorism, and the Holocaust. Finally, the third, "mundane," deals with issues such as victim compensation, or notification of proceedings against the suspect. (An example of the last can be found in the study conducted by Mesch and Fishman, 1998.) Finally, it could probably be stated that the victims have no place in the criminal process, except for submitting complaints and giving testimony in the police investigation and/or the trial.

Police

General Overview

The Israel National Police (INP), from its inception in 1948, has been a national, highly centralized force, commanded and managed by a commissioner (known as the inspector-general) from INP headquarters in Tel Aviv (and from Jerusalem since the Six-Day War). The country was divided into districts and subdistricts, each commanded and controlled by a local commander, operating from his own sub-headquarters. Careful lines of command and control were designed to facilitate the control ability of commanders and headquarters on different levels. In terms of structure and management, the INP followed a centralized military and tightly controlled example set by the British colonial police, and also by the military, from where many of the first top police officers were recruited. The military nature of the INP was further facilitated by the organizational climate: a predominantly authoritative leadership style, tight control over officers' professional discretion, strictly enforced discipline, and carefully maintained distance between commissioned officers and rank-and-file. Over the past four decades, the force went through three major reforms, culminating in the recent orientation toward the philosophy of community-oriented policing (Shadmi, 1998).

Today the INP is one national police service, under the charge of the minister of public security. The force is commanded and directed, operationally and organizationally, by its commissioner, who is appointed by the minister, almost invariably from INP ranks. This national force, with its headquarters in Jerusalem, is organized geographically into six regions or districts and thirteen subdistricts and delivers its services to the public from sixty-seven local police stations. The budget for the INP comes from central government revenue, excluding municipal taxes. Its commanding officers are selected by national and regional headquarters (town mayors or other heads of locally elected councils have no say whatsoever in these appointments).

A unified, unitary police service of this type permits rapid national response and deployment anywhere in the country, whether in response to terrorist attacks or to public order disturbances. Israel's long-standing security situation has led it to set up a network of strong national and regional service units to defend its internal security: special antiterrorist and bomb disposal units, the Border Guard (or the Border Patrol Police), and the special patrol units. All this has demanded massive investment of manpower, money, material, and other resources subtracted from investment in the local police stations that supply the greater part of services to the public. It is common for local station officers to be deployed elsewhere, wherever and whenever the need arises. Such circumstances inadvertently weaken the local stations and impair service to citizens (INP, official publication, 1996). Police roles and responsibilities, according to Article 3 of the Israel National Police Manual (new version, 1971), include the following:

- Prevent crimes

- Discover and investigate crimes

- Apprehend criminals and carry out criminal prosecution

- Enforce traffic laws

- Secure public safety and property

- Provide a secure environment for prisoners and detainees

- Secure internal peace (Israel National Police Annual Report, 1998)

The last function is a direct outcome of the Yom Kippur War and the terrorist events that followed thereafter. In 1974, the Israeli government imposed the responsibility for preserving internal peace on the Israel National Police. This extraordinary heavy burden took its toll on effective and efficient policing in the area of traditional police functions (Haberfeld et al., 1998).

The Border Patrol functions as an operational and professional unit of the Israel National Police, among other responsibilities, in the area of internal security and the war against terrorism. It can be compared, as far as its internal structure, to what is known in other countries as the *gendarmerie*.

The officers have the same authority as regular police officers; however, tactically, they are deployed in a semimilitary manner. Their function is unique and complex. They fight, protect, secure peace, and serve the public in various civilian service capacities—their functions and overall performance depend on specific needs and situational necessities.

In 1998, the Israel National Police was composed of 25,700 police officers, including the Border Patrol. Female officers constituted about 20% of the force (INP Annual Reports, 1998). Table 4-3 presents crimes recorded by the INP in 1997 and provides an illustration of the heavy burden of preserving internal peace.

Table 4-3a: *Crimes Recorded by the Police in 1997*

Type of crime	1997
State Security	1,042
Public Order	28,882
Against Human Life	2,986
Against Human Body	26,958
Sexual Offenses	3,098
Moral Offenses (included drugs)	14,546
Property	268,967
Fraud	11,635
Other	8,168
Total	366,282

Source: INP Annual Reports 1997

Table 4-3b: *Incidence of Property and Personal Crimes—Based on the Number of Criminal Investigations*

	Files (INP Annual Reports 1991–1996)[1]						
Year Crimes	Breaking and Entering	Violent Crimes[2]	Serious Crimes[3]	Sex Crimes	Drug Crimes— Personal Use	Drug Crimes— Trafficking	Drug Possession— not for Personal Use
1991	44,741	14,512	5,526	2,232	7,528	2,386	[4]
1992	51,939	16,725	6,554	2,544	6,581	3,529	[4]
1993	47,879	18,842	7,123	2,752	6,842	2,345	2,358
1994	44,421	18,809	6,686	2,825	6,594	2,033	2,801
1995	47,739	22,415	7,646	2,904	7,476	1,821	2,985
1996	51,621	24,445	7,362	3,001	8,821	2,038	3,677

[1]Some of the crime incidents are included in a number of categories.
[2]Included are murder and attempted murder, rape, sexual molestation, assault, aggravated assault, and robbery.
[3]Included are murder and attempted murder, rape and sexual molestation, robbery, blackmail, bribery, and arson.
[4]This offense in 1991 and 1992 was classified either as personal use or trafficking.

Both Tables 4-3a and 4-3b show that property crimes, as in the United States and other countries studied, outnumber crimes against persons.

Community-Oriented Policing

In 1994, having analyzed the needs of the INP and its public, the decision to make the transition to community-oriented policing was made. To carry forward this organizational change and realize the improvement in policing required by it, the Community Policing Unit (CPU) was inaugurated in December 1994. Directly answerable to the commissioner, the CPU has as its chief function to lead this organizational change process and assimilate the new approach into the INP's operational culture. The transition to community-oriented policing, the essence of which is the reorientation of police stations and their local communities, is planned to last until 2003 (INP Official Publication, 1996). Today, more than fifty cities in Israel are undergoing a change to community polic-

ing. Under the direction of the CPU staff, the police station and mayor in a given city are approached and asked if they are willing to undertake the change to community policing. The enthusiasm is usually great. Most of the mayors have immediately grasped the potential of such a change. As a first step, the police officers and the community leaders meet and are introduced to the working principles of this philosophy. The CPU works with steering committees, training them in problem-oriented analysis techniques, providing them with ideas and tested crime prevention partnership models, referring them to other cities where similar problems have been tackled, and assisting them in the evaluation processes. Seven cities going into their second year of implementation have, together with their local partners, reached a second stage of goal-setting—coordination with senior level management. During the first year of implementation, the commissioner decided that those implementing community policing (the station commanders) would be rewarded by a trip abroad to see how things are done in countries that have implemented the process. Not only was this a significant incentive, but it allowed the commanders to see how their counterparts in such countries as the United Kingdom and Holland had implemented community policing.

Community Policing Centers, "mini-stations," are being set up within neighborhoods in order to decentralize services and to help focus on local needs and problems. The neighborhood community police officer, who has been taken out of the main police station staff, collaborates with residents and local agencies and mobilizes volunteers to help implement crime prevention activities. Within the main police stations, a "Service Center" has been set up to provide citizens with "one-stop" response to all their requests and needs, from filing reports to receiving application forms for the licensing of personal weapons. The initial results seem promising (at least according to the INP official sources). More and more police officers are reporting a difference in the way they provide services, allowing them to target their services according to the needs of their specific communities. These officers have an increased level of satisfaction, and the hope that the new working methods will bring about real crime prevention in the long run.

Resource sharing has already produced increased police activity in areas that, until now, have been unattended, especially with respect to at-risk groups and enforcement of quality-of-life offenses. The officers are also reporting that in their newly formed neighborhood centers, an increased public cooperation with the police is noticeable (Geva, 1998).

Image and Accountability

Despite the efforts of the CPU, the overall public image of the police, at least as portrayed by the media, is very low. Prior to 1992, all complaints against police officers were handled internally by the police

department itself. During the last decades, this system came under criticism for being inappropriate and for its lack of objectivity and professionalism (Herzog, 1998a). Following public pressure and a gradual change in the attitudes of the Israeli police administration, especially with regard to the issue of accountability, the external-civilian Department for the Investigation of Complaints against Police Officers (known in Hebrew as *Machash*) was established in 1992, under the auspices of the Ministry of Justice. Less serious cases continue to be dealt with by the internal investigations unit within the Israeli police department. The role of Machash is to investigate every police officer suspected of committing offenses involving the illegal use of force as well as criminal offenses punishable by over 1 year of imprisonment. It also decides on whether a complaint is sustained or not. The board is headed by attorneys, but all of the investigators are police officers who were once part of the regular police force (Herzog, 1998b). In 1994, the numerous allegations about excessive use of force by the police led to the establishment of the Kremnitzer Committee to investigate such abuse. The Kremnitzer Committee was the third public committee established to investigate police misconduct. Previous committees included the State Comptroller's Committee and the Ministry of Police Comptrollers' Reports. The major recommendations of the committee were to speed up the process of investigation by investigating the complaints in the civil court, to discharge police officers even if the evidence does not warrant a criminal process, to enforce the standards of selective recruitment, to extend the probationary period from 1 to 2 years, to discharge officers who show violent propensity during the probationary period, to recruit more women, to prevent officers with a record of disciplinary violations from being promoted, and to photograph the investigative processes (Haberfeld et al., 1998). The Committee cited the positive changes that had been

Table 4-4: Police Budget and Its Distribution (1996; 1 U.S.$>Approx. 4 Israeli Shekels)

Direct budget	2,070,635	551,273	44,259
Expenses dependent on income	109,033	103,019	14,523
Other governmental offices	140,586	95,548	39,868
Total	2,320,254	749,840	98,650

Source: INP Annual Reports 1996

adopted by the police to ensure more successful treatment of police violence.

However, it also warned against "misunderstandings" stemming from clear messages on the declarative level rather than the operational level. It was the committee's opinion that the covert messages conveyed to lower rank officers become manifest in the field because of the police administration's emphasis on, or pressure toward, producing concrete results. These pressures bring about a disregard for declarative rules and regulations and a tendency to resort to various illegal means (Herzog, 1998b). The chief of police agreed to adopt all the recommendations. However, the media continues to portray a grim picture by reporting, almost on a daily basis, about instances of abuse of power and authority, problems with integrity, and police corruption. A recent survey of public opinion revealed that about half of the citizens of Israel do not have confidence in the abilities and effectiveness of the INP. However, at least as far as the use of excessive force is concerned, the public seems to be mistaken, as the INP proudly presents its recent statistics—citizen complaints against the excessive use of force went down, from 300 officers who faced indictment in 1995 to 229 in 1997 (Haberfeld et al., 1998).

Technology and Budget

The Israeli police are considered to be technologically up-to-date in comparison with their counterparts in the West. Among other technological inventions, the force uses video motion detection (VMD), digital traffic stop cameras, portable laptops in patrol cars, the Automated Fingerprint Identification System (AFIS), and DNA technology based on the polymerase chain reaction. Table 4-4 presents police budget distribution for the year 1996.

Prosecutorial and Judicial Process

At the end of the police investigation, the investigative files are transferred to the prosecutorial authorities of the state, which represent the people as the accuser in the criminal violation (article 11 of the Law of Criminal Procedure, hereafter referred to as "the Law"). The prosecutorial branch is headed by the attorney general to the government, and the state and district attorneys serve as deputies to the attorney general. Police prosecutors are allowed to represent the prosecution in misdemeanor cases.

The duties and responsibilities of the attorney general are rooted in the period of British rule in Palestine. However, contrary to the current situation in the United States and in England, where the attorney general is a political figure who serves also as a member of the government, in Israel the office of attorney general is a public office of high status. As such, it is not subordinate to the other branches of government in regard to the decision-making process. In addition to serving as the head of the prosecutorial process, the attorney general's duties include the following:

- To represent the state in courts at all the judicial processes

- To serve as a legal counsel to the government and to other governmental branches (including preparations for new legislation)
- To represent the people's interest

When the police investigative files are received, the prosecutor invokes the process of indictment and decides what criminal charges the suspect is going to face. Until the court hearings commence, the trial prosecutor has the right to amend/change the charges, and from that moment this right is transferred to the court (articles 91 and 92 of the Law). However, the prosecution is entitled to its own professional opinion, and therefore, it is allowed not to indict the suspect in one of the following instances:

- When it appears from the investigative files that there is not enough evidence to achieve indictment
- When the prosecutor decides that the evidence is not reliable (does not meet the desired standards)
- When the chances for a guilty verdict are low (the Israel High Court of Justice, 3846/91)

No public interest will be served by the indictment—here the legislators aimed at a desired balance between the indictment of the defendant and the public interest in a case of no indictment (see the High Court of Justice, 935/89).

During the entire prosecutorial process, the prosecutor has the right to offer a plea bargain to the suspect or his/her attorneys. If the plea bargain is accepted, the defendant (whether free or already incarcerated) pleads guilty to all or some of the charges included in the indictment and faces either a set of newly amended charges or a plea for a reduced sentence. Since its introduction, the plea bargain arrangement has been severely criticized, especially by the Israel High Court of Justice, because it is not secured by the Law of Criminal Procedure and the proceedings of this arrangement are regulated in case laws. For ex-

ample, it was decided that it is appropriate for the parties involved in the process to bring the written plea bargain agreement to the court and attach it to the investigative files, but the court does not have to pass its judgment based on the specific plea bargain.

Furthermore, the court is not tied to the agreement or any part of it (criminal request no. 523/71). However, during the past few years the plea bargain arrangement has acquired some legitimacy, and, to a certain degree, even some enthusiasm among prosecutors and attorneys.

In Israel, every criminal suspect or accused has the right to choose an attorney who will represent him/her. However, in reality, there is a major economic obstacle to this right, because a private counsel or attorney can be very expensive. Because of this obstacle, the court has the right, based on the defendant's request or its own initiative, to appoint an attorney (not only for the defendant/accused, but also for the free or already detained suspect), if the case involves an impecunious defendant (article 15(c)(d) of the Law). In other cases, if the defendant is not represented, this right of the court to appoint an attorney, free of charge, becomes mandatory (articles 21a and 15a of the Law) under the following circumstances:

- When the accused is brought to a hearing for a request of preventive detention until all the proceedings are over
- When the crime of which he/she is accused is first-degree murder, or the sentence for the crime committed is a death penalty or life sentence, or minimum sentence for the crime is set at 10 years' imprisonment or more
- When the accused is less than 16 years old and is brought to a court other than Juvenile Court
- When the accused is mute, deaf, or blind, or there is a reason to believe that he/she might be mentally insane or retarded

In 1996, because of the problems associated with finding an adequate number of attorneys who would volunteer to serve as public defenders, the office of public defender was established. The office employs both in-house and private attorneys. The main purpose of the office is to provide assistance in criminal cases, in cases in which the Law mandates the appointment of a public defender, and in cases in which the accused is an indigent person and cannot afford a private attorney.

Pretrial and Preventive Detention

According to the new Criminal Procedure Law (Law Enforcement and Incarceration Rights—1996), the police have to bring the arrested suspect in front of a judge (regardless of whether or not a warrant was issued) in order to extend the arrest warrant. If a suspect is an adult, this has to be done no later than 24 hours after the initial arrest was executed. If the suspect is a juvenile, he/she has to be brought in front of a judge no later than 12 hours after the initial arrest. During the hearings the judge has two options as to how to proceed (article 17 of the Law):

1. The judge can extend the arrest warrant, for not more than 15 days, providing that two cumulative circumstances are present:

   - There is an evidencial basis to assume that the accused is guilty as charged

   - There is a reason to justify the extent of his/her incarceration (that he/she might obstruct justice or compromise the outcome of the investigation, public safety might be in danger, and/or the seriousness of the crime committed)

2. The judge can release the accused and not extend the warrant, in an absolute manner, and also release the accused

on bail, with or without additional limitations (for example, by preventing the accused from leaving the country and taking away his/her passport). The amount of bail set does not necessarily reflect the damage caused or the profit gained from the crime; it is aimed at securing the appearance of the accused for the follow-up investigation, the trial itself, or part of the punishment (article 43 of the Law). If the conditional release is violated in any way, the accused is arrested or the bail money is forfeited to the state.

In two instances the judge does not have the authority to prevent the pretrial arrest:

- When the accused is a fleeing felon (article 17a of the Law)

- When the accused is suspected of committing a crime for which the mandatory sentence is either death penalty or life sentence, or was involved in one of the following crimes: prostitution, drug-related crimes, or blackmail (articles 34 and 35 of the Law)

When the indictment is submitted, the accused can be detained only on the basis of preventive detention that has been issued for the duration of all the proceedings, until the judicial verdict (articles 21a and 27a of the Law). If a person is arrested as a suspect and the prosecution does not request from the judge a preventive detention warrant, the suspect must be set free. As mentioned before, when the prosecution requests such a warrant, the accused must be represented by an attorney, unless he/she gives up this right.

Unless the accused is represented, the judge cannot issue this warrant for the duration of the proceedings, and a warrant can be issued for a limited period, not exceeding 30 days, each time.

Similar to the procedure followed during the extension of the pretrial arrest warrant, the preventive detention warrant can be issued while both of two cumulative conditions are present:

- Apparent evidence is present, in order to prove the accusation
- There is a reason for incarceration (as pointed out earlier)

However, the Law specifies that the accused should not be preventively incarcerated if either of the following is true:

- If more than 60 days have passed from the initial indictment to the beginning of the trial
- If more than a year has passed from the beginning of the trial to the time the verdict was issued (articles 52 and 53 of the Law)

The Judicial System

The Israeli regular judicial system (as opposed to the religious/rabbinical system) is adversarial in nature, with judicial proceedings and legal jurisdiction in the hands of professional judges only. The origin of the criminal court system can be traced to the British court model, during the British mandate in Palestine. The system is composed of a three-tier court: magistrates' courts, district courts, and the Supreme Court. Each tier has a different jurisdiction over criminal matters.

Magistrate's (or Peace) Courts

The magistrates' courts exercise criminal jurisdiction in crimes punishable by no more than 7 years of imprisonment or fine (article 51 of the Courts law). This upper limit is subjected to constant increases due to case overload. Until 1957, the upper limits rose from no more than 1 year of imprisonment to 3 and 5 years, and finally the limit reached 7 years in 1992 (Shacher, 1999). There are twenty-eight magistrates' courts throughout Israel. Most of the pro-

ceedings in these courts are conducted before a single judge.

District Courts

The district courts have a dual function: they deal with all criminal cases beyond the jurisdiction of the magistrates' courts, and also serve as appellate courts for magistrate's court decisions and other judgments.

These courts do not have discretion to reject appellate cases from the lower courts. During the appellate proceeding the courts can exercise the following rights: to deny the appeal; to amend the judgment of the lower court or to render a new judgment; or to return the appeal to the lower court with instructions as to the proceedings. There are five such courts in Israel. A three-judge panel is appointed in the following trials:

- When the crimes are punishable by death penalty (capital cases) or 10 years of imprisonment or more
- In appeals in which the final decisions are of severe nature

The Supreme Court

Israel's Supreme Court exercises jurisdiction over the district courts' decisions. Usually a case is decided by a three-member panel. In other proceedings, the number of judges is decided by the chief justice and the number is uneven. In special requests, there are instances when the Supreme Court consists of a single justice. In addition, similar to the English system, this court serves as the state's High Court of Justice.

In principle, in most of the hearings of the Israeli Supreme Court, three judges are present based on the personal decision of the supreme justice. Exceptions to this rule are made, for example, during additional hearings on cases that were previously

Table 4-5: *The Distribution of Criminal Cases According to the Various Israeli Courts, 1995–1997 (Central Bureau of Statistics, 1998)**

Court/Situation	Magistrate Courts			District Courts			Supreme Court		
Year	1995	1996	1997	1995	1996	1997	1995	1996	1997
Submitted	208,173	221,234	235,634	15,500	16,724	18,123	2,116	2,603	2,198
Closed files	201,677	209,143	233,228	14,848	16,824	17,811	2,061	2,608	1,963
Open files	96,634	111,132	114,841	5,194	5,131	4,698	1,028	996	1,015

*The number of files closed and open each year represents a total number of files dealt with in a given year, including files that were submitted in prior years.

decided by the Supreme Court. Also, depending on the importance of the specific hearing, the supreme justice has the authority to increase the number of the judges (more than three, but always an odd number). However, section 26 of the Court Law (1984) states that there are three types of hearings in which a single judge can preside over the Supreme Court:

1. Hearing on interim warrants, temporary warrants, and requests for suspended warrants
2. Hearings on appeals of the district courts' interim decisions, district courts' verdicts reached by a single judge, verdicts or decisions of the municipal courts
3. Hearings held prior to the appeal

The Israeli High Court of Justice, known as *Bagatz*, functions as an administrative law court to provide judicial review of official administrative actions. The grievances against a government authority can be brought by citizens or organizations. The significance of the Israeli High Court of Justice has grown in recent years: on one hand, defending the rights of the citizens against the state's actions and the state's involvement, when their basic rights are apparently violated by the government; on the other, intervening in constitutional, political, and even religious issues. This phenomenon has been referred to as "judicial activism" and has brought about vigorous opposition by the orthodox religious parties.

The judges in Israel are elected by a public committee composed of representatives from the Supreme Court, the government, and the representatives of the bar. Overall, judges in Israel command the respect of the population. However, the judicial system in general is characterized by case overload, which leads to significant delays in the hearings and rendering of judgments. These deficiencies are caused mainly by inadequate number of justices in comparison to the rising number of hundreds of thousands of cases currently processed by the magistrates' and district courts. Table 4-5 presents the distribution of criminal cases in the three courts during recent years.

This grim situation has brought about the establishment of a public committee headed by the Supreme Court Justice to review the court system in Israel, in an attempt to streamline and modernize its functions (1997). The main recommendation was to change the present structure of the judicial system based on redesigning of all the three courts and their hearing jurisdictions. The recommendation is still pending the government's approval.

Penalties and Sentencing

The criminal process in Israel is composed of two stages: the trial and the sentencing process.

During the first stage, the evidence is gathered and brought, together with the witnesses, in front of the judge by the two sides and the cross-examination takes place. The judge is also entitled to cross-examine and ask questions; however, this right is rarely exercised. Upon the completion of the first stage, the judge ultimately decides whether the accused is found guilty or innocent, based on the indictment and the material evidence. The witnesses are not sworn, but are warned against committing perjury. The accused, who serves as the first witness, is not obligated to testify and is allowed to remain silent. Despite the fact that this right to remain silent is perceived as an attribute for the prosecution, the guilty verdict cannot be based solely on the silence of the accused; additional, independent proof, is required. Every individual is eligible to serve as a witness and it is his/her duty to serve as such (with exceptions for immediate family members, who cannot be called as the prosecution witnesses). If an individual fails to appear in court as a witness, the judge can issue a bench warrant against him/her and can impose a prison sentence or a fine (as in the case of "hostile witnesses"). With regard to the mentally ill, their ability to testify is judged based on the capacity to understand parts of the events, and the ability to recall and convey. For the underaged, their ability to testify is based on their understanding of the need to testify truthfully. Hearsay testimony is not admissible in criminal cases.

Rules of Evidence

The statement or admission of guilt given to the police by the accused, is admissible in court, providing it was given out of a person's free will. However, a person cannot be found guilty based solely on his admission of guilt, additional and independent proof is required. If the defense team claims that the admission of guilt was forced and not given out of the suspect's free will, a subtrial is set in motion to investigate the claim. In general, the rule of evidence in Israel allows all other types of evidence to be introduced in court and deems them admissible, unless the judge finds otherwise, based on the severity of the offense and the potential harm to the accused. During the last few years, a gradual tendency to accept the legal doctrine of "exclusionary rule" has been noticed.

Sentencing

If the accused has been found guilty, the hearing about the severity of the sentence commences. Additional witnesses are allowed to testify for both parties as to the character of the accused, and to provide additional information to the judge, for sentencing consideration. At this point, the judge has the right to and must (if the accused is less than 21 years old) ask a probation officer for a report, which includes the social and personal background of the accused, as well as a recommendation for the sentence. In most the instances, the judges accept the recommendations included in the report (Fishman et al., 1982). Each side is entitled to an appeal (for both the guilty verdict and the sentence itself), which has to be submitted in less than 45 days from the sentencing day. However, the appellate courts tend not to annul or even intervene in the lower courts' decisions.

A great deal of individualization is allowed in the sentencing process, predominantly because the criminal law determines only the upper range or limit of the punishment, expressed by maximum years of imprisonment (with the exception of the crime of murder, where since 1954 the mandatory punishment has been life imprisonment). In light of this situation, the judge is allowed to sentence the accused to any length of sentence, as long as it falls below the maximum limit. The judge may also impose a more lenient alternative to imprisonment, such as one of the following:

1. *Open imprisonment.* In 1987 the criminal law was amended and the

judge was allowed to substitute the prison sentence up to 6 months of imprisonment, by sentencing the accused to open imprisonment with community service in various public organizations.

2. *Fine*. Various levels of fines are possible, depending upon the offense committed, and the judge has the right to impose a fine up to four times higher than the original amount of damage caused to the victim or profit from the offense.

3. *Suspended sentence*. This can be imposed for periods between 1 and 3 years of imprisonment, with the conditions broadly or specifically defined.

4. *Probation*. The boundaries are set between 6 months and 3 years; the judge is not limited by the type of the offense committed or by the prior record of the offender.

5. *Community service*. This sentencing option is exercised when the probation office is convinced that the public and the offender will benefit from it in a more significant way than from the actual imprisonment. (The community service must be performed without any compensation, during free time, must be well-structured, and cannot exceed a period of 1 year.)

Death penalty or capital punishment as a punishment for first-degree murder was in existence during the British Mandate and even after the establishment of the State of Israel. However, in 1954, it was abolished and replaced by a life sentence, without parole. Presently, the death penalty appears as a possible punishment in crimes such a treason during wartime, crimes against humanity and accompanying offenses, and terrorism. To date, the only person executed has been Adolf Eichmann, in 1965, for his crimes against humanity and the Jewish nation. More-

over, a number of times military judges imposed the death penalty on convicted felons in cases of terrorist attacks. However, the policy of the various Israeli governments is not to demand the death penalty, and in all these cases of exceptions, the death penalty was replaced with life imprisonment (Sheleff, 1998). More recently, opinions have been voiced on both political and public fronts demanding the implementation of capital punishment.

The Prison System

Administration and Organization

As with the police force, there is only one national prison system: the Israel Prison Service (the IPS).

According to the formal policy of the IPS, its principal role is safe incarceration of inmates, and prevention of inmates from causing harm to the society. The IPS also claims to have a role in the rehabilitation of the incarcerated population (*The Prison Ordinance*, 1971). It is headed by the prisons commissioner, who is appointed by the minister of interior security, based on the consent received from the government. From the organizational standpoint, the national prison system has a pyramidal (hierarchical) structure, similar to the military organization, and includes three tiers:

- Main headquarters of the Israeli Prison System, which serves as a professional center, running the prisons throughout the country.

- Three territorial, regional headquarters (North, Center, and South), which serve as the middle link between the territorial headquarters and the field offices, in charge of overseeing the effective management of the field units. Field offices are outposts and subsidiaries of the regional headquarters operating units designed for community policing.

Prisons and Jails

There are fifteen prisons (including two jails for pretrial detainees) and a national medical center. Table 4-6 portrays the main characteristics of prisons and jails (detention centers).

The table indicates that only five of the prisons were built with the specific goal of incarceration of inmates and pretrial detainees. The remaining seven are located in former British fortresses (known as *Tegarts*) and three in other sites that were not intended to serve as detention centers either.

Three of these facilities house more than 800 inmates; four, 600 to 800; four, 500 to 600; and three, fewer than 500. The security levels differ. Two-thirds are designated as maximum security prisons, three are medium security, and two are minimum security. A number of prisons are intended to serve special populations: Neve Tirtza for female prisoners and detainees only; Sharon for juvenile delinquents; Ashmoret and Eshel for prisoners who require special security measures to protect them from other inmates; Ayalon, which includes psychiatric wards and special religious wards, to separate and isolate the religious prisoners; and a medical center intended to house sick inmates. Sharon and Eshel also offer special treatment wards for addicted inmates for drug treatments; Damon, Shata, Nitzan, Shekma, and Nafcha house inmates from the occupied territories who are serving time for terrorist activities against the State of Israel

One of the characteristics of the prison system in Israel is severe overcrowding, except for the newly built Tzalmon, which was built according to modern, Western standards (about 5.7 square meters per inmate), Neve Tirtza (3.8 square meters), and Sharon (4.2 square meters). An adult inmate in an Israeli prison has, on the average, an accommodation of about 3 square meters only (about 9 square feet). The size of the accommodation is far below the standards set by the United Nations (12 square meters) and is also below American standards (5.7 square meters) (Shavitt, 1998). Furthermore, the ratio between number of inmates and number of cells is very high in most of the facilities, with the exception of Tzalmon, in which the ratio is 1.4 inmates per cell. In 8 facilities, the ratio varies from 3 to 5 inmates per cell; in 5 facilities the ratio varies between 5 and 9; and in the Carmel prison it reaches an enormous high of 18.5 inmates per cell.

The Prison Population

Out of 8,683 inmates incarcerated in prisons and detention centers throughout Israel in 1998, three-quarters are residents of Israel, and the rest Palestinians from the territories (most of them males), two-thirds from the West Bank and one-third from the Gaza Strip. The Palestinians are subject to Israeli military law and are incarcerated predominantly for security offenses and various terrorist acts.

The Israeli inmates are predominantly adult males (87.3% of the prisoners and 12.6% of detainees in preventive detention) and 3.2% females, and 2.2% juveniles.

Table 4-7 shows the distribution of the incarcerated population during the recent years.

Based on analysis of trends in the incarcerated population in recent years (1987–1998), it is possible to identify two main themes:

- Up to 1993, the incarcerated population increased steadily (an increase of 18%), especially because of a gradual growth in the number of Israeli inmates (an increase of 46%).

- Up to this year, practically very little has changed. The number of incarcerated Palestinians did not change during those years

Table 4-6: Characteristics of Prisons and Detention Centers in Israel (Israel Prison Service's Report, 1998)

Sector	Name	Original Structure	Year	Security Level	Population	Special Divisions	Capacity	Area per Prisoner
	Damon	Stables	1953	Medium	Light convicted	Terrorist	517	2.7 s/f
	Kishon	New	1983	Maximum	Detained	-	90	3.3 s/f
	Shata	Tegart	1953	Maximum	Convicted	Rehabilitation, terrorist	806	3 s/f
North	Ashmoret	Tegart	1962	Maximum	Convicted, detained	Drugs clean	383	3.2 s/f
	Carmel	Tents	1985	Minimum	Light convicted	-	520	2.5 s/f
	Tzalmon	New	1996	Medium	Convicted	Drugs clean	720	5.7 s/f
	Sharon	Tegart	1953	Medium	Convicted	Juvenile	525	4.2 s/f
	Ayalon	Tegart	1950	Maximum	Convicted, security danger	Psychiatry, isolation, religious	571	3.5 s/f
	Mahasiahu	Shacks	1956	Minimum	Light convicted	Rehabilitation	891	3.2 s/f
Center	Neve Tirtza	Ayalon	1968	Maximum	Women (convicted/detained)	Rehabilitation	217	3.8 s/f
	Nitzan	Ayalon	1978	Maximum	Convicted/detained	Classification, terrorist	739	3 s/f
	Medical Center	Ayalon	1990	Maximum	Ill	-	114	4.8 s/f
	Eshel	New	1970	Maximum	Convicted	Rehabilitation, security	914	3 s/f
South	Kidar	New	1984	Maximum	Detained	-	631	3.2 s/f
	Shekma	Tegart	1968	Maximum	Security	Terrorist	693	2.5 s/f
	Nafchah	New	1980	Maximum	Security	Terrorist, workers	702	3.5 s/f

Table 4-7: *Prisons' and Detention Centers' Population in Israel, 1987–1997 (Israel Prison Service Report, 1998)*

Year	Israelis Convicted	Rate per 100,000 Citizens	Israelis Detained	Palestinians Convicted and Detained	Total Imprisoned in Israel
1987	3,914	88.80	586	4,049	8,549
1988	4,290	95.80	682	4,082	9,054
1989	4,589	100.49	1,026	4,034	9,649
1990	4,981	103.23	936	3,914	9,831
1991	5,133	101.22	924	4,053	10,110
1992	5,715	109.79	395	4,008	10,118
1993	5,785	108.34	395	3,868	10,048
1994	5,790	105.78	627	2,940	9,357
1995	5,743	102.17	467	2,965	9,175
1996	5,260	89.41	1,055	2,225	8,540
1997	5,704	96.00	727	2,252	8,683

From 1993 a steady decrease in the number of incarcerations and detentions (about 14%) can be observed. One possible explanation can be found in the parallel decrease in the number of Palestinians arrested and detained, an outcome of the peace treaties signed with the Palestinian Liberation Organization and the establishment (in 1995) of the Palestinian Authority (decrease of 44%).

The ratio of Israeli inmates per 100,000 citizens, during recent years, is similar. The same trend can be observed for an increase in the numbers of inmates until 1993, followed by a steady decrease. In comparison with other countries around the world, Israel occupies a place in the middle, similar to the ratios acceptable in other modern, democratic countries (Kuhn, 1998).

The most common way of easing the pressure of prison overcrowding seems to be the "early release" system, which is administered through an early release committee. Eligible inmates are those sentenced for a minimum of 6 months, after serving two-thirds of their sentence. The early release committee is composed of a district judge, representative of the prison systems (usually a high ranking social worker) and a physician, representing the Ministry of Health. In addition, the district attorney's office and the probation board are also entitled to representation. The committee bases its decision on the outcome of an interview with the inmate and the report submitted by a social worker.

These early release options vary, depending on the length of the original sentence. For inmates serving sentences up to 2 years of imprisonment, the release is unconditional, in contrast to inmates serving prison terms that exceed 2 years of incarceration. For the latter, the conditions are (1) the individual must not commit a crime and (2) he/she must report once a month to a local police station for a follow-up report. In 1997, about 7,400 inmates appeared before the committee, and only about 36% were released.

For inmates serving sentences of 3 to 6 months, the early release is conditioned only upon receiving an administrative warrant from the prisons commissioner, after the inmate has served two-thirds of the initial sentence. Inmates who were sentenced for less than 3 months of incarceration are not entitled to early release. It is important to mention, that in addition to the early release program granted by the committee or through the administrative warrant, the president of the State of Israel has the right to grant clemency both for early release and for a decrease in the original length of a prison sentence. This decision becomes valid after a recommendation is received from the minister of justice.

Table 4-8 presents the main characteristics of the incarcerated population: recidivism rate, length of sentence, and type of offense committed.

In 1997, 3,527 correction officers were employed by the prisons system. Almost 80% of the positions are filled with correction officers who secure and serve the inmate population. The remaining 20% represent the command staff and various administrative functions. About 1,000 staff positions are filled by commissioned officers, two-thirds males and one-third females. The overall budget for the year 1998 was set at 618 million Israeli new shekels (about 150 million U.S. dollars). The budget is allocated for salaries (two-thirds), sundry expenditures (a little over one-fourth), and inflation (about 5%). In addition, the Ministry of Internal Defense allo-

Table 4-8: *Characterization of the Convicted Population in Israel in 1997 (in Percent; Israeli Prison Service's Report, 1998)*

Variable	Values	Israeli Convicted	Palestinian Convicted
Recidivism (imprisonment)	First time	32.6	55.3
	Second time	19.4	27.6
	Third time	13.3	9.5
	Fourth time	10.4	3.8
	Fifth time	8.7	1.8
	Sixth time or more	15.6	2.0
Prison time (in years)	Less than 1	10.0	18.9
	From 1 to 2	17.9	10.5
	From 3 to 5	22.7	9.9
	From 5 to 10	17.4	14.7
	More than 10	9.9	15.6
	Life sentence	5.0	23.0
Type of actual offense	Property	32.2	13.4
	Public order	13.1	3.2
	Security	8.6	66.9
	Human life	5.6	9.2
	Drugs	18.5	Included in Other
	Human body	8.4	Included in Other
	Sex	6.2	Included in Other
	Fraud	3.8	Included in Other
	Other	3.6	7.3

cated an additional 105 million Israeli new shekels (about 25 million U.S. dollars) to build new facilities and improvement of the existing infrastructure.

Miscellaneous Services

1. *Health.* General medical services, including dental treatment, are offered to the inmates in each facility. In addition, general practitioners visit the facilities on a daily basis, and psychiatrists once a week. The Medical Center in the Ayalon Prison houses a number of medical units: general, X-ray, operating room, and specialist unit. The medical services are rendered to all the inmates and detainees.

2. *Treatment of drug addicts.* About half of the prison population in Israel either uses various illegal substances or is already in the stage of addiction. The trend is on the rise. In 1997, about 2,700 inmates participated in programs targeted at the addict populations. About 1,500 of the latter were housed in special wards, for inmates not affected by drug addiction.

3. *Social services.* Each facility has its own team of social workers, who are supposed to maintain direct contact with each and every prisoner and to provide group sessions in various topics. Because of the inadequate number of positions, the social workers suffer from a very heavy work overload.

4. *Education.* In each facility there are a number of educational programs offered to inmates, including formal programs, such as basic skills classes and supplementary educational classes, and informal lectures and special sessions.

5. *Work programs.* According to the rules and regulations of the prison system, every inmate must work.

However, in reality, more than half of the inmate population is not employed, especially the ones with medical problems who are kept in solitary confinement, those serving time for terrorist activities, and those who refuse to work (Wozner, 1998). Approximately half of inmates are employed in the service areas of the facilities, and the salary range is 10% to 40% below the average salary in Israel. In addition, some special training/vocational courses are offered to the inmates.

6. *Leaves.* After serving one-fourth of the original sentence, inmates are allowed a leave. The duration of the leave varies from 24 hours to 4 days depending on the severity of the offense and prior criminal record.

7. *Religious services.* The prison system provides religious services to all inmates, regardless of their religious affiliation (Jews, Arabs, or Christians). There is a separate ward for the religious Jews, and the opportunity to rehabilitate through various religious activities is also possible and offered, both inside and outside the prison facility.

Extradition Procedures and Treaties

The extradition laws and treaties in Israel are codified in the Extradition Law enacted in 1954.

These laws define conditions and procedures to be followed while extraditing people from and to the State of Israel. In 1978, these laws were amended and according to the new, amended laws, an Israeli citizen cannot be extradited from Israel to another country, regardless of the offense committed, unless this offense was committed prior to his/her becoming a citizen of Israel (article 1a of the Law). This amendment presents a significant limitation on the ability of the state to extradite suspects, accused, and convicts to another state. According to the Law, the State of Israel is allowed to extradite a person (who is not an Israeli citizen) if two of the following, cumulative conditions are present (article 2 of the Law):

- If there is an extradition agreement between Israel and the country that requests the extradition, and this agreement binds both countries

- If the accused is charged with committing a crime in a foreign country and this crime is also defined as crime in the State of Israel; if the punishment for the crime committed is the death penalty; or if the punishment is set for 3 years (and above) of imprisonment (with exceptions defined in the Law)

In a case in which both of these conditions are present, the minister of justice is allowed to order that the accused be brought in front of the district court in order to establish whether or not he/she can be extradited (if extradition conditions are met), and to establish if there is enough evidence to bring him/her to justice in Israel (articles 3 and 9 of the Law). If the accused is pronounced as extraditable, he/she will be extradited to the country requesting the extradition, together with all the documents and other evidence that can be used against him/her in the court of law (article 21). However, articles 8, 10, and 17 of the Law specify and define the circumstances under which the accused cannot be extradited to the requesting country. These five conditions are as follows:

1. The accused was already brought to justice in Israel for the specific crime and was found not guilty.

2. Alternatively, the accused was found guilty and has already served the sentence.

3. The statute of limitation can be applied to the crime or the punishment.

4. He/she received clemency for the crime committed.

5. The district court that handled the extradition request has found reasonable grounds to believe that the nature of the crime committed was political and/or the extradition request is motivated by racial or religious prejudice.

If the extradition treaty does not provide sufficient assurance that the accused will not be subjected to death penalty or any punishment contrary to Israeli law or double jeopardy, the Israeli Government will reject the original extradition requested.

Conclusions

As we enter the twenty-first century, it appears that the criminal justice system in Israel faces numerous problems that are partially universal and partially unique to this state. An attempt to form a modern, democratic state based on the Western European model in the midst of the absolute monarchies of the Middle East was an experiment doomed to face not only challenges, but also inevitable failures. Historically, since the criminal justice system is rooted in the hegemonies of the Ottoman and British Empires, these challenges and obstacles cannot be understated. Both empires were governed by sets of powerful legal systems that influenced heavily the newly formed State of Israel. The process of transformation of the entire legal foundation and structure from the English-based model to Israeli laws that reflect the realities of life in Israeli society and its current needs has not yet been completed. Much has been accomplished; however, the task is not finished. In addition, the influx of population from all over the world, labeled as "Jewish" but nevertheless worlds apart, as well as constant external and internal threats (the internal ones predominantly from the social unrest cultivated by diverse ethnic and religious backgrounds), did not provide solid grounds for experimentation. A closer look at each branch of the criminal justice system reveals the omnipresent struggle with soaring crime rates; high representation of juvenile delinquents, especially in drug-related offenses; new forms of organized crime; an upward trend in violent crimes; and prison overcrowding.

Furthermore, it is important to recognize the significance of two very different views and attitudes regarding the central issues of the criminal justice system, such as commitment to the Law, normative and nonnormative behavior, and the legitimacy of the criminal justice in general (as opposed to other forms of social control).

These diametrically different views are held by the very different demographic groups in the Israeli society: religious versus secular; Arabs versus Jews; Ashkenaz versus Jews; new immigrants versus native-born; conflicting political factions, etc.

Additionally, a particular and unique aspect of the system can be observed in the area of policing. Since the INP was charged with securing internal peace, which practically reordered its priorities and budget and manpower allocation, what emerged was an unusual law enforcement body that had to operate based on a double standard. The INP had to operate in a situation in which enforcement of the "traditional" criminal laws was either impossible and/or ineffective. A country that has the same, if not higher, crime rates as its Western counterparts deserves a full allocation of resources to traditional policing.

When the resources have to be divided among two main priorities, effectiveness of law enforcement response diminishes significantly. This effectiveness suffers even further when paired with differential response to two sets of populations. One set is represented by traditional criminals; the second is composed of terrorists, both Arab and Jewish. Illegal force is employed quite routinely, during arrests, while dispersing demonstrations, in criminal investigations, and even in traffic control situations.

The INP seems to be suffering from a low public image based on its ineffective response to traditional criminality and various abuses of the rights of the office, such as excessive use of force and corruption for gain. The corrupt and ineffective behavior appears to be an outcome of a number of factors. First, since the INP was heavily involved in securing internal peace (serving more as a military force than a traditional law enforcement body), it had to give up, at least partially, the "war" on traditional crime.

Furthermore, while fighting the "war" on the traditional crime front, it had to rely on nonnormative and unethical means (such as excessive use of force) in order to show some efficiency. This reliance on illegal means was a direct result of its military, rather than traditional law enforcement, role.

Second, because the INP served as a military entity, the "real" enemy was the Arab/Palestinian terrorist, while Israeli criminals were treated with relative leniency, which allowed a certain degree of "street justice." This "relative leniency" is lenient only in comparison to the way the "real enemy" is treated. Overall, the Israeli criminals are treated in a rough and ruthless manner. Unmistakably, the degree of "street justice" is probably higher than the one exercised by other democratic police forces. As soldiers—figuratively, fighting the war for internal peace, and practically, as the vast majority of the INP officers are former soldiers (army service is mandatory in Israel)—they were allowed to use force against the enemy. The practical question emerges: how does one differentiate between the political enemies and criminals? How can the military training be obviated, and its orientation toward the state enemy replaced with an orientation toward control of traditional crime and criminals? The inevitable consequence is that all suspects, regardless of their ethnic, religious, or political affiliations, are treated more or less as "public enemies" from a very militaristic perspective.

Finally, it can be stated that the "war zone" generates corruption among the military, the masses, and the political ruling class. It remains to be seen how the Israeli criminal justice system in general, and the INP specifically, will walk this complex and problematic path created by political necessities and internal and external pressures. The future of effective law enforcement is inevitably tied to a peaceful solution to the internal and external conflicts brewing in, and around, the state of Israel.

Discussion and Review Questions

1. How do acts of the Israeli Parliament become laws of Israel?

2. When does an act or behavior become a crime in Israel?

3. When is a single judge required in the Israeli Supreme Court?

4. Since Israel, like Great Britain, has no written constitution or bill of rights, where are the Israeli laws derived from?

5. Compare and contrast organized crime in Israel and the United States.

6. What are the similarities and dissimilarities between Community-oriented policing in Israel and the United States?

7. What are the advantages and disadvantages of centralized and decentralized systems of policing?

8. What are the differences between the "blue" and the "green" (border patrol) police? What do you think about the cross and overlap between the military and police functions?

9. What are the major problems facing the Israeli national police in the new millennium?

10. The State of Israel has been shaped by the ancient and modern history. Discuss how the Israeli criminal justice system has been influenced by the various changes in the country's history.

11. What are the advantages and disadvantages of a country not having a written constitution?

12. What is judicial activism? Do we have such a phenomenon in the United States?

13. What is an adversarial judicial system?

14. Compare and contrast the prison systems in the United States and Israel.

15. How are crimes classified in Israel?

16. Israeli prisons are overcrowded. Compare the Israeli overcrowding with that of the United States.

17. What are the miscellaneous services offered to inmates in Israeli prisons?

18. Discuss the extradition procedures and treaties in Israel.

19. Name at least five countries that have extradition treaties with the United States or your own country.

20. What is the place of Israeli women in the Israeli national police?

5

The Criminal Justice System in Argentina

Obi N. I. Ebbe and Reuben G. R. de Olano

Introduction and Brief History

Early History

Prior to the advent of the Europeans in South America, the territory we call Argentina today was inhabited entirely by Indians, otherwise called Native Americans. They subsisted by agriculture in the coastal lands of their great rivers such as the Colorado, Rio Negro, and Rio Salado, and some hunting on the pampas. On the pampas were nomadic and marauding Indian tribes with their livestock. Kingdoms and leadership structures were maintained among the Indian tribes.

As in traditional Africa, the native Indians abhorred the presence of strangers within their territories, as was the practice worldwide throughout the Middle Ages and the early modern times. In effect, the native Americans resisted foreign penetration into their towns and kingdoms. The family played a pivotal role in social cohesion and harmony within each tribe. Social order was maintained through immemorial customs, traditions, and ancestral religious practices in which the earth, the stars, the Moon, and the Sun were used as intermediaries between humanity and the Supreme Being (God). Intertribal conflicts were rife, but there was relative peace and tranquility in the region compared to what was to unfold after the coming of the Europeans.

In 1615 A.D., the first European expedition commanded by Juan Diaz de Solis landed in Argentina at the northern bank of the Rio de la Plata estuary (Sobel, 1975). Shortly after their arrival, de Solis was killed by a Native American. Between 1615 and 1807, many other European nations in addition to Spain wanted a piece of the agricultural and maritime wealth of Argentina. After many battles to ward off the invasion of other European imperialists, Spain established itself as the colonial master of Argentina despite native opposition. Spain colonized Argentina in the sixteenth century. Argentina was then ruled as a dependency of the Viceroyalty of Peru until 1776, when the Viceroyalty of Rio de la Plata was established (Sobel, 1975). The last attempt to take Argentina from Spain was made by the British in 1806. British forces entered Buenos Aires in 1806 and occupied it in an attempt to oust the Spaniards, but were defeated in battle by combined forces of the Spanish militia and the native Indians in May 1807. In accordance with the peace treaty of September 9, 1807, the British left Argentina.

By 1800, Europeans had occupied most parts of Argentina. Many native Indians had been massacred in struggles for their land and resistance to colonization by a foreign monarchy. In the process of colonization, Europeans missionaries were used to change the ancestral religious beliefs and values and replace them with European religious values, norms, and laws. The European religion was Christianity, particularly Roman Catholicism, which spread in the region like an autumn burn fire in a savannah region. By this period (1800s), most Argentine citizens were descendants of European immigrants. The spirit of nationalism had begun to germinate in the minds of many Argentines. In effect, the period 1810–1816 marked an era of Argentine independence revolution against Spanish hegemony. It was also a period of emancipation from the clutches of colonialism. Undeniably, the movements for Argentine liberation and independence from Spain were motivated by the North American and French revolutions.

On July 9, 1816, a Congress of Representatives of the La Plata Provinces took place in Tucuman and a declaration of total independence from Spain was issued (Levene, 1937; Sobel, 1975).

Spain mustered its forces and fought back to retain control of Argentina, but was crushed by Argentine forces under the command of San Martin, who proceeded at the same time and liberated Chile from Spain on February 12, 1817, at the battle of Chacabuco (Levene, 1937; Sobel, 1975; Newton, 1977).

Although the independent republic of Argentina was declared in 1816, political instability gripped the region and continued for a long time. It was only in 1853 that a constitutional presidency was established in the Argentine nation (Levene, 1937).

Contemporary History

Today, Argentina is a multiethnic society with 97% of the population being persons of European descent (The World Almanac and Book of Facts, 1990).

Citizens of Spanish and Italian origin predominate. Other European–Argentine nationals include English, German, French, and other East and West European descents. Among other ethnic groups are Japanese, Jews, Mestizos, American Indians, and Arabs. The official language is Spanish. Other languages spoken are English, French, Italian, and German.

Argentina has a population of 32.6 million (1989), and Buenos Aires is the federal capital with a population of 2.9 million. But Greater Buenos Aires with ten large cities has a population of 5.3 million. It is fitting to say that Argentina is the eighth largest country in the world, and second largest country in South America in population as well as in land mass (Sobel, 1975). The people are 94% Catholic.

Argentina has experienced many upheavals in the political, economic, and social spheres. The people have seen a series of dictatorships and totalitarian regimes. However, after many years of the totalitarianism of Peron and the military dictatorships after him, Argentina returned to democracy in 1983.

The Legal System

The Constitution of 1853 still forms the basic laws of Argentina. The penal law of the country does not find antecedents in aboriginal (American Indian) laws and customs. Instead, it evolved through various periods of foreign administration—the offspring of European-imported legislation and doctrines. One of the most important manifestations is the Penal Code of Baviera (1813), which formed the bulwark of Argentine Criminal Code. This code originated from the old, repressive German law.

The Constitution of 1853, which was amended in 1994, gives the national congress exclusive power to make laws for the country covering criminal, civil, maritime, and commercial matters, and each provincial legislature has power to make laws specific for the welfare of members of each province. Suffice it to say that Argentina's legal system is almost entirely Roman law with some influence of German law, especially in the areas of criminal law. Since the Europeans exterminated most of the

American Indian tribes, the informal criminal justice system died with the natives and has no place in present-day Argentina. The territory's legal system is based on European norms, values, and standards, with the European constitutional principle that all citizens are equal before the law. In Argentina, therefore, resolving a criminal act outside the confines of the European-based courts is a crime.

The nomadic and marauding tribes of the pampas of Argentina undoubtedly have their traditional norms and customs as well as an informal justice system. Unfortunately, virtually no one has investigated their structure and place in Argentine criminal justice system.

There are also laws for certain categories of government institutions. One is the military penal law, which is a kind of criminal law to be applied to the military for military crimes. In this situation, a military penal code that applies to some specific situations is used, and the accused is tried by a military tribunal. Another law pertains to the Islas Malvinas, the lands situated between territorial Argentina and Argentina's Antarctic region known as the Falkland Islands. They have been occupied by the United Kingdom since 1833. The United Kingdom does not recognize Argentina's sovereignty over the islands called Kelpers. However, the inhabitants do not consider themselves to be British citizens or subjects. They prefer to live and die as Argentine citizens; hence Argentina's special laws over the inhabitants of the Islas Malvinas.

System of Government

Today, Argentina is a democratic republic. The government is made up of a bicameral national congress and an executive president. The national congress is made up of 69 senators and 243 members of the Chamber of Deputies (House of Representatives). The senators are elected by members of each provincial legislature, at least, two from each province and the Federal District. The senate members from the Federal District are elected by direct vote. The members of the Chambers of Deputies are directly elected, one from each 85,000 inhabitants in the provinces and the Federal District (Newton, 1977; Sobel, 1975).

The Constitution of 1853, with articles similar to the United States Constitution, still governs the people of Argentina. Like Nigeria, Argentina is a federation. There are twenty-two provinces and the Federal District that make up the Argentine Federation. Each province has its own legislature led by a provincial governor. The provincial governors and the provincial legislatures serve as "regents of the Federal Government for the execution of the Constitution and the law of the nation" (Newton, 1977; Sobel, 1975; Whitaker, 1956).

The executive president of Argentina is elected by popular vote for 4 years and may not seek reelection immediately after his/her term. As in the United States, the president appoints the cabinet ministers, and he/she is the commander-in-chief (CIC) of the armed forces. The president of Argentina can introduce a bill in the national congress and has veto power. He appoints the members of the judiciary, and he has the right, subject to senatorial confirmation, to grant pardon or commute sentences. Additionally, the president has the authority to declare a state of emergency or siege and "suspend constitutionally granted civil rights" (Sobel, 1975; Whitaker, 1956; Newton, 1977). It is noteworthy that Argentina is the first country in the Western Hemisphere to have a female executive president and head of state.

Members of the Argentine national congress have immunity from arrest, but this privilege can be revoked by a two-thirds majority vote of the House members against a member. Interestingly, the constitution empowers the president or the national congress to remove any provincial governor or other provincial official from his/her post for some constitutional violation, and replace him/her with a federal intervenor who must be responsible to federal authority that appointed him/her.

How Laws Are Made or Revoked

The simplest process for making or revoking a law in Argentina is known as *ordinary* and goes from the initiation of a bill, called a *project*, to its publication as a law. This process is regulated by the constitution, which established the ability of congress to legislate for the whole country. Synthetically, a project of law (the beginning of the process of promulgating a law) can be introduced by (1) any legislator in his/her own Camera (the Senate or the Chamber of Deputies) or (2) the executive in either of the two Cameras (Article 52, Constitution of 1853). The Camera where the bill is first initiated is called "Camera of origin." The other Camera will act as a revisory Camera. The project (bill) is dealt with by a commission, depending on the subject, and then, an official writ of commission is produced counseling the approval or rejection of the bill. If the bill is approved, it goes to the alternative Camera, where each article of the bill is discussed in general and in specifics, and then voted on one by one. If after the debate both

Cameras pass the project, they sanction it as a law and send it to the executive president. If the president (executive) expressly approves it, or does not return it by a total or partial veto in ten working days, it is then promulgated and published as the law of Argentina. Uniquely, in Argentina, any law can be in force before its publication, a way to oblige citizens to know about it.

Graphically, the process of making a law in Argentina is demonstrated in Figure 5-1. There are four ways that a bill can become a law of Argentina. (See Figures 5-1 to 5-4.)

The Crime Problem in Argentina

As in the United States, poor integration in a multiethnic, capitalist society breeds all kinds of property crimes and crimes against persons (Merton, 1968). Additionally, Argentina is highly urbanized with a multiplicity of ethnic Europeans, Mestizos, and Native Americans. This multiethnic structure beings its cultural conflicts, leading to conflicts of norms and to crime (Sellin, 1938). Despite an overpopulation of people of European origin in Argentina, the country is a poor nation. Buenos Aires has a high concentration of poor people, just like Mexico City and New York. Crime is a fact of life in the slums of large cities in Argentina, such as the Federal District of Buenos Aires (pop. 30,344,268), Buenos Aires (pop. 9,774,529), Cordoba (pop.

Figure 5-1: Process of How an Unopposed Bill Becomes a Law of Argentina

5-1 is the ordinary process. If the revisory Camera passes the project but has modified it, two alternatives are possible 5-2 and 5-3. In case of a partial veto from the president (executive), process 5-4 applies.

If neither of the Cameras attains a two-thirds majority of votes to override the veto, the project cannot be sanctioned and cannot be dealt with again during the current year. If the veto is partial, the part rejected may be sanctioned as law, if it is not contrary to the spirit of the original bill, and if it still keeps its autonomy.

Figure 5-2: *A Bill Modified by a Revisory Camera that Becomes a Law of Argentina*

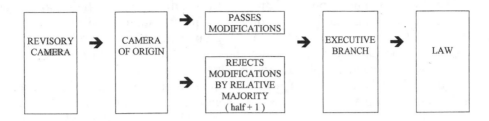

2,177,132), Santa Fe (pop. 2,518,586), Mendoza (pop. 1,026,178), Entre Rios (pop. 914,469), and many other cities with over half a million population.

In every city in Argentina, there are large populations of both the "haves" and the "have-nots." Widespread corruption in the governments of Juan Peron, Isabel Peron, and the military regimes that followed, coupled with ruthless murders and assassinations of innocent citizens in the military regimes, provided unemployed youths of Argentina with a rationale for engaging in armed robbery, hired killings, gang burglary, drug trafficking, and rape. The military regimes also increased the operation of organized crime in Argentina. With the large expanse of Argentine coastline, international smuggling of contraband goods is very easy to accomplish, and the poor economic conditions that gripped Argentina throughout the military regimes and Isabel Peron's era made crimes of all types, including narcotics drug smuggling, a way out of abject poverty and perpetual indigence among the underclass.

Throughout the major cities of Argentina, property offenders cause problems to the police and the courts. There are many cases of crimes against persons, but property crimes by far outnumber these.

Crime has always been an instrument for diverting the attention of the elite from national crises in Argentina, then blaming the criminals. The fear of crime is used as an instrument of social cohesion. The only enemy of the society is the violent offender. Politicians use him to divert attention from

the issues most important to the community. In other words, crime is used to distract attention from priority subjects and create an irrational fear of defenseless minorities. In reality, when it comes to crime, the police have their hands full. However, white collar crime and organized crime, as in other capitalist democracies of the Western world and Africa, cost Argentina fifty times more in monetary terms than the terrifying street crimes.

Police

Argentina, like the United States, has a decentralized police system. There is an Argentine federal police, and every province has it own police force. The federal police force is under the Ministry of the Interior, with headquarters in Buenos Aires. There is a detachment of the federal police in every province. The provincial police force is under a different ministry according to the order of the provincial cabinet. Commonly, provincial security institutions, including the police force, are under a ministry of a provincial government, but the hierarchical order is determined by the executive. In Cordoba Province, for example, the provincial police force is under the Ministry of Institutional Affairs.

Unmistakably, the administration and operations of the police forces (federal and provincial) are managed by the executive through its political organs and functionaries. Uniquely, it is not necessary in Argentina for the chief of police to be a member of the police force. The law empowers the governor to designate any person from his political party to take the position of chief of police for the province, and the appointment will be made by the president (the executive). However, a high-ranking person in the political arena is always appointed by the executive.

The Role of the Police

The police concentrate much of their efforts on crime prevention and control. The main function of the police is national security and protection of the lives and property of citizens. The police have the role of assisting the judiciary in bringing offenders to the attention of the courts and prosecution of cases. The police ensure that criminal procedure is followed and the rights of offenders respected.

Functions assigned to the police to control crime depend on three factors:

1. Ideas, images, and concepts about crime and delinquency

2. The model of intervention or control chosen

3. The police force's own concept of its function

In a modern industrial society, the police have many responsibilities. The nature of their function has made the agency the most visible in the whole legal system, converting it into a symbol of law and order. The discretionary powers of the police, their authority to arrest suspects and question suspects, and their legal possession and carrying of firearms make them celebrities in the perceptions of the citizens and the press in Argentina. However, the complex strategies employed by the police in social control have also stigmatized the police and have contributed to the recent interest in studying police operations in the country. In the process, it has been shown that the police are selective and discriminatory in their law enforcement operations. In the main, the police are influenced more by social class and ethnic factors than by the objective merits of their goals.

There is an organic and juristic debate regarding the organic and functional dependency of the police on state powers. The first phase of the debate deals with the idea of professionalism—the necessity to endow, equip, and train police functionaries, and to structure the force in accordance with modern technological

Figure 5-3: *Another Method of How a Modified Bill Could Become a Law in Argentina*

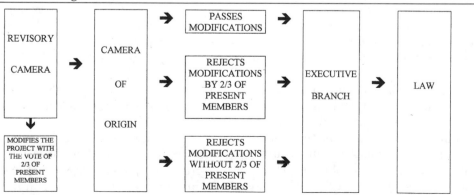

changes. The second phase is an ideological or political debate, and it is about the nature and function of the police. It is concerned with the possible abusive exercise of discretionary powers: corruption, control over political dissidents, and insensitivity to social changes. The third phase includes all concerns about effectiveness of police operations and the outcomes of police functions. The fourth phase responds to the interaction between the police and the community (society): citizens' image of and attitudes toward the police; how to reorient the police to meet the community's demands; and getting the police and the community to have common interests in the maintenance of order.

Unfortunately, in Argentina and throughout Latin America, the role of the police is primarily in behavior control, and their interaction with the citizens is considered secondary or minor. Thus the police force, as an armed instrument of the state, finds open challenges and major resistance from individuals, consequently generating a high degree of ambiguity and uncertainty in their daily operations. This kind of situation frustrates the police, leading to their use of excessive physical force.

In Argentina, the state is manifested as overdeveloped, interventionist, authoritarian, omnipresent, and serving foreign interests. In effect, the police are repressive, protecting an international order of division of labor for capitalist production. The people have experienced a time in recent years when the police concentrated on arrests of males in rural populations because of the official perception that this type of people support insurgent caudillos, who threaten the elite groups in whose hands lie control of the state machinery.

The Judiciary

The judiciary in Argentina, like its police system, and as in Nigeria and the United States, is decentralized. There are federal courts and there are provincial courts. On top of all of the courts is the Argentine Supreme Court. At the federal level are the Supreme Court and federal district courts.

The Supreme Court

The Supreme Court of Argentina is the final court of appeal in the country for both criminal and civil matters. The Supreme Court is composed of five judges. It has original jurisdiction only in constitutional matters. Appeals come to the court from the federal district courts. According to the Argentine Constitution, to be a judge of the Supreme Court, a lawyer must be at least 30 years old, must have been a citizen of Argentina for 6 years, and must have 8 years of professional experience as a practicing lawyer. Until 1994, federal judges were appointed by the president with the approval of the senate. There were no safeguards on the independence of the judiciary. In effect, the judiciary did not like the constitutional provisions for the appointment and dismissal of federal judges. Consequently, the 1994 constitutional amendments provided some safeguards against arbitrary appointment and dismissal of federal and provincial judges. The revised constitution provides bylaws related to the judiciary and safeguards to ensure the independence of judges. The revised constitution created some special courts for matters involving dismissal of judges and public officials.

Federal District Courts

Below the Supreme Court are federal district courts located in every province of the country and the Federal Capital District. They are courts of original jurisdiction in all criminal and judicial matters. One justice is assigned to each federal district court. The judges of the federal district courts have privileges similar to those of Supreme Court judges.

Provincial Courts

Each province has its own court system. The provincial courts are called "Ordinary Justice."

The provincial courts handle cases of crimes committed in the province that are violations of provincial laws. Crimes committed in each province that are violations of federal law go to the federal district court in that province. The judges of provincial courts are appointed by the governor of the province. The 1994 constitutional amendments provided the provincial court judges protection against arbitrary dismissal similar to that accorded to judges of federal courts.

Prosecutorial and Judicial Process

Both federal and ordinary courts have an attorney's office headed by a prosecutor who has served in the judiciary as a judge's or prosecutor's secretary. He or she must have accumulated much knowledge, experience, and practice in criminal/penal cases. Additionally, there is a general prosecutor for the federal government and for each provincial government. The general prosecutor is a political appointment. The general prosecutor is a link between the judiciary and the executive.

There are certain distinctions to be made in Argentine criminal law:

1. *Material Penal Law (or Substantive Law).* This is the branch of Argentine law that defines crime and its consequences (e.g., criminal participation or gang membership).

2. *Adjective Penal Law (or Processal Law).* These are legal rules imposed for penal law violations. They regulate the way court judges determine the criminal responsibility of the accused. Basically, the steps are as follows: accusation (charges); evidence (demonstrated); defense; and sentence.

Thousands of incidents and circumstances complicate the process of determining the material truth of the offense with which the accused was charged: to know whether the crime existed and to determine who committed it, fundamentally guaranteeing "the right of defense" to the accused.

The main expressed guarantees are in the constitution (Article 33). The rights of the accused are perfectly established in the penal code. For example, in the case of pretrial detention, the code orders the judge to apply the law that is more convenient to the accused. Let us use a hypothetical situation to explain this judicial process: A murder is committed, and 6 months later a man is charged with it; as murder is a crime without bail, he goes to prison for pretrial detention. A year later, he is judged, found guilty, and sentenced to 20 years of imprisonment. But suppose that at the time he committed the crime the law was in force, then was changed while he was under pretrial detention, and was changed one more time 2 years after he was sentenced. Well, as a general principle, the Argentine penal code establishes that the most benevolent law must be applied to the offender without considering which portion of the process he was in when he was charged, judged, or sentenced. However, in this case the law must be entirely analyzed by the judge to determine if it is really benevolent to the offender. That means a law may favor the offender's pretrial detention, and a different one his sentence, and both of them have to be applied. If the trial leads to a conviction, it is so declared; the next step is called execution penal law, in which the convict gets a prison term, and he is taken care of by the state.

The country has a federal penitentiary law that regulates a prisoner's life (to apply the law allows determination of the *modus vivendi*). The state diagnoses the offender's personality and the cause of his criminal behavior. After that, an internal criminological council studies case by case

Figure 5-4: How a Bill Introduced by a Legislator Can Become a Law of Argentina After Presidential Veto

to establish an adequate treatment (education, acquisition of positive habits). The treatment meted out to the convict is made according to his behavior, disciplinary sanctions, and others. By this approach the state is able to determine if the sentence objective is positively carried out to support conditional freedom of the offender.

Penalties and Sentencing

Penalty in Argentina is not reparative but retributory (it is retribution against the guilt of the offender and is nontransferable). It has both specific and general deterrent effect. The specific effect is to socially deter the offender to prevent him from committing a crime again. The general effect aims at deterring the rest of the society from engaging in a similar act.

There are some constitutional guarantees with respect to punishment. Under no circumstance should a citizen of the nation be punished without a finding of guilt based on law in force before the offense, and the case must be adjudicated in a court of law. If the offense is administrative, the executive branch has a tribunal for administrative offenses. A person accused of an administrative offense is given a fair trial and sentenced according to administrative law. All sentences must be legally founded and cannot consist of corporal punishment as in Singapore. The crime of treason against the nation is determined by a spe-

cial law and tribunal that have to be legally determined by the congress.

The Penal Code (Article 58) established the unification of penalties in different sentences to the same offender even though the cases were adjudicated in different jurisdictions. Two cases exemplify this situation, but we will develop only the first one because the second one requires extensive knowledge of Argentine jurisprudence.

1. If after a stable sentence, the same person had to be tried for a different crime while serving a prison term, the rule requires the following:

   - The condemnatory sentence must allow for an appeal.

   - The person must be sentenced to serve the sentence in an unconditional, effective manner.

   - The crime with which the offender is charged must derive from the previous offense that led to the present sentence.

   - The sentence must not have been served.

   - The new sentence (punishment) must be unified with the previous one, as decided by the judge of the present case.

2. Simply, we remark that this situation takes place if some articles of the Penal Code (Articles 55, 56, and #58) were violated when two or more

stable sentences were prescribed and the rule is applied only if there is an interest in its unification. The judge (federal or ordinary) who sentenced the offender in the first case is the same judge who must adjudicate in the new unified sentence.

Types of Penalties in Argentine Penal Code

Penalties include denial of freedom (imprisonment, confinement) and fines (forfeiture, confiscation of property. In decreasing order of severity, the penalties are death penalty, confinement, prison, forfeiture, and disablement.

Perpetual penalties means life imprisonment, and other penalties are temporary. Maximum punishment is imprisonment and seclusion for 25 years. The minimum imprisonment is 4 days, and 3 months for seclusion.

It is only in the military justice code that death is in force as a penalty. The death penalty can be invoked if the facts developed during national emergency, when a person may be executed after a brief trial for treason or other crime against national security. In peacetime, all procedural guarantees are observed, including for capital offenses. Capital punishment was revoked for political crimes, but it was in force in the nineteenth century during the periods of tyrannical government.

The Prison System

"The prisons of the nation will be healing and cleanly, for security and not for corporal punishment of persons detained in them. They must not aggravate the harm inherent in the penalty" (Article 18 of the Argentine Constitution). The preceding statement portrays the ideas of the nineteenth-century framers of the Argentine Constitution—a more humane approach

than the conceptions of the elite of twentieth-century North and South America. Certain factors, however, impinge upon the smooth running of Argentine prisons today. Stalking, laziness, industrialization, over-urbanization, modernization, immigration, alienation, social disorganization, and badly trained and paid personnel add together to frustrate smooth rehabilitation of offenders. Consequently, it becomes very difficult for a prisoner to bear punishment with so many unnecessary inconveniences, such as the lack of adequate space to keep different types of criminals, and inadequate and uncomfortable surroundings for visits by relatives of inmates. Additionally, Argentine prisons do not provide vocational training to help an inmate to secure a job after the period of incarceration. Worst of all, prisons in Argentina do not have adequate medical, psychological, and social assistance. In short, there is no professional staff for meticulous monitoring of the criminal's behavior during and after incarceration.

Drugs and violence, discrimination and apathy, prison gangs and mafias, and more are the common codes of conduct in both federal and provincial prisons. There is a move to build new prisons, but building new prisons is not a panacea for long and persistent correctional problems. For instance, to support a prisoner per year in Argentina costs at least three times more than support for a prisoner in the United States, which runs from $25,000 to $30,000 per year.

Argentina has a decentralized prison system, just like the United States. There are federal prisons and provincial prisons. The federal prisons are located in different provinces, but there is only one director of all federal prisons. Each province has its director of all provincial prisons in the province. Prisons are classified as in the United States, as maximum-, medium-, and minimum-security prisons.

The prisons in Argentina need reorganization and restructuring. Recidivism is high. To reduce recidivism, inmates must be rehabilitated before they leave the prison so that they do not come back again. The problem with prison reform, however, is that the prisoners, including those who work in the prisons, do not constitute a political force. Consequently, they do not draw the attention and interest of politicians. The politicians do not see what they could gain by reducing recidivism. Instead, they see that they could gain from contractors by building new prisons. This is unhealthy for society.

Discussion

Argentina has a good body of penal laws. But we can find some structural failures in this system of laws. Philosophically and theoretically, the laws are based on the interests of the nineteenth-century elites of Argentina. The laws are well developed according to the origin, customs, and social morality of society in the nineteenth century. Technically, there appears a kind of breakdown when the laws are applied to certain situations, because of various factors such as lawmakers not being in a close relationship with one another and with the executive (president), who has the duty of regulating the rule to establish how it will work. Unfortunately, neither the lawmakers nor the executive have in mind the concrete resources the law needs for its efficacy and efficiency. Consequently, the law fails.

Argentina needs fewer but more effective laws. Rosy, declamatory, but dictatorial laws give neither correct nor necessary answers to the economic problems of an organized, technocratic society. Rules have to be born through scientific discussions and measured by the guiding principles of criminal policy, indicating to the legislature how penal law should be stated; rules should also be in agreement with the society's historical evolution. Additionally, if we recognize that crime is not an isolated thing but a phonomenon and a complex one, we have to consider criminology and criminologists as very important parts of the social and legal systems, who have to indicate the necessity of regulating or upsetting a human subject. Legislation must be congruent with reality and social change.

Argentina still suffers from too much judicial insecurity. If good penal law reflects only a very small portion of the judicial insecurity, then comparing criminal justice systems between developed and developing countries can be an arduous task, because a criminal law that works perfectly in one system may not be successful in another. For example, Argentina copied the institution of probation and laws against drug trafficking entirely from the United States. But they turn out to be irrelevant for Argentina. A country should not import laws that do not suit the values of the society. Foreign legal systems can be used as a model and modified to suit the borrowing society's system of laws. Unmistakably, in every society, criminal law is an idea of someone who got the support of the powerful. Suffice it to say that a good legislative exercise is a coordinated work toward a body of laws that can be perfected.

Discussion and Review Questions

1. A society's cultural legacy can philosophically influence its criminal law. How?

2. What are the key factors in Argentina's success in its war of independence?

3. To what extent are American Indian norms and values embodied in contemporary Argentine criminal law?

4. What are the sources of law in Argentina?

5. Somebody broke into an interprovincial bank in the province of

Cordoba. Which type of court will try the case in Cordoba?

6. How does the constitution of 1994 differ from that of 1853 with regard to the independence of the judiciary in Argentina?

7. Critically evaluate Argentina's legislative process.

8. Compare and contrast appointment of the attorney general and Supreme Court judges in Argentina and the United Sates.

9. Indicate five unique features of the criminal justice system in Argentina.

10. What do you understand by a bicameral legislature? Name four countries with bicameral legislatures. What are their local/national names?

11. What are the advantages and disadvantages of decentralized and centralized systems of policing? In what system of government is the decentralized system of policing most suitable?

12. Worldwide, women are underrepresented in the police forces of nations. Is it an international conspiracy? Explain in detail.

13. Criminal law is dynamic. What does that mean? Explain fully.

14. What is "Material Penal Law" in Argentina?

15. What is meant by "Adjective Penal Law" in Argentina?

16. Argentina practices "retributive justice." What does this mean?

17. Compare and contrast specific deterrence and general deterrence.

18. What are some of the features of the U.S. Constitution that can be found in the Argentine Constitution of 1853?

19. In your opinion, why did Argentina decide to make some amendments to their constitution of 1853 in 1994? What are some of the amendments to the Argentine criminal justice system?

20. Ebbe and Olano criticized the prison system in the North and South America as not being rehabilitative. Give at least ten solutions for prison reform in order to reduce recidivism in your country's prisons.

6

The Criminal Justice System of Sierra Leone

Bankole Thompson

Introduction

From an American perspective, this study concerns one foreign criminal justice system, providing some knowledge about the practices of the West African state of Sierra Leone. The main motives for comparative and international criminal justice have been mentioned in Chapter 1. To this account one might add that scholars have identified at least five possible models for studying criminal justice from a comparative perspective. These are (1) the anthropological–historical approach, (2) the institutional–structural approach, (3) the political–legal approach, (4) the social–philosophical approach, and (5) the analytical–problems approach (Terrill, 1984). Each model has its own strengths, and the nature of any particular criminal justice system may lend itself more easily to treatment by one of these models than by another. The socio-philosophical model, for example, would resolve such questions as: What are the prevailing views about the causes of crime and deviancy in a society? What philosophical approaches are used to resolve or cope with these views in the penal context? The institutional–structural approach, on the other hand, would seek a panoramic view, exploring the institutions, policies, and processes that give structure to a country's criminal justice system, and surveying the organization, structure, and

function of the police, the courts, the correctional services, and the juvenile justice process. It is this approach that we will take in examining Sierra Leone. Key features and elements of both substantive criminal law and criminal procedure in that country will be highlighted, providing grounds for a summary critique of its administration of criminal justice.

Brief History

Sierra Leone is a relatively small West African country with an area of 27,925 square miles and a population of 3.7 million people. It is bounded on the west and north by Guinea and on the east by Liberia. The country is made up of many ethnic groups such as the Mendes, Ternnes, and Limbas. Most of the remaining population is composed of the Krios, or Creoles, who are largely Western in culture and still legally classified as "non-natives." The indigenous peoples are designated as "natives."

Throughout its modern history, and despite its British occupation, the country has retained the name Sierra Leone, thereby preserving its historical link with the Portuguese sailor Pedro da Cintra, who sailed into a huge bay on the west coast of Africa in 1462 and named the surrounding country for the mountain ranges above that bay, which he believed resembled lions. Like most African countries, Sierra Leone blends

Western cultural values derived from its British heritage with indigenous African norms. Part of its history is enmeshed in the slave trade that attracted sea captains to the west coast of Africa in the sixteenth and seventeenth centuries. By 1792, the British government had established a settlement in Sierra Leone, and Lieutenant John Clarkson had become the first governor of Freetown. The little settlement was administered by the Sierra Leone Company, which was formed in 1791.

In 1808 the settlement was taken over by the British government as a crown colony. The new colony became a base for the Act of Parliament (1807) abolishing the slave trade, with a naval squadron court set up in Freetown to try slave traders. After the Napoleonic Wars, the other European nations agreed to abolish the slave trade, and the naval squadron court was supplemented by Courts of Mixed Commission. Thousands of slaves were freed as a result of these events, and most chose to settle in Sierra Leone. These liberated Africans—Krios or Creoles as they were called—came from all parts of Africa. By 1861, through treaties of cession, the colony had been extended to include the whole of the Sierra Leone peninsula, Sherbro Island, and various other small islands. In 1896 the surrounding territory was declared a British protectorate (Kaplan et al., 1976; Fyfe and Jones, 1968).

Sierra Leone's blend of cultures and historical background have enormous significance and implications for the present organization of its legal system, and for its criminal justice system in particular. One important result has been the country's dual system of justice, British oriented general law courts on one hand, and local or customary law courts on the other. We will examine the organization, structures, and functions of these courts later in the chapter.

Crime Profile

Constructing crime profiles for most developing nations in Africa is, without exaggeration, a Herculean task. Many of these countries do not have accurate or reliable means to measure the amount of crime committed within their borders (Clinard and Abbott, 1973). This is true of Sierra Leone, where the only official source of indirect crime information is the Annual Statistical Digest. The Digest aims to present in one volume statistical data of interest to general users of official statistics, but while it covers a wide range of subjects, it does not give priority to factual crime reporting. No edition has ever reported crime facts. Other than information on road traffic accidents and casualties, the Digest does not provide data on numbers and types of crimes committed in Sierra Leone. Even in relation to road traffic accidents and casualties, there is some duplication of reporting. For example, the 1989 edition provides figures on one subject for the period 1983–1987, whereas the 1990 edition, evidently attempting to consolidate data, covers that same subject for the period 1979–1988.

On the rare occasion when statistical data relating to crime are reported in the Annual Statistical Digest, the method of compilation is penological, focusing on the number of persons committed to prison annually rather than on the numbers of crimes occurring yearly. The analysis proceeds on three levels. The first level enumerates (a) the number of inmates on remand and (b) the number of persons sentenced to imprisonment. Category (a) is broken down separately for each sex into those awaiting trial, those convicted but not sentenced, and others; category (b) is broken down separately for each sex into those sentenced to imprisonment without option of a fine, those in default of payment of a fine, and those sentenced to death (see Table 6-1).

The second level enumerates persons sentenced to imprisonment, classifying them by (i) sex and (ii) duration of sentence (see Table 6-2). The third level itemizes separately for each sex and year the number of previous convictions of persons sentenced (see Table 6-3). The Digest's penological approach to crime reporting has the serious limitation of not revealing either the seriousness of crime in Sierra Leone, or its demographic and ecological distribution.

Some criminologists doubt that the best available indices of crime rates are "crimes known to the police" (Hagan, 1987; Siegel, 1989), and the state of affairs in Sierra Leone would thoroughly justify this doubt. Poor police–community relations and a lack of adequate resources for the detection and investigation of crime allow numerous crimes to go unreported and undetected. In addition, strong socio-cultural attitudes and beliefs in traditional indigenous culture militate against the reporting and detection of crimes such as ritual murder and cannibalism. In the case of white-collar and economic crimes, crime reporting and detection are constrained by political influence, status, power, and affluence. Another real constraint is fear of retaliation or reprisal by the offender in such cases as rape, incest, and assault with intent to ravish. Many in Sierra Leone, furthermore, believe the police force to be one of the most corrupt institutions in the country, and this can influence both how the police report crime and how they record it. Police have been accused of underreporting of crime, and of deliberately obliterating evidence that a report was made and recorded.

Because of these constraints, this crime profile has been based largely on the ethnographic observations and perceptions of the author as a member of Sierra Leone society and a former judge of that country's High Court. It will interpret empirical indicators such as (a) media accounts of crime, (b) government releases on the crime problem, (c) public concern over crime, and (d) pressures for legislative reform of the criminal law. Ethnographic observational data gathering is, of course, subjective; but such qualitative research can be used to substantiate criminological explanations for the causes and incidence of crime.

It is both fair and accurate to say that crime continues to escalate in Sierra Leone. The trend goes back to the late 1960s and derives mainly from the major socioeconomic changes that have taken place in that country since independence. Conventional crimes continue to be highly visible and are committed by both adults and juveniles. Specifically, one sees significant acceleration in murder, manslaughter, rape, wounding with intent, causing grievous bodily harm, child abuse, robbery with aggravation, robbery with violence, simple robbery, burglary, housebreaking, simple larceny, and receiving stolen property. Since the 1970s, the rise in violent crime has generated much anxiety, fear, and insecurity in the Sierra Leone population.

Any criminological inquiry into criminal behavior and tendencies in contemporary Sierra Leone, especially any dealing with personal or property crimes, must take into account the key role of socioeconomic factors. Crime rates in Sierra Leone have no consistent correlation with punishment, whether viewed from a retributive, a deterrent, or a rehabilitative perspective. The level of criminality can be better explained and understood in the context of whether people: (i) protect, or have the means to protect, themselves from felonious acts; and (ii) secure, or have the means to secure, their property from damage or loss.

Crime rates may also have escalated in Sierra Leone because local government authorities are not able to provide the basic infrastructural security facilities that would allow citizens to go about their daily business without threats to their life, lib-

Table 6-1: *Persons Committed to Prison During the Year*

Type of Inmate		1979	1980	1981	1982	1983	1984	1985	1986	1987	1988
On Remand											
Awaiting Trial	Male	16373	8119	16578	21367	18188	16887	18286	17358	14357	8409
	Female	400	335	217	297	397	364	475	411	498	320
Convicted Unsentenced	Male	3187	2835	2821	4150	2788	4868	4561	4418	4286	4251
	Female	61	32	69	45	31	35	100	84	76	86
Other	Male	52	52	294	1456	377	392	38	59	66	38
	Female	1	2	—	3	9	1	—	3	6	2
Sentenced to Imprisonment Without Option of fine	Male	18554	17232	17956	22194	19990	20643	16830	21198	18425	17549
	Female	386	311	220	286	363	303	383	299	311	267
Default of Payment of fine	Male	1002	842	752	549	384	308	303	350	324	346
	Female	27	13	21	15	13	20	12	17	20	37
Sentenced to Death	Male	2	—	—	—	9	4	3	2	12	—
	Female	—	—	—	—	1	—	—	—	—	—

Source: Prisons Department, Freetown
Extracted from the 1990 edition of the Annual Statistical Digest

Table 6-2: *Persons Sentenced to Imprisonment Analysis by Sex and Duration of Sentence*

Duration of Sentence (months)		1979	1980	1981	1982	1983	1984	1985	1986	1987	1988
Less than 3	Male	553	513	419	411	210	131	146	131	138	173
	Female	14	4	12	13	2	1	—	—	3	13
3 and less than 6	Male	569	523	467	551	363	445	140	165	166	332
	Female	14	5	19	6	9	10	6	3	3	15
6 and less than 12	Male	624	610	681	664	619	665	331	240	256	266
	Female	14	10	17	11	2	11	3	6	6	7
12 and less than 18	Male	618	508	468	517	466	634	325	278	259	811
	Female	12	5	6	4	6	13	5	2	6	5
18 and less than 24	Male	404	311	270	266	363	458	297	225	184	209
	Female	9	3	4	6	--	6	3	4	4	3
24 and over	Male	376	222	288	278	349	488	470	367	325	363
	Female	8	3	5	2	3	1	5	5	28	11
Sentenced to Death	Male	2	—	—	—	9	4	3	2	12	—
	Female	—	—	—	—	1	—	—	—	—	—

Source: Prisons Department
Extracted from the 1990 edition of the Annual Statistical Digest

Table 6-3: *Persons Sentenced to Imprisonment Analysis by Sex and Duration of Sentence*

No. of Previous Convictions	1979	1980	1981	1982	1983	1984	1985	1986	1987	1988
Males										
None	137	187	384	966	1046	1333	1510	1174	1385	1026
1-2	1300	900	1124	2924	1202	2718	3221	2336	1960	2917
3-5	800	900	925	1046	596	1061	479	933	924	327
6- 10	641	700	587	640	308	143	250	34	76	19
11 and over	361	200	95	30	13	5	36	—	7	—
Females										
None	20	14	25	25	30	27	87	76	74	79
1-2	26	20	44	23	10	9	13	11	8	9
3-5	16	—	—	—	—	—	—	—	—	—
6-10	—	—	—	—	—	—	—	—	—	—
11 and over	—	—	—	—	—	—	—	—	—	—

Source: Prisons Department, Freetown
Extracted from the 1990 edition of the Annual Statistical Digest

erty, and property. Other factors include (i) the lack of discipline at home and at school, (ii) unemployment, and (iii) housing conditions.

In the mid-1970s, armed robbery, robbery with aggravation, and robbery with violence reached peak levels in Sierra Leone and caused such widespread panic that the government resorted, for the first time in its history, to enacting the death penalty. Armed robbery and robbery with aggravation became offenses punishable by death, but the wording of the statute became problematic in application, with much legal controversy over its legislative intent—specifically, over whether the prescribed penalty of death by firing squad was mandatory or discretionary. Sentences imposed by the courts varied between these two schools of thought, and the matter was never judicially settled. Many of these crimes were perpetrated by two notorious youth gangs that acted under such names as "The Black December" or "The Black September." These gangs especially perpetrated felony murders, and two cases in particular provoked much public revulsion and made national headlines: the "Wellington Street Murder Case" and the "Mammy Yoko Street Murder Case." After full-scale police investigations, no effort was spared in bringing the perpetrators to justice.

Another personal crime rampant in some parts of the indigenous communities in Sierra Leone is ritual murder. From the author's knowledge (having himself successfully prosecuted charges of ritual murder), this type of homicide is committed out of some strong socio-cultural mis-perceptions that ritual killings promote the welfare of the group, family, clan, or community and are instrumental in gaining power and leadership. Two recent and notorious cases of ritual murder in Sierra Leone were "State v. Alimamy Khazali" and the "Bureh Town Ritual Murder Case."

In addition to the increase in conventional crime, white-collar, corporate, and economic crimes predominate in Sierra Leone today, although statistics, as usual, are hard to come by. "White-collar crime" refers to offenses committed by individuals for self-enrichment in the course of their occupations and to offenses of employees against their employers. In this sense, the term is being used synonymously with "occupational crime" (Hagan, 1987); "corporate crime," on the other hand, consists in offenses by the corporation itself. "Economic crime" refers to any nonviolent, illegal activity that principally involves deceit, misrepresentation, concealment, manipulation, breach of trust, subterfuge, or illegal circumvention (Clifford, 1977). Empirical indicators show that white-collar crimes became noticeable after independence, escalated in the 1970s, and reached crisis proportions in the 1980s.

Specifically, over the past two decades there has been a marked rise in crimes committed within and against the bureaucracies of Sierra Leone. Such crimes have especially detrimental effects on allocation and utilization of public resources, derived from both internal and external sources, and on socioeconomic development, particularly in relation to agriculture, housing, trade, health, education, and similar projects. In the recent past, such funds have been embezzled practically into nonexistence. White-collar and economic criminality reached epidemic proportions in the late 1970s and early 1980s and culminated in the unearthing by the police of a huge fraud conspiracy within the civil service, later described as the "Vouchergate Fraud Cases."

It would be an oversimplification, then, to explain crime in contemporary Sierra Leone by reference to a single cause theory. Patterns of criminal behavior in that country rather seem to reflect a peculiar combination and interaction of these various factors: (i) the process of modernization and its socioeconomic dislocations, (ii) traditional cultural attitudes and beliefs, (iii) social ties and networks based on the extended family system (these account in part for the high level of white-collar-type criminality), (iv) the inefficiencies of the criminal justice system, (v) nonlegitimacy and political manipulation of the British style legal system, and (vi) lack of knowledge and interest in criminology as a social science.

Organization and Functioning of the Criminal Justice System

In Sierra Leone, the task of preventing and combating crime is assigned to three institutions that together constitute the criminal justice system. They are the police, the criminal courts, and the prison system. Basically, their organization, structures, and functions are patterned after the English criminal justice system. In Sierra Leone, as in England, the police are the first agency with whom a person suspected of crime comes into contact.

The Police

It is difficult to understand the existing structure of the Sierra Leone Police Force without some historical insights into its origins. Right from its inception, the system of law enforcement in Sierra Leone has always been patterned after the British model of policing, though it would be incorrect to suggest that policing in the country currently functions at the level of sophistication, expertise, and efficiency usually associated with the British model. Lack of modernization is one of the main weaknesses of law enforcement in Sierra Leone.

Conceptually, however, the Sierra Leone Police Force still much resembles its colonial beginnings. It dates back to 1829 when twenty-six constables, half of whom kept order by day and the other half by night, were appointed in Freetown. By 1836, the core of a modern civil police force, consisting of an inspector, three subinspectors, and sixty constables, had emerged. The senior officers were usually drafted from a pool of retired military noncommissioned officers or civilian volunteers. The force maintained law and order in Freetown and in the villages of what was then called the "Colony" (now the "Western Area").

In 1861, the British annexed Koya and Sherbro Island to Sierra Leone, thus making a greater measure of law enforcement and an increase in manpower necessary. The need was met by combined deployment of garrisoned troops and the police force. When the troops were withdrawn, the police became solely responsible for the maintenance of law and order in the colony. In order to provide the police force with some military training, the commanding officer of the garrison in Freetown was appointed inspector general of police, and the force was housed in police barracks, armed with carbines, and given uniforms of white tunics and slacks with broad leather belts. At that time, the numerical strength of the force was two hundred. As the colony expanded, the police force took on the additional role of guard duties at the frontiers. In 1891 they were relieved by the newly formed Frontier Police.

In October 1894, the civil police was designated the Sierra Leone Police Force for the first time in the government Gazette. With the formation of a police band in 1900, the total strength of the force reached six hundred. In September 1909, Superintendent Brook became the first Commissioner of the Force. He is credited with having formed a special riot squad to deal with civil disturbances.

In 1948, the force was enlarged to one thousand under a new police commissioner. Africans were promoted to the rank of assistant superintendent.

In 1951, the Sierra Leone Police Force became affiliated with Interpol. The riot squad was disbanded, and every police officer began to receive instructions in riot control. In September 1954, the force was extended to the main towns of the protectorate, replacing the disbanded court messenger forces. The first policewoman was recruited in 1947. At independence, the police force had developed into a well-established, efficient law enforcement institution.

By late 1975 the overall numerical strength of the force (including all ranks) was about 3,900. The highest ranking officer in the force, Police Commissioner Kaetu-Smith, like the military Force Commander, was a member of the legislature and a minister of state without portfolio, reflecting the high priority that the government placed on internal security and defense matters.

Unlike its British model, the Sierra Leone force is centralized, a true national police service, and its management and control has always been the responsibility of the central government. The force is organized into five geographical divisions, including one for the special protection of the country's diamond industry. Each regional division is subdivided into a number of branches and departments, which include mainly the Criminal Investigation Department (CID), a special branch, and a traffic division. The CID is the elite corps, responsible (like the U.S. Federal Bureau of Investigation) for the detection and investigation of serious crimes. In the 1970s and 1980s, the CID, under Commissioner of Police (later Inspector General) Bambay Kamara, was a highly organized and efficient branch of the force. Its detection and investigation of serious violent crimes used skills comparable to those employed by Scotland Yard.

Under specific statutory powers granted by the Police Act of 1964 and the Criminal Procedure Act of 1965, the police force in Sierra Leone has responsibility to: (i) maintain law and order and protect persons and property; (ii) prevent crime; (iii) detect and investigate crime; (iv) arrest criminal suspects with or without a warrant on reasonable cause; (v) control road traffic; and (vi) decide whether or not to bring charges against persons suspected of criminal offenses. In addition, pursuant to the Law Officers' Act of 1965 and under the direction of the director of public prosecutions, they have responsibility for the conduct of prosecutions for less serious offenses, especially minor traffic violations. They also introduce evidence before magistrates' courts in preliminary hearings into felony charges. Some question whether the police in contemporary Sierra Leone make reasonable and fair use of their discretionary powers of arrest, search, seizure, and bringing charges against persons suspected of crime.

During the period of APC (All People's Congress, a political party) rule, policemen were frequently accused of abusing and misusing their powers of arrest, search, and seizure. It was also said that they solicited and accepted bribes or other favors from crime suspects or from agents or relations in exchange for leniency, and that they executed their duties in a manner that showed strong political biases and other extraneous influences. There are no empirical studies to support or refute these criticisms. Based on this author's official knowledge, the Sierra Leone police are not entirely without merit, and their errors and miscarriages in law enforcement can be explained in terms of (i) very low educational levels, (ii) lack of professional standards and ethics, (iii) very low wages, and (v) extremely low morale.

Recruits for the Sierra Leone police wisely have been drawn from all parts of the country. The majority of policemen in Sierra Leone have either elementary or junior high school education, have passed a physical fitness test, and have graduated from the Police Training School at Hastings after 6 months' training. At the completion of their training, they are usually appointed constables and given housing in the barracks (those who cannot be accommodated in barracks receive special housing allowances). Postindependence governments have adopted a policy of recruiting senior high school and university graduates into the officer ranks. Recruits at this level still are sent to the United Kingdom for advanced training because no such facilities exist in Sierra Leone. After this training, they are appointed to the force as assistant superintendents for 6 months of practical work. Successful candidates are then promoted to existing vacancies or wait for openings. At the present time, the force is headed by an inspector general, a Sierra Leonean lawyer who served at the officer level prior to passing the bar.

Apart from the regular police force, Sierra Leone has a Special Security Division (SSD). It is a reorganized and restructured version of the Internal Security Unit (ISU) set up in the early 1970s by the APC government. This force originally performed presidential guard duties, but later developed into a special countersubversive security force available for deployment during periods of internal disturbance and civil unrest.

The Criminal Courts

Scholars of Sierra Leone's legal history and constitutional law agree that the history of the administration of justice in the country dates back to the foundation of the settlement in 1787 by English philanthropists. Since that time, adjudication and judicial settlement of public disorders and private disputes has been administered according to the principles of English law. The first chief justice, Mr. Charles Stoddart, was appointed in 1788, and when Freetown was granted municipal status the mayor and aldermen of the municipality were constituted judges of the civil courts, while the governor and councilors were the colony's criminal court judges. Trial by jury, a core component of the adversarial system of justice, began during those early years of the settlement.

By 1925, courts of tribal rulers had developed, and also the Police Magistrate Court of Freetown, the Courts of the Dis-

trict Commissioners of the Bonthe and Headquarters judicial districts, the Coroner's Court, the Supreme Court, the Full Court of Appeal, and the Judicial Committee of the Privy Council (an English tribunal in London with final appellate authority for the British colonies).

The existing judicial structure reflects, as already noted, a dual system of justice, with general law (British oriented) courts and customary law or local courts. Both the historical and contemporary development of the general law courts have been shaped largely by the common law tradition of England. The local courts are essentially indigenous in character. Their evolution continues to be influenced by the country's tradition of customary norms and values, though efforts are being made to modernize their procedures. Like the English courts, the general law courts of Sierra Leone are organized on the basis of jurisdiction (by geography, subject matter, and hierarchy) and on the basis of venue, with adjudicated cases confined to specified political boundaries (a metropolitan or urban area, a village or group of villages, a district or group of districts). Judicial business in Sierra Leone reflects the familiar English common law bifurcation between civil and criminal disputes.

The criminal courts are the linchpin of the criminal justice system and have responsibility for the trial, conviction, and sentencing of persons accused of crime. In addition to the geographical limitations on their jurisdictions, the powers of criminal law courts may be either limited or general in terms of subject matter, and either original or appellate. Presently, the country has a five-tier court system exercising criminal jurisdiction.

Local Courts
At the bottom of the hierarchy are the local courts with limited jurisdiction. These adjudicate minor criminal cases, especially those involving customary law issues

where the maximum penalty is imprisonment for 1 year or a fine of 600 leones or both. Elders of the local area who are proficient in customary law preside, and their decisions are subject to review by the Customary Law Officer, who acts not formally as a court but in a quasi-judicial capacity. Despite the absence of statistics, it can be said that these courts dispose of a significant volume of minor criminal cases involving customary law throughout the country, because the vast majority of Sierra Leoneans are rural people who willingly live their daily lives in accordance with customary law.

Magistrates' Courts

Next in the hierarchy are the magistrates' courts. They, too, are courts of limited jurisdiction, but have both original and appellate functions. They are courts of record and judges of both facts and law, and in their capacity as original courts, they perform three main roles. These roles are based on the modern classification of criminal offenses into (i) indictable offenses that must be tried on indictment before a jury (all very serious crimes are in this category); (ii) indictable offenses that can be tried either on indictment or in magistrates' courts; (iii) offenses that are both indictable and summary; (iv) summary offenses in which the defendant can demand trial on indictment; and (v) summary offenses triable only in magistrates' courts.

On the basis of the foregoing classification, the first and chief role of magistrates' courts in Sierra Leone is the hearing and disposition of lesser criminal charges punishable by a maximum imprisonment of 3 years or a fine not exceeding 1,000 leones or both. This summary function was extended in 1973 to include perjury or subornation of perjury under the Perjury Act of 1911 and reckless driving as defined in the Road Traffic Act of 1964.

Summary jurisdiction, a second role of the first instance magistrates' courts of Sierra Leone, comes into play when a person is charged with an offense punishable by a maximum penalty of 7 years or a fine not exceeding 3,000 leones. If the court so determines, the defendant can opt at preliminary hearing to be tried summarily instead of on indictment. The magistrate will then hear and dispose of the case in accordance with the summary trial law.

In the course of a summary trial, magistrates' courts may commit a defendant to be tried on indictment if the circumstances of the case so warrant or on the grounds of some aggravating or compelling factor. This function is especially useful when statutes create offenses that specify the maximum penalty for conviction summarily and the maximum penalty for conviction on indictment. Legislation of this type clearly makes the crime both summary and indictable, but leaves the courts with no guidance for determining whether a particular case should be tried summarily or on indictment. In one case, the legislature of Sierra Leone conferred special jurisdiction on magistrates' courts in 1977 and 1981 over offenses committed within the country's territorial waters, or in any port, harbor, wharf, or airport. They now have power to try persons charged with such offenses and punish them, on conviction, with a maximum of 5 years' imprisonment or a fine of up to 25,000 leones or both. This is an example of legislation making a crime both a summary and an indictable offense because it gives the court discretionary power to determine whether to try the case summarily or on indictment. (A magistrates' court cannot exercise this power if it is staffed by lay justices of the peace.)

The magistrates' courts also play a third key role, holding preliminary investigations into felony charges. This is a very important task, because it determines whether a person charged with the commission of a serious crime is to face trial in the High Court or have the charge dismissed. Decisions are made on the basis of whether there is sufficient or prima facie evidence to warrant a committal. Where there is no such evidence, the court will dismiss the case and discharge the defendant. The procedure is analogous to that of the preliminary hearing and the grand jury in the United States. Magistrates' courts in Sierra Leone have, since their inception, committed for trial or indictment for such charges as treason, sedition, murder, manslaughter, wounding, causing grievous bodily harm, rape, robbery, burglary, larceny, forgery, and conspiracy to defraud.

Unlike some countries, there are no separate Justice of the Peace courts in Sierra Leone, but these lay officials do play an important role within the country's criminal justice system. They sit in a magisterial capacity and, generally, carry out the same functions as legally qualified magistrates. Their sentencing power, however, is limited: they cannot impose fines in excess of 300 leones or imprisonment for more than a year. One important aspect of the criminal jurisdiction of lay magistrates is adjudicating juvenile offenses (a subject addressed later in this chapter). It is thought that non–legally qualified magistrates bring to the administration of juvenile criminal justice a much needed lay perspective.

There are no fewer than twenty-five magistrates' courts in Sierra Leone, one in each of the six districts that make up the Northern and Southern Provinces, respectively, three in the Eastern Province, and about ten in the Western Area. (The uncertainty in the number of magistrates' courts in Sierra Leone today is a result of the creation of new magisterial districts by the new regime of a military government that assumed power on April 29, 1992.) They carry the bulk of the criminal workload within the country's criminal justice system. Respect for the law and confidence in the legal system in Sierra Leone often are linked with the adjudica-

tion of cases in the magistrates' courts. This is because their function as appellate courts provides the first intersection between the customary justice system and the general law courts system. As district appeal courts, they hear and determine appeals from decisions of local courts, ascertaining whether the court below applied the relevant rule of custom correctly to the facts of the case and whether, on the whole, the case was heard fairly. In exceptional cases the de novo procedure allows them to rehear an entire case, admitting additional witnesses who did not testify in the lower court. Appeal to the magistrates' courts is automatic following an automatic stay of execution of the decision of the lower court for a period of 15 days. Unlike procedure in local courts, attorneys have a right of audience before district appeal courts, which consist of the magistrate for the district sitting with two assessors selected from a list of experts in customary law drawn up by the district officer. District appeal courts dispose of a substantial number of criminal appeals emanating from the local courts. In light of the review jurisdiction of the district appeal courts, it is debatable whether the review authority of the Customary Law Officer over the decisions of local courts is desirable or necessary to retain. Magistrates are appointed by the Judicial and Legal Service Commission and are (except for lay magistrates) legally qualified and salaried.

The High Court

The next court in the hierarchy of criminal courts in Sierra Leone is the High Court. By far the most important forum in the structure, the High Court together with the Court of Appeal and the Supreme Court constitute the superior Court of Judicature of the State of Sierra Leone. The High Court is a court of records with general jurisdiction. Its powers are original, appellate, and supervisory. As an original court, it hears and determines all types of criminal cases, especially those involving treason and such serious felony charges as sedition, murder, manslaughter, rape, robbery, burglary, larceny, forgery, and conspiracy to defraud. The cases are usually tried by judge and jury; and, exceptionally, by judge alone (on the ex parte application of the director of public prosecutions). The work of the High Court is centered in the Western Area, but there is a High Court for the Southern Province, another in the Eastern Province, and an itinerant High Court judge for the Northern Province. In exercising its original criminal jurisdiction, the court is constituted by a single judge or by a judge and jury.

The High Court also hears and determines appeals from decisions of magistrates' courts, given either as trial courts of limited jurisdiction or as district appeal courts. The appeal procedure reviews the decision of the lower court to determine whether relevant law was correctly interpreted and applied to the facts of the case, and scrutinizes the records of the lower court's hearing to ensure that the proceedings were conducted fairly and properly. The High Court may also inquire whether the court below wrongly admitted or excluded evidence. As an appellate tribunal, the court can (i) dismiss an appeal, (ii) overturn a conviction and set aside its sentence, (iii) dismiss an appeal and leave a sentence unaltered or impose a substitute sentence, (iv) order a retrial, or (v) substitute an alternative conviction (e.g., attempt to commit the crime, or commission of a different crime) for the conviction given in the lower court.

When the court hears appeals from a district appeal court, it is designated a local appeals division of the High Court and constituted by a single judge with two assessors selected by him or her from a list of experts in customary law drawn up by the Customary Law Officer.

In its supervisory capacity, the High Court has authority in any given case (i) to force a magistrates' court to accomplish an act that is legally required of it by an order of mandamus, (ii) to require a magistrates'

court to send up the records of its proceedings for review by an order of certiorari, or (iii) to require the court below to refrain from proceeding with a matter not within its jurisdiction by an order of prohibition. The most important additional order in the supervisory legal armory of the High Court is the writ of habeas corpus, by which it can inquire into the legality of the detention of any person in Sierra Leone.

In the Western Area, the High Court is continuously in session except for the vacation period, which runs from July 17 to September 17. In the provinces, the sessions are not continuous, varying from two to three a year. In the Western Area, two or three courts sit separately, and there may be three courts sitting simultaneously; in the provinces, only one court sits. The cases—most of them committed by the magistrates' courts after a preliminary hearing—come before the courts in an order known as the "criminal calendar" for each session.

Exceptionally, there may be cases on the "criminal calendar" that have been sent up for trial on ex-officio ex parte information from the attorney general and minister of justice or from the director of public prosecutions. This procedure is often invoked in cases with a political complexion, such as treason, and in huge fraud cases involving heavy financial losses to the government. It is also used in felony murder cases, where an expeditious trial best serves the ends of justice. Virtually all serious crimes are tried by the High Court. High Court judges are legally qualified and are appointed by the president on the advice of the Judicial and Legal Service Commission, subject to the approval of Parliament. Such appointments are usually made from the pool of state attorneys employed by the government and from members of the private bar. An attorney who currently aspires to High Court judgeship must have at least 10 years' professional standing (formerly it was 5 years). All Superior Court judges hold office pending good behavior. They may opt to retire at age 60, but must retire at age 65. The High Court consists of at least 10 judges.

Court of Appeal

The Court of Appeal is the intermediate appellate tribunal in the general law courts system in Sierra Leone. As a criminal court, it hears and determines appeals from decisions and orders of the High Court. Because it is practically the final appellate court for most criminal appeals arising out of decisions of the High Court, especially in exercise of its original jurisdiction over felony cases, its workload is tremendous. In most cases, appeal is automatic. As a review tribunal, the court determines whether the High Court interpreted and applied the law applicable to the facts of the case correctly; and, after an examination of the records of High Court proceedings, whether the trial was conducted properly; or, in the case of an appeal, whether it was heard fairly. It can also inquire into whether evidence was improperly admitted or excluded.

After hearing an appeal, the Court of Appeal can (i) dismiss the appeal, (ii) overturn the conviction and set aside the sentence, (iii) dismiss the appeal and leave the sentence unaltered or impose a substituted sentence, (iv) order a retrial, or (v) substitute an alternative conviction (e.g., attempt to commit the crime or commission of a different crime). When dismissing an appeal, the court can claim that, though there is merit in the point or points of law raised on appeal, yet no substantial miscarriage of justice occurred. As in England, but not as in America, this statutory power safeguards against the use of legal technicalities to overturn convictions on appeal, especially where the evidence overwhelmingly points to the guilt of the defendant.

The court is constituted by three justices, with the most senior presiding, for the normal business of hearing an appeal, but by a single justice in respect of interlocutory matters. Justices of Appeal are legally qualified and are usually appointed from the pool of judges on the High Court bench on the basis of seniority rather than merit. In exceptional cases, an appointment may be made directly from the team of government lawyers or the private bar. As already noted, all superior court judges in Sierra Leone are appointed by the president on the advice of the judicial and legal service commission, subject to the approval of Parliament. Current aspirants for the position of Justice of Appeal must have at least 15 years' professional standing (formerly it was 7 years). The Court of Appeal consists of at least eight justices.

Supreme Court

The Supreme Court of Sierra Leone is the highest judicial organ in the country. Its jurisdiction is mainly appellate and limited to the hearing and determination of civil and criminal appeals from the Court of Appeal. In exercise of its criminal appellate jurisdiction, the court hears and disposes only of a limited number of appeals largely dictated by the court itself and the Court of Appeal. In Sierra Leone, a defendant who is dissatisfied with a decision of the Court of Appeal in a criminal appeal can either opt by right to appeal the decision directly to the Supreme Court or, if the case involves a substantial question of law or is of public importance, he or she can seek permission from the Court of Appeal itself to appeal its decision. He or she can also obtain special permission from the Supreme Court to appeal against any decision of the Court of Appeal. But in recent times the court has insisted that defendants not under an imposed death penalty first apply to the Court of Appeal for permission to appeal its decision before they file an appeal in the Supreme Court or seek its special permission to do so. By this practice, the court limits itself to hearing and determining only those criminal appeals that raise substantial questions of law or are of significant public interest. Because of this limitation, the court disposes of only 5 to 15 criminal appeals a year.

The Supreme Court also exercises supervisory jurisdiction over all other courts in the country through procedures similar to the certiorari, mandamus, and prohibition proceedings of the English House of Lords and the U.S. Supreme Court. It also has original jurisdiction, to the exclusion of all other courts, (i) in all matters relating to the interpretation and enforcement of the constitution and (ii) where any question arises whether an enactment is ultra vires. Also, any citizen of Sierra Leone who alleges that any of his or her constitutional rights or freedoms has been, or is being, or is likely to be, violated can apply directly to the Supreme Court for redress. These two functions are far reaching, but they certainly fall short of the substantive judicial review power that the U.S. Supreme Court possesses; nevertheless, they do act as significant due process safeguards.

The court is constituted for regular judicial business, whether appellate or original, by five justices, including the chief justice (or, in his or her absence, the most senior justice) acting as president. When hearing interlocutory matters, a single justice sits. Justices of the Supreme Court are legally qualified and are usually appointed from justices of the Court of Appeal, emphasis being placed on seniority rather than merit. Exceptionally, an appointment may be made from the team of government lawyers or the private bar.

The chief justice and other judges of the Supreme Court are appointed by the president on the advice of the judicial and legal service commission and subject to the approval of Parliament (the advice requirements are recent additions). The position of chief justice is preeminent, with the candidate being chosen from among persons qualified to be Supreme Court justices. Present candidates for the position of justice of the Supreme Court must have at least 20 years of professional standing

(formerly it was 10 years). The Supreme Court consists of at least five justices. During the period of APC rule, those appointed to the position of chief justice would be judges with considerable political leverage.

The Prison System

Like the other components of the criminal justice system, correctional institutions in Sierra Leone are fashioned after the British model with variations appropriate to local conditions. The main correctional facility in the country—the Freetown Central Prison—is indeed a relic of outmoded English penological theory, with an architectural design reminiscent of correctional institutions in late-eighteenth-century England. Since independence, there has been no major attempt to alter or modify the architectural design of that correctional institution.

The administration of correctional services in Sierra Leone falls within the responsibilities of the minister of social welfare, but the services are centered in Freetown, the capital city, under the direction and supervision of the director of prisons. There are several provincial correctional facilities, including Bo, Makeni, Kabala, Kailahun, Sefadu, Mafanta, and Masanki. Ideally, and by statute, prison inmates are to be grouped and segregated according to sex, age, those awaiting trial, and those already convicted. Except for the Freetown facility, there are no correctional facilities in the country providing for complete physical segregation of male and female inmates, and females sentenced in the provinces ought normally to be transferred to Freetown, but in practice this does not happen. In a developing society like Sierra Leone, where economic resources are very scarce, funds for the improvement of correctional institutions will necessarily receive very low priority. Hence, the system does not reflect the traditional English classification of prisons into local, short-term training, medium-term training, and long-term training. In 1976 the National Development Plan envisaged the expansion of the main provincial facilities to accommodate more inmates. There was also provision for the development of industries in the Freetown Central Prison. But these plans were never fully implemented because they lacked adequate funding.

The key philosophy underlying the prison system in Sierra Leone is that inmates must either work or learn basic skills, the emphasis being on rehabilitation. Judges in Sierra Leone, however, focus on retributive justice in their sentencing practices. During the period of incarceration, inmates are taught such trades as carpentry, tailoring, shoemaking, printing, bricklaying, weaving, and painting. Courses are also given in basic reading and writing. Funds are not presently available to secure necessary new and additional equipment and machinery for teaching these trades and skills.

As with the police force, recruits in the prison service are drawn from all parts of the country. The majority of prison personnel have either an elementary or a junior high school education and have passed a physical fitness test. As an incentive for highly educated persons to enter the prison service, successive governments since independence have adopted recruiting policies favoring senior high school and university graduates. After some in-service training, these specially recruited officers are appointed to the rank of assistant superintendent, with the opportunity of being promoted to ranks such as chief superintendent, assistant deputy director, deputy director, and director.

Prison sentences in Sierra Leone range from 1 month to life imprisonment depending on the nature and gravity of the offense. Persons convicted of treason, murder, armed robbery, and robbery with aggravation may be sentenced to death.

There are also special correctional facilities for juvenile offenders. The issue of prisoners' rights in Sierra Leone has never raised much controversy, except as a result of criticisms emanating from Amnesty International on the issue of political detainees.

Juvenile Justice

In Sierra Leone, juvenile justice is regulated by the Children and Young Person Act of 1945. The juvenile justice process in the country is based on the British model and focuses on rehabilitation with a social welfare emphasis. Two main goals are pursued—first, to fulfill the needs of juveniles for care, protection, and supervision. When a juvenile is found wandering and seems not to have any home, settled place of abode, or visible means of existence, he or she may be brought before a juvenile court in Sierra Leone as one in need of care and protection. The second main goal of the juvenile justice agencies is to protect society against juveniles who violate the criminal law and threaten the fabric of society. A juvenile found guilty of an offense punishable, in the case of an adult, with imprisonment may be committed to the custody of an approved school until age 18 or for a shorter period of time.

The agencies responsible for addressing the problem of juvenile delinquency in Sierra Leone are the legislature, the courts, the police, prosecutors, defense attorneys, prison, probation officers, approved schools, and remand homes. The Children and Young Persons Act of 1945 and subsequent amendments give statutory provisions defining the scope of the legal authority of these agencies, prescribing procedures for the determination of guilt and for the hearing and disposal of juvenile cases. The term "juvenile" is defined to include both the "child" and the "young person," a child being under age 14 and a young person being between ages 14 and 17.

As in most countries, the bifurcation of the system of justice into juvenile and adult proceedings in Sierra Leone manifests itself in two sets of institutions and procedures with distinct goals and objectives: one set addresses juvenile delinquency and the other adult criminality. This is part of the British common law heritage. But although the juvenile justice system does have formal goals and procedures, its processes tend in practice to be more flexible and informal because of the large element of discretion granted to agencies handling juvenile cases.

On the whole, juvenile proceedings differ from adult proceedings in certain significant respects. The age boundary between the juvenile justice system and the criminal justice system for adults is 17 years. Generally, the language of adult proceedings, with its denunciatory connotations and stigmatizing effect, is not used in juvenile proceedings. When a juvenile is adjudged guilty or not guilty, reference is not made to a "conviction," a "sentence," or an "acquittal," but to an "order" (the only exception is homicide, in which case a juvenile is tried as an adult). Unlike in the United States, magistrates hearing criminal charges against juveniles (who are not charged with adults) sit in different buildings or rooms from those used for ordinary court sittings. Except for homicide, a child is not sentenced to imprisonment. The same applies to a young person, unless the court finds no other statutory disposition suitable. Again, except for homicide, policy dictates that an imprisoned young person should be segregated from adult prisoners.

The entire panoply of due process safeguards afforded the defendant in adult criminal proceedings are not available in juvenile proceedings. Juvenile court hearings take place in camera (meaning, in a judge's private room or place; in a private place, not in public), and only members and officers of the court, relatives of the defendant, parties to the case, their attorneys, and other persons directly concerned

are allowed to be present. Other persons cannot attend except with the permission of the court. The court can grant special permission to credentialed representatives of the press to attend. Strict statutory requirements preclude the disclosure of the name, school, or any other identifying information of the youth except with the permission of the court.

When a juvenile is adjudged as having committed a crime, the court will hear evidence of the juvenile's character, antecedents, home life, occupation, and health so as to determine what disposition should be made in the juvenile's best interest. So long as a juvenile has been adjudged guilty of an offense other than homicide, the court may make such custodial or noncustodial orders as (i) a conditional discharge on the juvenile's own recognizance, with or without sureties, to be of good behavior; (ii) a fine, compensation, or costs order against the parent or guardian, or against the juvenile, where the parent or guardian cannot be located or did not condone the crime; (iii) repatriation of the juvenile to his or her home or district of origin; (iv) a release to the custody of a fit person or institution; and (v) a release to the custody of an approved school. The court may also order that any custodial or noncustodial measure be supervised by a court-appointed probation officer.

Juvenile courts in Sierra Leone also dispose of cases involving status offenses, acts done by juveniles that, by virtue of the offender's status as a child or young person, may require care, protection, and supervisory jurisdiction from the juvenile justice system. Status offenses include begging or receiving alms; wandering without home or settled place of abode; and falling into such bad associations as the company of a reputed thief or a common prostitute. This jurisdiction also extends to cases where the juvenile is a victim of acts such as parental abuse, neglect, abandonment, or being in the custody of a parent or guardian who is criminally disposed or who is violent and alcoholic. Juveniles who are so victimized may be made wards of the court. In such cases, the court may order (i) that the juvenile be sent to an approved school; (ii) that the juvenile be committed to the care of a fit person, whether a relative or not, or to an institution; or (iii) that his or her parent or guardian guarantee to give him or her proper care and guardianship.

As in England and the United States, there are both pretrial and trial juvenile procedures in Sierra Leone. Pretrial procedures are called referrals and are essentially an intake process. Although no supporting statistics are available, it is evident that referrals to the juvenile court in Sierra Leone have increased over the years because of the country's economic decline. Most referrals come from the police. Parents and relatives rarely make referrals except as a last option, an attitude rooted in both the European and the African strands of Sierra Leone culture and tradition. A delinquent child brings moral opprobrium on the family, and it is thought that rehabilitation can be handled better within the family than by legal and institutional procedures. After a referral, the court must make three key decisions: (i) whether to detain an arrested juvenile pending investigation of the case, or to release him or her on bail on his or her own recognizance or that of his or her parents or guardian; (ii) whether or not to file formal charges against him or her; and, when it has been decided that the juvenile is in need of care, protection, and supervision, (iii) whether to file a formal petition for any appropriate statutory order. The fact that juveniles are not afforded the same comprehensive set of due process rights has not been controversial in Sierra Leone. Essentially, juveniles are afforded the right to bail; the right to cross-examine prosecution witnesses; the right of appeal; and the right to an attorney—but unlike in the United States, not at the expense of the state.

Some key aspects of trial procedures have already been covered in this section, especially with regard to the in-camera nature of juvenile proceedings, and the specific orders that the court can make both in exercise of its criminal jurisdiction and in the context of the adjudication of status offenses. When a juvenile is charged with a criminal offense other than homicide, the substance of the charge is explained to him or her in simple language. The court then gives him or her an opportunity to explain or else to admit to the allegation. If the juvenile's statement amounts to a plea of guilty, the court will record that the charge is proved. If the allegation is not confirmed, or the explanation does not amount to a guilty plea, the court will proceed to hear the evidence of the prosecution witnesses. At the close of the evidence of each witness, the court will ask the witness any questions necessary and desirable to establish the truth of the allegation or test the witness's credibility. The juvenile is also given the opportunity to question the witness, and the court will make sure that this is done, particularly when the juvenile is unrepresented. When all the prosecution evidence is in, the court will hear defense evidence, including any further statement the juvenile may wish to make, if it finds that a sufficient or prima facie case has been made against the defendant.

In Sierra Leone today, there are three penal facilities for juveniles. They are probation, approved schools, and remand homes. They function under the control and supervision of probation officers and managers who are in turn supervised by the court.

Conclusion

Criticisms of the social control mechanisms of criminal law and of criminal justice systems are inevitable because their application concerns the extremely delicate and sensitive issue of marking boundaries between individual liberty and the punitive power of the state. In many countries criminal law and criminal justice processes are perceived as conservative, and in the developing state of Sierra Leone, it would be difficult to contest this generalization. One historical reason adduced for the current lack of a Sierra Leone criminal code is the opposition of a legal profession that has always prided itself in uncritical adherence to the inherited common law system. The state of affairs is all the more anomalous for the fact that Sierra Leone has a permanent law reform commission whose specific functions are to eliminate anomalies found in the law, to repeal obsolete and outdated enactments, to consolidate enactments, to introduce and incorporate new areas of law, and to modernize and update the law. In spite of a truly elaborate and comprehensive mechanism for the reform of law in Sierra Leone, some key catalysts for law reform are missing, to wit, a lively public opinion, an importunate press, and an insistent academic legal community.

It is arguable, therefore, that criminal law and the criminal justice system in Sierra Leone are seriously in need of refurbishing. This is necessary, if they are to achieve their avowed goals and objectives as a social control mechanism, adjusting and responding to the rapidly changing socioeconomic realities and attendant criminogenic effects in a developing society with a strong common law heritage. For instance, unlike in the United States and in England, there has been no major effort either to devise a rational body of criminal law or to reform in the light of new realities some of its underlying principles and specific offenses. Sierra Leone has no counterpart to the U.S. Model Penal Code or the English Theft Act of 1968. Change is needed, and a legion of issues critical to the functioning of the criminal justice system ought to be addressed; but for our purposes it will suffice to identify the main ones: (i) whether or not the criminal jurisdiction of the local courts, whose adjudications are not based on due process, ought to be preserved; (ii) the role of the jury in trials on indictment; (iii) the effectiveness

of the criminal justice system as a whole in dealing with crime; (iv) the growth of white-collar crime, and (v) the goals of juvenile justice.

With regard to whether the criminal jurisdiction of the local courts should be preserved, undoubtedly the ideal for any country is to have one law and one judicial system for everybody (Roberts-Wray, 1959). The bifurcated legal system of Sierra Leone preserves normative disparities by keeping the customary law jurisdiction and the general law jurisdiction separate, and such disparities can inhibit modernization and progress toward industrialization in a developing country. However, two potentially compatible forces are at work in the modern socio-legal setting of Sierra Leone. On one hand, inherited English law is undergoing constant adaptation and modification in response to the changing socioeconomic realities of a pluralistic society that includes both the values of Western liberal democracy and indigenous African norms and beliefs. On the other hand, customary law rules are being refashioned and reformulated to ensure the rights and obligations of persons of indigenous culture. These complementary forces eventually may lead to the integration of the general law system with the customary system of justice (Thompson, 1991). The problem with this idea is that we cannot successfully eliminate a society's cultural values and standards entirely.

The second critical issue arising from the administration of criminal justice in Sierra Leone today concerns whether juries in trials on indictment perform their important duty effectively. The issue has not been seriously addressed in recent times in the country, nor has it evoked much public concern. Nevertheless, in one or two isolated cases in the postindependence period jury verdicts have been suspected of being tainted or perverse, and the press has questioned the usefulness of the institution. This problem should be addressed, not by searching for a better system of trial, but by considering new rules for jury eligibility and qualification. It is well known in Sierra Leone that the level of education of persons who qualify for jury service and who actually do serve as jurors seriously compromises the system. The need for reform here cannot be overemphasized.

The criminal justice system of Sierra Leone, as presently organized, is clearly incapable of dealing with the country's escalating crime rates. The law, the courts, the police, and the correctional services currently do not have sufficient resources to address all the manifestations of criminal behavior. Street crimes, white-collar crimes, and corporate and economic crimes are epidemic. The Criminal Investigation Department's various operational crime units certainly need increased manpower and logistical resources to do their jobs.

Furthermore, there is the malfunctioning of the heavily burdened criminal courts. Again we encounter the recurrent theme of scarcity of resources: criminal justice is not accorded a high place in governmental priorities. The courts have excessive caseloads, heavy backlogs, and protracted delays both in trials and in the hearing of appeals. The High Court typically spends 3 to 6 months adjudicating some ordinary felony cases; and 2 to 3 years can pass while trying difficult and complicated fraud cases. Cases on appeal never get determined more quickly than 2 to 4 years after they have been listed. On the trial level, vital witnesses, especially medical experts, may leave the country during protracted judicial delays, making prosecution when the case comes up for trial impossible. This happens frequently in homicide cases, where law requires the medical cause of the victim's death to be established conclusively. In the provinces, witnesses may not be able to attend trials because of scarcity of public transportation. It also should be noted that the criminal courts are often criticized for allegedly poor quality of justice and for failure to resist politicization of the criminal justice process.

The growth of white-collar crime in Sierra Leone manifests not only a lack of political will to fight this brand of criminality, but also a lack of expertise in the Criminal Investigation Department's fraud unit to unravel the complex financial malpractices that take place inside and against bureaucracies and corporate bodies. The difficulty is compounded by the powerful political connections often wielded by businessmen engaged in questionable commercial practices, and by the semblance of legitimacy they acquire from corrupt accountants and tax consultants.

Finally we address the critical issue of the goals of the juvenile justice system in Sierra Leone. As in most countries, juvenile justice in Sierra Leone can be properly characterized as the neglected sister, the "Cinderella" of the two justice systems. But Sierra Leone, unlike the United States and Britain, shows no concern about the future direction of juvenile justice. There has been no move to improve its process or to redefine its goals in the light of new realities, nor have rises in juvenile deviance provoked any significant impetus in that direction.

Discussion and Review Questions

1. Why are many crimes unreported and undetected in Sierra Leone?

2. What is ritual murder?

3. Which crimes predominate in Sierra Leone today?

4. Patterns of criminal behavior in Sierra Leone reflect a combination and interaction of many factors. What are these factors?

5. What is one of the major obstacles to effective law enforcement in Sierra Leone?

6. Name six major roles of the Sierra Leone Police Force.

7. What are the major criticisms against the police in Sierra Leone?

8. Compare and contrast the U.S. Supreme Court and the Supreme Court of Sierra Leone.

9. What is the main philosophy underlying the prison system in Sierra Leone?

10. Compare and contrast correctional ideology in Sierra Leone and Denmark; Sierra Leone and the United States.

11. Name five ways in which a juvenile offender can be treated in Sierra Leone.

12. Compare and contrast juvenile courts in Sierra Leone and the United States.

13. Thompson raised five issues of critical concern in the Sierra Leone justice system. What are they?

14. What is the role of the Law Reform Commission in Sierra Leone?

15. Name two cases of ritual murder in Sierra Leone in recent years.

16. What is economic crime?

17. What factors influence patterns of criminal behavior in Sierra Leone?

18. The modern police force was introduced in Sierra Leone in 1829. Is there any link between this period and Sir Robert Peel's London Metropolitan Police of 1829?

19. What do you understand by centralized policing in Sierra Leone?

20. Who was the first Chief Justice of Sierra Leone (1788)?

7

An Overview of the Criminal Justice System in Hong Kong

T. Wing Lo

Introduction and Brief History

Hong Kong, a special administrative region of the People's Republic of China, covers a tiny area, but by 1998, it had an estimated population of 6.7 million. It was a British colony from 1842 to 1997, governed by the British-appointed governor, assisted by a chief secretary, financial secretary, attorney general, and a group of secretaries (similar to ministers). The secretaries were senior civil servants in charge of various functions, such as economy, education, transport, security, and health and social welfare. There were two advisory bodies: the executive and legislative councils, comprising official and appointed unofficial members for the majority of the time. The executive council functioned as the cabinet of the governor. The legislative council was similar to a parliament. Apart from lawmaking, it had the powers to scrutinize public income and expenditure, and to monitor the work of the government. The judiciary, led by the chief justice, was independent of the central administration and legislature.

On 1 July 1997, Britain handed Hong Kong over to China under a Joint Declaration, signed between the two governments in 1984, which recognized the principle of "one country, two systems." That is, the capitalist system of the Hong Kong Special Administrative Region is to be retained for 50 years from the handover date, as com-pared to the socialist system on the mainland of China. Hong Kong will maintain high-level autonomy. Under the Basic Law, the constitution of Hong Kong and the criminal justice system will continue, together with the political, legal, economic, and social systems. After the transfer of sovereignty, the governor is replaced by a locally elected, small number of elite, but Beijing appointed the chief executive. The attorney general is renamed the secretary of justice, and other features of the government have remained basically unchanged.

Legal System

The criminal law of Hong Kong has a colonial origin, following the British legal system, and thus has no comprehensive codified criminal law. The principal sources of law are equity, common law, and criminal statutes. When the last two come into conflict, statutory law prevails. In some circumstances, the statutory law defines the punishment but the elements of crimes, such as murder and manslaughter, are established by the common law (Bindzus, 1991). A few conditions of Chinese customary law also apply in Hong Kong regarding the use of land, but they are not related to criminal law. Some international treaties and agreements have impact on the development of the common law, but they do not become part of Hong Kong law unless they are incorporated by legislation.

Despite the handover, Hong Kong retains the vast majority of its criminal law and procedure. In addition to the Basic Law, the laws of Hong Kong are those previously in force and those enacted by the provisional legislative council. However, there are some changes that deserve particular attention. In order to be in line with the International Covenant on Civil and Political Rights and probably with the negative memory of the June 4th Tiananmen Incident in Beijing, the legislative council passed the Bill of Rights Ordinance after hot debates in the early 1990s. In effect, two ordinances were amended, because they were considered to contravene the freedoms of association and assembly, i.e., the Societies (Amendment) Ordinance 1992 and the Public Order (Amendment) Ordinance 1995. The compulsory registration requirement for societies was abolished, and the requirement to obtain a license from the police before holding a public demonstration was also waived.

Both amendments were strongly criticized by the Beijing government, who declared that they reserved the right to repeal them in the future. In the few months before the handover in July 1997, when Beijing influences dominated the legislative council, the two ordinances were reamended to return them to their earlier forms. Moreover, the police were empowered to refuse or cancel registration, and to "prohibit the operation of a society where this is deemed necessary in the interests of national security or public safety, public order or the protection of the rights and freedoms of others" (Dobinson, 1997:181). Similarly, the police have the powers to prohibit public assemblies and demonstrations on the same ground.

Since the term "national security" is defined as the safeguarding of the territorial integrity and the independence of the People's Republic of China, the public, especially the pro-democracy group, was concerned with how this definition would be interpreted and applied by the authority concerned. Coupled with this was the possibility of enactment of law by the Hong Kong government, laid down in Article 23 of the Basic Law, to prohibit treason, secession, sedition, and subversion. There was a general fear that Beijing's increasing influence on the enactment and interpretation of law would pose a serious threat to civil liberties in Hong Kong.

Before the introduction of the Bill of Rights, some police powers authorized by statutory law could infringe upon a suspect's human rights. For instance, Section 160(1) of the Crimes Ordinance stated that any person who loiters in a public place has to give a satisfactory explanation for his presence there; otherwise, the person shall be guilty of an offense. In 1992, the ordinance was amended and this section was repealed; it now becomes the responsibility of the police to provide evidence of intent to commit an arrestable offense.

Crimes and Victims

In general, law and order in Hong Kong is not regarded by the public as a very serious problem. According to police statistics, the number of offenders per 100,000 population between 1990 and 1996 was 855. Between 1994 and 1996, the total number of crimes reported to the police was around 80,000 to 92,000, with a detection rate of 50–52%. The most often reported crimes were burglary and theft, followed by violent crimes against person and property. It must be noted that according to Table 7-1, Hong Kong has encountered problems on illegal immigration, dangerous drugs and corruption, whereas triad-related offenses were not as serious as expected.

The first crime victimization survey was conducted in 1979. Since then, it has been conducted once every 3 to 5 years. It provides useful information concerning the

Table 7-1: *Crimes Reported to the Police and the ICAC*

	1994	1995	1996
Violent crimes against person	9,462	10,177	9,950
Violent crimes against property	7,770	6,910	5,241
Burglary and theft	44,852	46,763	38,907
Fraud and forgery	3,201	4,093	4,167
Sexual offenses	1,256	1,289	1,298
Serious narcotics offenses	4,618	5,701	4,645
Serious Immigration offenses	4,021	4,117	3,302
Criminal damage	5,154	5,216	5,222
Unlawful society offenses (triads)	1,512	1,445	1,134
Possession of arms and weapons	870	738	536
Other crimes	5,088	5,437	4,648
Total crimes reported to police	87,804	91,886	79,050
Total crimes detected by police	44,142 (50.3%)	47,780 (52%)	40,741 (51.5%)
Corruption offenses reported to ICAC	6,284	5,183	4,547

Source: Independent Commission Against Police Corruption (ICAC) Committee Review Reports 1994, 1995, and 1996.

nature and extent of crime, reasons for not reporting crime, socioeconomic and demographic data, victim–offender relationships, circumstances of crime occurrence, etc. The objective of the survey is to assist the administration of criminal justice professionals; it is less concerned with the welfare of crime victims. Not until 1996 did the government pass the Victim's Charter to set out the duties and rights of crime victims and to improve the standards of services for them.

As stated in the Charter, apart from the duty to help maintain law and order, crime victims have the right to be treated with courtesy and respect by criminal justice professionals. Law enforcement agencies shall give a prompt and proper response to complaints of crime. Victims shall be provided with the necessary information related to the complaints, such as the progress of investigation and prosecution, their role as witnesses in court, the final disposal of the case, and even the date of the offender's pending release, or escape, from penal custody. In court, victims shall be provided with proper facilities so that

they are not made to feel intimidated. Their circumstances and views on prosecution and sentence shall be channeled to the prosecutors and the court. Their privacy shall be maintained and their information kept confidential. If necessary, testifying from outside the court by means of video facilities can be adopted. Victims also have the right to seek protection, compensation, remedies, and welfare services, and to have their property returned promptly after its use as evidence. Despite these favorable features, it is argued that some of the provisions are unlikely to reach the vast majority of victims, who are also not adequately taken care of in and by the community (Chan, 1998).

Police

Administration and Organization

Although Hong Kong was a British colony, its police were not modeled on the civilian police of London's Metropolitan Police Force. Like the Royal Irish Constabulary, its police officers are armed. The arrangement was to support a small military presence in the early days of the colony (Traver, 1994). Thus the police has an extensive paramilitary role (Traver and Gaylord, 1991). To uphold British control in the colony, senior ranks were traditionally filled by British officers. Since the signing of the Joint Declaration regarding the handover of Hong Kong to China, local Chinese officers have gradually replaced their British counterparts on the top level of the hierarchy.

Hong Kong has a relatively large police force. In 1997, in a force of 34,143, about 28,000 were disciplined staff (police officers). In addition, the Auxiliary Police Force had an establishment of 5,721 disciplined staff. Combining the strengths of the two forces, there was approximately one police officer for every 200 citizens. Between 1990 and 1997, the ratio of regular police per 100,000 population was 454. Auxiliary officers are part-time staff. They wear uniforms, carry weapons, and hold the same legal powers as regular police officers when on duty. Police officers are remunerated with an attractive salary. In 1997, there were 17.7 applicants for each inspector's post and 10 applicants for each constable's job. For the latter, the minimum educational qualification is form five (U.S. sixth-grade level). Increasingly, university graduates are recruited to the inspectorate. Basic training for inspectors lasts for 36 weeks, and 27 weeks for constables. Command courses are offered at different levels for senior officers.

The police have a headquarters comprising five departments: operations; crime and security; personnel and training; management services; and finance, administration, and planning. The force is further divided into six regions for operations. Each region is largely autonomous in its day-to-day policing and management. As regards its operations, there are different units, task forces, or bureaus responsible for commercial crime, narcotics, organized crime and triads, criminal intelligence,

witness protection, child protection and child abuse investigation, bomb disposal, anti-smuggling and illegal immigration, criminal records, fingerprint, ballistics and firearms identification, crime prevention, and liaison with Interpol. Services related to forensic pathology and science are provided by the government laboratory and the department of health.

The police devote a lot of time and resources to maintaining order, but they are not always necessarily related to the fighting of crime. They are heavily involved in traffic control, crowd control during major public events, responding to emergencies, and the licensing of various activities concerning the registration of societies and public order, such as massage parlors and pawnbrokers. Moreover, they have to settle family and neighborhood disputes, promote road safety, and participate in school talks and other community relations activities, such as the production of television programs.

The commissioner of police is responsible to the chief executive of Hong Kong. In 1997, the total number of complaints against police officers was around 3,000. Such complaints are handled by the Complaints Against Police Office and the Internal Investigations Office. Invariably, there have been voices urging that the two offices be made independent of the police force, based on the argument that they cannot conduct fair investigations if they are within the force. The government responded by forming the Independent Police Complaints Council, comprising non-police appointed members from all walks of life, to oversee the work of the two offices. This, however, did not satisfy the liberals. They continue to advocate the establishment of an independent investigation office separated from the police force.

Independent Commission Against Corruption

Corruption in the police force and a strong police–triad alliance in the postwar decades prompted the colonial government to set up Hong Kong's second police force, the Independent Commission Against Corruption (ICAC), in 1974 (Lethbridge, 1985; Lo, 1993). Its commissioner is formally and directly responsible to the chief executive. Its staff are not subject to the purview of the Public Services Commission, although they are financed by public revenue. Its work, however, comes under the close scrutiny of an independent advisory committees comprising prominent social figures. Such independence ensures that any investigation of corruption is not interrupted or influenced by any bureaucratic or political forces.

Being one of the largest anti-corruption forces in the world, the commission has a staff force of more than 1,200, working in three functional departments. The Operations Department, the largest of the three, is responsible for investigations. The Corruption Prevention Department is responsible for the examinations of the practices and procedures adopted by government departments and public bodies to identify opportunities for corruption and give advice on how to eliminate them. A private organization may also seek its advice if such a need arises. The Community Relations Department undertakes measures to enlist public support, educate the public on the evils of corruption, and monitor community responses to the commission and public attitudes toward corruption. The "three-pronged attack" on corruption is a unique feature of this graft fighter.

Supported by a powerful anti-corruption ordinance, the commission enjoyed draconian powers of investigation and prosecution, many of which were criticized as infringing upon human rights (Downey, 1976; ICAC Review Committee, 1994). For example, these included the powers to search premises without a court warrant, to seize any documents from passports to bank accounts, to forbid the mass media to disclose the identities of suspects, to detain anyone on the premises for up to 3 hours, and to put the burden of proof of

corruption on the accused civil servants. Since 1994, following the recommendations of a review committee, its power has been curbed; some of its powers are to be exercised by the court on application by the commission.

The Judiciary

The Courts

The judiciary, headed by the chief justice, is completely independent of the executive arm of the government and of the legislature. It handles all prosecutions and civil disputes in the following courts: the Court of Final Appeal, the High Court comprising the Court of Appeal and the Court of First Instance, District Court, Magistracy, and Juvenile Court. There are some other special courts such as the Lands Tribunal, Coroner's Court, Labor Tribunal, Small Claims Tribunal, and Obscene Articles Tribunal.

The Magistracy is the lowest court of Hong Kong and handles the majority of criminal cases. It is responsible for summary offenses and some indictable offenses. Its powers of punishment are restricted to a maximum of 2 years' imprisonment or a fine of HK$100,000. In some offenses, however, the convicted offenders can be sentenced to a maximum of 3 years' imprisonment or HK$1 million fine. The Juvenile Court is presided over by a magistrate who tries all offenses (except homicide) committed by persons 7 to 16 years old. To protect the juvenile, the trial is not made public, although bona fide representatives of the press can be admitted (Bindzus, 1991). Serious criminal offenses other than murder, manslaughter, rape, armed robbery, serious drug offenses, etc., are tried in the District Court, which sits with a judge without a jury. The judge has the authority to impose prison sentences for a maximum of 7 years. The Family Court is a part of the District Court. It deals with divorce, adoption, and other family-related cases.

The Court of First Instance and the Court of Appeal form the High Court. In the trials of the most serious criminal offenses at the Court of First Instance, a single judge sits with a jury consisting of seven or nine jurors. In deciding whether the accused is guilty or not guilty, a majority vote of five to two or seven to two is required. Normally no lower courts sit with jury, except when an inquest with a jury (of three) is required in the Coroner's Court. The Court of First Instance is also the appeal instance for decisions from the Magistracy and Juvenile Court. The Court of Appeal receives appeals from the Court of First Instance and the District Court. It makes rulings on questions of law submitted by the lower courts.

The Court of Final Appeal is the last instance of appeal from rulings in criminal and civil matters. When sitting, the court will comprise five judges, including the chief justice, three permanent judges, and one non-permanent Hong Kong judge or one judge from other common law jurisdictions. Before the handover, the court of final appeal was the Judicial Committee of the Privy Council of Britain. The two courts are similar in their procedural rules and regulations and in the type of case heard (Dobinson, 1997).

Appointment and Dismissal of Judges

The Judicial Officers Recommendation Commission, an independent statutory organization composed of judges, lawyers, and eminent social figures, makes recommendations to the chief executive of Hong Kong for the appointment of judges and judicial officers. They are recruited from Hong Kong or other common law jurisdictions on the basis of their professional and judicial qualifications as well as their maturity of character. Judges have security of tenure and may only be removed by the chief executive on the recommendation of a tribunal appointed by the chief justice, for misbehavior or inability to discharge duties. The tribunal is comprised of not less than three local judges. If the chief justice is the target of investigation, the tribunal has to be appointed by the chief executive and consists of no less than five local judges. Any appointment or dismissal of judges of the Court of Final Appeal and the chief judge of the High Court has to be endorsed by the Legislative Council, and the Standing Committee of the National People's Congress of China has also to be informed of such a decision.

Independence of the Judiciary

Hong Kong, one of the most crowded city-states in the world, has invariably faced a population problem. Immediately after the handover, the Provisional Legislative Council passed the Immigration (Amendment) Bill to empower the government to send back mainland-born children with Hong Kong parents who arrived in Hong Kong without proper documents. Under normal circumstances, they have to apply for an entry permit to Hong Kong from their local authorities, but this would take several years. Since the status of this group of people is vaguely defined in the Basic Law, and the power of interpretation of the Basic Law rests with the National People's Congress of China (NPC), many people believed that the independence of Hong Kong's judiciary and common law system was under threat.

In January 1999, however, the children won their right of abode after appeal. The Court of Final Appeal ruled that "Hong Kong courts can interfere with acts of the NPC if they breach the Basic Law. Interpretation of the Basic Law is to be carried out by the Court of Final Appeal, not the NPC, if the main issue in the case is within Hong Kong's autonomy. Additionally, the

Court of Final Appeal, not the NPC, will decide whether a case should be referred to the NPC. Courts should be reluctant to allow restrictions to be imposed on human rights enshrined in the Basic Law" (Buddle, 1999:1). The immediate effect of the ruling was that legal experts in mainland China fiercely attacked the decision of the Court of Final Appeal with the argument that the verdict challenges the powers and supreme status of the NPC, China's lawmaking body.

As a long-term effect, a large but unknown number of children born in mainland China with Hong Kong parents will be getting their right of abode in Hong Kong. This will create tremendous pressure on the territory's population as well as the demand for social services. The ruling is definitely against the wish of the government and the general public. In the 2 years following the handover, there was inquietude that the court would shrink from ruling against the government and the mainland China, but the fear has been dispelled after this landmark ruling. The decision of the Court of Final Appeal reconvinced Hong Kong people and the world that Hong Kong court will act to maintain the independence of the judiciary and the common law under the principle of "one country, two systems."

Prosecution and Criminal Procedure

Prosecution

In the Department of Justice, there are five distinct legal divisions responsible for prosecutions: civil law, criminal law, law drafting, legal policy, and international law. The director of public prosecutions (DPP) heads the Prosecutions Division, which controls all criminal prosecutions. Apart from handling almost all appeals, government counsels conduct prosecutions of offenses in the district and high courts, and occasionally in magistracies

when the trials involve important points of law and particular public interest. Counsels on fiat are regularly briefed to prosecute in the district courts and magistracies on behalf of the Division. The majority of prosecutions in the magistracies are conducted by court prosecutors (lay prosecutors) under the supervision of a senior assistant prosecutor. The court prosecutors are not qualified lawyers but have been trained for this work by counsel. In daily practice, the majority of prosecutions are routine matters and are thus directly dealt with by law enforcement agencies, but they will seek the advice of government counsel in dealing with serious and complicated cases, or when the prosecutions involve complex points of law.

The secretary for justice, who heads the Department of Justice, is directly appointed by the chief executive; yet she is not subject to any instruction or directions from him. Being a member of the Executive Council, she is the principal legal adviser to the chief executive and the government. On the one hand, she represents both the government and public interest in the court, and on the other hand, she becomes the defendant in all civil actions against the government. She has overall responsibility for the conduct of prosecutions, which are free from any interference. It is for her alone to rule whether a prosecution should be instituted in any specific case or group of cases. She will consider not only the sufficiency of evidence but other relevant matters, such as those affecting public policy and public interest.

The consideration of the secretary of justice in prosecution can be illustrated by the well-known *Hong Kong Standard* (a local newspaper) circulation fraud case in 1998–99. Ms. Aw Sian, the boss of Sing Tao News Group and a member of the Chinese People's Political Consultative Conference, was named as a co-conspirator, but no charge was laid against her. The secretary of justice later explained that apart from the possibility of insufficient evidence, she also made a "public interest" consideration. However, she defined public interest to include keeping a big international enterprise afloat. She did not charge Ms. Aw because the prosecution might lead to the collapse of Sing Tao enterprise and would thus create much unemployment and send an unfavorable message to the international community. Incidentally, the chief executive is a former director of Sing Tao. Following the explanation given by the secretary for justice, there was strong public pressure to call on her to step down in order to salvage public confidence in the legal system.

Criminal Procedure

Arrest and Pretrial Detention

The police determine who will go through the criminal justice system. Police officers are authorized to stop anyone in a public place and request to see the person's proof of identity, or search the person to check whether the person is carrying an offensive weapon if they have reasonable suspicion. They can arrest a person to prevent the commission of crime or to assist with further inquiries, or in some cases, to initiate a prosecution. There are certain procedures to safeguard the person under arrest. During the arrest, police officers should give the arrested a caution that he is not obliged to make any statement; however, if it is made, it will be written down and may be used as evidence. The arrested suspect is to be taken into custody in a police station, where the duty police officer is informed of the reason for the suspect's arrest, but not in any other place or facility.

The suspect may be granted bail if the charge is not a serious one, or may be discharged on recognizance, subject to the obligation to appear in court on a specified day. Then the process of identification, photographing, taking fingerprints and measurements, etc., takes place. Later,

a senior police officer has to decide on the charge to be filed against the suspect, and the advice of the Department of Justice is sought if necessary. A charge sheet containing the statement of the offense and other related particulars are delivered to the accused/suspect.

At this stage, if the accused is kept in custody, he must be brought before a magistrate as soon as practicable, normally within 48 hours of arrest. If a warrant of arrest or deportation order is granted, the arrested suspect can be detained for 72 hours. If the police wish to detain the accused for a longer period, they will apply to the court to have the accused remanded back into police custody to assist with further inquiries. The magistrate may accept the police officer's request, or put the accused into the custody of the court as administered by the Correctional Services Department. Thus the arrest is now over and further detention becomes the court's responsibility (Heilbronn, 1990).

Superintendents' Discretion Scheme

This is a diversion program. Under this scheme, senior police officers of the rank of superintendent and above have the discretion to caution, rather than prosecute, young offenders aged 18 or below. There are several criteria for cautioning. First, there is sufficient evidence to support a prosecution, which would be the only and inevitable alternative. Second, the offender voluntarily and unequivocally admits the offense. Third, the offender and the offender's parents agree to be cautioned (Lee, 1998; Working Group on Review of the Superintendents' Discretion Scheme, 1994).

When these conditions are satisfied, the police officer will consider other relevant factors before making a judgment, such as the nature, seriousness, and prevalence of the offense, the offender's previous record, the complainant's attitude, and the attitude of the offender's parents. Normally, an offender will be cautioned once; only in exceptional cases will the same offender be cautioned twice. After the cautioning, the police officer may refer the offender to the Social Welfare Department, the Education Department, or the Juvenile Protection Section of the Hong Kong Police Force for follow-up. Cautioned young offenders may also participate, on a voluntary basis, in the guidance and supportive programs organized by the community support service schemes run by nongovernment organizations.

The Decision to Prosecute

The decision to prosecute an offender depends on a number of factors concerning the offense, including its seriousness, the sufficiency of evidence, the existence of extenuating circumstances, and the suspect's attitude. Moreover, prosecutors will also consider the practical effect of a prosecution, the effect of the prosecution on other people, and whether "the consequences of the prosecution will be out of proportion with the seriousness of the offense or with the penalty to be imposed by the court" (Raffell, 1994:100). If there were a conviction, how seriously a court would take of the offense is also an essential point for consideration.

If the police decide to prosecute, they will issue a summons against the suspect, or charge the suspect in court. No one will be tried or punished for an offense for which one has previously been convicted or acquitted. All indictable offenses originate before a magistracy. But the secretary for justice may apply to have a case transferred to the district court or committed to the High Court depending on the seriousness of the case. During the prosecution process, plea bargaining is common. The accused may enter a guilty plea in exchange for some concession. However, plea bargains are always negotiated with the prosecutor rather than the judge.

Rights of the Accused

Before a trial, the accused has the right to obtain detailed information regarding the nature and cause of the charge. He can meet his family members, remain silent, and seek legal assistance and representation. One of the principles of defense is equality before the court. The accused has the right to a fair and public trial by a competent, independent, and impartial court. The presumption of innocence is upheld and the burden of proof lies with the prosecution. The standard of proof is one of "beyond reasonable doubt." In presiding over trials, members of the judiciary maintain absolute independence. They are accountable to the law itself and protect civil rights.

The accused is given sufficient time to prepare his defense. He is tried in his presence and without undue delay. He has the right to call witnesses and secure their presence in court, and to cross-examine prosecution witnesses. He can enjoy free interpretation service, or remain silent in court. A convicted offender can appeal against conviction or sentence and has the right to bail pending trial or appeal subject to the gravity of the offense and other related circumstances.

Sentencing Options and Procedure

The age of criminal responsibility is 7 years old. No children under this age may be found guilty of an offense. Moreover, no children under 14 years of age may be sentenced to imprisonment. A young person under 21 years of age may be sentenced to imprisonment only if there are no other appropriate alternatives. In this circumstance, youth prisoners must be separated from adult prisoners.

Unlike Singapore, corporal punishment and the death penalty are no longer used as sentencing options in Hong Kong. Punishment for murder was death by hanging, which was abolished in 1993. In fact, there had been no such executions since 1966 (Bindzus, 1991). Corporal punishment in the form of caning was abolished in 1989. Currently, the following sentencing options can be used by the court: unconditional discharge, conditional discharge of the offender on his entering into a recognizance, fines, confiscation of equipment and money related to the crimes, compensation order, hospital order, or suspended sentence. For young offenders below 16 years of age, a supervision order or care and protection order can be granted. In addition, offenders may be sentenced to attend other correctional and rehabilitation programs outlined next.

Rehabilitation programs are run by two government departments, the Social Welfare Department and the Correctional Services Department. The Social Welfare Department, staffed mainly by social workers, adopts social work methods to run both community-based and residential services for offenders who are 7 years of age or above and whose crimes are regarded as less serious. Its rehabilitation programs include probation orders, community service orders, detention orders, probation homes, probation hostels, reformatory schools, and community support service schemes. The Correctional Services Department, formerly the Prison Department, is a disciplinary force. It administers a detention center, drug addiction treatment centers, training centers, and prisons for offenders who are 14 years of age or above. In addition, its halfway houses offer temporary shelter for young offenders during their adjustment period after release.

To determine which rehabilitation program is most appropriate for an offender, the court obtains and considers information about his character, physical and mental conditions, schooling, employment, and family circumstances. This information is provided through a variety of reports prepared by the two departments, such as social inquiry reports, suitability reports for different sentencing options, and reports submitted by social workers,

psychologists, and psychiatric and medical professionals. If necessary, the Young Offender Assessment Panel, comprising representatives of the two departments, will examine specific cases thoroughly and advise the court on the appropriate sentence. In order to make these assessments, a convicted offender may be remanded for a period not exceeding three weeks before sentencing.

Rehabilitation Programs

Probation Orders

Under a probation order, a convicted offender 7 years of age or older is placed at liberty under the supervision of a probation officer for a period of 1 to 3 years. The philosophy of probation is rehabilitation, which emphasizes changing the offender rather than control and punishment. Probation officers provide supervision and personal guidance to probationers, and if necessary their family members, through regular home visits and interviews during the probation period.

Detention Orders

Young offenders between 7 and 15 years old who are not willing to be placed on probation orders can be sentenced to detention orders. That is, they are requested to reside in a place of detention, normally a remand home, for a period of not more than 6 months. Since it emphasizes short-term custody rather than educational and vocational training, the detention order is applied sparingly to local people. At present, it is mainly used to deal with young illegal immigrants.

Community Service Orders

For offenses punishable with imprisonment, convicted offenders 14 years of age or older can be sentenced to community service orders, which aim at rehabilitation, reparation, and constructive disposal. They have to perform unpaid work for not more than 240 hours within a year. This allows them to continue living in the community with the least disruption to their lives and to contribute to society through community service. Through structured work placements, they are helped to observe regulations, to enhance their sense of responsibility and self-worth, and to regain a law-abiding life.

Reformatory Schools, Probation Homes, and Hostels

Young offenders under 16 years of age may be sentenced to receive residential training in reformatory schools or probation homes run by the Social Welfare Department. Through counseling and academic, prevocational, and social skills training, they are helped to change their negative behavior and attitude. The period of residential training in a reformatory school does not exceed 3 years; normally, it ranges from 12 to 18 months, depending on inmates' responses to the training. Upon the completion of the training, they are provided with aftercare service, such as counseling, home visit, assistance in their accommodation, and job and school placement.

Those sentenced to probation orders may also be required to reside in a probation home or probation hostel for a period of not more than 1 year. Reformatory school and probation home are closed institutions, whereas probation hostel is an open institution for young offenders of 15 to 20 years of age. While residing in the hostel, they attend school or take up a job in the community.

Community Support Service Schemes

Community support service schemes provide services to probationers aged 7 to 20 through highly structured and intensively supervised activities. There are counseling or supportive groups, skill learning classes, adventure and outdoor activities, and volunteer and community service projects. Services are also extended to probationers' parents or foster homes who have experienced difficulty in supervising their children. Through these activities, social workers attempt to reintegrate the young offenders into the community, redirect their energies into constructive and legitimate channels, develop acceptable behavior, and reduce their likelihood of recidivism. Similar schemes are also run by nongovernment organizations but financed by the Social Welfare Department to help young people who are placed under the supervision of the Police Superintendent's Discretion Scheme.

Detention Center

The Detention Center, running a "short, sharp, shock" program for male offenders, emphasizes strict discipline, hard work, physical training, and foot-drill. The short-term disciplinary training aims at teaching offenders to have respect for the law and deter them from further law-breaking through rigorous training. The rule of silence must be observed by inmates except during meal time and counseling group. To meet the criteria for Detention Center, young offenders have to be convicted of an offense punishable with imprisonment but have not previously been detained in a training center or youth prison. They must be certified as physically fit and mentally sound.

The sentence is indeterminate, ranging from 1 to 6 months for young offenders (14–20 years old) and from 3 to 12 months for young adults (21–24 years old). A progressive system is employed. The progress, attitude, effort, and response of each inmate is assessed every month. Inmates must have secured suitable employment or a school placement before they can be discharged. After discharge, they are subject to 1-year statutory supervision.

Training Center

The target groups of Training Center are those who are found physically or mentally unsuitable for "short, sharp, shock" training, have previous penal experience, or require a longer period of comprehensive corrective training because of their criminal background. When compared with Detention Center, it focuses more on productive activities and character training for inmates. Education, vocational training, physical education, and community service programs, such as the Duke of Edinburgh's Award Scheme, Boy Scouts, and Girl Guides, are organized. Inmates are helped to develop good work habits and skills, and to regain recognition through serving the community.

The period of training is indeterminate, ranging from 6 months to 3 years, depending on the inmate's progress in training and his or her motivation to lead a law-abiding life upon release. The average training period is about 18 months. Inmates will be released when they have reached their peak in training and secured employment or a school placement. After release, they are subject to 3-year statutory supervision.

Drug Addiction Treatment Center

Notwithstanding the crimes they committed, the court may sentence convicted drug addicts aged 14 or older to a drug addiction treatment center for a period of 2 to 12 months. This provides an alternative for the court to sending a drug-dependent person to prison while undergoing treatment. The sentence is indeterminate and the actual period of detention is decided by the commissioner of correctional services, who will take into account the individual's progress and level of recovery. In 1995 and 1996, the average length of detention was about five and one-half months. The treatment program consists of three phases: restoration of physical health, removal of psychological and emotional dependence on drugs, and reintegration into the community. Upon release, the ex-addicts are subject to 1-year statutory supervision.

Prisons

In prison, the Correctional Services Department is responsible for the rehabilitation and safe and humane custody of offenders. Unlike the detention center and training center, the duration of imprisonment is determined by the court. However, prisoners can gain early release if they behave well during detention; this normally accounts for one-third of their sentence.

The prison system in Hong Kong, unlike in the United States, is centralized. As in the United States, there are three major classifications of prisons in Hong Kong: maximum-security prisons for violent and very dangerous offenders; medium-security prisons for offenders whose crimes do not require more than 3 to 4 years of incarceration; and minimum-security prisons that are equivalent to German open prisons. The minimum-security prisons are prisons without walls. They are like boot camps in the United States. The inmates of minimum-security prisons are not dangerous to society.

There are a total of seventeen prisons in Hong Kong, one detention center, three training centers, and four halfway houses. The halfway houses are for offender reintegration into society after spending 3 or more years in a prison facility. The inmates of a halfway house can go out in the daytime and come back to the halfway house in the evening. They can hold daytime jobs. Their stay at the halfway house ranges from 3 to 6 months.

Discussion and Conclusion

Hong Kong was a British colony. But when compared with former British colonies in West Africa, where prisoners were poorly fed and given insufficient medical care in poorly staffed prisons (Arthur, 1991, see Chapter 16), the standards of Hong Kong's penal institutions have been more advanced and developed. Unlike these African nations, Hong Kong has gradually walked away from the path of retributive justice. The death penalty and corporal punishment have been abolished. The powers of prison officers are scrutinized by the Bill of Rights. The Ombudsman has stepped into penal institutions to receive complaints from inmates. Moreover, the Correctional Services Department has experienced litigation about inmate rights. Its power has been challenged and even defeated by inmates in court.

Although physical abuse of inmates by individual correctional officers still occurs (Leung, 1998; Vagg, 1991), the humane custody of inmates is still largely upheld and becomes an underlying philosophy of penal institutions. Of 1,094 complaints that the Correctional Services Department satisfactorily dealt with between 1992 and 1996, only one-quarter were related to physical abuse (Lo et al., 1997). In general, the level of violence in Hong Kong prisons is not as high as in Brazilian prisons (See Chapter 17).

Unlike Sierra Leone, where juvenile justice is a "neglected sister" (See Chapter 6) Hong Kong has paid much attention to the welfare of young offenders. However, it is argued that an ethos of "disciplinary welfare" prevails in Hong Kong's juvenile justice system (Gray, 1991, 1998). Justice professionals have tended to use probation, residential care, and custody as a means to tackle juvenile delinquency. They increase discipline to solve the welfare problems of young offenders, resulting in "punitive treatment" (Parker et al., 1981). Vagg (1991) even suggested that the rehabilitative practice is in the context of strict and paternalistic discipline, surveillance, and control. Obviously, there is a gap between Hong Kong and Western welfare ideology.

On the other hand, human rights groups argue that the protection of children's rights is far from enough. For instance, there are constant demands from welfare groups to raise the age of criminal responsibility from 7 to 10 or 14 (Hong Kong Federation of Youth Groups, 1998). The same age for England and mainland China is currently 10 and 14, respectively. In this regard, it seems that Hong Kong is far behind international standards. As a government response, the Law Reform Committee released a public consultation paper in early 1999 to explore the possibility of changing the age of criminal liability.

There is positive development in other areas, too. A new Rehabilitation and Development Division was formed inside the Correctional Services Department in 1998 to take charge of all the operation and development of rehabilitation services. Previously, these were under the Operations Division, but operations and securityconcerns had taken precedence over rehabilitation matters (Lo et al., 1997). Moreover, the number of aftercare officers was also increased in the same year. This indicates that Hong Kong is making continual improvement in its correctional programs. Furthermore, the use of community service orders has been extended to the District Court, and community support service schemes have been permanently supported by government funds (Lo, 1998). This also shows Hong Kong's continuous commitment to community-based rehabilitation.

Insufficient sentencing options available to the court is an area criticized most by judges and magistrates (Lo et al.,1997). In criminal cases in Hong Kong, unlike China, Japan, Nigeria, and other West African countries, there are no arbitration and mediation programs between victims and offenders. Unlike Australia, New Zealand, Nigeria, Sierra Leone, and Ghana, Hong Kong has no family group conference and restorative justice to deal with juvenile offenders. There are no combination orders and attendance center orders as in Britain, whereas criminal justice in Hong Kong is of the British tradition. Certainly, there is still room for the development of more sentencing options.

Both mainland China and Hong Kong adopt a "disciplinary welfare" approach in their juvenile justice systems (Gray, 1998). However, unlike mainland China where informal justice has been extensively used (See Chapter 8) there is no systematic means to involve unpaid and elected representatives in supervising offenders in the neighborhood. Moreover, Hong Kong has no volunteer probation officers as in Japan (See Chapter 5) but volunteers are sometimes used by probation officers to assist and befriend young offenders in the community. Basically, the whole criminal justice system is run by full-time, paid legal, welfare, and correctional professionals according to the rule of law. As such, the sentencing philosophy of mainland China, "leniency for self-confession, severe for resistance" (See Chapter 13) is totally disregarded. Those valuable elements of the common law, such as the right of silence and presumption of innocence, are upheld absolutely.

Since the handover of Hong Kong to China, many people have worried whether Hong Kong would sustain its rule of law and judicial independence, whether the death penalty would be reintroduced, and whether the ICAC would continue to maintain its independence. Writing in early February 1999, the writer concluded that the landmark ruling of the Court of Final Appeal on mainland-born Hong Kong children has eased some people's minds as to the feasibility of "one country, two systems" when it is applied in the criminal justice system. Moreover, it also proves that unlike Nigeria under military regimes 1966–1979, 1983–1998 (Ebbe, 1996), Hong Kong's judiciary is absolutely independent of the government. Nonetheless, Hong Kong is still a rich man's paradise. As in the United States, the rich and famous are sometimes beyond incrimination (See Chapter 2). The case of Aw Sian suggests that there is one law for the poor and another for the rich in Hong Kong. Tycoons can escape punishment for crimes for which the poor go to prison. In this regard, the principle of "equality before the law" has been damaged.

Discussion and Review Questions

1. What is the Basic Law of Hong Kong?
2. What are the rights of victims?
3. What are the rights of persons arrested by the police?
4. What is the court system?
5. What is the landmark ruling made by the Court of Final Appeal regarding its relationship with the NPC?
6. What are the factors affecting whether or not to prosecute an accused?
7. What are the similarities and differences between the Social Welfare Department and the Correctional Services Department?
8. Name the community treatment and custodial programs that the court can use to dispose offenders in Hong Kong.
9. What is meant by disciplinary welfare?
10. Suggest the alternatives to increased sentencing options for the court.
11. What are the sources of law in Hong Kong?
12. Of the three sources of law in Hong Kong, which one prevails in a case of conflict of the laws?
13. In what aspect of social control in Hong Kong does the Chinese customary law apply?
14. While crime rate is low in Hong Kong, what crimes are most frequently reported to the police?
15. Compare and contrast the following:
    (a) London Metropolitan Police Force
    (b) Hong Kong Police Force

(c) Royal Irish Constabulary

16. There is, approximately, one police officer for every 200 citizens in Hong Kong. Compare this police-citizen ratio in Hong Kong with the ratio in your own country, state, or city. Does the ratio of the number of police officers to the general population of your city, state, or country have anything to do with crime rate in your area?

17. What is ICAC? What are its roles in the Hong Kong criminal justice system?

18. What are the roles of the Judicial Officers Recommendation Commission?

19. What is the age of criminal responsibility in Hong Kong?

20. What is the place of corporal punishment and death penalty in the Hong Kong criminal justice system?

8

The Criminal Justice System of China

Yingyi Situ and Weizheng Liu

Introduction

In China, as in any other country, the criminal justice system is a particular sector of the national political system. Thus its development is greatly affected by changes in Chinese government. During the past century, China has experienced a number of social revolutions that changed an established legal system, and created a new one. Until the late 1970s, all attempts to establish a stable legal system failed because of the frequency of these social revolutions. The last such upheaval, the Great Proletarian Culture Revolution initiated by Mao Tse-tung, then Chairman of the Chinese Communist Party, ended with Mao's death in 1976. Since 1978, a new generation of Chinese Communists has begun to establish a more formal and stable criminal justice system, one more modern than Mao's from an international point of view.

Although the legal codes, institutions, and procedures of the Chinese criminal justice system have been altered constantly in the past century, one striking characteristic has remained constant in Chinese legal tradition: the society has been regulated not by one, but by two judicial systems. The first is a formal system composed of governmental institutions. The second is an informal system based on community vigilance. Both mechanisms influence revisions in the Chinese criminal justice system.

This chapter will provide a brief history of the Chinese criminal justice system, and then review its present formal and informal characteristics.

Chinese Legal Tradition

Chinese legal tradition can be traced as far back as 2,100 years ago, when one of the warring states began to use law as an instrument for maintaining social order (Chen, 1973:7). However, a sound, formal legal system based upon written law was never established in Imperial China (221 B.C.–1911) because of resistance from the dominant Confucian philosophy. This ideology emphasized social obligations and self-sacrifice. It required that individuals or groups in conflict resolve their differences through discussion and compromise (Brady, 1982). Under the state philosophy of Confucianism, legal procedures were not designed to protect individual rights or to give litigants redress, but served to discourage them from litigation, which was regarded as an extreme form of self-assertion (Brady, 1982; Lubman, 1983). The defendant, witnesses, and litigants alike were tortured, made victims of extortion, and humiliated in a casual and routine fashion throughout the judicial or penal processes (Brady, 1982). As a consequence, fear of encounters with the legal system prevailed.

Traditionally, the administration of law was handled by a governmental magistrate at the county level. The magistrate served as a general administrator of the area. He was a Confucian scholar, untrained in legal matters, and never regarded enforcement of the law as a function or specialty of the government. He would prefer that conflicts be resolved informally (Lubman, 1983).

Given the relatively large size of each magistrate's jurisdiction and the official animus against litigation, laws were rarely applied to local communities. Below the county level, groups—landlords, the village heads, the merchant guilds, the clan (which united all descendants from common ancestors) and the family—played a significant role in settling both civil and criminal cases.

The informal justice process usually was called mediation. The first line of settlement was the family or clan. Clan mediation was usually accomplished by the older males or local gentry who provided the clan's political leadership. Mediation between members of different clans was accomplished by the local government of the village. In such a case the locally appointed village constable or village headman often decided the course of compromise and/or punishment (Brady, 1982:38–39). The determination of wrongs and negotiation of punishments through mediation was not bound by legal codes. As in official courts, the informal justice followed the contours of power and wealth. Thus the decisions of clan, guild, or village mediator-elites considered both the facts of the case and the wealth, prestige, and political power of the conflicting parties (Brady, 1982:39).

Imperial history ended in 1911, when the Qing dynasty was overthrown. The postimperial Republic of China was spotted with warlordism, civil wars, war against the Japanese, exploitation from abroad, and corruption within the regime. The Kuomintang (Chinese Nationalist) attempts to reform the legal system were lim-

ited to the cities and compromised by corruption and ineptitude. The longstanding imperial social heritage and the disorder of the Kuomintang's ruling period kept China from developing a sound legal system during the first half of the twentieth century.

The ouster of the Kuomintang regime in 1949, and its replacement by the People's Republic, marked the beginning of a new and more interesting era. After seizing power, the Communist government immediately abolished all the laws of the Kuomintang, because it believed that those laws represented only the interest of the bourgeoisie, landlord classes, and feudal society. During the first 30 years of the Communist regime, the abolished laws were not replaced by new codes but by a mixture of statutes, rules, decrees, orders, Party regulations, and directives that were subject to changes based upon the ruling Party's whims. Political policy of the Party was the major guideline for the adjudication process.

The judicial system developed since the mid-1950s in Communist China adapted formal to informal tradition. The formal justice system was composed of three branches: the public security organ (the police), the people's court, and the people's procuratorates. A suspected offender would be arrested by a Public Security Bureau, formally indicted by a procurator, and convicted by a hierarchy of courts. Although on paper the judiciary was formally distinct from other Party and state apparatus, in practice it remained essentially subordinate to the Party. Since the Civil War days, the Communist Party has enjoyed judicial power in its base areas. At that time, all arrests and death sentences to be carried out were examined and approved by the area's Party committees. After the founding of the People's Republic of China (PRC), the Party continued this tradition. In serious cases, guidance from the Party committee was the major basis of adjudication: examinations and approvals by Party committees were required (*Encyclopedia of New China*, 1987).

The informal justice system (popular justice), which applied the forms for popular tribunals and mass movements, provided two functions. The first function was to apply punitive sanctions to "class enemies," thus handling "antagonistic contradictions." The second function handled "non-antagonistic contradictions" among working classes by "criticism and self-criticism" and mediation (Mao, 1966).

For the first 30 years of Communist rule, the informal or popular justice took precedence over bureaucratic justice: the Communist Party continued its radical revolutionary policies until 1978, shortly after Mao's death. The revolution finally fell into chaos during the Great Proletarian Culture Revolution (1966–1976), when bureaucratic justice was essentially abolished. Popular justice meant suppression of class enemies: landlords, rich peasants, capitalists, counterrevolutionaries, "bad elements" (all kinds of lawbreakers), rightists (those who disagreed with the Party's radical policies), "revisionists" (those Communist governmental officials who advocated professionalism), and intellectuals. This proletarian dictatorship was operated by radical Communist leaders and supported by radical students, poor peasants, and unskilled workers. Millions of "class enemies" were arrested and prosecuted by the "revolutionary organizations." They were tried without defense attorneys by "people's Tribunals," convicted and sentenced without a right to appeal.

The "cultural revolution" ended in 1976 with Mao's death and the arrest of his fellow radical Party leaders. Since then the pragmatic Party leaders have begun to restore and develop a formal legal system, but allowed it still to remain under the control of the Communist Party.

In 1979, the National People's Congress adopted the People's Republic of China's first code of criminal law and criminal procedure law. In the same year local Party organizations' power of examination and approval of cases was limited by abolishing their political–legal committees. The judicial institutions began to exercise more independent power. From 1976 to 1979, several important legal institutions and systems were established: the Legal System Commission of the Standing Committee of the National People's Congress, a legislative institution; the Ministry of Justice; the People's Procuratorate; the People's Courts; a lawyer system; a notarization system; and legal personnel training institutions.

In short, prior to the 1980s, the Chinese legal system underwent many changes because of evolution of the political system. But the development from a feudalist society, to a semifeudalist, semicolonial country, and then to a communist nation did not alter two characteristics of the Chinese criminal justice system. First, the tradition of combining both formal and informal mechanisms into an indistinguishable control entity has remained constant. Second, a well-developed formal legal system never appeared. Only in the 1980s did the Chinese criminal justice system enter a new constructive era.

We will now review the contemporary formal and informal justice systems in the People's Republic of China.

Formal Justice System

The present formal Chinese justice system[1] is composed of public security organs, state security organs, people's procuratorates, people's courts, and judicial administrative departments. The public security organs are responsible for investigation of crime, detention of suspects, formal arrest and pretrial custody, and preparatory examination. State security organs are charged with cases involving counterrevolutionary organizations and espionage operations. The people's procuratorate is responsible for approving arrests, conducting procuratorial control (including investigation), and initiating public prosecutions. The people's courts are responsible for adjudication. Finally, the judicial administrative departments are responsible for the execution of court judgments and decisions.

Court System

The people's courts in China consist of a unified, hierarchical system of four courts: basic people's court, intermediate people's court, higher people's court, and the Supreme People's Court. Additionally, there are special courts with special jurisdictions. The basic people's courts, established in each autonomous county, include criminal tribunals, civil tribunals, and economic tribunals. Most ordinary civil and criminal cases are handled in first-instance cases by the basic people's courts, although law requires that certain sorts be heard directly by the higher people's courts. In large geographical jurisdictions, the basic people's courts can establish separate people's tribunals according to the specific circumstances. The judgment and decisions of the people's tribunal carry the same weight as those of the basic people's courts.

The intermediate people's courts maintain criminal tribunals, civil tribunals, and economic tribunals, and they establish other tribunals when necessary. The cases handled by the intermediate people's courts are of four categories: (a) first-instance cases within their jurisdictions, such as counterrevolutionary cases, cases in which there may be a sentence of life imprisonment or death, and cases involving foreigners; (b) first-instance cases transferred from the basic people's courts; (c) appeals and counterpleas made by people challenging the judgments and decisions of the basic people's courts; and (d) cases protested by the people's procuratorate at the corresponding level.

The higher people's courts include criminal tribunals, civil tribunals, economic tribunals, and other tribunals established when necessary. Cases handled by the higher people's courts are of four types: (a) first-instance cases within their jurisdiction, including major criminal cases that affect an entire province; (b) first-instance cases transferred from the lower people's courts; (c) appeals and counterpleas made by people dissatisfied with the judgments and decisions of the intermediate people's courts; and (d) cases protested by the people's procuratorate at the corresponding level.

The Supreme People's Court (seated in Beijing) includes criminal tribunals, civil tribunals, and economic tribunals, and other tribunals set up when necessary. Cases handled by the Supreme People's Court include (a) first-instance cases exclusively within its jurisdiction, including major criminal cases with an impact on the entire country; (b) cases appealed and counterpleaded by people dissatisfied with the judgments and decisions of higher people's courts and special people's courts; and (c) cases protested by the Supreme People's Procuratorate according to supervisory proceedings. Judgments and decisions of first-instance or second-instance cases made by the Supreme People's Court all constitute judgments and decisions of the last instance, and they become legally effective the day they are announced. The primary function of the Supreme People's Court is to exercise leadership over lower level courts.

Special courts, established according to law for special departments or special cases, include military courts, maritime courts, and railway transportation courts. They handle cases within their own organizational systems. The military courts handle cases of violation of military codes and criminal cases involving servicemen. The maritime courts handle cases related to maritime affairs and businesses. And the railway transportation courts handle criminal cases that occur along rail lines and aboard trains, as well as cases of economic disputes related to rail transportation.

In China's unified, hierarchical court system, courts at higher levels oversee the administration of justice by those at lower levels. The Supreme People's Court, the highest judicial organ, supervises the administration of justice by local courts at different levels and by special courts. Its judgments and rulings are final. Few cases are tried at first instance by the Supreme People's Court.

The people's court is composed at each level of judicial officers: the president, vice-president, presiding judges, deputy presiding judges, judges, and a number of assistant judges. Judicial officers are elected and appointed by the organ of the state power. The presidents of different levels of courts are elected by people's congresses at corresponding levels. Vice-presidents, presiding judges, deputy presiding judges, and judges are appointed and dismissed by the standing committees of the people's congresses at corresponding levels. Assistant judges are appointed and dismissed by the courts at the same level. Assistant judges can act for judges at the suggestion of the president of the court and with the approval of the judicial committee. The courts are accountable only to the people's congresses at corresponding levels.

China's judicial organization includes special judicial committees that are set up at different levels of the people's courts. These committees do not try cases directly, but discuss and make decisions on the most important or difficult cases handled by collegiate benches of judges. They are also responsible for reviewing judicial actions and making recommendations on judicial work. The judicial committee exercises collective leadership over the judicial activity within each people's court. Members of the judicial committee are appointed or dismissed by the standing committee of the people's congress at the

request of the president of the court. Membership on the judicial committee is generally delegated to highly qualified professionals in the judiciary system who have considerable legal and political experience. Their meetings are presided over by the president of the court, and they follow the principle of majority rule.

Cases of minor criminal offenses and private prosecution can be tried by one judge. Adjudications of serious criminal cases in the first instance are conducted by a collegiate bench composed of one to three judges and two to four people's assessors, depending on the nature of the case and court level. Adjudications of appeals are final and are conducted by a collegiate bench composed of three to five judges. The people's assessors are lay people elected or invited temporarily. Citizens who have reached the age of 23 and are eligible to vote and stand for election may be elected as people's assessor. In carrying out their duties at the people's courts, people's assessors are component members of the courts in which they participate and enjoy equal rights with judges. When the collegiate bench conducts its deliberations, if opinions diverge, the minority defer to the majority, but the opinion of the minority is entered in the record. At the discretion of the presiding judge, major or difficult cases can be submitted to the judicial committee for discussion and decisions. The collegiate bench is obligated to carry out decisions made by the judicial committee.

The courts try cases and pronounce verdicts publicly. Cases that are not subject to an open trial as specified by law include those involving state secrets, privacy, personal secrets, and juvenile delinquency.

The accused in a criminal case has a right to self-defense. He or she has the right to argue the case, explain his or her innocence, or request mitigation or relief of punishment. The accused also has the right to hire a lawyer. The defense attorney can also be recommended by the accused's employer or by a citizen allowed by the court. Also, the accused can ask a close relative or guardian to defend his or her case in court. In such necessary cases as a trial with a public prosecutor, the court can appoint a lawyer for an accused with no one to speak in his or her favor.

Basically, the Chinese court system is an inquisitorial one in which the burden of proof rests on the accused, and the judge takes the leading role in the proceedings. Facts such as hard evidence, testimonies by witnesses, and the defendant's confessions are the basis for decisions made by people's courts. During the examination of facts, the defendant enjoys few of the due process rights that are commonly recognized in adversarial court systems such as that of the United States. The presumption of innocence, the exclusionary rule, protection against self-incrimination, the right to a jury trial, and protection against "double jeopardy" are alien to the Chinese courts.

Unlike such common law courts as those of the United States, Britain, Canada, Nigeria, or Ghana, the Chinese courts do not enjoy the power to make law. Judicial precedent, therefore, does not figure in the Chinese system of justice. Consequently, Chinese judges handle cases flexibly, according to the needs of the state at any given time, and do not strive for doctrinal consistency (Leng, 1982).

Procuratorate

The people's procuratorate is set up at levels corresponding with those of the people's courts. At all levels, a people's procuratorate does the following:

(a) Exercises its procuratorial power in cases of treason, national separatism, and ser-ious sabotage of the imple-mentation of state policies, laws, and governmental decrees

(b) Investigates those criminal cases that it directly handles

(c) Examines cases handled by public security organs to decide whether or not to issue arrest warrants, and whether or not to initiate and prosecute cases

(d) Supervises investigative pro-cesses to ensure that the public security organs conform to the law

(e) Supervises prosecution processes to ensure the legality of the judicial activities of the people's courts

(f) Reviews the legality of court judgments

(g) Supervises the execution of judgments in criminal cases

(h) Monitors the activities of prisons, detention houses, reformatories, and reform-through-labor establishments

People's procuratorates exercise a very important function in criminal cases. They approve arrests made or to be made by public security organs and determine whether or not to initiate prosecutions. It is also their responsibility to ensure equal treatment for criminal defendants as well as to discourage interference by other governmental agencies, officials, or private persons.

Public Security Organs

Public security organs (police) carry out the following main tasks: (a) investigation, detention, and making arrests; (b) securing the populace and maintaining public order; (c) safeguarding state organs, enterprises, and other institutions and establishments; (d) executing administrative punishment; and (e) handling administrative routines, such as residence registration and citizen exit and entry.

The public security organs are both hierarchical and local in organization. The

Ministry of Public Security of the central government directs the national police force through its provincial and local bureaus. In time of emergency, every local police officer can be mobilized through this vertical command system. In the meantime, public security organs at different levels are under the horizontal supervision and leadership of government agencies at the same levels. For example, the Ministry of Public Security is under the leadership of the State Council and the Beijing Public Security Bureau is a department of the Beijing Municipality.

The formal structure of the current system is described by a leading official of the Ministry of Public Security as follows:

The Ministry of Public Security is under the State Council, and the Social Security Bureau is a professional bureau under the ministry and consists of a criminal investigation department, and an institute of forensic science and technology. The public security bureaus of the provinces, municipalities directly under central government, and autonomous regions have social security and criminal investigation departments. The public security bureau at the prefecture level has a social security and criminal investigation section, and the public security bureau at the county level, a social security and criminal investigation team. In cities, the public security bureaus have their social security and criminal investigation divisions or sections. At the grass roots are located their police stations (Brewer et al., 1988).

In the police's hierarchical system, the most effective organization in social control may be the neighborhood police station. The neighborhood police handle all kinds of activities such as criminal investigation, peace keeping, residence registration, legal education, foot or bicycle patrol, and visiting offenders and their families within the jurisdiction. The police motto holds that the local police officers belong to the people, are not functionally and structurally separate from the masses,

and should be active in community affairs (Johnson, 1978). In order to promote good relations between the police and the masses, the neighborhood police officers serve the people in kindly ways such as sending sick to the hospital; helping the lost find their homes; shopping for the aged; removing garbage around the community; taking part in mediation to resolve conflicts; and educating the young and potential offenders. They also listen to people's comments and opinions in order to provide them with better services. In return, the neighborhood police require the residents to cooperate in crime prevention and investigation, and in watching out for potential offenders and strangers.

According to the Security Administration Punishment Act, which was first passed in 1957, republished in 1980, and amended in 1987, the police have the power to order and carry out "administrative punishment" in cases of minor crimes and public-order offenses by means of warnings, fines, and detention in police cells. The maximum fine is 400 yuan (the average monthly salary was about 100 yuan in 1987), and the maximum detention period is 15 days. A dissatisfied defendant has the right to appeal his sentence, first to a higher level in the Public Security Bureau, and ultimately to the courts. In minor cases the police alone carry out apprehension, adjudication, and correction without reference to the procurator, the courts, or the correctional institutions (Bracey, 1989b). The Security Administration Punishment Act made the police the most powerful organ in the Chinese criminal justice system.

State Security Organs

State security organs are secret police bureaus handling cases of counterrevolutionary (i.e., anti-Communist and/or anti–current government) organizations and foreign espionage. Little is known by the public of their organizations and tasks. Their subject matter jurisdictions are claimed to be similar to those of the public security organs in criminal cases (*Encyclopedia of New China*, 1987).

Lawyers

Traditionally, China had no formally recognized "lawyer system." An experiment in the legal profession was conducted in the mid-1950s, but was discontinued after only 3 years. The system was reestablished in response to the 1979 code of criminal law and criminal procedure law. By 1993, there were about 4,100 law firms and offices with 50,000 lawyers in China (Zhang, 1993).

The function of lawyers is to offer legal aid to state organs, institutions, people's organizations, enterprises, and citizens in order to ensure the correct implementation of state laws. Furthermore, the lawyers are to protect the interests of the state, collectives, and the lawful rights and interests of citizens. Lawyers are allowed the following scope of operations:

(a) To accept engagements from state organs, institutions, social organizations, and enterprises to act as their legal advisers

(b) To accept the authorization of parties to civil cases and act as agents taking part in prosecution

(c) To accept the authorization of parties to criminal cases or appointments of people's courts and act as defenders

(d) To accept the authorization of private parties in private prosecutions, injured parties in public prosecutions, or their immediate family members, to act as agents and take part in prosecutions

(e) To offer legal aid upon the authorization of parties involved in disputes, and to act as agents

taking part in mediation or arbitration

(f) To answer questions on law, and to draft indictments or complaints and other legal documents on behalf of parties to a lawsuit

In China, private legal profession is not permitted. Lawyers work either for government legal-advisory offices or in lawyer associations. Judges and procurators receive separate legal training and are not lawyers. In a criminal lawsuit, lawyers are not seen as defenders of individual rights or as protectors of opposition to the government. A lawyer is first and foremost responsible to the court, not to the client. If the client has confessed to his lawyer that he committed a crime, the lawyer must plead his client guilty of the offense: it is a criminal act in China for a lawyer to shield a guilty client. Since the notion of presumption of innocence is not accepted by the government, "seeking truth from the facts" has become the standard in criminal cases. Under this principle, a lawyer who has discovered that a client committed a criminal act cannot plead "not guilty" for him or her. The most the defense attorney can do in such a case is ask for leniency. Thus, as indicated by Ingraham (1987), Chinese lawyers emphasize substantive justice much more than procedural justice.

Corrections

The judicial administrative organs are responsible for all correctional activities except for juvenile work-study schools used for reforming minor juvenile offenders, and police jails used for short-term administrative punishment. The Ministry of Justice of the central government, and bureaus and departments of justice at various levels, have been judicial administrative organs since 1983, replacing the Ministry of Public Security.

China has more than six hundred correctional institutions with 1.1 million inmates (Chen, 1993). Correctional institutions include provincial and municipal prisons, reform-through-labor camps, and juvenile reformatories, where convicts serve fixed term imprisonments, life imprisonments, or death sentences with a suspension of 2 years. Most serious offenders are assigned to reform-through-labor camps.

Punishment and rehabilitation are both included in Chinese corrective philosophy, and both are carried out by the policy of reform-through-labor. This policy is based on the belief that people are basically good, albeit corruptible; that bad examples and bad company can lead individuals astray; that education is the best tool for systemic and individual reform; and that people are malleable throughout their lives (Bracey, 1989a; Munro, 1977).

The process of reform-through-labor relies on combining labor production with political education. All prisoners with the physical ability to do so are required to work. The prison administration operates factories and farms and obtains subcontracts from outside enterprises. Inmates are not paid beyond a small regular allowance, since labor is one way to repay society for their wrongdoing. The products of prison labor are turned over to the state. The length of labor is generally limited to 9 or 10 hours daily. During the busiest production seasons, the length of labor is 12 hours a day, at most (*Encyclopedia of New China*, 1987:186). Juvenile convicts are organized to do appropriate light labor, taking into consideration their age and health needs.

In both juvenile and adult institutions, political education is used to rehabilitate and reform. Political education includes legal education such as study of laws and regulations, and moral education in socialist ideology (e.g., positive attitudes toward work, acceptance of collectivism) and social ethics. Self-criticism and mutual criticism are an important part of the process. Everybody is supposed to confess his or her crime and make self-criticism in public. Juvenile inmates, as well as adults, may receive cultural education at their own level—from elementary school through college. Vocational education is available in most of the institutions.

By their policy of meting out rewards, correctional institutions give convicts a chance to perform meritorious services to atone for their crimes. Convicts with good records are given oral commendations, are offered material rewards, have their terms of imprisonment reduced, or are granted parole. On the other hand, those who either refuse to repent or refuse to accept reform-through-labor are punished. Those found to have committed additional criminal offenses or new sorts of crimes during their term of reform-through-labor are referred to the people's procuratorate.

Often the Chinese correctional system has been regarded as a humane, natural, and practical model for the West (Allen, 1987). However, it is necessary to realize that Chinese authorities' patience has not been unlimited. Their intolerance can be found in three different situations. First, if the correctional officers' genuine commitment to help inmates bears no fruit, they may terminate further efforts. Second, "punishing one to warn a hundred" is an accepted correctional principle, and its implementation has resulted in the execution of thousands of habitual criminals and dangerous offenders who committed crimes ranging from murder, rape, and bribery to political dissension. Third, in the political and judicial campaigns against various specific offenders, severe penalties can be imposed on convicts without allowing for the possibility of reform. These campaigns are usually launched by the central or local governments and are designed to "frighten the criminal, encourage healthy trends, give publicity to the legal system and educate the masses" (*Questions and Answers*, 1986:147).

According to a 1983 decision of the Standing Committee of the National People's Congress, sentences are allowed to exceed the maximum punishment fixed in the criminal code during campaigns against some offenders (Xu, 1992:18). For instance, in the current campaign against smuggling illegal immigrants into foreign countries, the legal secretariat of the Party's Central Committee declared that in order to stop such illegal activity effectively, the organizers of smuggling must be punished severely, and the death penalty is one of the alternatives (Ren, 1993).

Thus, both rehabilitation and punishment are considered philosophies of Chinese correction, and the Chinese correctional system is capable of being lenient on one hand and severe on the other.

From the preceding discussion, one can tell that the functions of formal Chinese criminal justice institutions are designed to support each other when handling criminal cases, and to provide checks and balances. For example, the procuratorate supervises investigations by the public security organ, examining and approving arrests and prosecutions. It also oversees trials and deliberations of verdicts by the court. Also, if the public security organ disagrees with a procuratorial decision such as not to arrest or to sue, it can ask for reconsideration. If its suggestion is rejected, it can ask for review by the procuratorate at a higher level. If the court finds that the facts are unclear or insufficient to support the procuratorate's prosecution, it can return the prosecution to the procuratorate for a supplement. If the case is not important enough to follow up, it can ask the procuratorate to retract its suit or refuse to accept it.

One must also realize the importance of the relationship between the Chinese Communist Party (CCP) and the Chinese criminal justice system. Although the CCP has separated considerably from the state legal system since 1978, Party policy still plays a key role in judicial work. The justice system does not enjoy actual judicial independence in most significant cases. Under the principle of "strengthening party leadership," which is considered one of the four cardinal principles for modernizing China, one cannot expect the influence and control of the CCP to disappear in the near future.

Informal Justice System

More than in most other nations, informal justice[2] is an organic part of the entire Chinese criminal justice mechanism. The formal system and the informal system are connected with each other and are often fused. The teaching of proper behavior and the controlling of lawbreaking run a parallel course through formal and informal methods (Krase and Sagarin, 1980). The current policy of comprehensive treatment for social order focuses not only on formal judicial measures, but on informal combining of all political, economic, executive, educational, cultural, and judicial methods. The implementation of informal justice relies heavily on the activities of neighborhood public security committees (PSCs), people's mediation committees, and the security departments of enterprises and institutions.

According to the 1982 Chinese Constitution, each urban neighborhood committee and rural village committee is made up of a public security committee, a people's mediation committee, and other public affairs committees (Article 111). These unofficial organizations are grounded in citizen participation through a network of committees composed of unpaid, elected representatives who are usually retired governmental cadres and workers.

The public security committee (PSC) can be used by local police for mobilizing the residents to participate in crime prevention. In 1992, there were more than 1.17 million public security committees nationwide and more than 12 million PSC members (Xu, 1992). The major functions of the PSC are as follows:

(a) To assist the judicial organs in criminal investigations by (e.g.)

cordoning off the scene of a crime, informing the police of any suspect, conducting surveillance of the defendant prior to trial, and supervising the convicts on suspended sentences or parole, or when they are out of custody for medical treatment.

(b) To patrol, inspect, and safeguard the neighborhood. In the daytime, safety sentries are posted in key areas, and at night, foot patrol is widely used.

(c) To identify and advise potential offenders. The PSC analyzes and identifies those who have criminal histories and are potential offenders in the neighborhood. PSC members are assigned as advisors to potential offenders in order to help them resolve usual problems such as residence registration, employment, marriage, and family. The advisors also educate and discipline potential offenders to drive them back into conventional society.

(d) To investigate and determine the causes of some minor offenses such as petty larceny and fist-fighting. In this case, the PSC plays the role of police and judge. Punishment could be a written self-criticism.

(e) To popularize legal concepts and advise citizens to observe the law.

(f) To help mediators to settle civil disputes and prevent such controversies from developing into criminal offenses.

The PSC has yielded positive results by discovering, controlling, halting, and preventing crime. In 1988, 35,985 criminals of all kinds were apprehended by PSC members and other informal justice organizations in three municipalities—Beijing, Shanghai, and Tianjin. The PSC also helped the police uncover 19,193 criminal cases (Xu, 1992).

Another important informal justice agency is the people's mediation committee (PMC). According to the 1982 Constitution of PRC, Article 111, there must be a people's mediation committee under each neighborhood committee in urban areas and under each village committee in rural areas. People's mediation committees may also be set up in enterprises and institutions. By the end of 1988, there were about 1 million mediation committees in China with 6.37 million mediators (Si, 1989).

The history of mediation in China can be traced back 2,000 years to when the principles of Confucianism reformed the Chinese people's behavior. The Confucians believed that criminal punishment could not bring people to awareness of high morals in human society; educating the offenders and the general public in moral principles, on the other hand, could assure knowledge of the correct way to behave. Therefore, only the most serious offenses would be left for the formal justice authority to deal with by punishment. The vast majority of civil disputes and less serious criminal offenses were disposed of locally, most of them through mediation that was regarded as a form of moral education.

Although some changes have occurred in the structure and process of nonjudicial conflict management, the basic principles of out-of-court mediation of conflict have remained in contemporary dealings between persons and organizations.

People's mediation committees operate under the guidance of local governments and local people's courts, and the legal assistant of local government is in charge of mediation committee affairs. Members of the people's mediation committee are elected by the people living or working in the PMC's jurisdiction. They are volunteers and "solid citizens"—retired or current workers and petty officials, usually older and respected, maintaining close links with the masses, enthusiastic in promoting public welfare, and having some legal knowledge.

The system of people's mediation is a necessary element in mass self-government, self-control, self-administration, and self-education. The mediator works at the request of the people involved in a conflict and can also intervene directly in a conflict without being requested to do so. Because the mediator lives in the community, he or she is usually able to respond to the incident quickly. The service is free. In settling a dispute, the mediator is not entitled to use any forceful administrative or legal measures. The basic method of response and intervention is reasoning and persuasion. During mediation, laws and policies are explained to the parties concerned. Public morale is discussed and the interests of each party are balanced, commonly resulting in compromise. In the 1980s, about 7 million conflicts were resolved annually through mediation (Si, 1989).

Entering mediation is based on the principle of voluntariness. Not every disputing party must go through the process of mediation. If one of the parties refuses to enter mediation, or if the mediation effort fails, or if one of the parties decides to bring the case up again after having first accepted the results of mediation, he or she can file a lawsuit directly at a court or request the local government's decision. However, according to the "People's Mediation Committee Organic Rules" (1989), once the parties concerned enter mediation and once a mediated agreement is reached, each party should carry out the agreement. In other words, the mediated agreement has the force of law, and any violation of the agreement may result in a lawsuit (Ai, 1989).

The people's mediation committees are responsible for settling ordinary civil disputes and minor criminal cases. They also familiarize the people with laws and government policies. Ordinary civil disputes occur over such issues as neighborhood relations, housing, debts, marriage, family,

compensation for losses, inheritance, division of family property, provision of livelihood for aged parents, and support of children after a divorce. Minor criminal cases include such offenses as minor physical injury, maltreatment, petty larceny, encroachments, scuffles or fist fights, and slander. Generally, the people's mediation committee procedures are quite casual, unhurried, and nonstandardized. However, there is some formality: keeping of records, preparing of agreements, and standardizing of the physical arrangements of the mediation sessions (Clark, 1989). Results of mediation are filed and written agreements may be issued at the request of the interested parties.

In addition to the resident neighborhood and village PSCs and PMCs, security departments are also set up in such large enterprises as factories, companies, universities, and government bureaus, as part of the informal criminal justice system. The personnel of such security departments are generally full-time professionals, many with military or police experience. When necessary, they can carry weapons for enforcing the law. Functions carried out by the security departments are quite similar to those carried out by the public security committees: they assist the police in investigating crimes inside the enterprise; they handle some minor offenses, both investigating and punishing; they safeguard properties of the enterprise; they supervise probationers and parolees in the enterprise; and they popularize laws and regulations, advising employees to observe the law. Working together with other formal and informal judicial agencies, the security departments play a very important role in crime prevention and in settling minor offenses.

All of these informal justice mechanisms have significantly regulated behavior, controlling crime and maintaining social order, but they are not informal justice in the sense often meant by Western criminologists. These committees and departments are part of the local administrative structures mandated by Chinese Executive Laws, and they are guided by the Communist Party and its governmental policies. Thus, in China, the state remains ultimately in charge of both the formal and the informal justice mechanisms. It not only implants its ideology in these informal agencies, but actually controls their operations. These organizations are informal in the Western sense only by their use of persuasion, reasoning, and administrative methods to settle disputes and combat crime, instead of mobilizing the police, going to court, and sentencing an offender to imprisonment.

To summarize, Chinese society historically has been regulated by two criminal justice systems. The formalized bureaucratic justice based on the centralized government emphasized punishment and reforming the convict. Popular, informal justice is rooted in community associations and emphasizes mediation and education. Basically, formal justice deals with the serious offenders, punishing them for their misconduct, and reforming them into "new people"; informal justice manages minor and potential offenders, helping them to resolve problems that may result in criminal activity, and educating them by promoting laws and public morals. The two systems complement each other, sharing a common aim: shouldering and pressuring the deviant back into tracks set by the society's norms and the nation's power base.

Notes

1. The discussion of the formal criminal justice system in this section draws heavily on *The Criminal Law and the Criminal Procedure Law of China* (1984); "The Criminal Procedure Law of the People's Republic of China" (1982); the *Encyclopedia of New China* (1987); Felkenes, "Courts, Sentencing, and the Death Penalty in the PRC" (1989); McCabe, "Structural Elements of

Contemporary Criminal Justice in the People's Republic of China" (1988); and Min Zhang and Shan Changzong, "Inside China's Court System" (1990).

2. The major sources for this section include our personal experiences; Y. Fang, "Public Security Organization" (1988); Clark, "Conflict Management outside the Courtrooms of China" (1989); and the *Encyclopedia of New China* (1987).

Discussion and Review Questions

1. Why did imperial China have no written constitution?

2. Compare and contrast individual rights in China and Denmark.

3. What are the three branches of the formal justice system in China?

4. Why were the Kuomintang laws abolished in 1949?

5. What are the two main functions of the informal justice system in China?

6. What is meant by popular justice in China?

7. What is the modus operandi of popular justice in China?

8. What are the four categories of cases handled by intermediate people's courts in China?

9. What cases are handled by the Supreme People's Court?

10. Describe briefly the role of Chinese judicial committees in the criminal justice system.

11. What are the functions of the Procuratorate?

12. What are the functions of neighborhood police?

13. Compare and contrast customary courts in Nigeria and the Chinese informal courts.

14. Compare and contrast the role of lawyers in American and in Chinese criminal justice systems.

15. What are the functions of public security committees?

16. Briefly explain the following:
    (a) Urban Neighborhood Committee
    (b) Rural Village Committee
    (c) People's Mediation Committee

17. Who are People's Assessors? How does a person become a member of People's Assessors Committee?

18. Write a short account on the following:
    (a) Security Administration Punishment Act.
    (b) People's Mediation Committee.
    (c) Trial by a single judge.
    (d) State Security Organ.

19. To what extent is the independence of the judiciary practised in China?

20. How many correctional institutions are there in China? How many inmates were there in Chinese prisons in 1996?

Part III
Comparative Policing

9

Separate but Equal

Nondiscriminatory Policy and Practice in British and American Policing

Ian K. McKenzie

Introduction

In the American capital lies the nation's conscience. The National Archives in Washington, D.C., contains the paperwork of nationhood: the original documentation of the American Constitution, the Declaration of Independence, and the Bill of Rights. Alongside these historic records stands an exhibition of oppression: the persecution of the Native Americans, the injustice of the "peculiar institution" of slavery, and the oppression of religious minorities. There is a link in this historical collection between two nations that share a "special relationship": the United States of America and the United Kingdom.

Ignore the fiscal incompetence of King George III; dismiss the outcome of the Revolutionary War; set aside the Churchillian notion of "two nations divided by a common language": the link is far more fundamental. In the Archives, close to the American documentation, lies a 1297 version of Magna Charta, presented by Ross Perot, its presence intended to show to the nation the source of the idea of codification.

The shared heritage of these two nations also includes direct involvement in slavery, active participation in genocide, and religious oppression of such an order that many of the American colonies were founded in order to escape it.

That darker link remains a shared concern. Although there has been improvement in equality and equal opportunity for minorities and special needs groups, continued improvement remains critically important. This paper will address equal opportunities issues in law enforcement, particularly police activities in relation to three specific groups: women, members of ethnic minorities, and homosexuals.

The Structure of Policing

Before considering hiring and employment practices for these three groups, we shall briefly discuss the nature of policing in the two nations. The land mass of Britain (England and Wales, Scotland, and Northern Ireland) is about the same size as Georgia, but Georgia has a population of about 4 million while Britain's is close to 55 million. Britain has three separately administered units of police activity that differ significantly: England and Wales, Scotland, and Northern Ireland. Northern Ireland has one single, national police force—the Royal Ulster Constabulary (RUC). Policing in Scotland and in England and Wales, which was once centered in villages, towns, boroughs, cities and counties, is now administered and controlled in Scotland through eight regional forces, and in England and Wales through 43 constabularies.

There are a number of commonalities between these three elements of British policing. Every force is supervised by a chief constable (called a commissioner in the two London forces), and each constable has independent authority. Only one police force in England and Wales has fewer than 1,000 officers, and the average establishment has approximately 3,500 sworn staff. Some of the resources for British policing are centralized, and slightly more than half of the necessary funding comes from the central government, but each chief constable is autonomous and is theoretically able to interpret British constitutional law free from political interference, especially in "operational matters" (McKenzie and Gallagher, 1989). Currently, chief officers have considerable security of tenure, with some serving for 10 years or more. Supervision of police activity is undertaken by officials of the Home Office and through the Home Secretary of the British Cabinet. Also, the public has a limited involvement in policing through "police authorities," a partly elected body of people loosely analogous to public safety committees in the United States.

The law and the administration of law, however, do differ in each of Britain's three major geographical areas. The RUC, the regional police forces in Scotland, and the 43 forces in England and Wales are considered, for all practical purposes, separate entities. Much of what follows is, to some extent, applicable to all these entities, but hereafter we will concentrate on equal opportunity (EO) issues as they apply to England and Wales, with no reference to other parts of the United Kingdom.

The constitutional autonomy of the chief constable means, in practice, that the Home Office does not seek to impose direction of either policy or practice on individual chief constables. The Home Office, rather, issues "memoranda" that each chief can accept, adapt, or (in theory) ignore. In many areas, this procedure has produced disparate policy and practice, in some cases making comparisons difficult.

In the America, the 17,613 police departments (McKenzie and Gallagher, 1989) are a complex and multifaceted, multitiered arrangement, defying taxonomy. Jurisdictional conflicts and direct political involvement, including involvement in operational matters are (by British standards) commonplace. Departments can range in size from fewer than ten officers to thousands, but 98.1% of departments have fewer than 200 sworn staff (McKenzie and Gallagher, 1989). Chiefs cannot depend on security of tenure, particularly where their post requires popular election.

Access to Work: Legislation and Background

England and Wales

In Britain, access to work is controlled theoretically by the provisions of the Race Relations Act (1975), the Sex Discrimination Act (1975), and the Equal Pay Act (1970). This legislation encouraged employers to exercise fairness in hiring and retention practices and was intended to prevent overt discrimination. At the same time, the legislation attempts to ensure that the ethnic majority does not suffer unfair disadvantages. Two government-funded bodies support this national and legalistic approach to equality: the Commission for Racial Equality (CRE) and the Equal Opportunities Commission (EOC). Both seek to mediate complaints of discrimination, but neither often prosecutes.

The existence of two supervisory bodies, each charged with the oversight of grievance procedures and with necessary mediation, is an anomaly. The separation implies that race is a different problem from equality, a view supported by Fairmanner (1992), who cites the claim of the vice-chairman of the EOC that there remains "a clear delineation . . . between the duties of the CRE and those of the

EOC." The Home Office (Home Office, 1989a) has suggested that minority ethnic recruitment in policing should not be considered under the category of "discrimination," but rather under the more general category of "equal opportunities." Nevertheless, the Race Relations Board has continued to exist, and the notional separation in other social and work areas will continue.

United States

In America, equal opportunity to work is controlled by the Equal Opportunity Act of 1964 (42 USC, 2000e et seq.), the Equal Pay Act of 1963 (29 USC, 206(d)), and the Age Discrimination Employment Act of 1967 (29 USC, 261 et seq.). The Equal Opportunity Employment Act, otherwise referred to as Title VII of the Civil Rights Act of 1964, prohibits preferential treatment of minorities and has "created more litigation than the other two acts combined" (Yett, 1989).

The Department of Justice has declared its intention to use vigorously "litigation and the threat of litigation to achieve the hiring rights of minorities and women" (Raphey, 1979). However, this has effectively limited the potentials of the legislation. Fortunately, the litigation itself has nullified these limitations. The possibility of some employers not obeying the Equal Opportunity Acts, and of women and minorities suffering discrimination without government intervention, is eliminated in the United States through litigation, as the Acts did not provide for a stringent enforcement mechanism. Case law and the interpretation of the statutes have produced a system that seeks to ensure that selection and retention criteria are "job related," and thus, in theory, not discriminatory in any direction.

Practices Prohibited under American Equal Opportunity Legislation

Disparate treatment cases (Subsection (a)(1)) are those in which a claimant alleges that an employer has treated him or her less favorably than others because of his or her race, color, religion, sex, or national origin (*International Brotherhood of Teamsters v. United States,* 431, US 324 (1977)). Burden of proof rests on the plaintiff; and because one form of disparate treatment is failure to hire or promote based on unjustifiable and discriminatory grounds, this provision has been interpreted as meaning that "everyone is part of a protected class. Black males are part of a protected class, but so are white females, black females, Hispanic males, Hispanic females, Italian males, and white males" (Yett, 1989 and *McDonald v. Santa Fe Trail Company,* 427 US 273 (1976)).

A disparate impact case (subsection (a)(2)) is a form of class action case. The attack is on a specific employment practice. Written tests, specific objective requirements, or height/weight requirements might be included in such cases. Burden of proof shifts in such cases from the plaintiff to the defendant and back again (*Albermarle Paper Company v. Moody,* 422 US 405 (1975)). Proceedings are complex because each side attempts to establish that the criterion under discussion either is or is not job related. In addition to federal law, there are state laws of similar nature: examples would include the Municipal Civil Service System set out in Chapter 143 of the Texas Local Government Code, the Texas Commission on Human Rights Act of 1983, and similar legislation in other states.

Comparisons

What happens in the United States today, they say, will happen in the United Kingdom in the next 10 years. Nowhere is this clearer than in the legislation produced in each country to deal with discrimination in the workplace. But whatever one might say of equal opportunity legislation and its trends, discriminatory behavior in hiring and retention has been combated more successfully by American reliance on litigation, and through associated developments such as the Civil Service Reform Act of 1978 and the Equal Opportunity Commission's requirements that one avoid unfairness in hiring and maintain equality and job relatedness in on-the-job evaluations. The multi-million-dollar awards made to successful litigants in some cases have encouraged employers to search for positive discrimination programs, affirmative action initiatives, and other avoidance behaviors. In Britain these are so few as to be almost nonexistent.

Approaches in the United Kingdom have been very different. Resorting to litigation has been the exception rather than the rule. According to research, many police officers believe that "positive discrimination is degrading and insulting" to serving minority officers (Taylor, Ainsworth, and Gallan, 1990). This perception is used as a lever to ensure that both positive discrimination and quotas are avoided (Scarman, 1981).

There is no legislation in the United Kingdom that allows the central government to restrict funding to constabularies that fail to comply with equal opportunity requirements. In North America there is the Canadian Employment Equity Act and the American law for "Contract Compliance" (i.e., denial of federal funding to public and private organizations that fail to meet "formal hiring quota" objectives set as part of the funding contract). The "mediate, mollify, and minimize policy" of the British approach, by contrast, fails to address the critical need for minority ethnic representation in policing.

Litigation in Britain is confined to hearings before tribunals; criminal or civil hearings like those in America that assess financial liability through jury deliberations

are not available. Although many Americans and non-Americans are critical of American litigation, substantial financial liability (or the threat of it) is a powerful force toward compliance. In Britain awards are generally "capped,"[1] and no such fiscal levers operate.

Access to Policing

Minority Ethnic Groups

In 1981, street riots occurred in Brixton, South London. The Brixton Street Disorders were precipitated by the intervention of police officers after a black youth had been stabbed in a street incident. A large crowd of people that gathered around the scene of the incident claimed that the police had caused the injury. When the police officers decided to take the youth to a hospital in a police vehicle, the angry mob began to throw stones, starting a general street disorder that continued for 3 days.

The underlying causes were later determined in the "Lord Scarman Inquiry" to have emanated from the neighborhood's distrust and suspicion of the police practice of "stop and search" procedures, and as a consequence of a special operation (called Swamp 81) designed to control thefts and robberies in the area. This special operation entailed large numbers of police officers patrolling the Brixton area (both on foot and in cars). Lord Scarman considered the strain of such patrols on police–community relations to be excessive (Scarman, 1981).

Lord Scarman's report suggested that steps should be taken to eliminate or control overt racist behavior by police officers against minority-group citizens, and to increase the number of ethnic minority police officers. In later reports, it was argued that efforts toward recruiting ethnic minorities were needed to ensure that "all officers understand that . . . the effect of months of hard work by officers at all levels can be destroyed by an isolated act of rudeness or insensitivity" (Home Office, 1982). The report also indicated a need to "make it clear that black and Asian[2] officers are treated the same as white officers by their colleagues and supervisors."

The Brixton Street disorder also prompted an offense of "racially discriminatory behavior" to be added to the national discipline regulations of the Police and Criminal Evidence Act (1984). Although this disciplinary offense apparently addresses police–citizen encounters, it could also be used as a sanction in police versus police encounters. So far, it has not been so used.

Pettigrew (1989) proposed that the single best predictor of a riot is the number of minority police officers in a police department: a conclusion that must be deeply insulting to law-abiding minority group members who feel underrepresented in the policing of their community. The Home Office committed itself to resolving underrepresentation in British policing in 1986. This commitment, however, turned out to be a fudging exercise of the first order. Although the Office declared that it intended to achieve clear policy objectives and to demonstrate a viable and effective race relations policy by chief police officers, it refused to undertake direct intervention, choosing instead to adopt a supportive role.

This supportive role allows each chief officer to develop his or her own program of recruiting, monitoring, and retention— as it must do under British constitutional law. Many critics of this approach (Holdaway, 1990; Luthra, 1986) believed that attempts at reform without a clear, centrally directed strategy would be beyond the abilities of individual police organizations, especially in cases of promotion, appraisal, and the management of organizational change. At a national police seminar on equal opportunities, Skitt (1991) tried to introduce and explain such a centrally directed strategy by pointing out that true equal opportunity would require both individual and organizational

change. He added that the hierarchical and militaristic structure of policing led officers to believe that any group that did not conform to required behaviors could be labeled and dealt with as troublemakers; therefore, complaints of discrimination by both ethnic minority officers and women had been crushed and/or dismissed as mendacious. The view that litigation produces change rather than mediation was supported in *Nottinghamshire Constabulary v. Constable S. Singh* (1990),[3] where the finding was in favor of the plaintiff. The court also noted that the Home Office, Her Majesty's Inspector of Constabulary, and the Association of Chief Police Officers had admitted that the problem did not solely relate to the force named in the case, nor solely to the specific difficulty of selecting detectives.

In the United States, as in Britain, many of the attempts to improve minority representation in policing resulted from street disorder. As Holdaway (1990) points out:

> "Civil disturbances acted as a catalyst to a public consciousness of civil rights and a protest movement among black Americans. Legal change followed, first within a framework of equal opportunities. Affirmative action then developed as a prelude to the acceptance of positive discrimination and the setting of formal hiring quotas."

There are a plethora of cases in the United States that relate specifically to law enforcement (e.g., *Afro American Patrolman's League v. Duck*, 503 F, 2d 294 (6th Cir. 1974); *Hervey v. City of Little Rock*, 787 F. 2d 1223 (8th Circuit; 1986)).

Sex

Equal opportunity combats not only racism, but sexism as well. The lot of women in policing, despite an earlier entry than ethnic minority group members, has been and continues to be difficult. A review of literature, however, shows no cases of riots over underrepresentation of women in policing. Many women believe, however, that access to various positions will not guarantee promotion and unbiased appraisal.

The recently abandoned minimum height requirement for British police forces was effectively a form of institutional racism. Such implicit forms of discrimination against ethnic minority group members differ from the overtly discriminatory grounds on which women are rejected. Rejection on racial grounds has often been based on intellectual capacity, motivation to work, and acceptability to the public. Rejection on grounds of gender has been, in the main, based on negative assessments of physical competency, leadership ability, motivation to become a police officer, reasons for continuing to serve, and stress proneness (Coffee, Brown, and Savage, 1992). Of these, policemen's perceptions about women's physical competency have been most damaging. The stereotype of the "little woman" who is "only fit for two things and the other one's making coffee" has minimal justification, but tremendous power.

Studies in both the United Kingdom and the United States have repeatedly shown, despite beliefs to the contrary, that there is little difference between females and males in the measures of physical competency, leadership ability, motivation to become a police officer, reasons for continuing to serve, and stress proneness. In any case, the first of these factors may well be based on overvaluing of the importance of physical strength in patrol tasks. Furthermore, in an overview of a number of American studies, Balkin (1988) found that female officers performed as well as male officers in a wide range of assignments.

Nevertheless, it is the alleged physical danger of police work that predisposes male officers to use "protect the little woman" as a rationale to exclude women from policing: it is said that women should not be exposed to physical injury and death, and that in the event of life-threat-

ening duty a male officer should feel obliged to show "good breeding" by laying his life on the line. Such responses epitomize male attitudes toward female officers. According to research on both sides of the Atlantic, females can expect to achieve the full confidence neither of their supervising officers nor of their working colleagues, and they cannot expect to achieve the full range of duties attainable by male officers (Martin, 1979; Jones 1987). Past research did suggest that some women in policing lacked career ambition, avoided promotion, and sought only to fulfill a feminine role in police work (Martin, 1979), but this trend seems to have changed.

Coffee, Brown, and Savage (1992), who asked women about their own experiences and compared their answers with the experiences of their male colleagues, demonstrated "that serving police women do aspire to specialist duties but are often inhibited from . . . applying in the first instance or believe that they are thwarted from being appointed because of perceived prejudice." Similar trends have been noted in Scotland (CPS, 1989).

Americans can cite Chiefs Elizabeth M. Watson (Austin PD, TX), Cathleen Manchester (Norway, Maine), Mary Ann Viverette (Gaithersburg, MA), Joan M. Henderson (Decatur, Michigan), Linda K. Wait (Union City, Michigan), and Linda K. Weaver (Johnstown, PA) as examples of women's freedom of access to head administrative positions in policing; Britain, however, cannot cite any examples, and this includes Scotland and Northern Ireland. McKenzie and Gallagher (1989) submitted that it was safe to refer to Chief Officers in the United Kingdom as "him" because in 1988 there were "no female chiefs yet." Since then, nothing has changed.

In the early months of 1992 there was more action in equality efforts than ever before, at least in policing circles. Alison Halford, an assistant chief constable (ACC) in the Merseyside police, took action through the Equal Opportunities Commission against the Home Office, against her chief constable, against one of Her Majesty's Inspectors of Constabulary (HMI), and against the Northamptonshire police authority (roughly the equivalent of an American Public Safety Commission) to whom she had applied for a post as deputy chief constable. The case was brought on the grounds that she had been denied access to a higher rank (viz., deputy chief constable) because of her sex. Halford was the first of three female officers to rise to the rank of assistant chief constable. She claimed that she was denied nine applications made for higher posts, and that the posts were awarded to officers who were her inferiors in merit and experience. The respondents countered with allegations of homosexuality, excessive alcohol consumption, and unprofessional conduct.

Halford's problems began, by her own admission, when she responded to a publication by Lock (1987). Lock posed a question about the likelihood of appointing a woman a chief officer by asking, "How long must she wait?" Halford (1987) cynically replied: "Until the twelfth of never." This response was used against her. In that article, Halford spoke of the "inability of some very senior men to cope with a woman of comparable rank," of "strong but covert resentment or mistrust of the competence of a woman," and of male perception of an "oddness" in a woman wanting to progress in her career at the expense of a male competitor, "who after all has a family to support."

The Halford case highlighted many embarrassing macho elements in policing, even at a high level. Following weeks of sensational allegations of repeated drunkenness and gross and sexist behavior (Independent, 20 July 1992), all made and carefully reported in painful detail, the blinding glare of publicity proved too much for the plaintiff. An out-of-court settlement was the only viable alternative, and it was consummated.[4]

Because the case did not achieve a final conclusion within a judicial or even quasi-judicial process, the question of women's rights inside the British police has not been resolved. Women in British policing were poorly served, and some people have shown some concern about it (Bevins, 1992).

In 1992 about 15% of all officers in the United Kingdom were women. Home Office figures (July, 1992), however, showed that 14 of the 43 forces had no female officer at ranks higher than inspector (roughly equivalent to lieutenant or second-level supervisor), and that 2 of those forces had no female officer higher than a sergeant. Of the remaining 29 forces, 3 women held the rank of assistant chief constable. There were 11 chief superintendents and 29 superintendents (Bevins, 1992). Behind the scenes, the Home Office, Her Majesty's Inspectors of Constabulary, and the Association of Chief Police Officers probably have accepted that (as in the Singh litigation) the problems go beyond Halford's particular force, and beyond the particular issue of promotion of women to the highest levels of the organization. As Commander Sally Hubbard, an Assistant HMI, put it (Independent, July 26, 1992), "The Halford case has made police forces around the country realize that their policies and procedures are not as equitable as they thought."

British sex-discrimination cases, as in the case of racial discrimination directly related to law enforcement, are few. In U.S. law, on the other hand, multitudes of cases have taken place, with both the litigation itself and the attached financial awards having a positive effect. Two cases particularly stand out. In *Thorne v. City of El Sequenda*, 726, F2d 459 (9th Circuit, cert. denied, 469 US 979 (1984)), a female applicant for a position as a police officer proved that sex discrimination kept her from being hired. The defendant showed that responses in a polygraph examination relating to her sexual activities had affected her prospective employer's hiring decision, and these were seen by the court as being irrelevant. In *Curl v. Reavis*, 740 F. 2d 1323 (4th Circuit 1984), a female deputy sheriff won her sex discrimination case upon showing that she had been denied promotion to a road patrol position by the sheriff. The latter contended before the court, "There is no way I would put a woman on the road in uniform."

However, an attempt to ensure female representation in higher ranks was overturned on arbitration in *City of Fort Worth, Tx. v. Police Lieutenant Thomas J. Brown* (American Dispute Resolution, Inc. Case No 206-122LA, Arlington, Tx.), where a female lieutenant had been promoted to the rank of captain over the heads of two male officers who had higher grades on a current promotion eligibility list. The arbitration court, relying on *Price, Waterhouse v. Hopkins*, 190 S. Ct 1775 (1989), held that the promotion was unlawful. All things being equal, promotion on the grounds of gender alone was prohibited.

Sexual Orientation

The lot of both male and female police officers who happen to be homosexuals and whose sexual orientations are known resembles that of independent heterosexual women. The homosexual officer and the emancipated female officer are considered a threat to the family institution.

The emancipated woman and the homosexual may both be denigrated on the basis of religious dicta. According to Anthony (1992), in the context of police hiring, retention, and promotion practices, homophobia flourishes under cover of a lack of clear and unambiguous guidance from the top of the organization. This complex area, beset with ethical, moral, and legal difficulties, was even addressed in the U.S. presidential election of 1992, in which the two main candidates took different sides on the employment of homo-

sexuals in the armed forces. President Clinton's decision to admit homosexuals was based on the fact that there were only four reported cases of sexual misconduct of a homosexual nature among nearly 200,000 American troops deployed in the Gulf war, while there were six courts-martial for rape and sixteen official complaints of sexual harassment. As President Clinton asserted, perhaps it is conduct rather than sexual orientation that is important. Homosexuality, he inferred, is less of a problem than heterosexual men harassing women.

Anthony's recent research (1992) demonstrated that those who denigrate the role of women in policing rely on unfounded assertions about "public opinion." The logic of the cited stereotypes is not, however, consistent. If heterosexual women are unsuited to policing because of innate tenderness, or some such thing, the supposed "butch" characteristics of homosexual women should make them more, not less, suitable for police work.

Jones (1987) and Whittacker (1979) have suggested that the real problem lies in male officers' resentment toward women who are capable of undertaking police work without resorting to stereotyped "masculine" behaviors. The same apprehensions arguably may also exist when, in the absence of fully stereotypic male behaviors, homosexual officers are found to be quite capable of doing the job. Darryl Gates, former chief of the Los Angeles Police Department, showed the wisdom of this contention when he suggested that "female homosexual officers were to be admired because of their well developed upper body strength" (Interview, 20/20, NBC TV, 1990).

Resistance to overt homosexual police officers is based on three separate but interlinked factors: ignorance, fear of corruption, and an alleged instability. There is a commonly held negative stereotype of the homosexual as a camp, limp-wristed, transvestite, would-be transsexual and child abuser, with transvestism and transsexualism assumed to be chosen, deviant ways of life.

In addition to viewing homosexuals stereotypically, many believe that a person can be corrupted, that a heterosexual can become a homosexual merely by association, or through the teaching of homosexuality as an alternative lifestyle. The result of this is fear of homosexual assault. The likelihood of such assault is low, but problems should be anticipated. Female officers fear harassment by male officers and the potential for sexist abuse, and supporters of equal opportunity seek to develop mechanisms of redress in such cases. If an officer of either sex were to use such mechanisms to deal with a homosexual harassment problem, one wonders how the authorities in question would respond. The heterosexual officer's fear of harassment by a homosexual colleague is made more acute by apprehension that the homosexual assailant might claim that his or her advances had been invited. Munyard (1988) contends, however, that, "Because of the social prejudice that exists, lesbians and gay men are, in fact, generally much more reticent than heterosexuals and would usually be very cautious about doing anything which could be misconstrued as a sexual advance." Smith (1988) suggests that it is personality integration, maturity, and the acceptance of societal homophobia that are the critical issues in achieving equal opportunity for homosexual officers. In other words, sexuality is not important. What is important is the extent to which the individual has come to terms with his or her own sexual identity. Here the American approach again wins hands down.

In Britain, beyond a certain patchy application of IQ testing, no psychological screening of applicants for the police service takes place (McKenzie and Gallagher, 1989). In the United States, applicants to police departments must be psychologically evaluated, and where an acknowledgement of homosexuality is made, the investigators must assess the extent to which psychological integration has taken place. Although homosexuality per se has been removed from the mental illness categories of DSM III-R, lack of integration can be assessed and classified on the basis of existent DSM III-R criteria (302.90 Sexual Disorder NOS). No such opportunity is provided in the British selection process.

Many patrol officers, supervisors, chiefs, and certainly many psychologists would deny employment on the basis of homosexuality. But hiring of homosexuals is just as important in exposing the majority to the minority as are quotas in the hiring of ethnic minority officers and females. In Britain, much has been left undone in the usual British manner, and it is covertly believed that keeping minorities invisible will solve the problem. Only thirteen of forty-three police forces have seen fit to include the words "sexual orientation" in their Equal Opportunities statements. Despite the existence of a very small support group of gay and lesbian officers (the Lesbian and Gay Police Association, LGPA), there is still considerable doubt about openly declaring sexual orientation at the time of application for a job as a police officer. To date, no case law in Britain reflects the court ruling in *Society for Individual Rights v. Hampton*, 63 FRD 399 (ND Cal. 1973), which held that an employer could not discharge a person merely because "he is a homosexual." Even if such a case were brought in the United Kingdom, no punishment more severe than a slap on the wrist would be given, and it is unlikely that it could bring any major and ongoing benefits.

Changing Behavior and Modifying Attitudes

Gender, racial or ethnic background, and sexual orientation are certainly complicated and divisive issues, and there could be little doubt that in both Great Britain and the United States of America, homophobia, racism, misogyny, and misandry will take a long time to die. One must settle, therefore, for two sorts of goals, long and short term. In the long term we must seek to eliminate unacceptable values and attitudes. In the short term, we must aim to keep these attitudes and values under control.

Some say it is impossible for legislation to alter attitudes. This may be true regarding the long-term goal of eradicating unacceptable attitudes, but the short-term aim of controlling attitudes may not be so difficult. An attitude of mind may be an inaccessible internal and personal collection of ideas, but a person's attitude can be inferred from a person's behavior, and psychologists have long argued that modification of attitudes is obtained through modification behavior. Equal opportunity (EO) legislation has the power to modify behavior. According to psychologists, mere punishment is an inadequate method for changing behavior, but the opposite is true of reinforcement—both positive and negative.

Negative reinforcement is not punishment (with which it is often confused), but prompted avoidance behavior. Behavior that successfully avoids a noxious stimulus is likely to increase in frequency. In Social Learning Theory (Bandura, 1977), if a person sees another severely punished for an act, he or she will obviously avoid that behavior. Thus, where people are seen punished for espousing discriminatory practices, there will be an effect on others, provided that the punishment is seen as "sufficient." EO legislation supported by powerful sanctions is therefore of paramount importance because it serves as a negative reinforcer, increasing the likelihood of nondiscriminatory behavior. However, EO legislation that offers mere mediation and minimal financial liability for noncompliance has only slight attitude-changing ability. Where mediation is the norm, mendacity is the standard, but where financial liability and withdrawal of government approval are present, as in the United States, the likelihood of behavior change is increased.

Conclusion

One other reason should be mentioned to explain why the extent and effectiveness of EO legislation is greater in America than in Britain: the written U.S. Constitution. William Gladstone, a British Prime Minister, described that document as "the most wonderful work ever struck off at a given time by the brain and purpose of man: The U.S. Constitution and the Bill of Rights the nation's conscience."

The written nature of the U.S. Constitution and its interpretation by the U.S. Supreme Court give a leverage to the EO debate not seen in the United Kingdom. Of course, Great Britain has a constitution, but it is a "hotchpotch of legal documents, gentlemen's agreements, and democratically agreed statute law" (McKenzie and Gallagher, 1989), which provides "implicit" rights in contrast to the "explicit" rights of the American documents.

To be sure, the interpretation of the Constitution by the U.S. Supreme Court has sometimes been divisive rather than inclusionary, as with "separate but equal" educational practices. But at least it gets interpreted openly. The implicit nature of British rights leads to two consequences. First, there is no open discussion of the ethical and moral nature of individual rights. Second, in the absence of judicial decisions about rights that lead to further litigation, each individual case is dealt with on its merits, and no "collective consciousness" develops.

By contrast, the dynamic American litigation approach has had a marked professionalizing effect on many aspects of law enforcement (McKenzie and Gallagher, 1989; Gallagher, 1992) and has led to specific avoidance activity. For example, when civil service promotion regulations are breached by chiefs of police, or when hiring practices are found to be discriminatory, substantial financial penalties may be imposed. In an effort to avoid future conflicts and financial outlay, litigants and others operating in the same arena change their behavior. In Britain, the approach is more "laid back," less confrontational (one might also call it the "play it down model" or the "if you ignore, it will go away" paradigm). It has brought far fewer significant results.

Although racism, sexism, and homophobia continue to be seen in U.S. policing and in the entire society, powerful figures from the Supreme Court are seen to be actively involved. In the United Kingdom, by contrast, the control and limitation of unacceptable aspects of human nature is left in the hands of a faceless and tiny handful of CRE and EOC staffers. The penalties, furthermore, for noncompliance with EO legislation are laughable.

I strongly maintain that until British EO legislation and the attached sanctions echo those of the United States, Britain will remain far behind in its search for the Holy Grail of equality, in both law enforcement and broader social life. Women, ethnic minority group members, and those of minority sexual orientation will continue to be equal but separate, theoretically supported by the law but unable to obtain true and complete participation.

Notes

1. British law allows only an absolute maximum payout of (£)10,000 plus costs. By American standards, this is a paltry sum.

2. In British vernacular, the expression "Asian" refers to those who come from the Indian subcontinent. Those from China, Vietnam, etc., are referred to as Oriental.

3. In which an Asian officer claimed that selection procedures for detective work were of an institutionally discriminatory nature.

4. At the maximum permitted level (see note 1) and with secured pension rights. Halford agreed to retire on an "ill-health" pension, a practice she had denigrated while a serving officer.

Discussion and Review Questions

1. In the United Kingdom the chief constable has constitutional autonomy. Discuss and comment.

2. What is a "disparate treatment case"?

3. In a disparate treatment case, who has the burden of proof?

4. What is a "disparate impact case"? Name one case of this nature that reached a United States court in 1975.

5. What were the consequences of the Brixton, South London, street disorder of 1981?

6. What steps are being taken in both Britain and the United States to reduce street disorder?

7. In policing in the United States and Britain, what are the stereotypical images for discrimination against women and minorities?

8. What do you understand by Social Learning Theory?

9. In your own opinion, what is the essence of equal opportunity legislation?

10. What was British Prime Minister William Gladstone's opinion of the American Constitution?

11. What makes equal opportunity legislation more effective in the United States than in Great Britain?

12. What is the nature of the British Constitution?

13. What are the two consequences of the implicit nature of British rights?

10

Policing and Public Disorder in the United Kingdom

Michael Bullock

Quality of Service! A Police Department puts out a product to maintain peace and reduce crime and violence so that people feel safe. Our goal should be customer satisfaction, but rarely do we bother to find out what the customer wants.

Gates and Shah, 1992

Introduction

The preceding quote does not originate from England, where a considerable effort is being made to achieve high-quality service to the community, but from the biography of Daryl F. Gates, retired chief of police of Los Angeles. The use of the terms "Quality of Service," "customer satisfaction," and "find out what the customer wants" illustrates the argument put forward in this chapter. Gates appears to have made the link between service and disorder, connecting action with community consultation and identification of customer desires, although he gives final primacy to agreement of expectation. Here, then are our central themes: namely, that consultation will affect the quality of service and standing of the police in the community, which will lead in turn to shared responsibility for policing the community and a reduction in the levels of disorder. The evidence for this hypothesis comes from research

undertaken by the writer in 1992 and from data collected from American police departments and English police forces.

In this chapter we will consider what is meant by quality in police service in the United Kingdom, how such quality relates to the service function, and the need to consult with the community to achieve tranquility. Communities have asked for a more caring police service, and police responded initially through service programs such as Metropolitan Police "Plus" and Thames Valley Police "Make Contact." These were undertaken by individual forces, and there was a need for a national approach; consequently, in October 1990, the British Association of Chief Police Officers (ACPO) met to launch "The ACPO Statement of Common Purpose and Values" (Hirst, 1990). Work undertaken to identify the police role in society in the 1990s had shown that such a statement would be helpful (Birch, 1990).

In 1975 the public considered the U.K. police poor performers, and subsequent surveys also recorded falling levels of public satisfaction with the police. The disturbing numbers of incidents of public disorder during the late 1970s and early 1980s were interpreted as symptoms of a loss of confidence in the police (Smith, 1982; Reiner, 1992), which was reflected in research. Studies carried out in those decades showed a public loss of trust and confidence in the police (Jones, Young and

MacClean, 1982). The Statement of Common Purpose and Values sought to set a standard that would counter claims of poor service. It may be, however, that the loss of confidence in the police was actually a response to the style of policing by the police taking part in public disorders, an issue only partly addressed by Scarman (1981) in his seminal report on the Brixton Disorders in London.

The community disorders of the 1980s were also partly attributed to mistrust and hostility toward the police (Benyon, 1987), with the Bristol City riots and the Brixton Disorders in London seen as a watershed for British policing. But they were neither the first disorders (Geary, 1985) nor the last, as was clear in 1985, 1990 (Metcalf, 1990), and 1991. Were these disorders primarily linked to a loss of confidence in the police, or was the policing style of the 1980s a contributory factor? If it was the latter, then changing the style and improving the quality of police service may be one way forward. If the former, can we expect a mere improvement in service quality to restore police standing in the community? In the United States, several police initiatives have been described varying from COP+ (Glensor, 1990) to problem-solving (Goldstein, 1990) and community policing (Skolnick and Bayley, 1986). But it is not clear that these initiatives deliver the quality of service that the British police forces seek or that they were ever intended to do so. Some work in quality service has been done in America since the early 1980s; Goldstein (1977) argued that problem-oriented policing would answer many of the community concerns being raised by the changes in society, and would overcome the insular culture of the police.

The Dilemma of Police Service

All police services face the dilemma of how to deliver quality service acceptable to the community, while simultaneously exerting a coercive force over that community to maintain order. One commentator suggests that quality service is determined by the discretion of individual officers, and concludes that emphasis on quality service is a mere cloak for the coercive function of the police and does not eliminate it (Brown, 1988). This criticism could be evaded if quality service consistently were linked to consent and accountability, and not to response time and image, as is often the case in the United Kingdom at present. Current initiatives will be unlikely to succeed if they are arrived at without community consent, consultation, or internal support. But can this be achieved when trust and confidence in the police have fallen and civil rights issues have grown, when the media increasingly question the police role and court convictions are overturned on appeal? Objections are also made to any assumption that the community is one homogenous group; there are many communities or "customers of the police," each with its own profile, hopes, expectations, and needs.

If policing in the United Kingdom is now primarily measured by provision of quality service, one must define both quality and service. Quality means an excellence of disposition, a mental or moral attribute, trait or characteristic, an accomplishment or attainment. It relates to professionalism and varies from best to acceptable, unacceptable, and worst. In management terms, quality is the result of a carefully constructed cultural environment. It must include the whole fabric of an organization, not just a part of it. Services of good quality often are assumed to be customer driven, meeting customers' agreed requirements at lowest cost, first time and every time (Crosby, 1990), but it might be said that goals should go beyond even this. Quality should be an ongoing process, always aiming to improve. Achieving this requires cultural change through training, planning, identifying and understanding customer needs and expectations, and developing a process for their accomplishment. From such analyses can be deduced a logistical formula for quality: the frequency of deficiencies (defects, errors, failures) divided by the opportunity for deficiencies (hours, beats, manpower levels) (Juran, 1989). Quality in policing might be defined as the totality of features or characteristics of a police service that bear on its ability to satisfy a given need; in other words, the provision of the right service at the right time, and at a reasonable price.

A "service" is a branch of public employment or body of public servants concerned with some particular work or supplying particular needs. The British Police serve the sovereign, the state, and the community. They also serve to enforce laws and maintain order as representatives of the community. It should be noted that this last point is not universally agreed on. Some insist that the police role is law enforcement and order maintenance only, that "such a role (service) does not belong to police work" (Kinsey, Lea, and Young, 1986). This point of view gains support from a number of police officers who do not regard service jobs as "real" policing. Some may think that the main police service is coercive action, but one must also take account of how the British police themselves view their role. The ACPO statement has been devised to support the following key service areas, all of which have been recognized by the central government in advice on monitoring police performance: (1) public contact management; (2) crime management; (3) traffic management; (4) public tranquility; and (5) community partnership and reassurance.

Demands for community services from police, however, must be balanced against demands for police coercion and readiness to meet conflict: successful police forces will combine these two. Only once this balance has been attained will quality considerations enhance the service provision. Goldstein argues that the ultimate objective for all efforts to improve the police is to increase capacity to deliver high-quality service and to equip police to do so in

ways that are consistent with, and support, democratic values. Weaknesses in police response came from their belief that the best possible service was being provided already, from autocratic styles of management, and from lack of shared or devolved responsibility; in short, there was a general failure to appreciate severe shortcomings in the police's management of their service role.

Police and the Community

Goldstein advocated quality service as early as 1977, when police clearly were becoming isolated from the community. Low police visibility and lack of regular contact with the community had caused citizens to feel that there was no one to define and enforce social norms, and that the police neither knew nor cared about them (Brown and Wycoff, 1986). The police responded that they did care, but their response was not communicated adequately.

Obviously, there is only tenuous evidence of police consulting with the community to identify needs and expectations. Such procedures have their problems, and police occasionally believe that members of the community may not know what is good for them. Members of the community, however, know very well when they are not getting what they believe they deserve from the police. In the present writer's own experience of working through interagency approaches to crime with victim care schemes, crime prevention panels, and several other liaison groups, there has been a noticeable rise in demands throughout the community for more police time to be spent on service. The main qualities demanded today are concern, care and competency (not necessarily efficiency), effectiveness—and economy. Can such care be achieved in the face of constant demands for decreasing spending and increasing control from the central government? Recent government involvement in policing major industrial disputes that led to public disorder have continued a process which started as a response to the disorders of the late 1970s and early 1980s.

Under Conservative government, the U.K. Home Office has pursued national police policy demands for Value for Money (VFM). Police were notified of this policy through the Home Office Guidance Circular 114 of 1983, which introduced the three essential components of VFM: efficiency, effectiveness, and economy, supported by performance indicators designed to facilitate their measurement. The use of performance indicators can be regarded properly as a valuable tool for management, but the policy runs the risk of excluding the customer from decisions. It is unlikely that the police will ever give "value," whatever the cost, if the needs of the public are not addressed. The pursuit of efficiency probably would lead to a style of policing that leans more toward law enforcement than service provision, because the former can be more easily measured on a quantitative basis. Efficiency is easy to measure, but it leads to preoccupation with means rather than ends, and the goals of strategies based on efficiency tend to be short-term rather than long-term. Would this not create problems by failing to address the causes of community disorders? The police problem is not a Value For Money problem, but a crisis in policing itself and public confidence in the police. Quality is unlikely to be achieved through financial initiatives, and the present writer would suggest that the three "Cs"—competence, caring, and competition—will lead to greater public confidence in the police than the three "Es" of efficiency, effectiveness, and economy.

Confidence in the police will clearly be affected if the public observes police injustice, improper conduct, repressive measures, or coercion. Injustice especially can lead to disturbances, and hostility to the police can be a primary cause of disorder (Scarman, 1981). This view was supported by a survey of Londoners, which suggested that between one-third and one-half of resi-dent West Indians completely lack confidence in the police force, and that two-thirds have considerable doubts about police standards of conduct (Smith, 1982). In an independent inquiry into the disturbances at Broadwater Farm, Tottenham, London, conclusions confirmed the findings of the earlier survey of Londoners, but the evidence that was presented tended to be anecdotal and not subject to vigorous cross-examination. A report from the inquiry (largely critical of the police role) called for a strategy by which the police should cooperate at all levels with various agencies that represent the community in order to detect and deter crime (Gifford, 1986). But this argument generalized from London to the rest of the country, just as false a deduction as saying that the causes of the Los Angeles riot of April 1992 must have reflected the conditions in the rest of the United States. Policing must meet different needs in different communities and will require different strategies of crime and order control. A much wider British crime survey suggested that four distinct groups expressed most dissatisfaction in the police: young men, the unemployed, motorists, and ethnic minorities. In effecting any improvement in public confidence, there must be a drive for quality at both national and local levels, and it must be targeted at groups such as these that least trust the police.

Once one recognizes that police service provision has satisfied all of the community, one must ask questions about the gap between service provision and public expectation. Policing has always concentrated on crime, traffic, and order maintenance when not specifically responding to demands for family intervention, care of lost property, or issuing a variety of certificates. Little effort is, or can be, expended on public nuisance offenses such as litter, dogs fouling the footway, or noisy motorcycles. Yet, presence of public nuisances tends to dictate the public perception of the police. There are constant calls for more officers on the beat, pressures for greater victim care, and the need to address the fears of crime felt by nonvictims in the community. As a senior police officer said: "In neglecting to respond to the very real needs of those elements of the community we may appear to have lost the caring dimension in the quality of our service and in consequence undermined public confidence in the police" (Hirst, 1990). In fact, police tend to be apprehensive about social agency sorts of involvement, and about raising community expectations through such consultation and involvement. Because of conflicting requirements, whether national or local, they frequently have had to admit failure to respond or meet those demands. This conflict may be addressed by changing the culture of the police service. But in order to achieve that change, one must overcome any notion that the workforce alone is responsible for quality. Unless top management demands service-oriented quality, the workforce will lack motivation. To change behavior, one must change attitudes: individual officers must accept service as their role rather than perceiving service-oriented quality as being imposed upon them. Only then will real quality of service, in addition to law enforcement and order maintenance, be achievable. A parallel process must be followed in educating the public in the external consultative process. The police ought to make it clear that they seek partnership with their customers in the community.

The police must gain both public support and public consent to perform their role. However, in a society where conflict rather than consensus dominates political life, is that achievable? Some hold that society became deeply divided in the 1980s, and that this division precludes policing by consent of all of the community's members. In the United Kingdom, inner city problems, poverty, a weakened trade union movement, institutionalized groups, and racism all confront the police, and they will continue to do so. Police cannot work for the greater good merely in terms of some utilitarian calcu-

lation; rather, they need to pursue quality service for all in the community. If the traditional model of consensual policing is abandoned for one based upon coercive force, the police will continue to lose the confidence of the public. They will become further isolated in performing their role, looking inward and merely reacting to events around them. To improve the role of police in the community and achieve quality service, one must consult and gain consensus in order to succeed. A study of a 1990 survey showed that the public would prefer a service which worked with the community to solve crime matters, and that police discretion and crime prevention were the best means of dealing with crime (Birch, 1990). This has long been advocated through the problem-oriented approach.

While accepting the importance of experienced police judgment in deciding priorities, such judgment may be verified and strengthened through consultation. The question is, do police consult effectively? It might be said that the U.K. police do consult through the formal committees set up under Section 106 of the Police and Criminal Evidence Act (1984), but a Home Office review of these arrangements found that genuine community representation was difficult, if not impossible, to achieve; that ethnic members of the community were not attracted to the committee groups; and that some sections of the community deliberately distanced themselves from the consultation process (Home Office, 1989b). If quality service is a matter of meeting community expectations or needs, how are the police addressing their identification of those needs? Is informal consultation going on outside the parameters of the Section 106 committees where policing priorities are determined and policing operations agreed upon? It would seem that none are truly effective, and that the police in fact still decide their own priorities.

The present writer has undertaken research showing that quality-oriented U.K.

police have failed to adopt the central requirement for effective consultation in the
United States; for, in Britain, consultations
that occur in problem and community-oriented policing are not usually driven by
an identified need to provide quality service. In both countries, there has been a
series of innovations that have attempted
to overcome the alleged crisis which has
arisen in policing during the past 30 years.
Most of the innovations that aimed for
quality service (such as consultation, contact, consent, meeting of agreed needs, reduction in the use of coercive force) have
been carried out in the United States
(Skolnick and Bayley, 1986; Brown, 1988;
Sparrow, Moore, and Kennedy, 1990). Examples of particular team policing, contact programs, problem-oriented policing,
and community-oriented policing abound
in the United States, but can lessons learnt
in that country be brought back to the
United Kingdom?

U.S. and U.K. Innovations
in Quality of Service

In comparing the United States and the
United Kingdom, we will look at differing
types of police departments in the United
States that might be categorized as State
Capital, Mid State, Tourist City, and Big
City. These groups represent communities
of up to 2 million whose police officer establishments of up to 4,000 compare favorably with the U.K. police forces, where
the average police population and officer
establishment per unit area tends to be
much higher than in the United States. The
State Capital has a population of just under half a million and an officer establishment of more than 700. While the crime
rate is comparatively low, the management
style fosters community policing. As part
of the city structure and its overall requirements of management with accountability,
the department has adopted the city mission statement for quality of service that
states: "We want City X to be the best man-

aged and most liveable city in the country. We will accomplish this through
people who genuinely care and provide
responsive quality service." The city mission has always centered on a high standard of service, but recently even more
attention has been focused on the police
as public servants. Between 1990 and
1992, the city management plan gave "focus on customer service" top billing with
a common theme of quality service per-
meating value statements. The city emphasizes quality customer service and regards
the concept of community policing as a
priority, actively supporting the chief of
police in its achievement. To meet this
priority, the City Police Department has
decided that the key element in policing
style is police presence. He or she fulfills
an integral part of community policing
strategy by redeploying resources to ensure
that every police officer has a well-defined
area of the city to serve. As in China, each
community will have one or more identifiable officers responsible for it.

Another key element in the State
Capital's police service goals has been the
full adoption of the Stephens/Goldstein
model of problem-solving, whose entire
process is underpinned by qualitative
rather than quantitative performance measures. The force recognizes the practical
difficulties here, and has considered the
findings of one unpublished report that
quality of police service is absent from
most of the evaluative measures that are
now in use. Response time is easy to measure, but it is the quality delivered during
the initial call until the customer's request
for service has been met that is subjective
and difficult to evaluate. To negotiate this
difficulty, the department has appointed a
full-time officer responsible for total quality management and quality of service
within the State Capital Police Department. Having pursued reactive policing
and having failed to deliver a good service,
the department has changed its philosophy: it now can be proactive, but seeks to
be coactive through collaboration and con-

sultation. Quality of police service will emerge from the latter.

The Mid State, Tourist, and Big Cities Departments

The Mid State City is a relatively small department by English standards, with an establishment of 350 officers for a city population of 130,000. The city has an ethnic mix of white, African-American, and Hispanic reflecting the national average of 70%, 15%, and 10%. Its main source of income is tourism. Policing is community oriented, seeking to achieve three benefits: (a) improved delivery of police services; (b) improved community relations; and (c) mutual resolution of identifiable problems.

For some years this quality service approach to policing has been shown to be effective, and it closely resembles quality developments in the United Kingdom. Public attitude and satisfaction surveys are carried out biannually, and findings are now supported with internal staff surveys. The department uses three agencies to apply this data to its policing service objectives: (a) the Quality Assurance Bureau; (b) the Neighborhood Advisory Group (NAG); and (c) the Crime Analysis Unit.

The NAGs were much more effective at identifying community problems and expectations than the formal consultative groups in the United Kingdom. A plan for operational policing was agreed on that devolved community relations responsibilities, making the local officer accountable to the community.

The Quality Assurance Bureau coordinates departmental efforts to improve the service level to the community through consultation, external surveys, and internal surveys; it is now recognized by the Police Executive Research Forum as a model American program. Its strength lies in public consultation, and its success in such programs as community storefronts. Over the past 4 years, these successes have led to an increased level of public satis-

faction, and also to a reduction in community tensions and disorder.

Tourist City attracts visitors from around the world. Such cities are located over a wide area with a mixed population of about 1 million. The community tensions between African-Americans and Hispanics were also apparent between officers of both groups. The police department has more than 1,500 officers and practices traditional community policing. However, innovations have met public concerns that primarily relate to tourism and to the increasing number of immigrants to the city from the Latin countries. One innovation, "crisis intervention," mandates a unit of individually selected and trained officers to work directly with area commanders, and to design responses to community problems identified through analysis of calls, citizen complaints, or crime figures. The department also attends to the need for long-term solutions to community problems by encouraging joint interagency approaches. Projects have included derelict property cleaning and the establishing of city regulation to control behavior. The crisis intervention officers have increased the ability of the department to respond to the public through community-oriented initiatives addressed during the day across the city.

Big City Department is large and multicultural by any standards, with more than 4,000 officers serving a city of 2 million people. African-Americans and Hispanics are overrepresented within the community when compared to the national average. Relations between the two groups can be tense, as seen in very large cities of the United Kingdom. Several major policing programs have been developed; one, for example, encourages exchange of information between beat officers and neighborhood residents at community exchange meetings (often held in storefront premises). Police hope that this program will build community links through the consultative process, provide a forum for the exchange of information, and demonstrate care for the quality of life within neighborhoods. In practice, monthly meetings are held that bring together members of the police department and community representatives (including various civic groups). Each representative is responsible for reporting back to his or her group, and the meetings often achieve a change in police response to community or in identification of problems. The program resembles the Mid State Neighborhood Action Group concept, and it requires that beat officers encourage civic groups to discuss policing at the patrol officer rather than the management level. This will make it clear that it is local consultation that will make the project succeed.

Although the definition of quality has been far from clear in many cases, the concept of quality has been accepted generally by all U.S. departments and U.K. forces. Lack of a clear definition is not a problem, if all understand the philosophy under which a definition is being pursued; but not all do understand. State Capital's management-centered approach, which seeks to achieve quality through the adoption of the City Management Mission Statement, differs considerably from that advocated by Mid State. Mid State adopted a personnel model addressing community needs, combining public feedback on expectations with internal analysis of staff needs and expectations. The management model approach, although coactive with the community, allows management to re-

tain control of direction: the management staff determine priorities and employ their own professional judgments in their focus on customer service. The personnel model allows directional control to devolve to the community working with the lowest police ranks, with responsibility usually placed on a group that tends to be part of the Management Services, Force Inspectorate, or Audit Division. Of forces and departments surveyed, only thirteen forces (31% of total) and three departments (10% of total) clearly identified a group with full-time responsibility. Since respondents often reported these as problem-solving groups; Table 10-1 includes that category.

The actual use of problem-solving techniques to address either quality or style is limited, partially because the English approach quality neither through the personnel model nor through the management model, but through a combination of elements of both. The term "customer" is often used but not often clarified: although opinions on the issue are divided, it can be deduced that the customer is the community and not the internal members of the organization. Unfortunately, many police officers, both in America and in England, believe that the lower ranks and civilian staff are customers of the Chief Officer and the senior management team. The U.K. central government, however, takes the view that the term customer does not include internal employees of the police organization. If the police accept that the customer is the victim, service user or par-

Table 10-1: *Frequency of Problem Solving Groups Quality Circles and Quality Groups*

9		**Problem Solving**	Level	Q.C.	Level	QG	Level
		Policy	28%		24%		16%
U.S.	60%	Management	12%	24%	8%	40%	12%
		Other	36%	26%		20%	
		Policy	3%		0%	6%	
U.K.	38%	Management	6%	24%	3%	50%	6%
		Other	29%		21%		39%

Policy is represented by Chief Officer groups

Table 10-2: *Customer Groups-Consultation*

	U.S.			UK.		
	Informal	**Quality**	**Style**	**Informal**	**Quality**	**Style**
Statutory Agnecies	44	12	20	85	15	30
Non-Statutory Agencies	32	4	12	32	9	12
Victim Support	60	8	20	88	6	30
Political Group	36	8	20	17	6	15
Neighborhood Watch	80	8	20	88	3	27
Chamber of Trade	76	8	16	65	3	27
Schools	76	4	16	82	3	21
Churches	60	0	20	82	3	6
Race Relations	24	0	12	35	0	7
Tenants Association	40	0	0	70	0	0
Property Owners	32	20	0	18	3	0

ticipative user, and offenders, whom should the police consult to identify customer needs? The current state of affairs is summarized in Table 10-2, which indicates the percentage of forces and departments that consult informally, the percentage that formally consult on matters of quality of service, and the percentage that formally consult on policing style.

The groups listed in Table 10-2 are the ones most frequently cited for police consultation on behalf of the community. No such list, however, can be complete, and one might say that by selecting only certain customers for liaison, police still set the rules by which they will succeed. The survey data in Table 10-3 answers to this difficulty by being customer generated, indicating the most common demands by the community for police action; that is, the community needs.

The category "other" features strongly in English surveys, and most often contains demands for more information from victims about the crimes committed against them, along with demands for more action against burglars and car thieves, including "joy riders." This presents a further dilemma for the police, particularly in England. If they enforce this area of the law, some communities may react violently, as was the case in Oxford,

Table10-3: *Comparisons of Demands From Public for Police Action*

Demand for Action	**U.S.**	**England**
More Foot Patrol	12%	53%
More Community Involvement	12	29
Enforcement of Nuisance Offenses	16	26
Greater Victim Care	8	23
Control of Domestic Violence	20	6
Enforcement of Drug Laws	20	15
Juvenile Crime	8	18
Other	8	47
(Includes demand for action against Burglary and Car theft).		

Table 10-4: *Rank Attendance at Consultative Meetings*

U.S	Cop	Capts	Lieutenants	Sergeants	Patrol Offr.
	32%	20	12	20	36
U.K.	ACPO	Supts	Inspectors	Sergeants	Constables
	9%	70	50	23	9

Newcastle, and other large city housing estates in the United Kingdom in 1991. However, if the police do nothing, public satisfaction decreases. It seems that police need to rely on more data gathering mechanisms than mere public surveys, ones allowing a better understanding of the police role and an airing of public views through effective consultation.

The Differences between the United States and the United Kingdom in Community Policing

In America, problem-solving is accepted and practiced by many departments at the lower rank level, but in England the involvement of lower ranks is often poor. However, problem-solving is now being addressed internally, particularly in community consultation and problem identification. Such consultation will allow a redefinition of the police role and function. It is not sufficient merely to pursue order maintenance or crime control; rather, police and community must define what local problems exist and the appropriate response. Consultation can occur through a multiagency group, through a community group, or through local teams of police officers providing contact and reassurance, as observed in Mid State and Big City. If consultation is the seeking of consent, how effective is that process and with whom do the police consult? Table 10-1 indicates levels of problem-solving consultation within police forces and departments, while Table 10-2 indicates the groups most commonly consulted in the community on issues of quality and style. But are all these consultations true two-

way pursuits of consensus, or are they mere instances of contact such as a school visit or Neighborhood Watch talk? Consultation most often appears to be contact rather than agreement, used by the police as part of an information process in which they set their own priorities. This is highlighted by differences between English and American attendance of formal consultative meetings, as shown in Table 10-4.

Many informal meetings are regularly attended by lower ranking officers, but such meetings tend to be talks on offense prevention or safety; no informal meetings about policing style in England have become evident to this writer. Not only are there rank differences between officers who attend formal consultative meetings in the United States and those who attend in the United Kingdom, but the frequency of such meetings also varies (Table 10-5). One weakness in consultation programs is the limited opportunities they provide to discuss a response to problems as they arise. This is particularly noticeable in the United Kingdom, where formal meetings are held, on the average, once every 15 weeks. Another weakness is their tendency to represent a very large section of the area's population. Specific problems affecting only a local community would be less likely to be known and raised at large group meetings. The average U.K. Police and Community Consultative Committee represents just under 100,000 of the population compared to fewer than 30,000 represented in similar committees in the United States. However, this comparison is not altogether just, because participation in such groups is not a statutory duty in America. This makes the precise defining of formal consultation groups difficult.

Table 10-5: *Frequency of Formal Consultation*

	No. of Formal Consult. Groups	Frequency of Meetings	Average Population	Population Per Con. Group
U.S.	131 (8 Dept.)	8wks	0.47m	28k
U.K.	345 (28 Force)	15 wks	1.1 m	98k

One cannot easily gauge whether representation by such a large group is effective, but one can deduce from the infrequency of meetings that they are not a suitable vehicle for attempting to meet community expectations and needs. Formal community consultation, then, has great weaknesses in addition to its under-representation of the young, males, ethnically marginal groups, and offenders, whose unwillingness to attend such a formal forum compromises any hope that this style of consultation could achieve the goal of quality service. As a result, police will continue to choose their own policing style, subject to government pressures, and little effort will be made to address the causes behind lack of consultation.

In England, only 20% of forces surveyed felt that policing style had been changed to meet public demand: most interviewees felt that no real change had occurred. If changes in policing style and action do arise from community demand, police must evaluate the effectiveness of those changes by setting performance standards or targets (see Table 10-6).

If standards or targets in quality and style are not set, and feedback does not specifically address these aspects, how can the police know whether they are meeting community expectations and needs for quality? One alternative is to use an internal audit process by inspection departments. There are some 76% of forces and 40% of departments that allocate some responsibility to a specialist department or division, whether full-time (40% England, 14% America) or part-time (36% England, 26% America). This process was established for different reasons in each country—in the United States to meet accreditation requirements, and in the United Kingdom as a part of the "value for money" initiative. Quality, style, and communication may enable police to succeed, but if the young, the marginal groups, or the offenders are not consulted on these issues, it is no surprise when protest against authority and the police occurs. The disorders that affect society in the 1990s can be separated into three categories: those relating to issues, those relating to events, and those relating to com-

Table10-6: *Changes in Police Style Arose From*

	U.S.	U.K.
A Need to Meet Demand	64%	20%
Community Consultation	36	9
Crime Level Unacceptable	20	3
Evolvement of Style	8	21
Management Style Change	—	3
Style of Chief Officer	16	12
Need for Success	4	3
Other	—	3

munities. Although there will always be some overlap between the groups, the general patterns observed are a concern over a need to meet community demands; community consultation; unacceptable crime rate; evolution of style; changes in management style; style of the chief officer; and need for success (Table 10-7).

Table 10-7: Setting of Standard of Performance

	U.S.	UK
Are Standards Set	52%	41%
Quality Standards	40	29
Style Standards	80	12

Issues

Over 25% of forces experienced demonstrations in relation to political causes such as the Gulf War, animal rights, and anti–community taxation. Most passed with only a minimum of disorder. Others, such as the events at Trafalgar Square in March 1991, cannot be regarded so lightly; but they do not cause any real long-term problems. In the United States, abortion issues have led to disorder similar to that seen in parts of the United Kingdom.

Events

In recent years in England, illegal dance parties and the reemergence of the itinerant New Age Travelers have led to confrontations with the police and sporadic outbreaks of violence. Sports events also have caused disorders. Again, these present no long-term problem for the police.

Community

Community-oriented disorders are the sort that have, in the past years, been most frequent and crime related; usually they occur on large local authority housing estates and in areas of severe poverty. A solution to the problems encountered in such areas will only be found in long-term policing strategy. Developing an effective policing style will lead to an acceptable response from the community. Housing estate disorder affects nearly half of all forces in England, causes high levels of damage to community infrastructure, and reduces the general public satisfaction in the level of local policing. The frequency of U.S. housing project disorder is not as high as in England despite similar poverty, unemployment, and feelings of hopelessness observed among the disadvantaged. This is surprising given the added factor of racial tension between Hispanic, Asian, and African-American groups in the community. In Big City, the disorders relate to issues and rarely to the community, but this is not the case in other parts of the country.

The U.S. police do campaign against drug abuse, street crime, burglary, and vehicle-related offenses, but there is no protest against policing style, law enforcement, or police presence. Why isn't there as much hostility toward the police as in the United Kingdom? In short, American police consultation programs have strengthened their communities' abilities to address identified problems.

Community disorder in State Capital is comparatively rare and relates to issues that attract demonstrations rather than to community unrest. It might be argued that the managerial approach to quality helps in the maintenance of public tranquillity. But other factors such as low crime rate, low number of police officers leading to selective law enforcement, and the imposition of a curfew on young people in certain districts all play some part in community quality of life. In Tourist Town, the police respond to community disorder incidents through specialized units, supported by up to 200 officers trained in tactics, which very much reflects the U.K. approach. As noted earlier, there is an awareness of the problems with the Hispanic community and of public demand for police change. Since the West Coast riot of April 1992, greater "cultural sensitivity training" has been attempted to overcome the gap between the major Hispanic community and the predominantly white police department

In England, the police appear confused about their role. On the one hand, they seek to provide quality service, which could be achieved through community contacts; on the other hand, they continue to place emphasis not on consultation but on instant response and being available to exert a coercive force. Such constant response, often to repeat calls, does little to address causes—causes that might be identified if the police were to depend on responsible low-level consultation. Current management-oriented models for police quality will be unlikely to attain the prime objective of community policing, that is, enhancing relationships between the police and the community. It seems necessary to consider a new model for English policing that not only meets community expectations on crime control and order maintenance but also meets the need for quality of life and feeling of safety, neither of which exists now. Let us assume that police ought to provide the latter in the context of crime prevention, using the standard model of problem-solving.

The ACPO statement is a starting point, but it is general and poses public tranquillity as an overriding need. Such tranquillity can be achieved through innovation and a readjustment in the means of determining policing. There are many examples of this happening in both countries, all of which include community police teams assigned to a clearly defined area with a specific responsibility for that area, with authority to consult and respond and be coactive with the community. Such teams, while accountable to the local community, should be part of a much shorter management structure within the police. They should form part of a basic command unit that has gained greater autonomy, an autonomy attained by lowering the rank level

of formal community consultation in order to achieve three objectives. First, the formal group will represent a much smaller, more clearly defined section of the population; second, the community will take part in decision-making; and finally, a multiagency approach will be adopted within the community in order to consider both crime and its causes and to give some level of public ownership to the statutory agencies' response.

No more than a handful of forces and departments have changed their basic policing style, preferring instead to examine performance, improve response, and seek a more visible caring image. Police officers are, by and large, caring and concerned, yet they are blamed for many of the shortcomings in society. Focusing on quality alone is unlikely to curb disorder, because it is the police law enforcement culture itself that provides resistance. Senior management does not devolve responsibility beyond the ranks of superintendent or captain, and forces consistently fail to consult effectively. The police need to be more competent and caring than they are now in order to be effective, but the drive for efficiency and economy through use of a management style for quality rather than a personnel style may preclude any service-centered approach. The State Capital management approach to quality is not likely to have so good an effect in England as the community or personal approach practiced in Mid State City, but current English trends are toward the former rather than the latter. If possible, this should be changed. English policing needs to adapt to that philosophy of community policing that most empowers the local officer, and that links that officer with the community through effective consultation.

Can quality of service and community consultation reduce the number of disorders—particularly community disorders—that have been seen in the United Kingdom during the past 10 years? On their own, probably not. But if taken as part of a style of policing that effectively delivers

quality based upon consultation and devolved responsibility, one can be much
more hopeful. Consultation and quality
service within the community will reduce
community disorder, and "community
policing provides a powerful strategy for
the police to employ in reducing the likelihood of collective violence in cities, and,
arguably the most substantial short run
program for meeting urban social needs"
(Bayley, 1992).

Discussion and Review Questions

1. What does Bullock mean by the
   "insular culture of the police?"

2. The British police serve three categories of people. Who are they?

3. "Police service job is not real policing." Discuss and comment.

4. The conservative government of
   Britain introduced a policy of "Value
   For Money." What is meant by value
   for money?

5. What are the three essential components of value for money?

6. According to Bullock, what are the
   three factors that could lead to greater
   public confidence in the police?

7. What are the major problems facing
   the British police in law enforcement?

8. Policing based on coercive force
   versus policing based on consultation
   and consensus: discuss and comment.

9. What are the principles needed to
   achieve quality of police services?

10. The key element in policing is police
    presence. Discuss and comment.

11. What are the three major benefits that
    "Mid State" policing is designed to
    achieve?

12. What are the differences between the
    United States and the United King-
    dom in community policing?

13. There are three types of disorder that
    affect society in the 1990s. What are
    they?

14. According to Bullock, consultation
    and quality of service within the
    community will reduce community
    disorder. Discuss.

11

The Police System in the People's Republic of China

Zheng Wang

Introduction

The People's Republic of China, with its population of 1.2 billion (a fifth of the world's total population), currently is undergoing many changes toward the development of an open market economy. Under its new "open policy," China desires that its criminal justice system, including its police system, be understood. The police system in China has long been shrouded in secrecy and not been fully revealed to the West, and especially not by people of Chinese origin. This chapter attempts to provide an initial first-hand account of the police system in China. We will describe the historical development of the police force, its overall organizational structure, the types of police forces, dynamic factors influencing and controlling the system, the crime situation that has resulted from Chinese policing, and a comparison between the policing in China and policing in the United States.

In order to better illustrate the system, tables, figures, diagrams, and statistics collected over the past 12 years will be provided.[1]

The police systems in China are usually called the "people's police agencies," or "public security agencies," and policemen are called "public security personnel." Along with the other three major components of the criminal justice system—the

procuratorate, the court, and corrections—the police play a major role in maintaining social order in both city and countryside. Therefore, greater understanding of the Chinese police system will be a major step toward understanding China's criminal justice system at large.

Historical Development

The establishment of the public security system can be traced back to the early 1920s, when the Communist Party was an underground movement fighting against the Nationalist government. During the First Revolutionary Civil War (1924–1927), the Special Service Section was set up to lead the workers' union movement (Du and Zhang, 1990:124). In 1938, the Special Service Section was replaced by the Social Affairs Department (SAD) under the direction and jurisdiction of the Politburo (Richelson, 1988:274).

In October 1949, the Ministry of Public Security (MPS) was established under the supervision of the State Council (the central government). The MPS was responsible for countersubversion, counterintelligence, surveillance, protection of economic and military installations, border patrol, management of "labor reform" camps, census registration, routine police administration, and investigation of criminal cases.

Figure 11-1: *Overall Criminal Justice System in China*

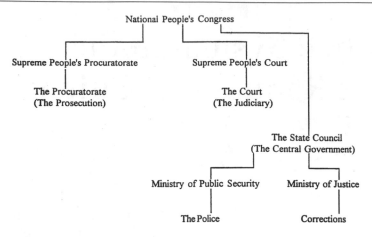

Organizational Structure

Like all the political and economic systems in the People's Republic of China, the current criminal justice system is highly centralized. Its four major components are placed under four different state ministries, with the police system under the supervision of the Ministry of Public Security, the procuratorate under the Supreme People's Procuratorate, the court under the Supreme People's Court, and the

Figure 11-2: *Vertical Structure of Public Security Organizations*

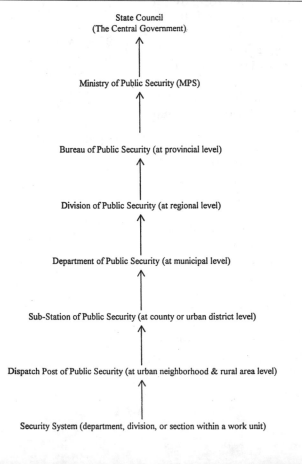

Figure 11-3: *Vertical Organizational Structure of Chinese Public Security*

Ministry of Public Security —	Regular Police and Armed Police
Ministry of Railroads —	Railway Police
Ministry of Forestry —	Forest Police
Ministry of Transportation —	Maritime Police
Air Administration —	Airport Police
Ministry of Defence —	Military Police

corrections division under the Ministry of Justice. (See Figure 11-1.)

On October 15, 1949, the first National Public Security Conference decided on a centralized public security organization, and agencies were to be established at various levels (Figure 11-2). Security systems were also set up within the military, government agencies, schools, institutes, and factories. These agencies are responsible for the public security within these units and are auxiliary apparatus of local public security organizations. Overall, the present police system in China still follows the pattern set up then.

The ministries besides Public Security that have their own public security systems are Railway Transportation (MRT), Forestry (MF), Transportation (MT), Air Administration (AD), and Defense (MD) (Figure 11-3). These police forces are responsible for public security within their respective jurisdictions.

Unlike the decentralized police forces in the United States, various security institutions in China follow a "dual supervision system." Each police agency is supervised by higher police agencies that reside under the jurisdiction of the MPS, which is in turn subordinate to the government (Figure 11-2). All public security agencies are armed forces and are charged with keeping public order in society.

The Ministry of Public Security, the highest police agency in China, is under the direct leadership of the State Council. Its major functions are to provide policy directions and coordinate criminal investigations that include more than one pro-

vincial jurisdiction. Within the Ministry there are thirteen bureaus and also several supporting bureaus such as the General Office, the Personnel Administration Department, and the International Cooperation Bureau. In addition, the Ministry runs three police universities and three research institutes. Figure 11-4 shows the organization of the MPS.

The major functions of the police bureau at the provincial level are (1) to handle major or heinous crimes occurring within that province; (2) to conduct forensic/criminalistics analysis of the evidence submitted by the local police stations; and (3) to provide professional supervision for the local police agencies.

At the municipal level, Chinese police departments have greater similarity to Western police departments than is generally the case otherwise.

In urban areas, local police district stations and local neighborhood police stations (dispatch posts) are grassroots agencies and carry the bulk of policing work, conducting criminal investigations, maintaining public order, administering census registration, managing special trades, controlling criminal activities, and doing routine patrols. We will illustrate with two examples of local police agencies.

Yan An Zhoung Lu Police Substation in Shanghai is considered a medium-sized agency. Its jurisdiction covers an area of 1.7 square kilometers and includes 14,500 households and 50,700 residents. There are 34 police officers and four supervisors in the agency whose average age is 31. They are not usually armed, but carry elec-

Figure 11-4: *Organization of the Ministry of Public Security*

The General Office

The Personnel Administration

The International Cooperation Bureau

The Headquarters of People's Armed Police

Bureau One: Special Investigation (International Crime)

Bureau Two: Traffic Control

Bureau Three: Public Order (Public Safety)

Bureau Four: Preliminary Hearing (Interrogation and Questioning)

Bureau Five: Criminal Investigation (Murder, Armed Robbery, Rape, and National Central Bureau of INTERPOL)

Bureau Six: Interior Guard (Protection of State Leaders and Foreign VIPs)

Bureau Seven: Residence Registration (Household Administration)

Bureau Eight: Border Control (Border Patrol, Border Check)

Bureau Nine: Education and Training

Bureau Ten: Fire Fighting and Prevention

Bureau Eleven: Technical Investigation (Surveillance)

Bureau Twelve: Scientific and Technological Development

Bureau Thirteen: Comprehensive Affairs (Budget, Finance, Supply, and General Service

Public Security University (Beijing)

Police Officers University (Beijing)

Criminal police College of China (Shenyang)

The First Research Institute (Police Equipment)

The Second Research Institute (Forensic Science and Criminalistics)

The Third Research Institute (Police System and Organization)

tric prods when necessary. In 1983, the agency investigated 23 reported criminal incidents, and 22 incidents in 1984. Eighty percent of these cases were solved (Allen, 1987).

The Keiko Road police station in northwest Jianan is an example of the PRC effort to integrate law enforcement within the community. The neighborhood has 11 household registration districts with 6,300 households, 27,000 residents, and some 60 factories and schools. The police station is a two-story, gray stucco building divided into a number of offices, and the staff (as usual) is small in number. The 15 members include the director, deputy director, 2 office workers, and 11 policemen, each

policeman managing household registration in 1 district (Johnson, 1983).

Within both large and small public security organizations down to the substation level, division of labor tends to be clear and fixed, as arranged half a century ago. Each separate responsibility falls within a specific unit, and certain tasks are designated for each unit. Generally speaking, there are twelve units in each public security agency: security for political affairs, criminal investigation, preliminary interrogation, security for economic and cultural affairs, public order, fire-fighting, security guards, reform through labor, reform through education, and armed police (Figure 11-5).

Figure 11-5: *Internal Structure of the Police Department*

Unit 1	Unit 2	Unit 3	Unit 4
Security Political Affairs	Criminal Investigation	Preliminary Hearing	Security for Economic and Cultural Affairs

Unit 5	Unit 6	Unit 7	Unit 8	Unit 9
Public Order	Fire Fighting	Household Registration	Security Guard	Border Patrol

Unit	Unit	Unit
Reform Through Labor	Reform Through Education	Armed Police

If we could say that the police district station or substation is the first level where there is some degree of specialization, the neighborhood police station is like a general management office for all community affairs (Chang, 1984). It emphasizes "educating the masses," which includes crime prevention efforts, classes on various aspects of the law, and working with juveniles and work groups to develop better lines of communication between the police and the people (Ward, 1985). All the police officers at the neighborhood station level are called census registration police, though in practice there is some division of labor.

Types of Police Forces

According to official data, there are 1.2 million police directed by the Ministry of Public Security, one-half of whom are armed. However, it is believed that the actual number increased to 2 million after the Tiananmen Square incident.

Figure 11-6: *Administration of Police Force*

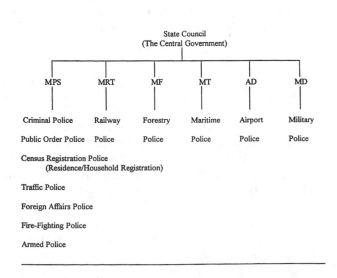

There are seven major types of police with different functions within the system: criminal police, public order police, census registration (residence/household registration) police, traffic police, foreign affairs police, fire-fighting police, and armed police. All are under the leadership of the MPS, are housed within one police agency, and are designed to cooperate with each other. The five additional security agencies governed by different ministries work side by side with the regular police force (Figure 11-6).

The criminal police force is the system's backbone agency. Its major tasks include on-scene response, collecting of evidence, investigation of major crimes (murder, robbery, rape, arson, etc.), conduct of criminalistic laboratory analyses, arresting of criminals, testifying at court, and enforcing sentences imposed by the courts. The subdivision within the criminal police force conducting criminalistic analyses are called criminal examiners; the rest are referred to as criminal investigators. The criminal examiners are subdivided further into those specializing in forensic medicine, forensic chemistry, physical evidence, and examination of disputed documents.

Census registration police are responsible for compiling statistics on population growth and movement. Every Chinese must register with a census police officer, and authorization must be obtained from the local census registration police station before anyone can move out of an old residence or into a new one. All births and deaths in the jurisdiction are recorded at the police station. Finally, census registration police are also responsible for supervising probationers and parolees.

Traffic police primarily patrol the highways and maintain an orderly flow of automotive and pedestrian traffic in urban areas. There is a police booth (post) at almost every major street intersection where one or two traffic officers are on duty, and one or two more direct traffic at the center of the street crossing.

Public order police generally oversee special trades, dangerous goods, and public places. Moreover, they concentrate on preventing, controlling, and handling crimes, act on violations of public order, and deal with disastrous accidents. In China, professions whose workers could provide tools for crime are regarded as special trades. A smith's shop, for instance, can produce a key for illegal entry; and a seal or stamp shop can forge seals or stamps for illegal use. Therefore, people working in these professions are required to report to the police if they discover that somebody has made a suspicious request. In terms of dangerous goods, public order police control certain sorts of equipment, and poisonous drugs and medicines. Guns and ammunition are strictly forbidden to individual use. Opium, morphine, and heroin are prohibited save with doctor's permission. Public order police also routinely patrol public places: railway stations, long-distance bus stations, parks, shopping centers, free markets, and certain "busy areas"—i.e., prostitution or gambling areas. Finally, public order police keep close working relations with hotels, motels, theaters, and pawn shops in order to detect any criminals or criminal activities.

Foreign affairs police work only at the municipal level, handling crimes and other incidents involving foreigners. Moreover, foreign affairs police examine and approve all applications for going abroad, either for study or for short visits (official and nonofficial). Finally, foreign affairs police issue passports to those who have obtained approval for going abroad.

The people's armed police force was established in the early 1950s, but was abolished in the mid-1960s. In 1983, as a result of the post–Mao Tse-tung disarmament, 1 million military soldiers were converted into an armed police force, thus reestablishing the armed police. This special police force has its own headquarters within the MPS and constitutes a special subsystem within the regular police force at various levels. Some regular police tasks have been transferred to the armed police, including border patrol and the guarding of major governmental and party institutions, foreign embassies, key installations (major bridges and tunnels, power and utility centers), airports, and ports. In recent years, antiterrorist duties have been added to armed police activities. Overall, armed police are housed only in provincial police agencies and in urban districts.

Fire-fighting police and armed police differ from the rest of the police in being not professional but obligatory. Their service resembles that of a soldier in the military and is paid accordingly. In 1988 the armed police started their own military-style ranking system: lieutenant-general, major-general, senior colonel, colonel, lieutenant-colonel, major, captain, first lieutenant, and second lieutenant.

Functions of the Police in the Judicial Process

According to Chinese criminal procedure law, there are several important functions carried out by the police.

The first function is registration of criminal cases. A criminal case is registered when the police department (and court and procuratorate) examine denunciations which inform them that a crime has been committed. The department also registers a criminal case when information is presented by those who surrender themselves to the law, confessing that they have committed a criminal act. A criminal case is formally registered only when the police department believes it necessary to hold the accused criminally responsible for the offense.

The second function is investigation. During this stage, the police agency conducts search and seizure, collects evidence, and handles criminal investigation. Except in emergency situations, police wishing to search must show the suspect a search warrant (Criminal Law, 1984:125–128). Finally, if they believe that the ac-

cused should be held criminally liable, the police draft a request for an arrest. This request, together with all relevant materials, is forwarded to the procuratorate, which can issue a warrant for arrest. The police must obtain an arrest warrant from the procuratorate before carrying out an apprehension or making an arrest (Leng, 1982). Only police agencies may execute arrests.

Persons under suspicion of having committed crimes may also be detained by the police for questioning prior to issue of an arrest warrant. Either in arrest or in detention situations, the family of the detainee or the arrestee should be notified within 24 hours of the time the arrest was made of the reasons for the arrest and the confinement. Interrogation must start within 24 hours after detention or arrest.[3] The detainee or the arrested party must be released without delay if no legitimate grounds for concern are established by the police. When the police department deems it necessary to declare a detainee arrested, the case is submitted to the procuratorate for approval within 3 days or, in special circumstances, 7 days. The procuratorate must either approve the arrest or order a release of the detainee within 3 days (Article 38-52).

The third function of the police in the judicial process is to conduct preliminary hearings for persons arrested or detained according to law. Such a hearing continues investigatory work and includes examination and interrogation of criminals before they are brought to court for trial (Du and Zhang, 1990:133). According to the law, during the preliminary hearings the police should gather all the facts surrounding the defendant's behavior and the relationships between the defendant and any other criminals in the case. The police must insist on the principle of seeking truth from facts, relying on evidence and investigation, and must refrain from extorting confessions by torture, threat, enticement, or deceit of any other illegal nature (Article 32).

The fourth function is to file a "memorandum of indictment" to the procuratorate for further examination. The procuratorate examines the materials submitted by the police agency. On finding the facts of the crime clear and evidence sufficient to hold the accused responsible for the crime, the procuratorate files an indictment against the accused. The case is then held over for trial by the court. The procuratorate must decide whether or not to prosecute a case within one month to one and a half months (Article 97).

Functions of the Police in the Social Arena

Besides their judicial functions in the legal process, the police in China are also mandated by law to play an important administrative role in crime prevention and social control.

According to the Security Administrative Punishment Act,[4] there are three types of sanctions that the police can implement in dealing with minor crimes or public-order offenses (prostitution, drugs, and gambling) without reference to the procuratorate, the court, and corrections. First, the police agency at the neighborhood level can issue a warning to a minor criminal offender. Second, the police agency from urban district level and above can order a fine up to 400 yuan ($50) and a detention at the police station (up to 15 days). However, a dissatisfied defendant has the right to make an appeal to a police agency at the next level up, and ultimately to a court that is under the supervision of the Ministry of Justice and not the Ministry of Public Security. If the individual wins the appellate case, the police agency as well as the police officer(s) concerned have to apologize to the victim and compensate him or her for any damages.

Reform-through-education[5] is another administrative sanction that police agencies at the urban district level and above can employ in dealing with "anti-societal"

behaviors. The police do not need to ask the procuratorate or the court for any approval, but do need to consult with the public security committee[6] in the defendant's neighborhood. The language of this legislation somewhat resembles that of the old vagrancy laws in England and the United States. Both the Security Administrative Punishment Act and the Decision of the State Council Relating to Problems of Reform Through Education require sanctions to be imposed on the following:

> [T]hose who do not engage in productive labor and those who behave like hooligans, . . . those who receive the sanction of expulsion from an organ, organization, enterprise, school . . . and who are without a way of earning a livelihood, . . . those persons who have the capacity to labor, but who for a long period refuse to labor or who destroy discipline, . . . those who do not obey work assignments or arrangements for getting them employment or for transferring them to other employment. . ." (English translation in Cohen, 1968:249–250).

The purpose of this sanction is twofold. First, it brings reeducation and moral reform to an unproductive person. Second, it forces the person to do compulsory labor. Before an offender is treated, the source of his or her problem with the law must be determined. Generally it is either as a result of ignorance of the law, in which case the offender needs reform through legal education, or the offender is too lazy to work, in which case he or she needs reform through labor.

Commonly a local neighborhood, school, work unit, or family may report to the police that somebody fits the definition of an "unproductive person." If the police and the local neighborhood committee agree after a review of a case, they make recommendations. Next, the case is sent to a district Reform Through Labor Committee that consists of representatives from the police, civil affairs, and labor officials. The committee can decide to send the person to a labor farm for a period of 1 to 3 years. The basic programs on the labor farm usually consist of agricultural labor, physical training, skill training, academic education, and political education. It is believed that such administrative sanctions could help an "unproductive person" to learn job skills and learn to labor.

Dynamics of the System

"Following the Mass Line" was a slogan that has directed police work from the early 1950s to the early 1980s. Ideally, this strategy is to call on the police to respect the people's opinion, to experience the people's lives, and accept the people's supervision. However, the police officials are the ones who finally define what the masses want in the field of public security (Bracey, 1989b).

In 1984, a new "Comprehensive Approach" was outlined, containing the following seven major objectives:

1. To call on society to show concern for the youth and further educate them in lofty ideals, moral codes, discipline, and legality

2. To promote mass participation in cultural and sporting activities and enrich young people's lives in their leisure hours

3. To clear away all pornographic publications and objects

4. To punish severely abettors who lead young people astray

5. To accomplish good school education and reduce the number of dropouts

6. To make use of retired officials, workers and teachers and encourage them to help and educate delinquents

7. To expedite the formulation of a law for protecting the youth (Jiang and Dai, 1990)

In essence, this new program is to organize all possible social forces to educate the young people and to promote a good social order. Since 1984, the police agencies at various levels have asked the members of public security committees to join the police in patrol and have organized them to do so. Public security committees are similar to the Neighborhood Watch or Guardian Angels programs in the United States. As of 1991, there were 1.17 million public security committees with 12 million members throughout China (Jiang and Dai, 1990).

Furthermore, the police also assist larger work in setting up civilian security forces (economic police) in big factories, mines, companies, and hotels. These economic police forces are quite similar to private security forces in the United States: they have their own uniforms; they are responsible for security and prevention of offenses such as theft and assault only within the work unit; and they are under direct supervision of the leadership of the work unit. In China, however, the economic police must report to the local police agency on their security work. Essentially, this program emphasizes partnership between the society and the police force to control crime and preserve social order.

Mass education is another strategy used in the Comprehensive Approach. According to Confucianism, human beings are born with the capability of developing a good nature through proper education and training. Moreover, all behavior results from an individual's ideology (values, morals, or viewpoints). The individual's ideology is shaped and influenced by social environment, including education. Deviant behavior also develops gradually over time. Therefore, reinforcing early education, intervention, and rehabilitation will, as they say, "nip crime in the bud."

For this reason, police and local governments in China constantly launch massive campaigns of legal education. Legal education is expected to fulfill two purposes. First, it can shape mass legal thoughts (awareness) about what is right and what is wrong. Second, it warns lawbreakers of the possible consequences of deviant behavior. The legal education takes various forms. The police agency may take to the streets to deliver speeches on laws, may offer legal courses in schools, or may help the court to organize a public trial of a defendant in his or her own work unit.

When mass mobilization and mass education fail in their persuasive functions, punitive measures are necessary to crack down on serious crimes. This is the third important component of the Chinese comprehensive program. The police authorities often relate the sudden increase in crime rates between 1981 and 1983 to an overemphasis on education and persuasion. Punishment and deterrence still have an important role to play in crime prevention. The "Anti-Crime Campaign" of 1983–1984 and the "Anti–Six Evils Campaign" of 1988–1989 directly resulted from this punitive principle. The second campaign focused on six new types of crimes: (1) prostitution; (2) producing, selling, and spreading pornographic objects; (3) kidnapping women and children; (4) planting, gathering, and trafficking in drugs without permission; (5) gambling; and (6) defrauding people of their money by su-

perstition. Chinese police officers believe that such law enforcement functions must supplement mass mobilization and mass education in order to improve social order.

The "Comprehensive Approach" brought crime under control by 1988 (see Tables 11-1 and 11-2). However, after 1988 the crime rate rose again, due in part to a rapid increase in juvenile offenses. According to official data, the conviction rate in 1989 was 36% above that of 1988. Major Chinese crime statistics from 1981 to 1987 are listed in the tables.

From the late 1980s on, regular patrol emerged as a new direction in police strategy. Contrary to trends in the United States toward community policing, the police in China are switching from "people's policing" to formal patrolling. There are several reasons for this new direction. First, as the economic reform gathers strength, more and more small private businesses are set up in urban areas. Thus, security and protection require immediate attention. Second, more and more young farmers are moving to urban areas for employment. This new transient population tends to be without permanent residence: therefore, the traditional neighborhood police

Table 11-1: *National Crimes Recorded by Public Security in the People's Republic of China*

Crimes	1981	1982	1983*	1984	1985	1986	1987
Homicide	9,567	9,324	—	9,021	10,440	11,510	13,154
Assault	21,499	20,298	—	14,526	15,586	18,364	21,727
Robbery	22,266	16,518	—	7,237	8,801	12,124	18,775
Rape	30,808	35,361	—	44,630	37,712	39,121	37,225
Larceny	743,105	609,481	—	395,319	431,323	425,845	435,235
(Grand)	(16,147)	(15,462)	—	(16,340)	(34,643)	(42,192)	(58,661)
Fraud	18,665	17,707	—	13,479	13,157	14,663	14,693
Counterfeit	1,649	1,763	—	707	491	497	436
Other	41,424	38,024	—	29,414	24,495	25,001	29,630
TOTAL	890,261	748,476	610,478	514,369	542,002	547,115	570,439

Source: Law Yearbook of China
(*) No official crime data available for 1983.

Table 11-2: *Rates of Crime in People's Republic of China*

Crimes	1981	1982	1983*	1984	1985	1986	1987
Homicide	0.96	0.92	—	0.88	1.00	2.10	2.31
Assault	2.16	2.01	—	1.41	1.50	3.36	3.81
Robbery	2.24	1.63	—	0.71	0.86	2.22	3.29
Rape	3.09	3.50	—	4.33	3.62	7.15	6.53
Larceny	74.72	60.21	—	38.36	41.43	77.83	76.30
Fraud	1.87	1.75	—	1.31	1.26	2.68	2.S8
Counterfeit	0.17	0.17	—	0.07	0.05	0.09	0.08
Other	4.16	3.77	—	2.84	2.34	11.57	5.10
TOTAL	89.37	14.02	59.81	49.91	52.06	51.41	54.10
Clearance Rate	73.1%	77.4%	—	76.9%	78.8%	79.2%	81.3%

Source: Law Yearbook of China
(*) No official crime data available for 1983.

cannot deal effectively with this new social element. Third, the degree of seriousness of crime has escalated: although nonviolent crimes such as theft or larceny have decreased, violent crimes such as robbery, armed robbery, rape, and murder have burgeoned. The police as well as the public are beginning to question the effectiveness of community policing. Finally, as China becomes a more open society, the traditional culture of collectiveness is being challenged (Wang, 1993). This means that the number of people interested in voluntary or low-paying public participation has decreased sharply (Fu, 1991a).

Since the late 1980s, police patrol of the big cities, such as Beijing, Shanghai, Tianjin, Guanzhong, Shenyang, and Xian, has increased because of social, economic, and cultural changes, and the concomitant public pressure for more police protection, professionalism, and visibility.

The police in China, like those in other countries, tend to be satisfied with the status quo, completely supportive of the government, and somewhat resistant to change (Ward, 1985). The most common complaints and criticisms against Chinese police are corruption, brutality, and too much discretion (Fu, 1991a; Seymour, 1987; Townsend, 1987; and Ma, 1986).

Recently, some efforts have been made to improve the situation.

Conclusion

The police system in China is the social product of the country's political and economic systems. Its nature and functions therefore must be analyzed in the Chinese social context.

The Chinese police operate under a highly centralized hierarchy with complex subdivisions. Unlike the police forces in Western societies, the Chinese police play important roles both in legal process and in the social arena; it is the social (administrative) functions that have enabled police to achieve a unique social control in Chinese society. Police in China and police in the United States use very different approaches, especially in terms of roles, scope of police power, and police discretion in both the legal and the social arenas. However, as political and economic reforms strengthen, the police system in China is facing its new challenges, including control of illegal police power, overprofessionalism, and waning public support.

Notes

1. The author expresses sincere thanks to Professor Robert Davidson of the Justice Studies Program at Northern Michigan University for his valuable comments and suggestions. Professor Davidson has visited China twice with the Office of International Criminal Justice Delegations.

2. The security system within the military differs from public security in that the military security personnel wear military uniforms, not regular police uniforms. The military also has its own prosecution and court system defendants who commit crimes within military jurisdiction and/or crimes involving military secrets.

3. The difference between "detention" and "arrest" is as follows: detention is the emergency apprehension and confinement of a suspect without an arrest warrant for the purpose of investigating whether there is sufficient evidence to justify arrest. Arrest is apprehension and confinement or continuing confinement of a suspect on the basis of an arrest warrant for the purpose of investigation, and to determine whether there is sufficient evidence to justify prosecution (Leng, 1982).

4. This Act was originally passed in 1957, then republished in 1980, and amended in 1987.

5. Reform-through-education and reform-through-labor are two different types of punishment. The former is an administrative sanction determined by the police agency at the urban district level and above, whereas the latter is a formal judicial punishment levied by the court.

6. The Public Security Committee and the Mediation Committee are two major components in a Neighborhood Committee. Most members are retired workers, officials, teachers, or housewives. The members of the Public Security Committee patrol the neighborhood and report to the local neighborhood police station when they find a suspicious person in the area (Bracey, 1989b:134–136).

Discussion and Revision Questions

1. What are the duties of the Ministry of Public Security (MPS) in the Chinese criminal justice system?

2. What are the four components of the Chinese criminal justice system?

3. What are the divisions of the MPS?

4. Local police district stations and local neighborhood police stations are China's grassroots agencies. Discuss.

5. What are the functions of the following:
   (a) Criminal police force
   (b) Criminal examiner
   (c) Public Order Police
   (d) People's Armed Police

6. Which agency issues arrest warrants in China?

7. What are the functions of the police in the judicial process?

8. What are the functions of the police in the social arena?

9. Compare and contrast police services in Great Britain and China.

10. What is meant by "Following the Mass Line"?

11. Compare and contrast public security committees in China and the Guardian Angels in the United States.

12. What are the six evils of the Chinese "Anti–Six Evils Campaign"?

13. What is the most influential traditional value system in China?

14. What are the most common complaints against the police in China?

15. Compare and contrast the role of the police in China and the United States.

16. What is the administrative difference between reform-through-education and reform-through-labor?

Part IV
Comparative Judicial Systems

12

The Judiciary and Criminal Procedure in Nigeria

Obi N. I. Ebbe

Introduction

Criminal law creates both crime and the criminal; crimes and criminals create in turn judiciary and criminal procedures. For indigenous Nigerian society, then, where all such criminal justice concepts are alien, there could be no judiciary and no criminal procedure. This chapter will descriptively analyze the emergence of a Western judiciary and criminal procedure model in a formerly stateless society; how the new judicial system currently exists in symbiosis with customary law and procedure; and factors that have influenced the operation of the Western and Nigerian customary models.

Studying Nigerian judiciary and criminal procedures provides answers to why societies evolve from simple to complex, why rules change over time, and what impact a dual system of judiciary can have on societal order.

This chapter will give a brief history of how the concepts "crime" and "criminal law" emerged in Nigeria, and will also provide arrest and prosecution rates and offender disposal records. The account is based on this author's own ethnographic observations as a native of Nigeria, on his formal and informal knowledge of Nigerian history, and on a review of relevant literature on Nigerian judiciary and legal history.

Pre-English Legal System

Before its colonization in 1849, Nigeria was a stateless society made up of isolated clusters of "gemeinschafts" or communities. Some larger communities had kings, Emirs, OAS, chiefs, an elder, or a council of elders who judged disputes in the community. Relative order and solidarity prevailed in communities without a criminal or penal code.

Offenses in stateless Nigeria were conceived as abominations, taboos, offenses against the earth or deities or ancestors, and minor interpersonal victimizations. The highest authority in each community settled all interpersonal victimizations. Abominations, taboos, and offenses against earth, deities, and ancestors could be tried and disposed by the community as a whole according to the customs of the tribe. But none of these offenses was technically a "crime"; the concept of criminality did not emerge in Nigeria until 1861.

The Emergence of the English Legal System

In 1849 the British annexed Lagos and declared it a colony (Lagos was the capital of Nigeria until 1992). In time, the British gained control over the whole of Nigeria, whose several parts were the colony and protectorate of Lagos, the protectorate of Southern Nigeria, and the protectorate of Northern Nigeria. In 1861 a legislative council was created to control friendly and unfriendly populations, and to regulate business activities that included agents from many European and African countries (Burns, 1929; Niven, 1957; Dike, 1959; Arikpo, 1967).

The British consuls and the Royal Niger Company, who set up the legislative council, also established Courts of Justice and an armed constabulary to enforce laws and regulations. Between 1861 and 1874, ten different courts were created, only four of which were concerned with criminal matters: the Supreme Court/Police Magistrate Court, the Court of Civil and Criminal Justice, the West African Court of Appeal (WACA), and the Privy Council (Elias, 1963). The laws enacted by the colonial legislative council were based on laws, values, standards, and customs in England. It was during this period that the concept of "crime" emerged in Nigeria. In 1900 the British government took over direct administration of Nigeria from the Royal Niger Company, retaining all of the courts, laws, and regulations of the previous administration.

Nigeria has two codes of law and procedure, the Criminal Code and the Penal Code. How and why the two codes emerged will be discussed next.

The Criminal Code

In 1904, Lord Lugard, the colonial Governor of the Northern Protectorate of Nigeria, introduced a Criminal Code for the Northern Protectorate only (Elias, 1954, 1963, 1967; Nwabueze, 1963; Okonkwo and Naish, 1964; Adewoye, 1977). It was modeled closely on the code introduced into the State of Queensland, Australia, in 1899; the Queensland Code was in turn based on a criminal code drafted by British criminal law attorney Sir James Fritzstephen, in Jamaica in 1878 (Arikpo,

1967; Ailed, 1972). The Southern Protectorates of Nigeria were amalgamated in 1906, and in 1914 the Southern Protectorates were amalgamated with the Protectorate of Northern Nigeria. Lord Lagered subsequently made the Criminal Code of 1904 applicable to all of the protectorates in Nigeria.

The Nigerian Criminal Code and its antecedent colonial documents were based on the values of the English common law tradition and not on the values of the people governed; furthermore, the members of the central Legislative Council who drafted and approved the Nigerian Criminal Code of 1904 were all of British origin (Elias, 1954; Ebbs, 1985a). Therefore, the first Nigerian Criminal Code was determined by the interests and standards of British officials, and by what would constitute a crime in Great Britain (Lugard, 1913). The Criminal Code provoked conflicts of norms among the citizens of Nigeria because it criminalized some customary practices and normative standards of the Nigerian people. For example, Section 370 of the Nigerian Criminal Code prescribes 7 years' imprisonment for any person who marries another while his or her marriage partner is still living (Elias, 1954; 1972b; Ebbe, 1985a). According to this section of the Criminal Code, "Bigamy is the contracting of a second marriage during the lifetime of one's 'first' wife or husband. Section 35 of the Marriage Act declares such a second marriage as void, and there [are] penalty provisions in Section 47 and 48 of the Marriage Act" (Elias, 1954; 1972b). Section 370 of the Criminal Code was interpreted to mean that second marriages under Customary Law henceforward would be illegal.

The introduction of a bigamy statute into Nigeria was a gross error and would not have been featured in the Nigerian Criminal Code if it had been based on "customs, customary beliefs, ideals, values, and taboos" of Nigerian society, as consensus theorists assumed. Culturally and traditionally, polygamy is a cherished tradition in Nigerian culture: a Nigerian who marries a second or a third wife gets a handshake and a pat on the back, like a man who has scored a touchdown in American football. Furthermore, the Islamic Maliki Law, to which 49% of Nigerians are subject, allows its members a maximum of four wives (Ebbe, 1985a). After 35 years of political independence from Britain (1960–1995) and some amendments to the criminal code, Nigerians still have difficulties with its alien-based standards.

The Penal Code

In 1959, the current Nigerian Criminal Code ceased to apply to Northern Nigeria. Throughout the colonial era, the courts in the northern region of Nigeria had been without personnel with professional training in English criminal law, and the British judges had experienced difficulties with the Emirs regarding offense and punishment differences between Islamic (Maliki) Law and English criminal law. As a result, a panel of jurists introduced a Penal Code that would take into account the interests, values, and standards of the Muslims (Adewoye, 1977; Nwabueze, 1963). The new Penal Code was based on the Sudanese Penal Code, because the Sudan's Muslim laws were similar to those of the Maliki Code in Northern Nigeria (Elias, 1967).

The Northern Nigerian Penal Code law was intended to apply to all persons living in Northern Nigeria, thus solving some of the problems associated with having different laws for different groups. Occasionally a non-Muslim had been brought before an Islamic Alkali Court, with the defendant not even knowing the illegality of some acts in the Emirate (Karibi-Whyte, 1964). The Penal Code made the region's laws applicable to everybody; but because the majority of the people living in the region were Muslim, the Penal Code Law avoided any conflict with the dictates of the Holy Koran (Elias, 1967).

Customary Law

After the Criminal Code became applicable to the whole of Nigeria in 1916, most criminal cases were still governed not by the Code but by "Native Law and Custom." In Southern Nigeria customary law was unwritten, but Northern Nigeria had written customary law and even schools of jurists such as the Maliki School (Nwabueze, 1963; Allott, 1963). This created problems, especially in Northern Nigeria, where Maliki law and English law were frequently incompatible (Okonkwo and Naish, 1964). In Maliki law, for instance, the capital offense of homicide included any assault ending in death, regardless of intention. What the colonial criminal code considered manslaughter was interpreted as murder under Maliki law (Okonkwo and Naish, 1964).

It is not surprising, then, that colonial authorities attempted to abolish customary law in 1933 by dropping clauses protecting it in Section 4 of the Criminal Code.[1]

British administrators, however, realized that total abolition of the Maliki law would cause an intolerable backlash; therefore, Section 10 of the Native Courts Ordinance allowed customary law to continue, provided that its punishments did not involve mutilation or torture and were "not repugnant to natural justice, equity, and good conscience" (Elias, 1963).

Since independence in 1960, both the Criminal Code and the Penal Code of Nigeria have been amended many times to reflect the norms, values, and standards of the Nigerian people (Karibi-Whyte, 1964; Elias, 1972b; Ebbe, 1985a). Also, some Nigerian customs that were criminalized by the colonial administration have again been legalized. For example, by a 1970 decree, the anti-bigamy law was declared null and void (Elias, 1972b; Obilade, 1969; Ebbe, 1985a).

The post-independence legislatures have given more regard to customary law and its administration than the colonial regime. Indigenous Nigerian administrators understand and sympathize with the culture of the people and their traditional justice system more than the colonial administrators, and many customary laws were restored and others strengthened after the colonial regime (Keay and Richardson, 1966).

Today, Nigeria operates a tripartite system of criminal law and justice. First, there is the Criminal Code, based on English common law and legal practice; second, the Penal Code, based on Maliki law and the Muslim system of law and justice; and finally, Customary Law, based on immemorial customs and traditions of the people. These native laws and customs are conventional and unwritten in Southern Nigeria, whereas in Northern Nigeria they are written.

In order to understand the judiciary and criminal procedure in Nigeria, we will now discuss the nature of that country's crime problem.

The Crime Problem

The crime problem in Nigeria emanates mainly from modernization. By the time colonial rule ended on October 1, 1960, Nigeria had become the largest and most populous center of Western, Asian, and Middle-Eastern trade in sub-Saharan Africa. Nigerian cities had many racial and ethnic groups, with the precolonial gemeinschaft structure, or what Durkheim (1964) called the "mechanical solidarity" type of structure, having given way to an "organic solidarity." After 60 years of direct British administration of Nigeria, English laws, values, and education had been embraced by the greater part of the Nigerian people.

The heterogeneity of city population made English law seem most suitable for a country of Muslims, Christians, and African religions. However, such multiracial, multiethnic, and multireligious communities with laws of alien origin as a control

mechanism led inevitably to cultural conflict and crime (Sellin, 1938).

Crimes in Nigeria today are classified by seriousness (with felonies being very serious and misdemeanors less serious). They are also separated by the Nigerian police into offenses against persons, offenses against property, other offenses (crimes without victims), and offenses against local ordinance.

Felonious offenses include armed robbery, arson, auto theft, burglary, child-stealing, counterfeiting, conspiracy, drug offenses, forgery, fraud, kidnapping, murder, aggravated assault, rape, smuggling contrabands, theft of something of high value, strong-arm robbery, and treason. All other offenses are misdemeanors.

For the purpose of criminal prosecution, any person 17 or older is an adult. Young persons 12 to 16 years old are treated as juveniles, while ages 7–11 are regarded as children. The offenses of both children and young persons are handled by juvenile courts. The magistrate of a county and a layman and a laywoman constitute a juvenile court—i.e., an ad hoc informal court (Ebbe, 1988).

Drug offenses in Nigeria include possession or selling of cocaine, heroin, or marijuana. Unlike in the United States, all barbiturates and amphetamines are legal drugs that can be purchased easily as over-the-counter medicines.

Tables 12-1 and 12-2 show the rates of crime based on police records from 1986 to 1989, in terms of number of crimes reported (which includes crimes reported by citizens, crimes observed by citizens, and crimes observed by the police), percentage of cases solved by the police, and rate of crime per 100,000 population. Tables 12-1 and 12-2 do not include attempted offenses; nor do they include "offenses against local ordinance," for which much data is missing.

Systematic record keeping on crime data in Nigeria is still very cumbersome for the Nigerian Police Force (NPF), but Police Force Headquarters is making some

Table 12-1: Rates of Crime Based on Offenses Known to the Police—1986 - 1987*

Types of Offenses	1986			1987		
	Number of Crimes Reported	Cases Solved Percent	Crime per 100,000	Number of Crimes Reported	Cases Solved Percent	Crimes per 100,000
1. Armed Robbery	1,217	66.7	1.52	1,436	57.2	1.77
2. Assault (Aggravated and Simple Assault)	56,832	85.4	71.18	52,117	61.6	64.31
3. Auto Theft	5,139	41.7	6.43	6,288	36.4	7.75
4. Burglary	11,223	41.6	17.81	15,319	41.2	18.90
5. Counterfeiting	541	48.4	0.67	581	42.9	0.71
6. Drug Offenses	316	42.8	0.39	422	46.9	0.52
7. Forgery	283	39.7	0.35	189	41.3	0.23
8. Fraud	387	29.3	0.48	287	35.2	0.35
9. Manslaughter	738	65.2	0.92	618	54.9	0.76
10. Murder	984	54.7	1.23	849	61.5	1.04
11. Rape	1,238	49.4	1.55	1,116	42.2	1.37
12. Smuggling	449	28.5	0.56	364	39.8	0.44
13. Stealing (Theft)	68,322	48.5	85.57	69,767	45.0	86.09
14. Strong-Arm Robbery	826	49.9	1.03	944	49.9	1.16
TOTAL	151,495	—	89.76	150,297	—	185.47
POPULATION	70,835,000			81,035,000		

Source of Data: Annual Reports of the Nigerian Police Force 1986-1989 and Nigerian Year Book 1986-1989. The rates of crime are computed based on the police reports, and the country's population was estimated from the 1991 Nigerian census report of 88,569,226.

effort toward achieving that goal. The number of robberies and burglaries recorded by the Nigerian police constitutes only about 30% of the robberies or burglaries committed in the country, because many such crimes are not detected or reported. Furthermore, over 60% of crimes that should appear in police records are disposed without record at informal, customary criminal justice courts of the chiefs or councils of elders. Police crime record data from Nigeria can be used only with the full realization of its incompleteness.

The definitions of the crimes listed in Tables 12-1 and 12-2 are similar to English and American definitions, but the American concept of date rape is not a rape in Nigeria. Additionally, unlike in some states in the United States, in Nigeria a husband can never be said to have raped his wife.

From the state of the crime problem presented here, one can see that Nigeria has become more complex than in the precolonial period. It was unavoidable under such an amalgamation of ethnic groups, regions, and religious denominations that an English-based judiciary and criminal procedure should be introduced.

Judicial System

Administration and Organization

There are two classes of courts in Nigeria: federal courts and state courts. Federal courts include the Nigerian Supreme Court

Table 12-2: *Rates of Crime Based on Offenses Known to the Police — 1988 - 1989**

	1988			1989		
Types of Offenses	Number of Crimes Reported	Cases Solved Percent	Crime per 100,000	Number of Crimes Reported	Cases Solved Percent	Crimes per 100,000
1. Armed Robbery	1,529	46.5	1.83	1,398	44.9	1.61
2. Assault (Aggravated and Simple Assault)	55,334	62.4	66.31	54,116	53.0	62.97
3. Auto Theft	6,291	42.8	7.54	5,282	47.6	6.14
4. Burglary	13,862	41.8	16.61	12,678	49.3	14.75
5. Counterfeiting	488	37.7	0.58	472	41.7	0.54
6. Drug Offenses	593	45.9	0.71	588	45.2	0.68
7. Forgery	326	51.8	0.39	336	46.1	0.39
8. Fraud	457	43.3	0.54	492	37.8	0.57
9. Manslaughter	629	65.3	0.75	543	49.4	0.63
10. Murder	838	61.6	1.00	928	54.7	1.07
11. Rape	963	44.2	1.15	1,032	47.7	1.20
12. Smuggling	291	35.4	0.34	287	42.5	0.33
13. Stealing (Theft)	72,368	50.3	86.73	69,454	49.9	80.82
14. Strong-Arm Robbery	851	50.8	1.01	865	46.6	1.00
TOTAL	154,820	—	185.55	148.462	—	172 76
POPULATION	83,435,000			85,935,000		

*Source of Data: Annual Reports of Nigerian Police Force 1986- 1989 and Nigerian Year Book 1986-1989. The rates of crime are computed based on the police reports, and the country's population was estimated from the 1991 Nigerian censu report of 88,569,226.

and the Federal High Court. In the states, there are a variety of courts (Figure 12-1). Unlike in the United States, the states in Nigeria have no Supreme Court. The State High Court is the highest court in most states, although some have a High Court of Appeal.

We will first discuss the federal courts and then proceed to the state courts.

The Supreme Court

The Nigerian Supreme Court was established under the Constitution of the federation Order-in-Council, 1960, and revised by the Republican Constitution (1963). The Republican Constitution did not ensure the independence of the judiciary, but did provide for a Supreme Court

with the chief justice of Nigeria and at least five other judges. The Supreme Court is the final court of appeal and a superior court of records. It has exclusive jurisdiction on constitutional matters, and its judges are appointed by the president of the Republic.[2]

The Nigerian Supreme Court today has powers similar to those of the United States Supreme Court. Under the 1979 Constitution the Supreme Court and its judges became independent of the president and the legislature, and presidential appointments were made subject to the approval of both Houses of the Legislature (Kasumu, 1978). There are thirteen judges in the Nigerian Supreme Court including the chief justice. The judges must be certified lawyers who had served as judges at the federal or state court levels for a minimum of 10 years.

Figure 12-1: *Structure and Organization of the Court in the Federal Republic of Nigeria*

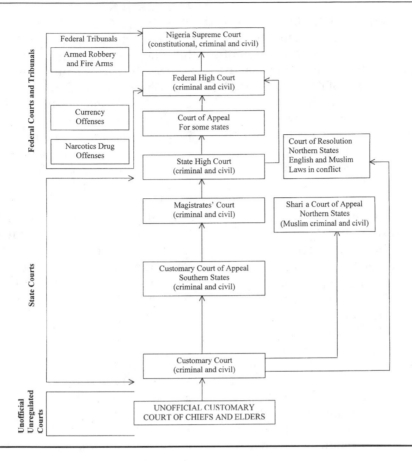

Unfortunately, the presence of a military head of state in Nigeria can adversely influence the roles and decisions of the Supreme Court. We will discuss the Supreme Court's procedure for hearing appeals in a later section on criminal procedure.

Federal High Court/Federal Court of Appeal

The Federal High Court is composed of a chief justice and at least five other judges, all of whom are appointed by the president of the Republic. The Federal High Court is a superior court of records, hearing cases involving the federal government versus individuals or states, or states versus states. Appeals from its decisions go to the Supreme Court. The Federal High Court may sit in any one of the states as an assize court, especially where the parties come from the same state. A case involving persons of different states may be filed in a Federal High Court in Lagos or Abuja. The court has both original and appellate jurisdiction in offenses involving violation of federal law such as smuggling contraband, counterfeiting, and possession of marijuana or narcotic drugs (drug appeals and currency offenses are now tried by special tribunals). Ten years of experience on the bench is required before a lawyer is appointed judge of the Federal High Court. The Federal High Court hears appeals from state high courts and states' courts of appeals.

State Courts

All of Nigeria's thirty states have powers under the constitution to establish state courts of appeal for the determination of appeals brought from a state high court (Elias, 1967). Where a state has a court of appeal, decisions from its high court cannot be brought directly to the Nigerian Supreme Court. Instead, appeals must first be made to the State Court of Appeal and from there to the Supreme Court.

The Court of Appeal
(Western States)

In the western states, a court of appeal was established by the Court of Appeal Edict, 1967 (Elias, 1972b). The provisions of the edict were given effect under Section 127 (2) of the Constitution of the Federation by the Constitution (Western Nigeria Court of Appeal) Order, 1967. The court consists of the president and four justices of appeal and receives appeals from high courts of western states. It has jurisdiction in questions concerning the interpretation of the state constitution, civil matters, murder, and all felonies requiring more than 5 years of imprisonment.

The Courts of Resolution
(Northern States)

The Court of Resolution of Northern Nigeria was established by the Court of Resolution Law (1960)[3] for the purpose of resolving any conflict of jurisdiction between the State High Court and the Sharia Court of Appeal. Today, the Court of Resolution of each northern state consists of the chief justice of the state (who is the president), the Grand Khadi, one judge of the high court nominated by the chief justice, and one judge of the Sharia Court nominated by the Grand Khadi.[4] No appeal can be made from the Court of Resolution to any other court.[5]

The Sharia Court of Appeal
(Northern States)

The Sharia Court of Appeal was established in the northern states in 1960 for hearing appeals from customary courts where Muslim personal law is involved. The Sharia Court of Appeal consists of a Grand Khadi and not less than two other judges well versed in Sharia law. The judges are appointed by the president after consultation with the Advisory Judicial Committee. Appeals from an upper area court in cases involving Muslim personal law go to the Sharia Court of Appeal. Appeals from the decision of the Sharia Court of Appeal on questions regarding the interpretation of the Constitution of the Federation, or that of a state, or questions about violations of fundamental constitutional rights, go to the Nigerian Supreme Court.[6]

The High Courts

The federal constitution of 1954 empowered the regional legislatures to establish courts for their respective regions, and in 1955 each region established a high court, magistrates' courts, and native or customary courts. When the regions were broken into thirty states, each state was granted power to establish its own courts in accordance with the federal constitution.

Under the constitutions of 1960, 1979, and 1992, the high court of each state consists of the chief justice of the state and other judges. Each state high court is required by law to have six or more judges (except in the state of Lagos, which requires five or more). The chief justice is appointed by the state governor. The other judges are also appointed by the governor, but the appointments have to be in accordance with the advice of the state Judicial Service Commission. During Nigeria's military regimes, the chief justice of each high court and the other judges of the court were appointed by the Supreme Military

Council after consultation with the Advisory Judicial Committee.

Each high court is a superior court of records having original and appellate jurisdiction. Since the Nigerian Civil War destroyed most of the customary court buildings in the Eastern States, customary courts have been abolished there, and the high courts now have original jurisdiction in their land causes and matters arising under customary law.

Magistrates' Courts

There are different grades of magistrates' courts from state to state. The Public Service Commission of each state is empowered to appoint magistrates, and there are grades of magistrates and magistrates' courts that vary from state to state. The magistrates are all certified lawyers with at least 5 years of experience on the bench. In the Eastern States, especially in the Ibo areas, the cases that used to be brought to the customary courts now go to the magistrates' courts.

Customary Courts

All judges of customary courts, including Sharia Courts, are lay judges without formal legal training. They are supposed to be persons who, by their age and experience, have a deep knowledge of the customary laws of their clans.

In the northern states, the customary courts are known as area courts. Area courts are of four types: Upper Area Courts, Area Courts Grade I, Area Courts Grade II, and Area Courts Grade III. The area courts are established by the chief justice of each of the states, and their judges are appointed by the state's Public Service Commission. Appeals go from an Area Court Grade I to II or III, or to the Upper Area Court having jurisdiction. Appeals from Upper Area Court go to the Sharia Court of Appeal in cases involving Muslim personal law, and to the High Court in other cases (Aguda, 1974; Elias, 1967; Nwabueze, 1963).

In midwestern states, all customary courts are now of the same grade. Customary courts are established by the chief justice subject to the approval of the state governor. The chief justice has the power to appoint persons as presidents or members of a customary court on the recommendation of the Advisory Judicial Committee (Elias, 1972a).

In the western states, customary courts are graded as A, B, and C; there was formerly a D grade that has been abolished. The Judicial Service Commission was empowered to appoint presidents of grade A and B courts presided over by legal practitioners. On the abolition of the Judicial Service Commission, the Local Government Service Board was empowered to appoint, dismiss, and exercise disciplinary control over all members of customary courts (Aguda, 1974).

All the courts discussed above have powers of criminal jurisdiction except some district courts in the northern states.

Special Courts

Special Criminal Offenses Tribunals:

Special criminal offenses are those for which trials cannot be originated in any of the courts just discussed. Such crimes are tried at special tribunals, including (a) the Armed Robbery and Firearms Tribunal (1970), (b) the Currency Offenses Tribunal (1974), and (c) the Illegal Drugs and Narcotics Tribunal (1986).

The Nigerian government set up these tribunals because people known to have committed these certain offenses were not paying the price for their crimes in regular criminal courts because of pettifogging legal arguments of defense lawyers. Each one of the tribunals is composed of five to seven officials such as retired court judges, senior military officials, retired senior police officers, or retired senior civil servants, most with no degree in law. The defendant is allowed to call witnesses and to have a defense attorney, and there is no prosecutor; the trial session consists of the defendant and his or her defense attorney facing a panel of unbiased judges. This system and its operation could be said to be the spirit of the Nigerian customary criminal procedure haunting the government's English judicial system. In effect, the adversarial system is disregarded in these tribunals in favor of the inquisitorial approach: instead of the accused being convicted only when evidence proves that he or she committed the offense beyond a reasonable doubt, the accused has to prove to the tribunal that he or she did not commit the offense.

Penalties for each of the three offenses are established by decree, with very little discretionary power given to the judges in sentencing: any person convicted of any of the tribunal offenses receives death by a firing-squad. It was only in November 1992 that Nigerian Head of State Ibrahim Babangida commuted the death penalty to life imprisonment for any person convicted of narcotics drug smuggling or possession. Whether a person convicted of narcotics drug smuggling has a prior criminal record is immaterial to the life sentence, and Nigeria has no parole system.

Juvenile Court

The juvenile court in Nigeria began in Lagos in the 1940s as a brainchild of British colonial authorities. After World War II it was introduced into the Western, Eastern, and Northern regions (Ebbe, 1988). Today the court is composed of a magistrate who is the president of the court, a layman, and a laywoman.

Juveniles adjudicated as delinquent are sent to approved schools, sent to remand homes, or placed on probation. A juvenile accused of murder is tried as an adult in a criminal court. If convicted, he or she is sent to a medium-security prison until he or she attains the age of 17 or 18.

Criminal Procedures

Both to Nigerians with some Western education and to those without Western education, the English system of criminal procedure can be a nightmare. It is not easy to adapt criminal procedures to a society for which any such system is culturally alien. In fact, in some rural towns and villages in Nigeria today, it will offend the whole town or village if any member of the community calls the police over any criminal victimization by a community member, or brings a lawsuit against any member for damages. This attitude has prevailed since colonial days. Most villages want to handle all criminal victimizations within the village in a traditional manner.

Nigeria is a country divided between literates and illiterates, with the literates holding firmly to Western ways and systems of justice; therefore, the English system of criminal procedure probably has come to stay despite its difficulties and despite local opposition. The controversial nature of the English criminal procedures, however, has made police operations in Nigeria very cumbersome and often ineffective.

Rights of the Accused

When the accused is indigent and incapable of providing a defense attorney, he or she is protected against self-incrimination by a public defender.

There has been no jury trial in Nigeria since the eclipse of the colonial administration of justice (Aguda, 1974). If an accused is brought before a magistrate's court and pleads guilty during questioning, the court will immediately refer him or her to a psychiatrist to determine whether he or she is in full control of his or her mental faculties. If he or she is found to be normal, the magistrate will then give sentence according to law without regard to his or her pleading guilty. (The court accepts the defendant's guilty plea, but—unlike the

American plea bargaining situation—there is no reduction in the severity of punishment for the offense.)

Arrest and Investigation

Suspects come to the attention of the police through victims or crime-scene observers, or suspects may be caught by the police on patrol. The police officer with greatest seniority at the station thoroughly investigates the case, and may take any one of the following three actions:

(a) Dismiss the case because of insufficient evidence

(b) In trivial cases, simply warn the suspect and discharge him or her on grounds that:

    (i) The suspect has no prior criminal record

    (ii) The crime has no victim

    (iii) The offender has agreed to compensate the victim

(c) When the suspect is a juvenile (less than 17 years old), refer the case to a juvenile court or discharge the juvenile

If there are grounds to detain the suspect, the police officer will do so and initiate an investigation of the case. If the investigation report shows that the suspect actually committed an offense, the case reports for the accused person are transferred to the office of the director of public prosecution (DPP). If the DPP finds inadequate evidence to charge the case to court, he or she dismisses it. If there is enough evidence to charge the accused of a crime, he or she places charges against the suspect in a magistrate's court.

A person charged with a misdemeanor is entitled to bail unless the DPP and the court see good reasons for not granting it. In felony cases, however, granting bail is at the discretion of the court. Should the offender fail to show up on the day of trial, the bailer is held liable. Bail can be granted by the court on recognizance with or without sureties to appear before the court. The court can deny bail and require an offender to be remanded in custody awaiting trial in a medium or maximum pretrial security prison. Law allows magistrates to detain a suspect for 30 days, but in practice detainees may be in prison awaiting trial for 6 months or even a year. Bail may be denied on the following grounds:

(a) The suspect refused arrest

(b) The suspect is a recidivist

(c) The suspect committed the crime while on bail

(d) The suspect is arrested for murder, rape, armed robbery, narcotics drug smuggling, counterfeiting currency, or any other heinous crime

(e) The suspect is an apparent danger to the public

(f) There is a need to protect the offender

(g) The suspect is an unruly juvenile

It is noteworthy that in the area of public prosecution, there are deviant factors that can make the police or the DPP not charge an offender with a legal violation. These are the interests and influences of top officials or politicians in the executive branch of the government, the justice department, corporate executives, and wealthy businessmen. These individuals can order or lobby the police or the director of public prosecution not to take a case to court, or cause a case to be dropped when it is already charged to court.

As in Britain, most criminal prosecutions are police prosecutions. The DPP and department prosecute only in more serious cases, particularly murder, armed robbery, and narcotics drug trafficking (Aguda, 1974). When the police prosecute, the prosecution may be in the name of the officer of the Nigerian or native authority police; or in the name of the commissioner of police of the state (for example, *Obi Okonkwo v. Commissioner of Police*); or in the name of the native authority of the area in which the offense was committed, or against whose rules the offenses were committed (for example, *Bobo Ikemefuna v. Orlu Urban Council*; or *Jim Jones v. The Inspector General*). In contrast, in the United States the accused is prosecuted in the name of the state or the people (e.g., *The People v. O. J. Simpson*).

There is no plea bargaining in the Nigerian criminal justice system. The defense in a criminal trial may claim self-defense or insanity (Brett and McLean, 1963), but intoxication is not a defense unless coupled with duress. Minor criminal cases that require negotiated settlements are referred at the discretion of the magistrate to a customary court that has jurisdiction over the parties involved in the case. In practice, if it is clear, unequivocal, and beyond a reasonable doubt, that the defendant committed the crime charged, Nigerian criminal procedure will not entertain denial of due process (e.g., failure to read the Miranda rule or judge's rule to the accused) as a defense in court. This constitutes a major difference between Nigerian and American criminal procedure.

Tables 12-3 and 12-4, which show offender disposal records for 1987 and 1988, indicate that most persons convicted of offenses in Nigeria are not incarcerated. Instead, they receive non-prison sentences, including warning, compensation, service at public projects, a fine, or time in a labor camp. Most arrested persons are not prosecuted, but most of those prosecuted are found guilty of the offense(s) charged (66.9% in 1987 and 81.2% in 1988). Rates of conviction are particularly high for murder, armed robbery, rape, burglary, counterfeiting, forgery, fraud, auto theft, strong-arm robbery, and drug offenses. Assault charges (except for premeditated aggravated assault) are less likely to lead to a sentence of imprisonment. Assault and battery are a traditional means of settling differences between friends in Nigeria, and social changes have increased their fre-

quency despite the fact that the British criminalized them; thus, they do not lead to incarceration of the offender in most cases today.

Dismissal or Discharge

Every criminal court in Nigeria, whether a court of first instance or a court of appeal, can dismiss a case and discharge the accused, if it finds no reasonable grounds to put the accused on trial or convict him.

It is provided, however, that the dismissal of a complaint or the discharge of the accused is not the same as an acquittal (The Criminal Procedure Act, Cap. 43 of the Laws of the Federation of Nigeria; Aguda, 1980). Also, if an accused has been tried by a court of competent jurisdiction for a crime and convicted or acquitted of the crime, he or she will not be tried again for the same offense; nor will the same facts be used to charge him or her with any other crime "for which a different charge from the one made against him might have been made before the court by which he was earlier on acquitted or convicted" (Aguda, 1980; Brett and McLean, 1963). Such a second trial would amount to "double jeopardy," also prohibited by law in the U.S. criminal justice system.

However, if an accused was tried for a crime and convicted or acquitted by a court that has no competent jurisdiction in the matter, he or she can be subsequently charged with and tried for the same offense without regard to the decision of the court where he or she was first charged and adjudicated (The Criminal Procedure Act, 1960; Brett and McLean, 1963; Aguda, 1980).

Right of Appeal in Criminal Cases

Both Federal and State constitutions in Nigeria provide for rights of appeal from subordinate courts to the appropriate high court and from the state high courts, in their original and appellate jurisdictions, to the federal high court or to the federal Supreme Court on constitutional grounds.

The constitutional provisions are the same, mutatis mutandis, for all of the thirty states in Nigeria and for the capital territory of Abuja.

Table 12-3: Offender Disposal Records Year 1987

	No. of Persons Arrested	No. of Prosecutions (%)	No. Discharged (%)*	No. Imprisoned (%)*	Death Sentences (%)*	Non-Prison Sentence (%)*	Found Guilty (%)**
1. Murder	716	441 (61.6)	38 (8.6)	147 (33.3)	256 (58.0)	—	91.4
2. Manslaughter	618	339 (54.9)	102 (30.1)	237 (69.9)	—	—	69.9
3. Armed robbery	1,012	579 (57.2)	66 (11.4)	125 (21.6)	388 (67.0)	—	88.6
4. Rape	1,116	471 (42.2)	113 (24.0)	358 (76.0)	—	—	76.0
5. Burglary	12,867	5,301 (41.2)	1,809 (34.1)	3,492 (65.9)	—	—	65.9
6. Stealing/theft	31,281	14,077 (45.0)	2,163 (15.4)	4,722 (33.5)	—	7,192 (51.1)	84.6
7. Assault (all types)	33,019	20,341 (61.6)	9,874 (48.5)	1,316 (6.5)	—	9,151 (45.0)	51.5
8. Smuggling	263	105 (39.9)	16 (15.2)	89 (84.8)	—	—	84.8
9. Counterfeiting	522	224 (42.9)	21 (9.4)	203 (90.6)	—	—	90.6
10. Forgery	121	51 (42.1)	19 (37.3)	32 (62.7)	—	—	62.7
11. Fraud	169	60 (35.5)	22 (36.7)	38 (63.3)	—	–	63.3
12. Auto theft and snatching	4,063	1,479 (36.4)	173 (11.7)	1,306 (88.3)	—	—	88.3
13. Strong arm robbery	623	311 (49.9)	58 (18.6)	188 (60.5)	—	65 (20.9)	81.4
14. Narcotic drugs offense	422	198 (46.9)	86 (43.4)	66 (33.3)	46 (23.2)	—	56.5
15. Other	814	464 (57.0)	132 (28.4)	152 (32.8)	—	180 (38.8)	71.6
Total	87,626	44,441 (50.7%)	14,692 (33.1%)	12,471 (28.1%)	690 (1.5%)	16,588 (37.3%)	66.9%
Population	81,035,000						

Source: Nigerian Police Force Annual Reports 1987
*Percentage of those prosecuted.
**Percentage of those prosecuted found guilty of the offense charged.

Table 12-4: Offender Disposal Records Year 1988

	No. of Persons Arrested	No. of Prosecutions (%)*	No. Discharged (%)*	No. Imprisoned (%)*	Death Sentences (%)*	Non prison Sentences (%)*	Found Guilty (%)**
1. Murder	876	540 (61.6)	42 (7.8)	189 (35.0)	309 (57.2)		92.2
2. Manslaughter	518	339 (65.4)	131 (38.6)	208 (61.4)	—	—	61.4
3. Armed robbery	1,214	5651 (46.5)	33 (5.8)	238 (42.1)	294 (52.0)	—	94.2
4. Rape	912	403 (44.2)	98 (24.3)	305 (75.7)	—	—	75.7
5. Burglary	10,961	4,582 (41.8)	914 (19.9)	3,553 (77.5)	—	115 (2.5)	80.1
6. Stealing/theft	43,119	21,689 (50.3)	1,224 (5.6)	8,731 (40.3)	—	11,734 (54.1)	94.4
7. Assault (all types)	35,866	22,380 (62.4)	7,361 (32.9)	4,406 (19.7)	—	10,613 (47.4)	67.1
8. Smuggling	213	76 (35.7)	24 (31.6)	38 (50.0)	—	14 (18.4)	68.4
9. Counterfeiting	364	137 (37.6)	11 (8.0)	113 (82.5)	—	13 (9.5)	92.0
10. Forgery	229	119 (52.0)	15 (12.6)	104 (87.4)	—	—	87.4
11. Fraud	332	144 (43.4)	9 (6.3)	135 (93.8)	—	—	93.8
12. Auto theft and snatching	4,158	1,821 (43.8)	53 (2.9)	1,768 (97.1)	—	—	97.1
13. Strong arm robbery	541	275 (50.8)	37 (13.5)	189 (68.7)		49 (17.8)	86.5
14. Narcotic drugs offense	517	237 (45.8)	26 (11.0)	135 (57.0)	76 (32.1)		89.1
15. Other	966	493 (51.0)	113 (22.9)	117 (23.7)	—	263 (53.3)	77.0
Total	100,786	53,800 (53.4%)	10,091 (18.8%)	20,229 (37.6%)	679 (1.3%)	22,801 (42.4%)	81.2%
Population	83,435,000						

Source: Nigerian Police Annual Reports 1988
*Percentage of those prosecuted
**Percentage of those prosecuted found guilty

Appeals to Magistrate's Court

At the customary court level, if a convicted party does not countenance the decision or order of a grade A or grade B district court or a customary court of appeal, he or she can appeal to the magistrate's court or the state high court within 30 days from the date of the lower court's order or decision (similar appeals are allowed 6 or 7 months to be lodged in the United States and 3 days in China). The cases appealed must involve a prison sentence or a fine exceeding N250 (250 naira) on conviction.

An appeal from a decision or order of a magistrate's court goes to the high court of the state where the magistrate's court is located. The appellant must give the registrar of the magistrate's court notice of appeal indicating the grounds on which his or her complaints are based.

If the appellant is in prison custody, the magistrate may "release him from custody on his entering into a recognizance, with or without securities," and at a reasonable cost that the magistrate thinks expedient to secure the appellant's appearance (Nigerian [Constitution] Order in Council, 1960; Brett and McLean, 1963). The magistrate will not grant a release from prison custody if any one of the following applies:

(a) The appellant has previously served a sentence of not less than 6 months' imprisonment

(b) The magistrate has a reason to believe that if released from prison, the appellant is likely to commit an additional crime

(c) The appellant is likely to abscond or disappear.

The magistrate has the discretionary power to release the appellant from prison custody or not to do so. However, if the magistrate refuses to grant the appellant a release from custody, the appellant can apply to the state high court, which also has the power to grant a release or refuse to do so. If the high court grants the release request and the appellant fails to show up on the day of the appeal hearing, the high court may take any one of the following actions:

(a) Issue a warrant for the appellant's arrest

(b) Dismiss the appeal or order the appeal hearing to be postponed, and order that, if the appellant is caught, he or she should be remanded in custody

(c) Order that the appellant's security or securities be forfeited in total or in part

The High Court in Criminal Appeals

The High Court, in its appellate jurisdiction in criminal cases coming from the customary courts and magistrate's courts, can respond to the appeals as follows:

(a) It can, after reviewing the matter, confirm the decision or order of the lower court and dismiss the appeal.

(b) If it sees that there is sufficient ground to interfere with the decision of the lower court, it can set aside the earlier decision and (1) acquit the appellant; or (2) retry the appellant on the same charge and/or on a new charge that might have been disclosed by the evidence, and then sentence the appellant as it deems just; or (3) order a retrial of the appellant on the same charge or on any new charge disclosed by the evidence; or (4) modify or substitute the decision or order of the lower court where the appeal was filed (Brett and McLean, 1963; Aguda, 1980).

An appeal court may not entertain an appeal made only because the decision reached by the lower court is "challenged on the ground of its being contrary to the weight of the evidence" (Aladesuru and

Others v. R. [1955], 39 Cr. App. R. 184, p.c.; Aguda, 1980). However, the court of appeal can hear the case, if it can be shown that the decision or order of the court of trial is "unwarranted, unreasonable, and cannot be supported having regard to the evidence" (*Chivo Adi v. R.* [1955], 15 W.A.C.A.G.; Aguda, 1980).

The Appellate Jurisdiction of the Nigerian Supreme Court

The federal Supreme Court has exclusive jurisdiction to hear and determine appeals from state high courts and the federal high court. In addition to civil matters, the Supreme Court has final say (1) in all criminal cases brought before the high court sitting at first instance; (2) in any criminal decisions addressing alleged violations of the constitutional rights of the accused; (3) in instances where a death sentence has been imposed by a high court, or decisions "in which the High Court has affirmed a sentence of death imposed by some other courts" (Aguda, 1980; Brett and McLean, 1963).

The Supreme Court allows an appeal against conviction from a high court if it thinks that the decision reached at the lower court "should be set aside on the ground that it is unreasonable and cannot be supported having regard to the evidence"; or it believes that a wrongful decision was made based on a question of law applied to the case; or "on the ground that there was a miscarriage of justice" (Brett and McLean, 1963).

If the Supreme Court allows an appeal against a conviction, it may set aside the conviction and order that the appellant be acquitted. Also, the Supreme Court may order that "the appellant be retried by a court of competent jurisdiction" (Brett and McLean, 1963).

A defendant in a criminal case who wants to take a case to the Supreme Court must "give notice of appeal or notice of his application for leave to appeal" (Aguda, 1980; Brett and McLean, 1963) according to the rules of the court and within 30 days. In some circumstances, 15 days may be added to help the appellant prepare.

The Supreme Court may, at any stage, appoint counsel to help an appellant. When the Supreme Court upholds the decision of the high court, the appellant serves the sentence imposed by the high court that led to the appeal.

Appeals may also reach the Supreme Court from the special tribunals for cases of armed robbery, which draws the death penalty; or for cases of counterfeiting currency and narcotic drugs trafficking, which draw a life sentence without parole.

Penalties and Sentencing

Sentencing Process

Nigeria has no presentencing hearings. The magistrate or a high court judge, in a state court, can sentence an offender to terms of imprisonment according to law on the very day the case is tried, if the accused is found guilty of the offense. Only rarely does a judge or magistrate postpone sentencing until a later date.

Only judges can give sentences. Victims have no sentencing role; nor do psychiatrists or social workers, although they may be involved in pretrial investigations.

Types of Penalties

Persons found guilty of misdemeanor offenses may be fined, warned, granted probation, or, as in Singapore, be given corporal punishment or a community service order. Persons found guilty of felonious offenses may be sentenced to some years of imprisonment, served either in a maximum-security prison or in a medium-security prison, depending on the gravity of the offense. Less serious felonious offenders are sent either to minimum-security prisons or to a labor camp.

Nigeria has the death penalty for murder, armed robbery, treason, and serious currency offenses. Until November 1992, illegal drugs and narcotics smuggling was disposed by death penalty. The punishment is now life imprisonment, which in Nigeria means that the offender will be released from prison only in a coffin. Once again, there is no parole program in the Nigerian criminal justice system.

House arrest, banishment, and exile are no longer used in the Nigerian criminal justice system. House arrest, however, may be applied to a political dissident.

Capital punishment is carried out publicly by a firing squad of soldiers with the offender tied to a stake. Sometimes the audience is an angry crowd of crime condemners; sometimes it is a sympathetic crowd.

Discussion

Every aspect of the Nigerian criminal justice system is still developing, partly because most of Nigeria's laws are based on alien customs and traditions, and partly because federal governments in Nigeria fall like ripe apples. Every new regime brings new decrees, a new constitution, and new organizational structures, and what criminal codes declare to be illegal acts depends on who occupies the seat of power. Changes in Nigerian law reflect changes in its ruling classes.

Contrary to Thompson's idea about Sierra Leone (Chapter 6), Nigeria does show that multiple systems of criminal justice—the English legal system, the Islamic legal system, and the customary legal system—can coexist and work in relative harmony with each other. The Muslim courts and the customary courts are very close to the people and are understood by the common citizens, because the legal arguments in those courts are based on immemorial custom, tradition, and revelation (Sharia)—that is, on the values and standards of the people. Cases are disposed of in these courts cheaply and expeditiously. But the English legal system, although entrenched in the Nigerian constitution, still appears alien and threatening to the majority of the people.

The English-based legal system has many loopholes through which a criminal can escape. It is a phenomenon of the urban areas, and so is crime: criminals take refuge and operate in the cities because customary law and its informal control mechanisms are too far away to apply. Finally, frequent military interventions in the governance of Nigeria weaken the independence of the judiciary and generally disrupt the normal course of the criminal justice system.

The judiciary in Nigeria is highly politicized. Arcane societies that unite some members of the judiciary, the military, and top civilians create disintegration and insincerity within the judiciary. In effect, partisanship has nullified the rule of law and due process, and the entire society has become disorganized. The military regime and violent criminals maintain their power through cold-blooded assassinations of persons who oppose the military clique; consequently, some murders are not truly investigated because they were ordered by top military commanders or their civilian cronies. The judiciary has failed to challenge the illegal regimes and their atrocities because many important members of the judiciary are party to political conspiracies and self-defeating political agendas.

Under this state of affairs, an offender who reaches the courts and gets convicted is one who has no money and no "godfather" in the military or among the top civilian population. Nigeria's criminal justice system has shortened prima facie cases against offenders with "godfathers," but for the poor and unconnected it has become a nightmare.

Conclusion

In nations without viable political systems, justice is denied; and Nigeria is such a nation. The Nigerian Constitution becomes obsolete with each change of government, and a new one is created in its place; the masses become disorganized and the judiciary is rendered powerless before the military. Worst of all, the Nigerian Supreme Court refuses to declare an act of the military junta or government unconstitutional. In effect, the military junta has criminalized any behaviors that fail to serve its interests. The Nigerian criminal justice system will never be reliable until the military undergoes an improvement of manners, adopts respect for human dignity, and submits to rule of law.

In summary, the advent of the English legal system in Nigeria in the late nineteenth century created new forms of crime and criminals. Contemporary Nigerian criminal law is based on English law, customary law, and Maliki law summed up in the criminal code and the penal code. Of course, customary law still stands apart from the two codes, making Nigeria effectively operate a tripartite system of criminal law and justice.

Nigeria has two classes of courts, federal and state, with the Nigerian Supreme Court being the highest court of the land. The 1979 Constitution gave the Supreme Court powers similar to those of the United States' Supreme Court, but the Nigerian military regimes have reduced the court to impotence. The most important lesson to be learned from the Nigerian criminal justice system is the use of lay judges, chiefs, or a village council of elders as mediators in disposing some serious crimes at very little cost to the victim, offender, or taxpayers. This customary court approach also reduces the number of undecided cases in the files of magistrates' courts and high courts.

Finally, as long as the military continues to abuse the constitution drafted by a preceding regime, Nigeria will continue to be an unjust society and a raped democracy.

Notes

1. Section 4 of the Criminal Code originally stated that "no person shall be liable to be tried or punished in any Court in Nigeria, other than a native tribunal, for an offense except under the express provision of the Code or some other Ordinance, or some law, or of some Order-in-Council made by his Majesty for Nigeria or under the express provisions of some statute of the Imperial Parliament which is in force in, or forms part of the law of Nigeria" (Okonkwo and Naish, 1964; Elias, 1967). It was amended to read that "no person shall be liable to be tried or punished in any Court in Nigeria for an offense except under the express provisions of the Code or . . . under the express provisions of some statute of the Imperial Parliament which is in force, or forms part of, the law of Nigeria" (Okonkwo and Naish, 1964; Elias, 1967).

2. Constitution of the Federal Republic of Nigeria 1963, Sec. III(2).

3. Northern Region Law Report, 94 of 1960.

4. Court of Resolution Law, Cap. 28, Law of Northern Nigeria, 1964 Revision Section 3(1).

5. Ibid.

6. Constitution of the Federation Sec. 119, Act No. 20 of 1963.

Discussion and Review Questions

1. What are the two codes of law in Nigeria?

2. The Nigerian Criminal Code of 1904 was determined by alien norms. Discuss and comment.

3. What is the consensus theorists' view of criminal law?

4. What is Maliki law?

5. What is Sharia court?

6. What is meant by the statement that "Nigeria operates a tripartite system of criminal justice"?

7. Compare and contrast the judiciary in Nigeria and the United States.

8. What are the common features of the Nigerian judiciary and the Sierra Leonean judiciary?

9. On what grounds can bail be denied an accused in the Nigerian criminal justice system?

10. What are the functions of the director of public prosecution (DPP) in the Nigerian criminal justice system?

11. What are the defenses available to one accused of a crime in Nigeria?

12. What factors will make a magistrate choose not to release an appellant from detention when his or her appeal is pending?

13. Under what circumstances can the Nigerian Supreme Court allow an appeal against conviction from a high court decision?

14. What are the capital offenses in Nigeria?

15. What factors politicized the Nigerian judiciary and made it unreliable in upholding the rule of law and due process standards?

16. Compare and contrast treatment of offenders in precolonial Nigeria and in contemporary Denmark.

17. How did the English legal system emerge in Nigeria?

18. What are "special tribunal" in Nigeria?

19. What were the roles of the West African Court of Appeals (WACA) and the Privy Council in London (UK) in the colonial times?

20. What is the purpose of the Court of Resolution in the Nigerian criminal Justice system?

13

The Court System in the People's Republic of China with a Case Study of a Criminal Trial

Robert Davidson and Zheng Wang

Introduction

The American and Chinese approaches to social control are enforced by two very different philosophical and experimental perspectives (Rojek, 1985). Indeed, they differ so fundamentally that they invite comparison in order to promote a better understanding of each. This chapter will attempt such a comparison focusing on the basic structure, organizational dynamics, and philosophies of the Chinese judicial system. In order to illustrate how the system works, a case study of criminal trial also will be provided. Finally, a summary of the trial will be given from a comparative perspective.

The present court system in China was first designed after the founding of the People's Republic of China in 1949, but has been remodeled several times since. Under Article 17 of the Common Program,[1] "laws and decrees promoting the people shall be enacted, and the people's judicial systems shall be established" (Important Documents, 1949:1–20). Later, the Ministry of Justice was set up, with the court system being one of the functions within the Ministry. On September 20, 1954, the first adopted constitution announced that the court system would be separated from governmental supervision under the Ministry of Justice and under an independent system, the Supreme People's Court. Septem-

ber 28, 1954, saw passage of the Organic Law of the People's Court, which laid out the present court system.

Overall Structure

According to the Organic Law of the People's Courts of the People's Republic of China, the judicial authority of the state is exercised through the Supreme People's Court, local people's courts, and special people's courts.

Special courts include military, maritime, railway-transportation, forestry, and other courts. The military courts handle cases of violation of military duties and criminal cases involving servicemen in the Chinese People's Liberation Army. The maritime courts deal with cases related to maritime affairs. There are eight maritime courts in the eight coastal and island river ports. Railway-transportation courts handle criminal cases that occur along rail lines and aboard trains, as well as cases of economic dispute related to rail transportation.

The major court system in China is divided into two levels: the Supreme People's Court at the national level and the local people's courts at the divisional levels. The local people's courts are subdivided into another three levels: the higher people's courts at the provincial, autonomous region and autonomous city level; the intermediate people's courts at the municipal or prefecture level; and the basic people's courts at the urban district level or rural county level (also called the District People's Court). See Figures 13-1 and 13-2.

There are five autonomous regions in China, each occupying an area inhabited predominantly by minority peoples. Their governments have the same basic responsibilities as the provincial governments in economic affairs, but enjoy more favorable national policies.

Three of China's largest and most important cities, Beijing, Shanghai, and Tianjin, are called autonomous or centrally administered cities. They are not subject

to provincial governments, but under the direct supervision of the central government or the State Council. Therefore, each of these three cities has a higher people's court, an intermediate people's court, and several district people's courts.

Prefectures lie within autonomous regions and county levels. Their main function is to provide a convenient administrative division for minorities who occupy areas larger than counties but smaller than provinces.

China's judicial system is a highly centralized (unified) and hierarchical organization. The Constitution gives the Standing Committee of the National People's Congress (NPC) judicial as well as legisla-

Figure 13-1: *The National Court System of the People's Republic of China*

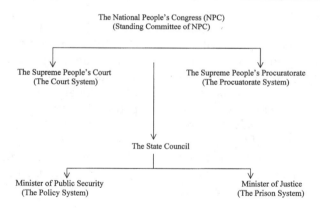

Figure 13-2: *The Divisional Court System of the People's Republic of China*

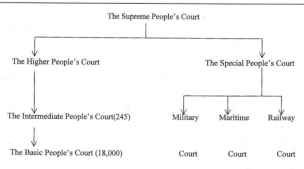

tive control of the country. The Standing Committee interprets the Constitution and various statutes, it enacts and amends statutes, and also supervises the work of the Supreme People's Court, the Supreme People's Procuratorate, and the State Council. This is unlike the United States, which limits constitutional interpretations to the highest judicial organ (the U.S. Supreme Court).

The Supreme People's Court is the highest judicial organ in China. It supervises the administration of justice by the various local courts, although these local people's courts also must answer to the Standing Committee of the NPC at corresponding levels. The Supreme People's Court has several important functions. First, it explains how laws and decrees should be specifically applied in judicial procedures. Such explanation by the Supreme Court usually occurs in two ways: in response to petitions from local courts and in notices issued to local courts in the region (Gong, 1989). Second, the Supreme People's Court deals with cases that will have significant impact on the whole judicial system of the country. When the Supreme People's Court decides a case, its judgment or order is final. Third, it hears appeals from higher people's court. Finally, it approves death sentences.

Few cases are tried directly by the Supreme Court. Since 1949, first instance trials have included only the cases of Japanese war criminals and the Lin Biao and "Gang of Four" cases. The court operates at four levels, consisting of four subcourts (also called divisions, chambers, or tribunals): the criminal court, the civil court, the economic court, and the administrative court. On certain occasions and for special purposes an additional court is set up.

The different levels of criminal court have jurisdiction over criminal cases. The criminal court within the higher people's court at the provincial level serves as a court of both first and second instance. As a court of first instance, it decides major cases that have an impact on the entire

province. As a court of second instance, it receives appeals from the criminal court of the intermediate people's court at the municipal or prefecture level.

The criminal court within the intermediate people's court hears the criminal cases of major crimes in the jurisdiction, such as murder, rape, robbery, bombing, arson, and grand larceny. Like the higher people's court, the intermediate people's court also serves as a court of second instance.

The criminal court within the basic people's court tries misdemeanor and minor felonious cases, such as theft, assault, and violations of public order. This level of the courts carries the heaviest workload in the judicial system. In recent years, some district courts in Beijing, Tianjin, and some other larger cities have also established neighborhood-based courts. These courts not only handle cases in their permanent offices, but also make a circuit of localities to try the cases on the spot. The procedure has allowed them to handle large numbers of civil disputes. Today, they handle some 70–80% of the civil cases and economic disputes accepted by those district courts (Zhang and Shan, 1990).

Every court is composed of a president, two or more vice-presidents, one chief judge (presiding judge of a given division), several deputy judges, judges, and assistant judges (Figure 13-3). The court president is elected by the people's congress at the corresponding level, while other members are appointed and dismissed by the standing committees of those congresses. Assistant judges can act for judges at the suggestion of the president of the court with the approval of the judicial committee, and they are appointed and dismissed by the courts at the same level.

Every court at every level must set up a judicial committee to deal with the most difficult or major cases. Instead of trying cases directly, the committee first discusses and then decides the most important or difficult cases submitted by collegiate benches of judges. Its members are

Figure 13-3: *The Composition of Each Court*

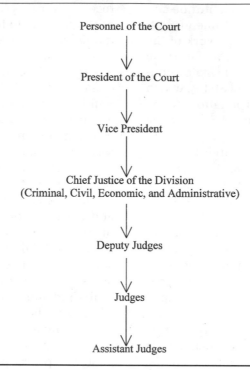

Personnel of the Court

President of the Court

Vice President

Chief Justice of the Division
(Criminal, Civil, Economic, and Administrative)

Deputy Judges

Judges

Assistant Judges

appointed by the Standing Committee of NPC at the corresponding level, upon the recommendation of the president of the court. The procurators at the corresponding levels have the right to attend the committee meeting as observers.

Major Procedures

The people's courts at various levels in China abide by the following procedures in their judicial responsibilities.

Pretrial

The court should send a copy of the indictment to the accused at least 7 working days before the trial, and also notify the accused of the trial's location. The court must also notify the victim, the defense attorney, the witness, the examination ex-

pert, and the translator at least 3 working days before the trial. Finally, the court also has to inform the procuratorate at least 3 days before the trial.

Right to Defense Counsel

The accused, apart from having the right to defend himself, has the right to choose to entrust a lawyer, relative, or lay advocate recommended by his work unit to plead on his behalf. The court may also appoint an advocate for the accused at its own discretion. However, the defense counsel may only consult the materials of the case, acquaint himself or herself with the circumstances of the case, and interview and correspond with a defendant held in custody. The counsel has no right to participate in the preliminary investigation (McCabe, 1989:123).

Trial

Criminal cases of both instances are heard in public, unless they involve issues of state secrets, privacy, or juvenile offenders under the age of 18. Occasionally, the criminal court even hears a criminal case in the work unit or college where the defendant is resident. There are several reasons behind this practice. First, as the court exposes and punishes the criminal in the hearing, citizens learn that criminal deeds are dangerous to society and lead to serious consequences. Second, this awareness should increase the citizen's sense of responsibility in obeying the law and fighting crime. Finally, the public trial warns potential criminals to give up their intentions and to become law-abiding citizens (Du and Zhang, 1990:103).

In local people's courts, cases of the first instance are tried either by an appointed judge for minor offenses, or before a collegiate bench consisting of an appointed judge and two people's assessors (jurors) (see Figure 13-4). The judge of a collegiate bench is appointed by the president of the court or by the chief judge of the division concerned. The two people's assessors may be the defendant's relatives or friends with the permission of the court. This is usually the case when the defendant is disabled, deaf, or mute. In most cases, the two assessors are the citizens elected by the defendant's work unit. Citizens who have reached the age of 23 and are eligible to vote and stand for election may be elected as people's jurors. Article 105 states that assessors have equal status with judges (Criminal law, 1984:147). The opinion of the majority prevails, but the minority viewpoint is recorded. [figure 13-4 here]

The purpose of the people's assessors is to ensure that the "mass line" is followed, and that the opinion of the people is considered at all court trials. Additionally, the people's assessors serve indirectly as educators. The masses can learn from the assessors in group discussions in work units or neighborhood associations (Rojek, 1985). In other words, this process increases the involvement of the community, bridges the gap between the community and the courts, and has the potential to reduce disparities in sentencing (Allen, 1987a)

There are two possible results of the trial. First, the court may find the accused innocent and acquit him or her immediately. Second, the court may find the accused guilty and sentence him or her at the end of the trial, sending the verdict in writing to the convicted offender and the procuratorate within 5 working days after the trial.

Figure 13-4: *Types of Trial in People's Rebublic of China*

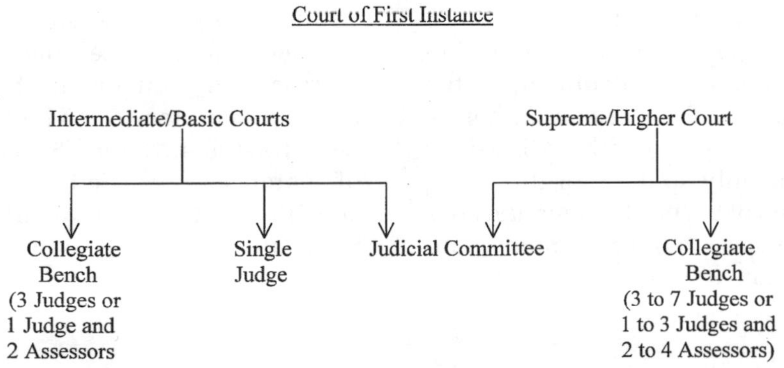

Court of First Instance

Intermediate/Basic Courts   Supreme/Higher Court

Collegiate Bench (3 Judges or 1 Judge and 2 Assessors   Single Judge   Judicial Committee   Collegiate Bench (3 to 7 Judges or 1 to 3 Judges and 2 to 4 Assessors)

Penalty

There are five major penalties and three supplementary penalties listed in Criminal Law. These five major penalties are control, criminal detention, fixed-term imprisonment, life imprisonment, and death penalty. The three supplementary penalties are fines, deprivation of political rights, and confiscation of property (*Criminal Law*, 1984:17–18). The five major penalties and three additional penalties can be meted out concurrently or independently.

The Chinese judicial system, like those of Nigeria, Ghana, and Sierra Leone, decides on both conviction and sentencing on the same day the trial ends, with the sentence taking immediate effect. This saves time and resources and also prevents any potential interference from outside. Two points need to be elaborated. First, control or surveillance, similar to "probation," ranges from 3 months to 2 years. The person sentenced to control can live with his family, continue to work, and enjoy his rights to citizenship; but he must report to the police regularly.

Second, according to the principle of combining punishment with leniency, the court can sentence a defendant to death with a 2-year suspension, depending on the circumstances. This means that the person will have a 2-year stay of the actual execution of the death sentence. During the 2-year period, the person is given a last opportunity to repent and mend his ways by reformation through labor. If he meets the requirements, the death sentence with 2-year suspension can be reduced to life imprisonment by the court upon the recommendation of the prison authority. The death penalty or death with 2-year suspension is only applied for those persons convicted of the most odious and atrocious offenses, such as murder, rape, counterrevolutionary offenses, and high-level official corruption (Felkenes, 1989:151).

The verdict of capital punishment must be reported to the Supreme People's Court for examination and approval, and becomes legally effective after it is approved. The death sentence must be pronounced or approved by the Supreme People's Court after reexamination by a higher people's court.

In 1983, a special statute was passed to stipulate that the higher people's court at the provincial level has the authority to approve the death sentence in cases of murder, rape, robbery, and explosion/bombing.

Appeal

Criminal procedure law stipulates the right to one appeal by either the accused or the procurator. When a person has been convicted and sentenced, he or she can appeal to a higher court within 10 working days after the trial, if he or she is dissatisfied with the decision of the court. If the person has been convicted for murder, rape, robbery, or explosion, he or she must appeal within 3 working days. The person can appeal either to the court of first instance, or go directly up to the court at the next level. By the same principle, the procuratorate at the same level may protest the ordinary criminal judgments or order of a legal supervisory organ of the state by appealing to a court at the next level within 10 working days. Cases involving murder, rape, robbery, or explosion should be protested by the procuratorate within 3 working days after the trial. If the accused makes appeal, the court can not increase the punishment, but an appeal by the procuratorate can increase punishment (McCabe, 1989:125). The execution of sentences is carried out as originally specified until some appellate body directs otherwise.

Second Instance

The second instance (or appellant instance) is conducted by a higher court, which reviews the verdict of the court of the first instance, when a party concerned appeals or the procuratorate protests against the verdict. Unlike practices in Britain, Nigeria, and the United States, the appellate court reviews both the facts and the laws of the case. A collegiate bench consisting of three to five judges examines the case and comes to a decision. The bench may rebuff the appeal or modify the original judgment. In these two instances, the judgment or order of the higher court is final.

The appellate bench may also withdraw the original judgment and return it to the original court for a retrial. In this case, the accused can appeal again if he disagrees with the new ruling. The court of second instance should notify the appealing party or the protesting procuratorate of its decisions within 10 working days after the review.

Major Principles

Mutual Restraint

In China, the police, the procuratorate, the court, and the corrections are the four major components in the criminal justice system, and are all state organs of law enforcement with separate responsibilities. These agencies not only coordinate but also restrain each other in order to guarantee accurate and effective enforcement of the law (Zhou, 1987). Specifically, the police are responsible for investigating crime and arresting suspects. The arrests must be approved by another branch, the procuratorate, which then decides whether to prosecute, exempt, or waive the case. In turn, the court decides whether to accept the case prosecuted by the procuratorate or return it to the same procuratorate for further investigation, or to request the procuratorate to withdraw the case. The procuratorate, on the other hand, may disagree with the decision of the court and may lodge a protest with the next higher court.

Independence

Article 126 of the constitution states that "the people's court exercises judicial power independently, and is not subject to interference by administrative organs, public organizations or individuals" (the Constitution, 1986:86). That is to say, that the court must try cases based on the facts and according to law, and its performance should not be subject to interference by individuals, governmental offices, or political parties. One measure that guarantees the independence of the judiciary is the appointment system. Unlike practices in some states in the United States, all judges except assistant judges are appointed and dismissed by the Standing Committee of the National People's Congress at the corresponding level. The government and the Communist Party otherwise should not interfere with the administration of justice by the court.

Equality

Everyone is considered equal before the law. The court should treat every citizen equally under applicable law without regard to nationality, race, sex, occupation, social position, religion, education, financial background, or length of residence. Any special privilege is forbidden.

Language

Citizens of all nationalities have the right to use their own spoken and written languages in court procedures. The court should provide interpreters for court proceedings if necessary.

Combining Punishment with Leniency

Article I of the Criminal Law states that the criminal law is "formulated in accordance with the policy of combining punishment with leniency in light of actual circumstances." According to this principle, the court takes into account subjective and objective conditions of crime within the range of the law. For instance, different sentences will apply to the primary culprit and the subordinate; to one who actively engages in crime and one who is coerced into a crime; to the first-time offender and the recidivist; to one who refuses to confess and one who surrenders himself to the police. The attitude of the defendant is very important in mitigating the sentence. Adult offenders caught *in flagrante delicto*, or who involve children in a crime, are punished severely. Finally, crimes against the state are treated very harshly (Felkenes, 1989:146).

Supervision by the Procuratorate

When a case is being tried, the procuratorate is required to attend the trial and to determine whether the court procedures conform to the law. The procurator can make a protest (counterplea) to the next higher court if he or she believes that the judge has made an error.

Some Factors and Issues Affecting the Court System

Because the judicial system is a part of the overall social system, it is greatly affected by certain social and political factors. This is especially true of the judicial system in China.

Function of the Law

One essential function of the court system is to administer justice according to law. However, the Marxist view of law has prevailed for some time in China and regards law as an instrument of class struggle or class oppression. According to this view, laws in a capitalist society aim at protecting the rich and exploiting the poor, whereas in China the law protects the ordinary people. This Marxist view fails to take two important points into account. First, laws in the West are used not only to protect or exploit, but also to readjust internal relations within the society, and further to regulate the life of the whole society. In effect, laws in Marxist China are used to achieve the same purpose—exploitation of the proletariat and protection of the life and property of every citizen. Second, if the law in China is nothing but an instrument of class struggle (or class oppression), how can one explain the laws on traffic, sanitation, forestry, and environmental protection?

In recent years, the debate over whether laws should be a function of class or of society has still gone unsettled. However, more and more people hold that the law should be divided into three categories: one related more closely to class structure, another oriented toward social life, and finally, one that combines elements of both. Criminal law falls within the third category, having a class as well as a social orientation. Overall, people throughout the society benefit from the implementation of the laws. Based on this legal ideology, the court keeps a neutral stand in dealing with criminal cases. However, when it deals with crimes against the state, or with "counterrevolutionary" crimes, it shifts to what the Party line directs.

The Party Line

In China, the Communist Party is still the ruling party, and it must play some role in the judicial system. The constitution emphasizes that the court should administer justice independently. In practice, however, the court is required to implement the policies of the Party or the "Party line." Such a practice is usually initiated and guided by documents or directives from Party organizations at various levels. Obviously, conflict between judicial independence and toeing the Party line occasionally arises. Up to this point, no sound solutions have materialized.

Further, if a Party or government official (or an official's relative or family member) violates the law, can the law be applied equally by the court? In other words, to what extent can the judicial system act independently? These issues remain controversial in China and the Chinese clearly are engaged in a good-faith effort to reform their practices. However, the question remains: to what extent do pressures or interventions by the Party vitiate the protection that the legal system purports to provide? (Gelatt, 1982).

Presumption of Innocence

The basic principles set forth in the introductory section of the Criminal Procedure Law do not clearly espouse a presumption of innocence, but do not negate or deny the presumption either (Gelatt, 1982). Basically, the presumption of innocence is a concept missing from the Chinese judicial system. The concept of presumption of innocence was raised during the French bourgeois revolution in opposition to the feudal principle of presumption of guilt. It played a certain progressive role in the struggle against feudal judicial arbitrariness. But in modern China, the concept of presumption of innocence has been regarded as a manifestation of idealism and metaphysics and has been rejected in favor of a more practical or pragmatic approach, for two reasons. First, China does not wish criminals to escape penalty under a presumption of innocence. Second,

China has its own guideline, the principle of "seeking truth from facts," with "facts" here referring to the evidence that both parties concerned can provide in court.

China would also disagree with the notion that the accused should be presumed innocent prior to the trial. In other words, according to the Criminal Procedure Law of PRC, when the court decides to try the case prosecuted by the procurator, the acceptance of the case by the court itself implies that the court agrees that the accused is guilty. This is because the case has gone through a two-stage pretrial investigation, a procuratorial determination, and a preliminary court screening; if the accused were presumed innocent the court would ask the procuratorate to withdraw the case. Also there is the influence of Confucian ideology. Unlike American society, which stresses the rights of the individual, Confucian ideology emphasizes public interest. Therefore, the judicial system is obligated to maximize protection of public interest first, or the innocent majority. Of course, this practice is maintained at the risk of sacrificing the rights of the accused. But the Chinese would reply that the whole is greater than the sum of its parts. In Western society, the dilemma is known as society versus the individual.

In the Anglo-American legal system, the probable cause standard for prosecution and the absence of an extensive pretrial procedure might make the presumption of innocence at trial seem easier to accept (Gelatt, 1982). In brief, the Anglo-American judicial system tends to categorize the accused as either guilty or innocent, while the Chinese judicial system tends to categorize the accused as either guilty or semi-guilty.

A Case Study

During the summers of 1991 and 1992, one of the authors participated in two study tours in the People's Republic of China

(PRC) sponsored by the Office of International Criminal Justice at the University of Illinois at Chicago. During the tour, the author was privileged to observe two Chinese criminal trials in addition to local mediation sessions. The trials were conducted by the Chang Ning District People's Court of Shanghai. The following section describes one of the trials and the related legal proceedings. The authors attempt to illustrate some of the Chinese court system via this example.

Charge

The defendant was arrested on March 11, 1992, by police officers of the Public Security Bureau of Shanghai, and charged with four counts of robbery. Under Article 151 of the Criminal Law (Criminal law, 1984:53), "whoever habitually steals or habitually swindles, or steals, swindles or forcibly seizes articles of public or private property of a relatively large amount is to be sentenced to not more than five years of fixed-term imprisonment, criminal detention or supervision." The trial was held on July 1, 1992.

Defendant's Background

The defendant was in his mid-twenties. He had no previous criminal record. He lived in the district where the crimes were committed and where the trial took place. He had a high school education, and he was unemployed at the time of the offense and trial.

The Circumstances of the Case

The defendant was accused of waiting outside a public bath house late at night and then robbing young females as they left the premises. The accused allegedly rode a bicycle rapidly past the victims and grabbed their bags, which contained clothing, money, purses, and other items of value. The total value of the items stolen was 900 yuen (about $165 in U.S. currency). In order to help put this figure into perspective, 900 yuen represents 4 months' average wages in China. Additionally, the defendant reportedly had worn some of the women's undergarments he stole. This became an important issue in the trial, because the defense attempted to convince the collegial panel that the defendant was psychologically disturbed. The defense pleaded that he should not be held fully accountable for his actions, and that he should be institutionalized for psychological treatment rather than being sentenced to prison.

The Trial

Jurisdiction

The Chang Ning District Court has jurisdiction over a 44-square-kilometer area with a population of 580,000 citizens. The court adjudicates cases involving criminal, civil, economic, and administrative issues. During 1991, the court heard 3,700 cases, over half of which were criminal cases (1,600–1,700 cases were civil).

District court is the lowest level of courts in the Chinese system. Those found guilty have the right of appeal to the intermediate people's court.

Physical Setting of the Court

The courtroom itself is not unlike some courtrooms in the United States and Europe. The participants were located at the four sides of a rectangle, facing one another. The judge presided over the trial from a central position behind the bench. He was flanked on either side by people's assessors. The defendant stood in a witness box facing the bench. He could view the judge and the assessors as well as the bench. Defense counsels were seated to the right of the bench, equally facing the others. Directly behind the defendant's box were several rows of seats for the public. This is consistent with the Chinese legal premise that trials should serve as a vehicle for public education as well as adjudication.

Components

Judiciary

A judge presided over the trial. More than 70% of the judges in China have university degrees. Chinese judges wear gray public service uniforms with red and gold shoulder boards. The judge headed a collegial bench (panel) that included two people's assessors, private citizens selected to assist the judge in reaching a verdict and sentencing. They have no formal legal training, but have authority that almost equals that of the judge.

One of the assessors is elected from the defendant's work unit. The other is selected from the defendant's neighborhood. The verdict is a product of majority rule, which, of course, could result in the judge being outvoted by the assessors.

The judge and people's assessors are active inquisitors in the trial process. Additionally, the judge also may have chosen to be active investigator in the case.

The Procuratorate

The procurator (the prosecutor) is the major figure in filing formal charges against the accused. Often the procurator chooses to play an active role in the investigation of the offense. During trial, the procurator represents the state interest against the defendant, and conducts a direct examination of the accused. The procurator also wears a public service uniform in court.

Defense

The defense was presented by lawyers from the Number Four Law Firm. Lawyers are usually provided for the defense by the court. However, if the defendant and/or the family can afford to hire lawyers of their own, this is permitted. The second option was exercised in the case observed. The two defense attorneys wore civilian clothing.

Summary of the Procedures

1. Court was called to order and the judge proceeded to introduce all of the participants.
2. The defendant was identified.
3. The charges were read.
4. The defendant was advised of his rights under Chinese law and the constitution.
5. The judge and people's assessors questioned the defendant.
6. The procurator made a statement, questioned the defendant, and verified evidence.
7. The defense entered a statement and questioned the defendant.
8. The procurator and the defense presented their arguments.
9. No witnesses testified other than the defendant.
10. The defendant was invited to make a statement and he did so.
11. The judge called for a 15-minute recess while he and the people's assessors deliberated.
12. Court was reconvened, a guilty verdict announced, and the defendant was sentenced.

Disposition

The defendant confessed to the offenses and was found guilty by a panel in a unanimous decision. During an interview with the judge following the trial, it was explained that the defense's position was that the defendant was psychologically disturbed or mentally ill, and was therefore not fully responsible for his actions. The collegial panel did not find this argument persuasive.

The Chinese law does not hold a legally insane person culpable of criminal behavior (*Criminal Law*, 1984:14). The test for insanity is based upon the accused being capable of understanding the difference between right and wrong.

The procurator, however, argued that the defendant knew his actions were wrong based on the planning and development of method employed in carrying out the offenses. The defendant planned the offenses and timed them for late night when visibility was poor and fewer people were on the streets, selected promising victims, and ensured that escape could be accomplished easily; therefore, the judge and the assessors found the procurator's argument more convincing. The judge added that the defendant apparently did have some minor psychological problems, but not of the sort to make his behavior uncontrollable and certainly not to the level of legal insanity. (The Chinese do not equate medical insanity and legal insanity.)

The preceding description illustrates some important differences between the Chinese legal system and that of the United States. First, the defendant's guilt is established through previous investigations (a two-stage pretrial investigation, a procuratorial determination, and a preliminary court screening). Once this disposition is reached, one is in the position of needing to prove one's own innocence. Second, the purpose of having a trial is to formalize the process, and to allow the defendant and the defense attorney to make statements, offering evidence and mitigating circumstances that would prove innocence.

Sentence

The defendant was sentenced to an 8-month "fixed term" in prison. The defense planned to appeal the verdict to the intermediate people's court.

Social Issues

The legal system in China is seen as a major form of social control and an essential element for progress and order in the socialist society. However, informal social controls are believed to be some of the most effective sanctions.

The basic organization of Chinese society is centered on the "work unit" or "the Danwei." The citizens work unit not only provides income, but also assigns housing. Housing police and local neighborhood committees also help to maintain order and settle minor disputes.

When a person is convicted of committing a crime and imprisoned or otherwise sanctioned, the workplace may not accept him or her back into the community. In this case, the individual must seek a new workplace, and may have to accept lower pay and less satisfactory housing if a new job is available at all. This situation affects not only the convicted offender, but also his or her family.

Points of Comparison

The following are some preliminary comparisons between the judicial system of China and the United States (see Table 13-1). Emphasis is placed on major contrasting points.

First, there are fewer persons involved in the Chinese collegial bench than in a jury in the United States. This may be due to limited resources in the Chinese judicial system.

Second, the Chinese collegial bench is inquisitorial, whereas the task of the judge and the jury in the United States is to over-

Table 13-1: *Summary of Points of Comparison*

China	United States
Public Security Bureau-Usual initial contact with the CJ system, and investigation	Police—same
Defense—provided by state	Same in United States if the accused is indigent
Collegial Bench—Inquisitorial	**Jury**
	Judge presides and referees over adversarial process
Judge may be active investigator	Judge does not take active role in investigation
Emphasis on protection of public and less on individual	Emphasis on protection of rights of the accused and less of the victim
More flexibility in investigation and interrogation	More restrictive—primarily through 4th, 5th, 6th, 8th, and 14th amendments of the US Constitution
Emphasis on excpediency: Quick capture of offender and successful prosecution effective method of crime control	Emphasis more on due process Protection of constitutional rights of the accused regardless of slow process and less efficiency
Emphasis on confession confession = light sentence no confession = more severe sentence	Plea bargaining—risk innocent pleading guilty for guaranteed light sentence
No presumption of innocence at trial	Presumption of innocence until found guilty
Trial mainly for review of facts, consideration of mitigating factors, and sentencing	Trial to determine guilt of innocence
Guilty party has a right to appeal	Guilty party has a right to appeal

see the adversarial process. The judge in China may even have been an investigator for the case.

Third, the people's assessors are active components of the court in which they participate, and enjoy the same rights as judges. In the United States, the jurors are the decision makers, but they do not ask the accused any questions.

Fourth, the court system in China is primarily responsible for the protection of public interest, whereas the U.S. court system places strong emphasis on the rights of the accused through due process.

Fifth, for certain practical and philosophical reasons, in China there is no presumption of innocence of the accused. In the United States, on the other hand, the adversarial approach is taken, and presumption of innocence is so important that the prosecutor representing the state must prove guilt beyond a reasonable doubt.

Finally, a trial in China is a final stage in the legal process in which the facts are reviewed and a final decision is made. In the United States, on the other hand, the trial is a critical moment in which the guilt or innocence of the accused is decided through adversarial process by judge and jury.

Conclusion

This chapter does not seek to judge which system, that of China or that of the United States, is better. Rather it is intended to illustrate and explain the Chinese system with a case study; comparisons are made to enhance understanding of the two systems. China is experiencing rapid changes in many areas, including in its judicial system. It is hoped that this analysis may eventually promote a movement toward a more democratic Chinese judicial system.

Finally, studying another system helps us to appreciate our own with greater sophistication and sensitivity than might be had under rote learning. Comparing crime problems and options for control in countries with different cultures and systems of government adds new perspective to the observation that democratic governments are faced with unusual crime control challenges.

Notes

1. The Common Program was the preliminary constitution for the People's Republic of China and was passed by the Chinese People's Political Consultative Conference on September 29, 1949.

Discussion and Review Questions

1. What are formal and informal courts in China?

2. What is the highest legislative body in China?

3. What are the functions of the standing committee of the National People's Congress with regard to criminal justice?

4. At the judicial formal court level, the Chinese judiciary and procedure are to some extent democratic. Discuss.

5. Why are some Chinese criminal court hearings held in the work unit of the defendant, or at the residence of the defendant, or at a college the defendant attends?

6. Compare and contrast the Nigerian High Court and the Higher People's Court of China.

7. Compare and contrast assessors in a criminal court in China and jurors in American criminal courts.

8. What are the five major penalties and three supplementary penalties in the Chinese criminal justice system?

9. Why is it that in the People's Republic of China, as in Nigeria, Ghana, and Sierra Leone, the defendant is sentenced on the same day that he or she is convicted?

10. Name the capital offenses in China.

11. For a capital offense conviction, an appeal must be filed within 3 days in China, within 30 days in Nigeria, and within 6 to 7 months in the state of New York in the United States. What are the merits and demerits of the different appeal deadlines in the three countries?

12. In China the interests of society are held to be superior to individual rights. Discuss this in the light of individual rights in the United States.

13. Give three reasons why China does not recognize the principle of presumption of innocence.

14. Compare and contrast the standard application of the insanity defense in China and the United States.

15. Consider the American adversarial versus the Chinese inquisitorial approach in criminal trials, discussing the merits and demerits of each approach.

16. Write a short paragraph on the following:

    (a) "Control" as one of the five major penalties in China

    (b) The nature of the Chinese death penalty with a 2-year suspension

17. In China, the Appellate Courts review both the facts and the law. Discuss this in the light of Court of Appeal hearings in the United States, Nigeria, and the United Kingdom.

Part V
Comparative Corrections

14

Guided Change in Japan

The Correctional Association Prison Industrial Cooperative (CAPIC) and Prison Industry

Elmer H. Johnson

Introduction

In 1973 and from 1979 to 1980, the oil producing nations of the Middle East increased the price of oil in several stages and gravely dislocated the world economy. Japan, which depends heavily on oil for its energy, suffered huge increases in the costs of imports, inflation of domestic prices, unemployment (despite a history of labor shortages), and an interruption of remarkable economic growth (Beasley, 1990:249–250).

Under the duress of this financial crisis, the national government of Japan told the Correction Bureau to eliminate the budgetary allocation for purchase of raw materials for prison industries. The prospect of a body blow to prison industries tested the commitment of the national government to continuing industrial operations. As we shall see, this situation turned out to be a "window of opportunity": the Correction Bureau's negotiations culminated in the establishment of the Correctional Association Prison Industrial Cooperative (CAPIC) as an additional participant in the prisons' industrial operation.[1]

A Window of Opportunity for Prison Industries

Penal reform sometimes takes place when demands for changes from outside the correctional agency create a situation favorable for the correctional agency to introduce policies or practices that the executives and personnel of the agency already desire. The reform agenda of the external change-agents provides a "window of opportunity" for the internal change-agents, because the external agenda is susceptible to modification by the correctional agency.

The Correctional Bureau's response to the external demand that it should eliminate the budget item for prison industries showed its vulnerability as a reactive institution dependent on developments in society generally and in government specifically. The Correction Bureau found that a crucial element in its budget had been threatened abruptly by a joint decision of the Ministry of Finance and the Ministry of Justice, and had to engage in political bargaining to meet this threat.

Windows of opportunity emerge and are exploited through the society's political process of governmental decision-making. Noting that there is no Japanese word for "opposition," Leiserson (1966:346, 394–395) points out that, from the Japanese perspective, political bargaining within the system (*taisei-gai*) is more likely to effect changes in policy than efforts seeking policy change from outside the system (*taisei-nai*): to have any chance for success, taisei-nai must strike some sort of alliance with taisei-gai. His terms resemble our earlier distinction between external and internal change-agents: internal change-agents must accommodate to the external change agenda in order to exploit a window of opportunity.

Before CAPIC was accepted as a solution, negotiations followed the usual budget-making process of the Japanese national government. The following circumstances and special conditions combined within that process to lead to the founding of CAPIC.

Several conditions surrounding this window of opportunity made it possible to preserve industrial prisons and provide for their richer future. The industrial prison was defined, its significance noted, and the conditions for its implementation outlined. It was found that prison labor played an important role in the development of modern Japan and that it has vital connections with private industry through subcontracting. Also, the external parties had a stake in the industrial operations. Furthermore, prison industry played an important role in the stability and purposes of the prison.

These conditions made both external and internal change-agents willing to bargain for the creation and implementation of CAPIC. The external change-agents had superior power in negotiations but also had an interest in preserving prison industries. The internal change-agents were indispensable for implementing any change agenda but depended on the external change-agents for necessary resources.

Factory System and the Prison

In the European putting-out system, the merchant-capitalist or his representative visited the homes of each worker, distributing raw materials, and later collecting the products. The factory system developed during the first industrial revolution (1750–1825) brought workers together in a central shop, and assigned each particular tasks in operating one of a series of specialized machines. Workers sometimes had been assembled in central workshops prior to 1750, but factory labor as a system arose with the development of suitable machinery. The factory system by definition combines the labor of many kinds of workers who tend with appropriate skills a series of productive machines (Taylor-Cooke, 1886:29).

Factory systems require rigorous discipline and regimentation. According to Barnes (1942:107), "It became necessary to issue certain rules defining the hours of labor, the assignment of industrial tasks, the attitude of the employee in his relations with the employer, details of conduct within the factory, and even the matter of orderly entering and leaving." Compared with the putting-out system, the factory system required closer control, supervision, and discipline of labor. A predetermined scheme of production assigned particular tasks to each worker in relation to specialized machines. If any worker came to the factory late or failed to show, he or she would delay the entire process. Failure to perform an assigned task would frustrate the industrial process, and the worker responsible for the failure could be identified easily.

By 1823, the Auburn Prison in New York had exploited the disciplinary potential of the factory system, providing "for the separate confinement of each prisoner in silence in his individual cell at night, and for the work of the prisoners in association during the day" (Lewis, 1922:86). Inmates were forbidden ever to converse with one another in order to prevent ill influences on morale, plotting against the keepers, or escape. Violators were subject to flogging.

The Auburn system enabled the private contractor to transform the prison into a factory at his own expense, to direct the inmate workers, and ultimately to sell their products on the open market. The industrial prison brought orderliness to the prisons, but as Melossi and Pararini (1981:129–130) note, radically changed the form of discipline. Productive work imposes regulations that dictate the form and timing of the interaction of inmate workers; the discipline for work replaces the discipline for purposes of prison custody. To motivate efficient task performance, the prospect of rewards is superior to the threat of punishment. Melossi and Pararini show this principle to have been behind evaluating working ability as a measure of "good conduct," commuting long sentences, and preferring of long-term prisoners for teaching of new work techniques.

Jeremy Bentham (1843:12) set the tone for arguments in favor of the industrial prison when he commented in 1778 on the proposal before the British Parliament to establish "houses of labor":

> The object in view in it, we see, is partly economical and partly moral: that such a project be drawn from the labor of the convicts as may altogether, or at least in part, compensate the expense of the establishment; and that the morals of the convicts may be improved by a habit of steady and well-directed industry.

Industrial Model in Japan

Industrial prison operations are favored in Japan by the centralized Japanese correctional administration. All correctional activities are carried out on the national level, unlike the American federal, state, and local subdivisions. Centralized admin-

istration encourages fiscal efficiency and uniformity in policy and practice, and enables use of a national system for recruiting personnel. Quality of personnel is further assured by a long history of in-service training. The official system for classifying adult prisoners supports the needs of industrial operations.

Japanese inmates' engagement in regular industrial labor contributes noticeably to the orderliness in prisons,[2] to the Correction Bureau's rehabilitation goals,[3] and to national revenue.[4] Both "economical" and "moral" purposes are served.

Violence against other inmates is unusual, and aggression against staff and escape attempts are even more rare. As in all custodial prisons, inmates' conduct is constrained by a regimented routine. Workshop assignments make up the greatest number of tightly scheduled daily activities of inmates who breakfast in their cells, begin work at 7:20 A.M., lunch in the workshop, and march back to their congregate cells at 4:30 P.M. for dinner. Silence is not required in the congregate cells, which usually have a half-dozen residents. Individuals whose behavior has caused problems are housed in single-occupancy cells and must assemble paper shopping bags for retail stores. Inmates who are physically unfit for workshop labor assemble paper shopping bags as well, but in congregate cells.

Both threat of punishment and promise of reward motivate task performance. Inmates may not contact one another while at work and must meet a daily work quota. Infractions peculiar to the workshops are violations of safety rules, looking aside while working, leaving the designated place, leaving a machine untended, making shoddy products, damaging products, and manufacturing unauthorized items.[5]

As positive incentives, inmate workers receive modest "remunerations," promotions in the progressive stage system, privileges earned by exceeding the production quota, and satisfactions for exceeding the quota. Not considered the privilege im-

plied by the word "wage," monetary remunerations come in ten grades according to task skill, length of time in prison,
and work attitudes.[6] Progressive stages are
from the lowest (fourth) at admission to
prison to the highest (first), with privileges
and chances for parole linked to promotion. If a work quota is exceeded, certain
freedoms, such as watching television, are
obtained. Competition between workshops
in exceeding production quotas expresses
the spirit of "*Gambare!*" ("Persevere!" or
"Endure!") that motivates great effort in
every facet of Japanese life. According to
Duke (1986:122–123) "Gambare is also a
major component in developing a strong
sense of competition, especially group
competition. Regardless of the group's
purposes or the ages of the participants,
the goals must be pursued through collective effort."

The influence of Japanese culture on
work motivation goes beyond the competi-
tive spirit. Previous socialization and the
messages of social institutions prepare
most inmates to accept the behavioral standards of the industrial prison. The inmates
come from a sociocultural system that pre-
fers the interests of the group over those
of the individual member. Ozaki
(1978:183) summarizes Western culture in
the statement: "Do your own thing and go
your own way." The Japanese statement,
on the other hand, would be: "Find your
own group and belong to it. You and the
group will rise or sink together. Without
belonging you will be lost in the wilderness. Apart from dependence there is no
human happiness."

In Western societies relationships tend
to be along the horizontal dimension, with
work colleagues, persons of similar age,
and other peers. In the prison factory, Foucault (1977:238) says, inmates "come together in a strict hierarchical framework
with no lateral relation, communication
being possible only in the vertical direction." The same pattern has been described
for the ordinary life in Japan. There,
Nakane (1981:36–37, 44, 68) argues, social

ties are vertical rather than horizontal
through attachments of *oyabun* (persons
of superior rank such as parent, patron,
boss) with the *kobun* (persons of subordinate rank such as child, client, employee).
The vertical dimension favors group cohesion in spite of rank differences among
members. Officer–inmate contacts draw on
the oyabun–kobun relationship, with the
officer expected to combine the roles of
moral educator, lay counselor, and security monitor. "Although some prisoners try
to reject their guard, because of the authority that he carries, the majority accept his
guidance and advice, at least on an emotional level" (Shikita, 1972:19).

Roots in Japanese History

Japan did not erect a modern prison system until the 1880s, and industrial prisons began even later. Yet prison labor existed in Japan before the eighth century,
when Chinese legal principles were followed in specifying penal measures: death
by decapitation or strangulation, exile to
Hokkaido, beating with a light stick, beating of offenders who lacked a sense of
shame with a heavy stick, and penal servitude. Those sentenced to penal servitude
were assigned to local confinement stations and, according to local needs and the
individual's strength, were ordered to perform a specific kind of labor for 12, 18, 24,
30, or 36 months. They were paid one-
tenth of an ordinary worker's wage, and
half of the daily income was held until
release (Ch'en, 1981:40–43).

The Ninsoku-Yoseba (Stockade for Laborers) was established in 1790 on the
small island of Ishikawajima at the mouth
of the Sumida River. Homeless persons
made lime or charcoal balls or paper there,
and were paid for their work. In 1820
criminals sentenced to forced labor and
exile were admitted (Kyokai, 1943:813;
Hiromatsu, 1972:44–49).

On January 3, 1868, a group of feudal lords engaged in a successful coup d'etat in Kyoto terminating the Tokugawa Shogunate that had isolated Japan from the outside world for almost two and a half centuries. The ensuing reform movement known as the Meiji Restoration made great efforts to modernize the socioeconomic infrastructure of Japan. Delegations were sent to Europe and the United States for quick studies of Western social institutions, including laws and prisons. Modern Japan gradually evolved as a combination of lessons from the West and indigenous customs (Beasley, 1972:1–2; Noda, 1976:41–48; Beasley, 1990:22–30, 85–88).

The central prisons of France were a model for Kosuge Prison near Tokyo, and the prison at Miyagi (still existing in modified form) duplicated the Central Prison at Leuven, Belgium. The central prisons in France, at the time of the Meiji Reformation, had initiated a version of the Auburn system in the mid-nineteenth century with its reliance on contracting, although in France and the United States, the industrial prison was under political attack and suffered general decline in the 1880s and later (O'Brien, 1982:23, 152–190).

The Meiji reformers began to establish a modern prison system while laboriously suppressing the 1877 Satsuma Rebellion by imprisoning 27,000 dissident samurai: rice warehouses and stables had to be hastily converted into provisional confinement sites. Rioting, arson, and escapes were frequent until new prisons were constructed (Hiromatsu, 1973: 31–32).

Prisoners participated directly in the development of Japan's infrastructure. They reclaimed land, labored in mines, and constructed the Asahikawa-Abashiri highway (1886–1891) in the northern island of Hokkaido while farmed out from Kabato Prison (opened 1881) and Kushiro Prison (opened 1885). Sorachi Prison (opened 1882) provided labor for coal mines. The government began operating the Miike coal mines in Kyushu in 1873 with both free workers and prisoners. Although privatized in 1888, the mines continued to employ prisoners but in declining numbers, until their use was discontinued in 1933 (Yokoyama, 1984:3–4; Hane, 1982:227; Hiromatsu, 1973:35–36).

Factory organization and techniques existed in Japanese prisons at the time of the Meiji Restoration. Sometime during the last two decades of the nineteenth century, Griffiths (n.d.:235–238) reported that Japanese prisons were places of detention, of reformation, and of profitable work. The visitors were surprised to find a couple hundred prisoners making machinery and steam boilers in the first workshop. One warder, carrying only a sword, was in charge of every fifteen men. The prisoners were working on contract orders for private firms, under the supervision of one skilled master and one representative of the firm giving the contract. Another shop contained woodcarvers. There were also paper-makers, weavers (who were making fabric for prison clothing), fan-makers, lantern-makers, and workers in baskets, mats, and nets. In one of the shops *jinrikishas* were being made, in another umbrellas were being elaborately carved, and in another every kind of pottery was being turned out.

The Key Importance of Subcontracting

Small businesses were a powerful force in the nineteenth-century industrial revolution of Japan, and they now account for a larger percentage of total enterprises than in any other industrialized nation (Tadao, 1979:157–158).[7] In the years immediately before and during World War II, manufacturers of military equipment shifted from producing everything themselves to relying on smaller firms through contracts (Nakamura, 1981:15)[8]. Contracting had existed in Japan before the war, but its popularity was stimulated afterward by advantages to "parent" companies such as lower wages, managerial skills in small firms, and willingness to work longer hours (Dore, 1987:172–173).

Primary contractors have direct ties with the parent companies; secondary and tertiary subcontractors are related indirectly to primary contractors. "It is not unusual to find several 'layers' of hierarchically organized subcontractors in a pyramid-like pattern, with each performing subcontracting operations for those at a higher level in the pyramid. Most commonly, the lower its stratum, the smaller the establishment" (Yoshino, 1968:155).

Parent companies contract with small firms because, when the economy is depressed, they then have the option of canceling the contracts while maintaining the jobs of regular employees, of postponing payments to contractors, or of lowering the rate paid to them (Nakamura, 1981:175). Kosai and Ogino (1984:72) present a different perspective: "In reality, a great number of Japan's small companies boast a high level of technology and efficiency and are valued by their parent company as a vital link in their organization." The parent company enters an agreement with such small firms when only a small order is needed, and when the small firm is reliable in delivery and product quality. The advantages for the small firm, Kosai and Ogino say, are avoiding the costs of sales promotion, gaining the benefits of stable work and profits, and being guided otherwise by the parent company.

By acting as secondary or tertiary subcontractors, the adult prisons of Japan are able to sustain their heavy involvement in industrial production. Their wide range of products generate different amounts of annual income (see Table 14-1). Metal work, tailoring, woodcraft (largely furniture), and printing contributed 74% of the 1990 total income. The table distinguishes projects using equipment supplied by the government from projects using equipment supplied by private contractors. For the four major industries, private firms supplied the equipment for 99.5% of project income. For total projects, privately supplied equipment accounted for 96.5% of the income. Government-supplied equipment was prominent in farming and stockraising, vocational training,[9] papermaking, and forestry; but only 0.4% of all income was obtained from those industries.

The staff of each prison, especially its industrial division, plays the primary role in obtaining subcontracts. All sectors of the staff have a keen interest in replacing an expiring subcontract in order to maintain an active inmate labor force. Some headquarters of the correction region may refer a contractor to an appropriate prison, or a local company may approach the prison seeking an arrangement in its own interest. The prison's correction fair displaying its goods may awaken a company's interest. Newspaper advertisements and suggestions by volunteers serving the prison also spread the word.

Oil Shock and Crisis for Prison Labor

The oil crisis of 1973 occurred after a long period of economic growth and expanding government revenue in Japan. The ensuing financial setback was especially untimely, because the fiscal budget of 1973 initiated an unprecedented public investment in social services. Pension benefits for employees almost doubled, insurance coverage of medical care for dependents increased, and free medical care was introduced for the aged (Collick, 1988:214–215). The government debated whether expenditures should be significantly reduced or whether they should be retained in order to prime the economy. Increased taxes were found to be politically impractical (Woronoff, 1986:241–246). When Finance Minister Aichi Kiichi died, Prime Minister Kakuei Tanaka appointed in his place Takeo Fukuda, a fiscal conservative. The fiscal year 1974 thus saw, for the first time, a prime minister and minister of finance who both wanted to reverse the growth of expenditures during the framing of the national budget (Campbell, 1977:259–260).

The national budget undergoes a year-long process in Japan. In April (the beginning of the fiscal year) the ministries begin drafting their budget requests for the following fiscal year. Usually the Ministry of Finance (MOF) expects an increase in budgets, though each ministry is asked to limit requests to no more than a 25% gain. The requests reach the MOF by August 31, and then are reviewed by the Budget Bureau of the MOF and discussed with responsible officials of the requesting ministries. In early December the draft budget is ratified, and sometimes modified, in a

ministerial conference of the MOF. In the weeks immediately following, the MOF receives appeals and doles out small amounts of supplementary funds. Diet members of the dominant political party also make requests in favor of their political constituencies. The Cabinet ratifies the final version of the budget that is sent to the Diet for passage (Campbell, 1977:9–11). The relative positions of the Diet and MOF in the budget-making process have changed at various times since the end of World War II (Campbell, 1977:9–11), but since 1955 the Diet had modified the MOF draft only three or four times, and all such changes had been minor. The MOF gained

Table14-1: *Income from Prison Industries by Types of Products and State's versus Contractors' Resources, 1990*

Types of Products	Total Income (Million Yen)	State Resources	Private Resources
		Percentages	
Metal work	5,421.9	0.7	99.3
(Assembly)	(3,164.9)	(—)	(100.0)
(Production)	(2,257.0)	(1.6)	(98.4)
Tailoring	3,622.9	—	100.0
Woodcraft	1,990.3	1.3	98.7
Printing	1,364.3	0.2	99.8
Leather work	997.6	—	100.0
Paper products	685.8	0.1	99.9
Farm stock raising	413.9	96.5	3.5
Chemical products	277.3	—	100.0
Paper bags	159.9	—	100.0
Auto repair	145.3	0.8	—
Ceramics	142.0	5.4	94.6
Vocational training	124.6	47.0	53.0
Spinning	90.8	—	100.0
Paper making	72.7	30.7	69.3
Forestry	24.6	100.0	—
Food processing	22.1	11.3	88.7
Others	1,195.5	—	100.0
TOTALS	16,751,63.5	3.5	96.5

Source: Ministry of Justice (1991:238-239).

influence during the postwar reconstruction and after the oil shock of 1973.

The budget for fiscal year 1974 limited growth of expenditures but did not impose zero growth. In 1975 the government obtained authority from the Diet to issue bonds in addition to its usual "red national bonds" for construction of bridges and similar projects, bonds that would help to bring revenue up to expenditures. Deficit financing rose from 11% of expenditures in 1974 to almost 35% in 1979 (Woronoff, 1986:241–246).

The drafting of the 1982 budget brought extraordinary fiscal pressures on the ministries from sources external to the government, for the mounting fiscal deficit necessitated zero growth in budgetary allocations. Furthermore, a semiprivate entity was introduced into the process. The Provisional Commission on Administrative Reform (RINCHO) was established temporarily in March 1981 to advise on improving public administration.[10] It issued five reports before being dissolved in May 1983. In addressing the opening session of the Commission, Prime Minister Zenko Suzuki instructed its members to assume the additional responsibility of helping to draw up the budget for the 1982 fiscal year in order to eliminate deficit financing (Daiichi, 1988:77–80).

Negotiations Culminating in CAPIC

In July 1982, the MOF requested all ministries to reduce their requests for the 1983 fiscal year by 10% of the previous fiscal year's budget. The imposed ceiling enabled the ministries to decide on cuts "during the relatively private and quiet process of request preparation during the summer, rather than in the noisy and highly political hubbub of final budget negotiations" (Campbell, 1985:512).

During negotiations at the ministry level, the MOF and the head of the Accounting Section of the Ministry of Justice noticed an item in the Correction Bureau's budget for 4 billion yen. The allocation for purchase of raw materials for prison industries amounted to 10% of the total budget for the Ministry of Justice. This discovery led to a demand from several parties outside the control of the Correction Bureau that the expenditure for raw materials be eliminated from the Correction Bureau's 1983 budget. Agents of external pressure here included the prime minister and the minister of finance, who had initiated the framing of a zero growth budget for the fiscal year 1983; RINCHO, which had been pressed unexpectedly into short-term assisting of the MOF in that budget program; and the Ministry of Justice itself, of which the Correction Bureau is a component—although that Ministry also negotiated for preservation of prison industries.

The head of the Correction Bureau Accounting Section told the MOF that eliminating the item would have profoundly adverse consequences for the Correction Bureau and for the government in general. Unless raw materials were available, the Bureau would not comply with Article 24 of the Prison Law: "Prison labor shall be imposed upon inmates, the sanitary condition and general economy of the prison taken into consideration, and also with due attention paid to the term of their penalty and to their health, ability, occupation, and future life, etc. . . ." The MOF would have an interest in the continued operation of prison industries, because Article 27 of the Prison Law requires that all proceeds from prison labor "shall be vested in the national treasury" rather than retained by the Correction Bureau.[11] Also, the employment of the majority of inmates in industrial production is a key element in the management of prisoners, the noteworthy tranquility of prison life, and the official position that inmates are being prepared for return to the free world.

The head of the accounting section had also consulted with officials experienced in prison industrial operations and was impressed with the possibilities of involving a private organization in the financing of raw materials and expanding the market. In usual practice, the funds for purchase of raw materials would result in the sale of the finished products, but the proceeds of such sales would go into the national treasury without replenishing Correction Bureau funds for further purchase of raw materials. A semiprivate organization would not be subject to this practice, but could furnish raw materials as a private contractor, sell the products, and compensate the Correction Bureau for the contribution of inmate labor.

To introduce a semiprivate organization into the budgetary process, funds would have to be provided for initial purchase of raw material. The semiprivate organization would be able to retain the raw material investment when the Correction Bureau's share of expenses were submitted to the national treasury. By retaining that portion of the proceeds, the semiprivate organization would be able to purchase raw materials at least twice during a fiscal year. The consequence would be that 2 billion yen a year—not 4 billion yen—would be sufficient to provide raw materials.

MOF agreed to provide a subsidy of 2 billion yen but insisted that it be spread over the years 1983–1988. Four hundred million yen would be paid each of 5 years for a total of 2 billion yen. There would be a shortage of 1.6 billion yen in 1983. MOF agreed to provide additional money for administrative and personnel expenses, and (especially) for paying interest on the 1.6 billion yen debt.

Taking Advantage of an Opportunity

The head of the Accounting Section faced two problems in accomplishing the proposed arrangement: the Correction Bureau had to be persuaded to introduce the plan, and a semiprivate organization had to be recruited. The emergence of CAPIC was accomplished in developments that demonstrate how a window of opportunity can be exploited successfully.

The executives and staff of an agency must be receptive to a change agenda proposed from an external source. The Correction Bureau personnel were reluctant to accept multiple use of funds in a fiscal year and concerned about sharing authority with an outside party, but agreed under threat that if they rejected the proposal, the budget item would be eliminated without a subsidy. After the Bureau accepted the change-agenda, its personnel contributed actively and indispensably to CAPIC's success, especially the industrial sections of the Bureau's headquarters and the prisons themselves. Retired prison executives, especially those experienced in prison industries, make up an important sector of CAPIC managers.

Because there was not enough time to create a completely new semiprivate organization, the Correction Bureau had recourse to the Japanese Correctional Association (JCA), a society founded in 1888 to improve prison practices and serve prison personnel. The JCA leadership and most of its staff are retired personnel, with the rest of its membership composed of active personnel and retirees. Its headquarters are located on the same grounds as those of the Tokyo Correction Region in Nakano.

The JCA is one of the *gaikaku dantai* (public corporations or extradepartmental groups), incorporated private associations, foundations, or unions initiated by the government bureaucracy. Each is an institutionalized private interest group that has an affiliated section of government as a client and is staffed predominantly by retired government officials.[12] In varying degrees, they rely on government funding (George, 1988:124–125). Through CAPIC, JCA received government funds; otherwise, JCA has had the Correction Bureau as a client for a long time.

The directors were reluctant to allow JCA to become a semiprivate organization as proposed. Membership dues were sufficient to support the Association's projects, and the large scale of the subsidized industrial activities made the directors doubt that JCA could manage them successfully. After a series of conferences with the Industrial Section in the Correction Bureau's headquarters, JCA agreed to add a special unit to its organization: CAPIC.

The Establishment and Aim of CAPIC

The head office and executive director of CAPIC are located in the JCA headquarters. Divisional CAPIC offices have been established in each headquarters of the Bureau's correction regions, and 68 local branches have been established at each of the prisons with industrial activities. Subsidy payments, including loans to CAPIC, were 1,034 million yen in 1983, 930 million yen in 1984, 767 million yen in 1985, 210 million yen in 1986, and 189 million yen in 1987. Of the total sum of 3,130 million yen, interest charges and administrative costs drew 1,130 million yen.

CAPIC has announced its major goals: "In the first place, it becomes possible to increase the opportunities of prisons receiving orders from outside through the flexible appropriation of funds for raw materials, without being bound by the budget, which serves for securing the stability of the value of work for inmates. Secondly, the introduction of corporate management systems makes it possible to strengthen the production control, time limits of delivery, costs, etc., and also to promote the development and research in new products and high value-added products" (Japan Correctional Association, n.d.:2).

CAPIC was expected to broaden access to the free market for prison-made goods. As a semiprivate organization, it would be more acceptable to the public than a government agency. To increase the volume of sales and to create a more stable market, private enterprises and individual consumers would be assured of a dependable supply and prompt delivery of high-quality products. A catalog of products is issued, and CAPIC participates in a large-scale annual fair displaying prison-made goods. The Correction Bureau has held a national fair in Tokyo for more than 30 years, attracting thousands of individual consumers. Many modest fairs are held at prisons throughout the country each year. Retail stores are located in Tokyo, in Nagoya, and at some prisons.

Economic returns would be enhanced by paying more attention to higher-value products and by introducing more sophisticated technology. The national government contributes to the renovation of workshop equipment and sponsors training of workshop supervisors to help them in their duties and in their improvement of inmate skills. CAPIC pays their secondary expenses for attending courses and seminars. The system's emphasis on prison industries makes regularity of production very important, and CAPIC ultimately hopes to safeguard such regularity by providing 20% of prison employment through its own projects.

CAPIC's Place in Prison Industry

CAPIC reports considerable progress in accomplishing its goals, but more progress is necessary. The costs of administration and of transportation of finished goods must be reduced.[13] Changes in markets and customer needs require constant monitoring. The nationwide operations involve an inventory of some four hundred products. For systematic management, plans should be advanced for developing a computerized database.

CAPIC uses three methods to increase sales and stabilize the market. First, CAPIC furnishes raw materials and prison labor, and sells the products. Second, CAPIC obtains orders from customers, provides raw materials, and the prison makes the products. Third, CAPIC purchases raw materials from the contractor and relays them to the prison, and then receives the finished products and sells them to the contractor.

CAPIC has not increased its share of total contracts obtained, but its financial contribution has been enhanced. From 1985 to 1991, CAPIC reports that its share of net revenue rose from 24.8% to 32.4%; and its share of inmate man-days from 13.2% to 23.4%. Its sales increased from 4.17 billion yen in 1983 to 15.89 billion yen in 1991, a 387% gain. For fiscal years 1989 to 1990, the customers were long-term contractors (46.4%), large-scale contractors (8.3%), government agencies (8.9%), the general public (23.5%), and annual fairs (12.9%). Gross profits were 3.9% of sales in 1983 and 11.2% of 1989

sales. However, operating costs also increased at a rate of 374%. In the initial years, net income was negative, but it has been positive ever since, reaching 442,784 thousand yen in 1991.

For all prison industries in Japan, metal work and tailoring alone employed 37% of all inmate workers in 1988 and made 53.7% of the revenue (see Table 14-2). Woodcraft (chiefly furniture), printing, and leather work employed 14% and supplied 25.9% of the revenue. Those five industries were disproportionately "profitable." Unlike proportions in non-CAPIC revenue, woodcraft and printing brought CAPIC more revenue than metal work and tailoring. The ratios in Table 14-2 indicate that (in addition to woodcraft and printing) CAPIC draws revenue most advanta-

Table 14-2: *Inmate Workers by Kind of Products; Comparing CAPIC and All Prison Industry by Revenue and Kind of Products, 1988*

Kind of Products	Inmates in all Industry Number	Pct.	Total Revenue From Industries In Million Yen	Pct.	Capic Revenue In Million Yen	Ratio*
Metal Work	8,909	20.7	5,389.9	32.6	726.8	.16
Tailoring	7,045	16.4	3,495.8	21.1	761.0	.28
Woodcraft	2,657	6.2	2,012.6	12.2	1,450.0	2.58
Printing	1,776	4.1	1,391.6	8.4	1,054.4	3.13
Leather Work	1,595	3.7	878.1	5.3	207.4	.31
Vocational Training	1,062	2.5	116.4	0.7	94.8	4.39
Farm Forestry, Stock Raising	228	0.5	257.5	1.6	24.1	.10
Ceramics	186	0.4	130.3	0.8	93.7	2.56
Auto Repair	122	0.3	123.0	0.7	116.1	16.83
Paper Work	68	0.2	74.1	0.5	19.8	.36
Others	19,395	45.0	2,666.0	16.1	49.4	.02
TOTAL	43,043	100.0	16,535.3	100.0	4,597.4	.38

*For the ratio, CAPIC revenue was subtracted from total revenue. The ratio is CAPIC revenue divided by non-CAPIC revenue.
Source: CAPIC

geously from industries contributing relatively less to total revenue: automobile repair and ceramics. CAPIC was especially
helpful in vocational training programs
that incidentally generated revenue.

Between 1986 and 1991, the value of
CAPIC sales rose an impressive 37% (see
Table 14-3). In 1986, woodcraft and printing brought the greatest financial return, but
tailoring, metal work, and leather work
scored greater gains. Woodcraft continued
to accrue the most revenue of all industrial
categories in spite of a very modest gain
proportionately. Printing made a small increase in absolute value of sales but failed
to keep pace with other categories.

Other Contributions of CAPIC

CAPIC contributed a total of 347,323 thousand yen to various projects for the personnel and programs of the Correction
Bureau in the 1985–1991 period. Among
the projects are financial support of over-
seas study tours for selected Correction
Bureau personnel, sponsorship of an ath-
letic marathon, sponsorship of a contest
in word processing, and establishment of
a research institute.

While president of JCA, Yoshiho
Yasuhara suggested that CAPIC sponsor a
new research unit, the Correctional Association Research Institute for Criminology.
The Institute is designed to remedy a lack
of private research centers in Japan dealing with the fields of corrections and criminology, and has a staff of [14]. Governmen-
tally sponsored variations on the Institute
have been developed by the Ministry of
Justice and the National Police Agency.

The Institute has five divisions. General
Affairs is responsible for administrative
support. The Investigation Division nego-
tiates with other research units in planning
projects, publishes a journal (The Bulletin of Correctional Research Institute for
Criminology), reports on the Institute's
projects, and prepares teaching materials
for personnel training conducted by the
Correction Bureau. Three of the five divisions specialize in particular areas of research.

The First Research Division examines
the causes of crime and delinquency, the
methodologies of prediction and trend
identification, and crime prevention. In
one project, analysis of event-history was
examined as a method for follow-up studies. In another project, the eight correc-

Table 14-3: CAPIC Sales by Products, 1986-1991 (A)

Types of Products	1986		1991		PCT.
	Sales	Pct.	Sales	Pct.	Change
Woodcraft	4,176.7	35.0	5,800.8	35.4	38.9
Printing	2,153.5	18.0	2,270.6	13.9	5.4
Tailoring	2,084.1	17.5	3,272.8	20.0	57.0
Metalwork	1,800.7	15.1	2,695.6	16.5	49.7
Leatherwork	704.0	5.9	1,127.8	6.9	60.2
Ceramics	235.4	2.0	328.6	2.0	39.6
Auto Repair	218.1	1.8	241.8	1.5	10.9
Other Products	444.7	3.7	498.2	3.0	12.0
Vocational Training	119.0	1.0	127.1	0.8	6.8
TOTAL	11,936.2	100.0	16,363.3	100.0	37.1

(a) Sales are in million yen.
Source: CAPIC

tional regions of the Correction Bureau gathered data for an evaluation of treatment methods.

The Second Research Division concentrates on the practical aspects of crime prevention systems such as punitive and protective measures taken against offenders, and rehabilitation-oriented programs. One project studied how prison industries are organized; another followed up prisoners who had completed vocational training.

The Third Research Division considers theories concerning therapeutic responses to offenders, the characteristics of criminals and delinquents, and the development of staff skills for treating offenders. Among the projects are studies of the drawings of family members by female inmates at juvenile training schools, problems encountered in counseling prison inmates suffering from AIDS, and characteristic responses of training school inmates in a sentence comprehension test.

Opposing Outcomes: U.S. and Japan

In nineteenth-century America some three dozen states adopted the industrial prison in the mode of the Auburn system, but opposition appeared soon after the system was created. As the decades passed, the share of inmates employed in industries declined consistently: 90% in 1885, 71% in 1895, 53% in 1932, 10% in 1979 (Funke, Wayson, and Miller, 1982:20–21).

Americans have a historical proclivity for joining associations, including political interest groups that mobilize efforts to gain advantages from government in a particular public issue. The American scene is especially congenial to the competition among interest groups. Federalism divides power between the national and state governments, offering several targets for exerting influence. Power is decentralized within two major political parties; politicians of various ideological persuasions are found in both major parties. Party discipline is weakened, and candidates for political office are very susceptible to the demands of interest groups (Keefe et al., 1990:306–311).

The decline in industrial employment of prisoners reflects the growing success of lobbying that persuaded state and national lawmakers to restrict prison-made goods. The prosperous contract industries attracted major opposition in the northern states. There were a series of investigations in eleven states during the 1870s and 1880s. Manufacturers in certain industries organized the National Anti-Contract Association in 1886. Reports prepared in 1905 and 1923, Gill (1931:84) declares, set forth "an array of evidence which leaves no doubt that prison industries, by underselling, by dumping, by false labeling, by unfair advertising, by unscientific accounting, by brutal treatment of labor, and by bad management, have been able to take advantage of free industry to the detriment of both labor and capital."

By 1950 the state-use and the public-works-and-ways systems[14] were the dominant forms of inmate employment. The final blow to the industrial prison was struck during the Great Depression with the Hawes–Cooper Act (1929) and the Ashurst–Sumners Acts (1935 and 1940) of the national Congress. These authorized state legislatures to prohibit in their jurisdiction the sale of goods made in prisons of other states, an exception to the U.S. Constitutional reservation of interstate commerce control to the federal government. The state legislatures reacted enthusiastically to the opportunity and also abetted lobbyists by pursuing further sanctions against the sale of goods made in their own prisons (Flynn, 1951:239–241).

In Japan there has been incidental opposition to prisoner-made goods, but resistance is uncommon, especially in times of prosperity and labor shortage. "Japan has experienced neither systematic opposition to prison industries from outsiders, representing business and labor unions, nor legislative action to limit the inmate's employment in order to protect the free

market" (Yanigimoto, 1970:216). Primary
or secondary contractors would seem the
most likely opponents, but they are the
primary sources of agreements with
prisons. These agreements are general
affirmations of prison-made goods, as Japan has consistently lacked an adequate
supply of blue-collar workers and skilled
manpower.

Japanese political experts usually favor
the elitist model of policymaking with a
tripartite power group composed of the
leaders of the Liberal Democratic Party
(LDP), senior bureaucrats, and big businessmen. The LDP has ruled the national
Diet almost without interruption since
1954,[15] but the Party depends on interest
groups (especially "big business") for campaign funds and on government bureaucracy for expertise and implementation of
policy (Fukui, 1977:22–24). "Although
organized economic interests, including
big business and the agricultural lobby,
enjoy an astonishing level of access to
policymaking in Japan," (Pharr, 1990:xi–
xii) notes, "when it comes to noneconomic
interests, the story is quite different." Interest groups especially concerned about
prison issues would be among those non-
economic groups with limited access to
policymaking at the national level. They
have little incentive to amass the resources
of an effective protest group.

CAPIC shows the Correction Bureau's
ability to succeed in negotiations when
the viability of the industrial prison is
threatened. The organization did not
emerge from a struggle between political
interest groups, but from bargaining between ministries in an unusual but general fiscal crisis. The Correction Bureau
was vulnerable to external pressures, but
was able to justify its advantageous functions within the structures of government
and private industry.

One could say that all of the circumstances of the case were uniquely Japanese:
the history of prison labor's contribution
to the nation's economy, the contemporary
linkage with private industry through sub-

contracting, the absence of vigorous and
organized opposition to prison-made
goods, the fundamental position of prison
industry in the prison's operations, CAPIC
as another example of *gaikaku dantai*, and
the Correction Bureau's orientation toward
taisei-gai bargaining.

Notes

1. This paper is among the products of
   research financed by a Fulbright
   award for 1990–1991. Collection of
   information was especially assisted by
   Kazuo Kawakani, former Director-
   General of the Correction Bureau, Keisei
   Miyamoto, head of CAPIC, and Takehisa
   Kihara, Director of the Industrial
   Division, Correction Bureau's head-
   quarters in Tokyo.

2. In 1834 a prison director in France
   responded to an official inquiry: "I do
   not know how to concede that work
   exercises an essentially reforming
   (emphasis in original) effect on them
   (the inmates). But I do consider work
   in any large prison to be the surest
   guarantee of order, peace, and quiet."
   (Quoted by O'Brien, 1982: 183–184).

3. The Ministry of Justice (1990:35–36)
   addresses the rehabilitative purpose.
   "Prison industry is organized so as to
   serve constructive purposes in the
   treatment of prisoners. Its objective is
   not only to provide inmates with
   vocational knowledge and skills, but
   also to strengthen their will to work,
   sense of self-help, and spirit of cooperation through working together in
   well-regulated circumstances. Thus,
   prison industry contributes to the
   correctional aims of resocializing
   offenders."

4. The budget for adult institutions in 1990
   was $1,028,391,361 and the "settled
   revenue" from prison industries
   $127,635,408 (130 yen per $1 U.S.).

5. The rules resemble those of a Japanese
   automobile factory in 1927: "Don't lose
   your spirit for work. Don't look around

while working. Don't think about anything else while working. Talking to someone who is working is prohibited in this factory." (Quoted by Allison, 1975:104).

6. When released from prison in 1990, a male inmate averaged 25,961 yen and a woman inmate 28,449 yen accumulated remuneration. The averages increased consistently with length of sentence: from 1,686 yen for less than 3 months to 53,923 yen for sentences over 3 years for males; equivalent range for women was 1,500 to 54,897 yen (Ministry of Justice, 1991:180). In 1990 the exchange rate was 134 yen per U.S. dollar.

7. "In large areas of Tokyo and Osaka back streets rarely visited by outsiders," Van Wolferen (1989:171) comments, "one hears the same incessant clickety-clack of small machines behind hundreds of wooden doors as one did ten or twenty years ago; but the clickety-clack produces entirely different things today."

8. Convinced that small and medium-sized firms would play the key role in postwar economic reconstruction, Yoshisuke Ayukawa purchased a commercial bank in 1952 and organized loans to small companies (Van Wolferen, 1989:388–389).

9. Income accrued from products made incidentally to vocational training courses.

10. Campbell (1985:507–511) relates the effort to deal with the deficit to the more general movement to reduce the size of the national government. He describes RINCHO as a blue-ribbon commission representing "big business" and this direct participation of big business in governmental affairs to be "actually quite a new development." However, RINCHO backed off from rigorous administrative reform in the face of "generally hostile bureaucracy."

11. MOF collects monies from several governmental institutions: primarily postal savings, insurance, national

pensions, and welfare pensions (Woronoff, 1986:127).

12. Public corporations pay their own way, provide services, and thus help to keep the Japanese tax rate comparatively low (Johnson, 1978:144–146).

13. By improved administration and accounting methods the prisons were able, by the end of 1992, to stabilize these costs, which previously had been increasing.

14. The state-use system produces goods and services exclusively for agencies and political subdivisions of the given state. Public-works-and-ways includes road construction and repair, reforestation, soil-erosion control, and other similar services.

15. At the time of this writing, LDP has lost control of the Diet.

Discussion and Review Questions

1. What are the advantages and disadvantages of the factory system of corrections prevalent in Japan, China, and Denmark?

2. Why did the factory system of corrections collapse in the United States but survive in major Asian and European countries?

3. Compare and contrast the Japanese congregate cells system and the American Auburn plan.

4. What are the goals of the Correctional Association Prison Industrial Cooperative (CAPIC)?

5. The Japanese Prisons System is self-sustaining. Discuss.

6. What are the reasons why Japanese prisoners accept the behavioral standards of the industrial prisons?

7. How is a stable amount of productivity maintained in Japanese industrial prisons?

8. What is the role of physically unfit inmates in the Japanese industrial prison system?

9. How are Japanese industrial prison products marketed?

10. What are the main unique features of the Japanese prison system?

11. What is CAPIC? How did it emerge in Japan?

12. What are the basic requirements of the factory system of prisons in Japan?

13. How did Jeremy Bentham set the tone for industrial prison in Great Britan?

14. Why is violence against other inmates and aggression against staff in Japanese prisons a rare occurrence?

15. When did Japan start to erect modern prisons?

16. How did the Meiji Restoration emerge in Japan?

17. CAPIC uses three methods to increase sales and stabilize the market. What are the three ways?

15

Japanese Version of Community Corrections

Volunteer Probation Officers and Hostels

Elmer H. Johnson

Introduction

In a videotaped presentation orienting the Japanese to the work of the Rehabilitation Bureau, a spokesman says in part:

> Japan is a peaceful and stable society. The system for rehabilitating criminals has played a large role in achieving this. . . . We hear about crime and juvenile delinquency in the newspapers and on television every day, but, to protect ourselves and to build a society where we can all live safely, it is not sufficient just to strengthen crime control or to punish criminals. We must work to insure that offenders are reintegrated into society and that crime is prevented. . . .

> The rehabilitation system is based on the concept of trusting people who unfortunately have committed crimes or have been delinquent so they can reform by developing a greater awareness of themselves and their circumstances. . . . Imprisonment isolates criminals from society, and they often return to crime when they are released. Consequently, the crime rate never decreases. Therefore, the prevention system is very important in

assisting offenders when they return to society, supporting their social rehabilitation and making them productive members of society. . . .

The Rehabilitation Bureau expresses the claims made for community-based corrections in the criminal justice and criminological literature of the West. Similarities in general purposes are suggested, but, unlike in the West, the Rehabilitation Bureau largely relies on private persons and groups for their achievement. Volunteer probation officers (unsalaried private persons) carry out almost all supervision of probationers and parolees. Rehabilitation aid associations operate the halfway houses, serve parolees chiefly, and receive government subsidies meeting only a portion of their operating expenses. This paper concentrates on this major aspect of Rehabilitation Bureau policy.[1]

This chapter will trace precedents in Japanese history for the use of volunteer probation officers (VPOs) and of private groups in aftercare (rehabilitation aid hostels), but also will show what such policies owe to the diffusion of foreign ideas following the modernization of feudal Japan. We will argue that the Japanese concept of "community" can help us understand how the participation of private citizens in community corrections came to be important in Japanese criminal justice. It was a concept formed under the Tokugawa rulers of the rural villages during the Tokugawa Era (1603–1867), the social control system of which brought centuries of unprecedented peace and security. The influence of the Tokugawa system lingers in the behavior and beliefs of contemporary Japanese.

Western nations forced Japan to end centuries of isolation from foreign influences and contributed to the Meiji Restoration, initiated in 1868, at which time Japan made a tardy but hasty effort to develop modern institutions and infrastructure. The social psychology of Japanese community has been affected by modernization, and the motivation and activities of volunteers in criminal justice activities will be assessed in that context. Modern societies believe that things can be changed, that human consciousness can bend destiny to its will. Modernization has contributed to an increasing crime rate, but Japan remains on the whole "a peaceful and stable society."

Modern Japanese society, like other modern societies, believes community correction to be a superior alternative to imprisonment, because it accords with the belief that things can change. The Japanese culture and the structure and operations of Japan's criminal justice system contribute to a remarkably low imprisonment rate, which has dropped from 65 per 100,000 in 1926 to 34 per 100,000 in 1989. The imprisonment rate in the United States, on the other hand, rose from 83 per 100,000 in 1926 to 271 per 100,000 in 1989 (Shikita and Tsuchiya, 1990:371; Ministry of Justice, 1991:24; Flanagan and Maguire, 1991:604).

Japanese criminal justice also authorizes the court, under certain conditions, to suspend a prison sentence after imposing it and to place the offender under "protective supervision" (Penal Code, Articles 25 and 26). Table 15-1 demonstrates that less than 5% of the courts' dispositions are imprisonment; that almost 3% are suspended imprisonment; and that, of those suspensions, only 0.39% are probationers. More specifically, only a small share of adult convicted offenders receive probation. Judges often are reluctant to require probationary supervision as a condition of suspension, when there are extenuating circumstances (Kouhashi, 1985:4-5). They treat probation as a punitive sanction.

Table15-1: *Disposition of Adjudicated Defendants by Courts of First Instance, 1989*

Dispositions	Number	Percentage
Total Defendants	1,306,214	100.00
Imprisonment	61,531	4.71
Fines	1,208,575	92.52
Penal Detention	79	0.01
Suspended Imprisonment	35,528	2.72
Simple Suspension	(30,409)	(2.33)
With Probation	(5,119)	(0.39)
Acquittals	134	0.01
Others*	367	0.03

Source: Research and Training Institute, Ministry of Justice
*"Others" include guilty but no penalty, time of legal responsibility was exceeded, and summary sentence was sent by mail but not received by the defendant.

Japan is a paradox among modern societies, because its programs of community corrections are greatly dependent on private citizens and do not extend the grasp of criminal justice agencies. People have objected to various community strategies in the United States on grounds that they capture a larger proportion of the population in a broader criminal justice network.[2] This criticism has not been borne out in Japan. Before the postwar expansion of community corrections in 1926, only 6.2 Japanese per 100,000 population were placed on probation, and the rate rose to 73.5 in 1950. Thereafter, the rate has dropped to 38.9 in 1970 and to 31.0 in 1988 (Shikita and Tsuchiya, 1990:369–370).

Twin Sources of Community Corrections

Prisons differ in details of procedure, exigencies of daily events, and the philosophies of those administering them, but there are also basic similarities that override variations in time, place, and purpose. "Perhaps this (the set of similarities) is due to a diffusion of ideas, customs, and laws. Perhaps it is a matter of similar social structures arising independently from attempts to solve much the same problems. Most probably it is some combination of both" (Sykes, 1958:xii–xiii).

One can observe both similarities and differences between community corrections in Japan and the practices and policies of probation, parole, and aftercare in Western societies. In the case of prisons, contemporary practices and policies may be attributed to cultural diffusion from the West and the lingering influence of indigenous traditions. Modern correctional systems emerged later in Japan than in most Western societies, especially community corrections. The development of modern Japanese corrections provides a fine example of the mingling of foreign ideas and institutions with indigenous customs and

ideology that took place in Japanese society starting with the Meiji Restoration.

Prisoners' postrelease difficulties drew the earliest concern. Once, for instance, the emperor granted amnesty to a burglar and gave him some clothes to wear (Satoh, 1989:1). In 1790 the Tokugawa Shogunate opened the *Ninsoku-Yoseba* (Stockade for Laborers) to control homeless wanderers in. After 1820, when it began to house persons sentenced to forced labor, it became a model for other penal facilities. The inmates were paid for their work to give them means for support after release. If those released were farmers, they were given a plot of land. Those from Edo (now Tokyo) were given a shop; otherwise, they were given tools of a trade or granted an allowance (Takigawa, 1972:45, 173–175; Hiromatsu, 1972:44–49, 57).

The Meiji reformers asked Emile Gustave Boissonade to draft a penal code on a French model, and it came into force in 1882. However, a new penal code, developed on a German model, replaced the French version (the "old penal code"), when the Penal Code of 1907 was still in force, although amended in some respects. The Code of 1882 did not provide for government involvement in community corrections, but the Code of 1907 provided strong government commitment to community-based corrections. Early on, the government endeavored to introduce community corrections but lacked sufficient resources. Therefore, "the government requested religious groups, mainly Buddhist organizations, as well as other voluntary organizations, to provide financial assistance and moral support for ex-offenders" (Satoh, 1989:1).

The Napoleonic Code of 1810 had provided for "surveillance"—that is, the supervision and control of released prisoners by the police as an additional punishment. On the other hand, a parole system had emerged from nineteenth-century French patronage societies. These had existed since 1823 and had expanded rapidly in France after 1885; they were private organizations, funded by private donations and partially by state subsidies, which recognized that released prisoners might have problems adjusting. The societies were privately directed but authorized by the government. In the parole system established in 1885, misdemeanants with good conduct could be released from the correctional institution after serving half the sentence and be supervised by a patronage society (O'Brien, 1982:25, 227, 251–254).

In Shizuoka Prefecture, Meisen Kinbara—a philanthropist troubled by a released prisoner who was rejected by his family—pioneered in 1888 the first halfway houses of Japan. In 1907 the government began to help with partial subsidies, and by 1891 two other private halfway houses were opened elsewhere; there were 26 halfway houses by 1900; 61 by 1910; and more than 100 by 1920. Buddhists, Christians, the Salvation Army, and prison personnel were especially active in the movement. The Offenders Rehabilitation Service Law (1934) specified joint responsibility between the government and voluntary organizations for aftercare of prisoners, but World War II stopped its implementation (Udo, 1990:1–2).

Probation of adults emerged in Japan almost as an afterthought, under the authority of the judge to suspend a prison sentence in case of "extenuating circumstances." Article 25 of the Penal Code limits the leniency to persons receiving sentences of 3 years or less (convicts who have served previous sentences must have satisfied those sentences at least 5 years previously).

Article 25-2 says that the person may be placed under "protective supervision" (probation). Of the total suspended sentences in 1961, only 18.7% were with probation and in 1989 probation took up 14.4% (Shikita and Tsuchiya, 1990:165).[3]

"Extenuating circumstances" that permit parole include the following: the defendant has no criminal record or a minimal criminal record, or is young enough to change his or her attitudes and lifestyle; the victim excuses the offender; the victim and defendant have agreed to terms of restitution; the offender exhibits readiness for rehabilitation; the offense was accidental, not deliberate. The judges regard probation to be punitive and are reluctant to add probation to the suspension (Kouhashi, 1985:3–5). Supervision is inconvenient for a person with such extenuating circumstances. If probation is required, the individual would be denied another suspension, if a new crime were committed; but suspension without probation would not render a new suspension impossible.

The Japanese Penal Code's provision for suspended sentences was modeled on the Franco-Belgian system (Ancel, 1971:22–26, 36–40). Alarmed by increases in rates of crime and recidivism, nineteenth-century France questioned the usefulness of imprisonment. Conditional suspension of prison sentences emerged in Belgian law in 1888 and in French law in 1891. The prison sentence was pronounced to intimidate the convicted individual, but the casual offender was believed to have the capacity to rehabilitate himself without assistance or probationary supervision. Suspended sentences without probationary supervision were preferred for deserving offenders—as they are today in Japan.

Conditional release from Japanese prisons was first officially specified in the Penal Code of 1881, which authorized police surveillance after three-quarters of a prison sentence had been served. The Penal Code of 1907 reduced the sentence-serving requirement to one-third, but granted parole on a limited scale. Probation was first formally recognized in 1905 and was incorporated in the Penal Code of 1907, but supervision was lacking. Probation in the full sense was yet to be introduced (Ogawa, 1976:633).

Modern probation and parole were founded after World War II. The Offenders Rehabilitation Law (1949) provides for the organization, principles, and procedures of juvenile law, juvenile parole, and adult parole. The Law for Probationary Supervision of Persons under Suspension of Execution of Sentence (1954) initiated adult probation for convicted offenders, whom the court granted a suspension of prison sentence with supervision. The Law for Aftercare of Discharged Offenders (1950) established criteria for voluntary referrals for postrelease assistance and outlined the principles and procedures for rehabilitation aid hostels (halfway houses) operated by private organizations. The Amnesty Law (1947) defined the kinds and variety of pardons. The Voluntary Probation Officer Law (1950) described the qualifications, selection, and duties of VPOs.

When the Japanese system of community corrections was established in 1949 and 1950, it was debated whether the probation and parole services should be professionalized as in many other countries. The decision was to combine professionals and unpaid volunteers. "It is true that the shortage of funds at the time precluded the realization of overall professionalism," the Rehabilitation Bureau recalls (Ministry of Justice, 1990b:13). "But the even greater reason making a determination to maintain volunteers obviously lies in the fact that the trust of the authorities in the potential of volunteer workers was so overwhelming."

Contemporary VPO and Hostel Programs

The Volunteer Probation Officer Law states that the VPO mission will be "to contribute to the welfare of the individual and the public by helping persons who have committed criminal offenses to improve and be rehabilitated and, at the same time, by leading public opinion for the prevention of offenses and by cleaning up the community, in the spirit of social service." The total number of VPOs for Japan is set at 52,500. They are allocated by the Min-

ister of Justice in "rehabilitation areas" fixed according to population, economic characteristics, crime rates, and other community circumstances.

The Minister of Justice either may delegate the authority to appoint VPOs to the chair of the regional parole board or may appoint them personally. VPOs receive 2-year terms, subject to reappointment, according to these criteria: confidence and popularity with the community in character and conduct; enthusiasm and time for the work; financial stability; and being healthy and active. Persons are disqualified if adjudicated as incompetent; as formerly sentenced to prison; or as having organized or been a member of any organization advocating the overthrow of the Constitution of Japan or the Japanese government by force and violence. No salary or allowance is paid, but expenses incurred in the course of performing duties are paid "within the limits of the budget."

There are fifty probation offices responsible for supervising probationers and parolees and for making referrals to rehabilitation aid hostels. These offices provide VPOs with three kinds of training: initial orientation training for recruits (materials for which are prepared by the Investigation and Research Section in the headquarters of the Rehabilitation Bureau); periodic refresher training; and special sessions bringing experienced VPOs together for study of specific topics.

Rehabilitation and hostels are defined by the Law for Aftercare of Discharged Offenders, which requires their certification by the Minister of Justice and delegates their supervision to probation offices. The hostels provide room and board to discharged prisoners, parolees, and probationers referred to them by a probation office. The hostel associations are private organizations and obtain funds from subsidies by the Rehabilitation Bureau and by private donations; they also may raise support by leasing a part of their land or property to private enterprises, or by other financial means. The 96 hostels have 470 full-time salaried staff plus volunteers. The paid personnel include persons who retired after years of probation or parole service.

The chief of the probation office refers persons to the hostels and sets the official time limit for the stay. For adult parolees, the maximum stay is supposed to be the unserved portion of the prison sentence. A discharged inmate is eligible for a maximum period of 6 months from date of release. The judge sets the length of probation, ranging from 1 to 5 years. Officially, the probationer may stay at the hostel for a full period of probation; but in practice, government funds available for subsidy determine the length of stay. The resident is always responsible for payments beyond that coverage.

Parolees were referred to hostels more often than probationers, and adults more than juveniles. In 1992, of the 13,098 adult parole terminations, 26.5% were referred. Others referred were 4.7% of the 4,384 juvenile parole terminations; 8.3% of the 46,695 juvenile probation terminations; and 2.7% of the 5,436 adult probation terminations. In 1992, 69.1% of released hostel residents had boarded in the hostel because they lacked relatives on whom to depend for help. Another 13.6% had been denied assistance by relatives, and 16% of the residents did not want to seek help from relatives. The remainder (1.3%) had been referred to the hostels to obtain "training for resocialization" (Ministry of Justice, 1993:126, 162–163).

The rehabilitation aid hostels' receipt of government subsidies is in keeping with the *gaikaku dantai* system—private associations, foundations, or unions incorporated at the initiation of the government bureaucracy. Each of these public corporations or extradepartmental groups has a section of government as a predictable client, is staffed predominately by retired government personnel, and is to some degree reliant on government funds[4] (George, 1988:124–125). Public corporations pay at least a portion of their own way, provide services, and thus contribute to the rela-

tively low tax rate of Japan (Johnson, 1978:144–146).

Tokugawa Controls and the Rural Village

Early Japan was a collection of feudal domains engaged in perennial warfare. Ieyasu, founder of the Tokugawa house, won national hegemony by military victories and in 1603 took the office of *Shogun*, nominally the emperor's military deputy but the de facto ruler of Japan (Beasley, 1990:3). To establish political dominance, he used clever military leadership, skillful political treatment of defeated adversaries, and giving fiefs to the *daimyo* (feudal lords) to bind them to him.

The Tokugawa Era (1603–1867) brought centuries of unprecedented peace and security. The *daimyo* who had been early allies (*fudai*) were distinguished from those who had submitted only after Tokugawa military victories (*tozama*). The latter were relegated to distant areas and required to send hostages to Edo (now Tokyo). After pledging loyalty to the Tokugawa regime, the *daimyo* were granted a domain as a fief. To discipline insubordination, the *Shogun* could transfer a lord, or reduce his domain, or confiscate it. By the end of the seventeenth century, bureaucratic administration had been established. The *Shogun* recruited the highest advisors from the *fudai* and sent auditing officials to the domains to check on their wealth, administration, military strength, and size of population (Duus, 1967:88-95).

Formation of a community in Japan was a normal social process that was, unlike in the West, "neither a special privilege nor a legal right to be discussed" (Tonomura, 1992:190). Legal rights such as that of assembly were never demanded from the aristocracy and the Tokugawa state, and the villages seem to have been nothing more than administrative and political arms of the central Tokugawa government.

Community solidarity of local people seems to have come from their resistance to the demands of the centralized government.

Although the system of neighborhood associations "was used principally as a political tool, it did nevertheless develop as an autonomous body of neighborhood families for the handling of community problems" (Masland, 1946:355–356). Villagers maintained community solidarity because the feudal system of social control accorded autonomy to the villagers as long as the Tokugawas' political purposes were served, and because of technological factors associated with rice agriculture.

The Tokugawa system of rule was designed to maintain law and order, to enforce official programs of frugality and morality, to collect taxes, and to suppress anti-Tokugawa activities. Only one castle town was permitted in each domain; all other strongholds were dismantled. The *samurai* were forced to live in a castle town and serve as salaried bureaucrats or to surrender their aristocratic status. "While the physical distance of the *samurai* from the farming land enhanced their bureaucratic character, it also restricted them from direct intervention in village affairs. With minimal involvement of the urban bureaucrats, the primary producers paid taxes and kept the local peace and order" (Tonomura, 1992:169).

The agricultural village had a central role in creating peace and order. With the *samurai* bureaucrats unable to interfere directly in village affairs, authority was delegated to villages to collect taxes, to maintain law and order, and to regulate the daily life of local persons (Sato, 1990:50–51). The village's headman was appointed by the government from among the local people and represented them in contacts with the government. He also was held responsible for the village in satisfying the tax assessment (calculated in units of rice), in overseeing the registration of members of households, and in disseminating the rulers' orders. Local officials were able to oversee conduct of residents because of the information provided by household registration: name, sex, occupation, birth, marriage, divorce, death, and movements of household members (Tonomura, 1992:172–174). Especially in feudal times, the rural hamlet exerted heavy social pressure for conformity with local community norms. Ostracism by vote had great force because of cultural emphasis on harmony among residents, and because agricultural production demanded the neighbors' cooperation (Smith, 1961:522–525; Steiner, 1965: 210–212). Rice growing was a group endeavor, and the entire village worked so closely at it that cooperation was second nature. Tasks were not specialized: everyone took turns at all chores. The work was repetitive from year to year. Perseverance was demanded more than innovation, and operations could be conducted through a consensus without strong individual leadership (Hayashi, 1988:87–92).

In 1597 Hideyoshi Toyotomi ordered that the peasants be organized into five-householder groups (the *gonin-gumi*). (The idea of organizing Japan in small community groups was borrowed from China.) The head of each group was obligated to make certain that the peasants lived frugal lives, worked hard, and paid taxes (Braibanti, 1948:140). In the Tokugawa era, this system for controlling the peasantry was again borrowed from the Chinese (Dore, 1958:255). The Tokugawa regime went deeper than Toyotomi in copying the Chinese village-oriented social organization. In ancient Japan, the *gonin-gumi* system had either imposed criminal liability on the offender's relatives (*enza*) or an unrelated person serving in the same office (*renza*). Later the responsibility had been extended to the offender's neighbors (Ishii, 1980:51, 58, 89).[5]

In the 1620s and 1630s, the Tokugawa regime acted to forbid contacts with Europeans because contacts were thought to encourage Japanese dissidents, and because Christianity was believed to corrupt Japanese values. Foreign trade was limited to a Dutch trading port and a few Chinese

junks. Christianity was savagely perse-
cuted (Beasley, 1990:22). Foreign intervention, however, eventually did succeed in
challenging the isolation and precipitated
Japan's entry into the modern age.

Twin Sources of the Meiji Restoration

Commodore Matthew C. Perry entered Edo
Bay in February 1854 with his Black Fleet
of eight American warships. In the following years, foreign powers forced treaties
on the Tokugawa government specifying
the principle of extraterritoriality; that is,
foreign nationals in Japan would be subject to the laws of their own countries, not
to the laws of Japan. The principle had
earlier resulted in the loss of China's independence and its domination by Western
imperialism. To avoid China's fate, the
leaders of Japan set out to create the military force and infrastructure of a modern
nation. The term "Meiji Restoration" refers to a coup d'etat carried out in Kyoto
on January 3, 1868, with a group of feudal
lords taking control of the Imperial Court,
terminating the Tokugawa Shogunate, and
proclaiming the Emperor's direct responsibility for government. Their series of reforms established the institutional structure of a new Japan. The process of institutional change was carefully controlled.
Delegations were sent to Europe and the
United States for quick studies of Western
social institutions (Noda, 1976; Beasley,
1990:22–30, 85–88, 142).

The feudal system of the Tokugawa state
had been in decline, and something like
the Meiji Restoration may have come without the intervention of foreign nations
(Craig, 1961:85–86). Also, the Japanese
differed from other Asian nations in their
reaction to foreign pressure because of factors internal to Japan. Entering the modern age well after the industrial revolution
in Europe, Japan confronted the foreign
threat with a common language and with

a set of values consolidated through two
centuries of isolation from the external
world.

Studies of Western institutions guided
the development of Japan's modern political and economic systems. The timing was
exceptionally appropriate for the examination of Western institutions, because "all
of the great powers at that time were engaged in organization-building on a major
scale" (Westney, 1987:11). State structures
of France were being refashioned into patterns appropriate to the Third Republic;
the unified German Empire was emerging;
Great Britain was striving for stability at
home and within the Empire; and the
United States was rebuilding its administrative structure after the Civil War.

The lessons learned from the West were
accommodated to Japanese values and social patterns. The ultimate outcome illustrates the principle that mass transfer of
foreign ideas encounters resistance: people
are slow to change their familiar ways, and
new ideas must be accommodated to existing institutions and values.

Community in Twentieth-Century Japan

Massive and sweeping changes since the
Meiji Restoration have affected community
solidarity and modified the nature of relationships among the local residents. In his
study of potters in Kyushu, Moeran
(1984:174–175) describes the effects of
such change on rural residents: "They still
share their lives; they still participate in
communal events. Everyone turns out to
help when it comes to building a new
house." Nevertheless, traditional solidarity grounded in the unity of all households
has been weakened by materialism and
erosion of the authority of traditional leadership. The appreciation of the classic pottery by outsiders has given potting households greater income than non-potting
households and introduced social stratifi-

cation. Recognition of the skills of master potters has undermined the traditional gerontocracy.

With the termination of the Tokugawa state, its system for controlling rural villagers was weakened, and new conditions altered the nature of community ties. After the Meiji Restoration, the new regime officially abolished the *gonin-gumi* with the intention of substituting reverence to the Emperor for loyalty to the immediate neighborhood (Braibanti,1948:1). Nevertheless, the groups survived, and neighborhood gatherings for weddings, funerals, festivals, harvesting, and care of the sick still exist.

For wartime mobilization of civilians, the Home Ministry of the national government in 1940 ordered the prefectures (equivalent to the American states) to enlist neighborhood associations. The rural *buraku-kai* were based on the traditional communal units. In urban areas, the *chonaikai* (district or block associations) were composed of 400 to 600 households. Legislation in 1943 authorized local governments to enlist the aid of the unit heads and to control the property and expenditures of neighborhood associations. Although the neighborhood associations were based on mutual cooperation and were examples of local self-government, their wartime functions recalled the services of feudal villages for the Tokugawa dictatorship (Masland, 1946:356–357; Shihgetoh, 1943:984–985).

Because the *chonaikai* were identified with wartime service to the military dictatorship, the allied occupation authorities ordered them disbanded. Also, postwar developments magnified the effects of migration and technological change on the social solidarity of local community groups. In rural areas, the need for neighbors' cooperation had been reduced by mechanization of agriculture. Electric cooking and heating eased the demand for communal forests. Other types of roofing replaced thatched roofs and ended the need for neighbors' assistance in rethatching (Steiner, 1965:224).

Social changes and the orders of the allied occupation have failed to eliminate the *chonaikai*, but the groups' nature has been modified. The *chonaikai* is unquestionably the neighborhood's most important and visible organization. In some senses it acts as "a semi-official local government, providing services to residents both at local initiative and at the behest of the municipal authorities" (Bestor, 1985: 126–127).

The *chonaikai* hovers between a group for communal fellowship and a semiofficial component of formal government. It is multifunctional in contrast to the specialized functions of government agencies. Households, not individuals, are members; membership is taken for granted rather than being a conscious or clearly compulsory act (Nakamura, 1968:191–192, 201–207).

Voluntary associations emerged only with the end of World War II, because previously "all groups were subordinated to the emperor system" and then were in practice "more or less dependent on government." Because political parties and labor unions had failed to deal with pollution and other postwar local issues, "the citizens felt that they had no organization that could support them and so they started a voluntary organization to tackle the problem" (Ishida, 1983:16–17). In contrast to the earlier *chonaikai* that served government, the postwar versions in urban fringe areas have opposed local governments by voicing demands of citizens who believe their rights have been violated in a given problematic situation (Aoyagi, 1983:105).

Groups especially interested in criminal justice issues, however, have little incentive to amass resources for organized political activities. "Although organized economic interests, including big business and the agricultural lobby, enjoy an astonishing level of access to policy-making in

Japan, when it comes to non-economic interests the story is quite different" (Pharr, 1990:xi–xii). The management of criminals ranks among noneconomic issues, especially in a nation with a crime rate as low as Japan's.

VPOs and Community Participation

The Tokugawa system of controlling villagers lingers in the attitudes of many contemporary Japanese. Plath (1964:141–142) notes "there is no doubt that the Japanese have tended to be more accepting than Americans of government surveillance and control of organizations." The difference is not universal, however. Plath also notes that some Japanese find active membership in community groups to be exciting, and some Americans "volunteered" for participation in PTAs and charities. However, Plath continues: "Americans tend to underline the voluntary aspects of association membership. Japanese are more aware of its compulsory facets of the moral pressure of the *waku*." The social control system (the *waku*) presses them to give priority to group interests over narrow self-interests and to seek participation in community groups as a duty.

In an interview, a Yokohama VPO told this writer that such a sense of duty had motivated his accepting the service:

> My father owns a Japanese restaurant, a Western restaurant, a Chinese restaurant, and an Italian restaurant. I manage the family business. Twenty-two years ago the prefectural government sent me to see youth programs in the Soviet Union, England, Germany, Switzerland, and Italy. The government decided to build a youth hostel. The officials said to me: "You spent the government's money to go abroad; now you should do volunteer probation work." My family expected me to do something without pay. I had no reason to say "no." So I said: "Okay! I will do that."

VPOs are drawn heavily from members of the middle classes who are likely to be active in other volunteer organizations and often leaders in the *chonaikai* (Anagata, 1990:4). "It was markedly apparent that Japanese small entrepreneurs over fifty years old in Arakawa ward (a section of Tokyo) as elsewhere who had some leisure time were apt to devote it to some form of voluntary community activities, such service is a recognized and compelling way to gain prestige within Japanese society" (Wagatsuma and DeVos, 1984:29).

Other long-term VPOs observed by this writer in Sendai also expressed the duty theme, but added more personal explanations for accepting the responsibilities: need to be active during retirement, the satisfactions derived from working with other persons, and the persuasion of a friend who was a VPO. The older Japanese are particularly public-service oriented. Frager and Rohlen (1976:266–268) believe that such "spiritual improvement will bring general social betterment." They continue: "The impression given to the cynical outsider is at best one of saccharine naivete, yet many of the country's great men participate in and frequently lead such efforts with a degree of personal devotion and energy that is amazing."

The competence and dedication of the older and experienced VPOs impressed this writer when he witnessed their discussions during a training session. Nevertheless, the VPO program has its problems. The volunteers in community corrections tend to be middle class and older, whereas their clients are drawn predominately from less affluent younger adults. The long-term trend has been away from occupational groups particularly apt to share life perspectives and hold the ready cooperation of their clients. From 1958 to 1990, the VPO occupations have shifted toward the unemployed, including retired persons and housewives, from 13% to 25.7%. Other major occupational categories have slipped in representation: fishing and farming, religious figures, government and company employees, and sales personnel. Women VPOs have consistently increased their presence from 7% in 1953 to 21.1% in 1990. The average age of VPOs was 53.2 years in 1953 and rose consistently to 61.7 years at the end of 1990. Meanwhile, the median length of service increased from 6.93 years in 1953 to 11.61 years in 1990 (Anagata, 1990:18–19).

Assessing the Volunteer System

"Without about 48,000 volunteer probation officers who are actively engaged in the offenders rehabilitation service across the country," declares former Director-General Kunpei Satoh (1989:17) of the Rehabilitation Bureau, "we have only 1,000 probation officers in 50 probation offices, to take care of about 100,000 persons placed under probation or parole."

As community leaders, volunteers are expected to be more familiar with the local scene than full-time professional probation officers (PPOs) who are more likely to be transferred to other communities. When PPOs are also volunteers in other social service programs, they have the knowledge of and accessibility to refer probationers and parolees, when the services are needed. Although representatives of government, the *hogoshi* (PPOs) are more likely to obtain client rapport and less likely to attract the neighbors' attention as private citizens. Not bound strictly by regulations and working hours, they are more flexible in service delivery than rule-bound PPOs. Responsibilities of PPOs end with termination of supervision, while personal ties of VPOs and clients can continue (Anagata, 1990:5; Hashimoto, 1983:185–186; Wagatsuma and DeVos, 1984:37). A leading official told this writer: "Volunteer involvement in the probation service has been well accepted in our country and instrumental over the past years, in particular, in terms of its aid-oriented service."

Article 20, the Offenders Rehabilitation Law, which specifies the relationship between the VPO and the PPO, states: "The volunteer probation officer provided for in the Volunteer Probation Office Law shall assist the professional probation officer and make up for inadequacies of the latter's work, and engage in the work coming within the scope of the specific function of RPB (Regional Parole Board) or the Probation Office. . . ." Instead of assisting the PPO, however, the VPO performs the treatment function. Anagata (1990:9) contends: "We are short of professional probation officers, and there is little prospect of a rapid increase of professional probation officers because of the presence of the VPO system." Since 1974 the probation offices in Tokyo and Osaka have found difficult cases require a level of supervision beyond the grasp of VPOs. In direct supervision units, several PPOs assume supervisory responsibilities for selected cases. Five PPOs in Tokyo supervise an average of 20 cases, compared with 150 or so cases managed by a PPO who works through VPOs. The offenders in direct supervision have general characteristics such as mental disorders not requiring hospitalization, gross environmental handicaps such as grave parent–child conflicts or mental disorders of parents, or foreigners unable to adjust to Japanese society.

As lay persons, VPOs tend to treat clients from particular personal experiences rather than on basis of principles. The PPO may not be properly informed on the client's actual situation. "When two probationers show the same progress," Hashimoto (1983:86) notes, "one may be discharged from probation based on the favorable reports of a lenient VPO, where the other may remain under the further supervision of a strict VPO." Competent VPOs are especially difficult to recruit for high-delinquency areas. The progressive effects of urban conditions on community solidarity make for difficult cases. Some volunteers are hopelessly out of touch with the clients' changing needs. VPOs may neglect supervisory duties because of their own business and family obligations (Wagatsuma and DeVos, 1983:37).

Recognizing that extended use of community corrections requires more emphasis on professionalism, the Rehabilitation Bureau plans to strengthen training of junior PPOs. It is hoped that promoting professionalism in rising PPOs will advance the quality of community corrections while preserving the advantages of the VPO services.

Shortage of funds, the Rehabilitation Bureau notes (Ministry of Justice, 1990a:19–20), compromises the administration of rehabilitation aid hostels. Those running profit-making businesses have an advantage but are exceptional. In fiscal year 1989, the halfway houses took in an average income of 26,790,069 yen from the following sources: reimbursement and subsidy from probation offices and family courts (49.6%); workshop income (20.6%); donations (9.6%); property dividends (5.8%); residents' board and room payments when they stay past subsidy (6.9%); local government subsidy (1.3%); membership fees (1.5%); and miscellaneous sources (4.7%).

The financial difficulties stem from the insufficiency of government subsidy payments which, in turn, may be traced to a combination of too few residents and short average stays. The number of hostels dropped from 150 to 98 in 1988, and the total authorized capacity from 3,921 to 2,400. In spite of these declines, the use of available bed space dropped from 74% in 1958 to 58% in 1988 (Udo, 1990:9). In 1992 the residents stayed in hostels for a median of 28 days (Ministry of Justice, 1993:167).

Conclusion

"The rehabilitation system is based on the concept of trusting people who unfortunately have committed crimes," the Reha-

bilitation Bureau announced in a public statement. By not trusting criminals, the Bureau implies, the prison isolates them from the curative powers of normal community relationships.

The idea of trust has particular implications for urbanites who inhabit a social world that is more complex and variable than social worlds of more direct and stable character. As Luhmann (1979:5–6, 20, 68–69) comments, the urban scene tends to lose its taken-for-granted familiarity, because daily experience can only envisage it in a fragmentary way. In personal trust, confidence is placed in other persons with whom one is in relatively intimate social interaction. System trust entails placing confidence in a long chain of events, without full knowledge or direct experience of the interactions that are supposed to deliver benefits. Trust in either persons or systems will figure in any motive for offering or refusing benefits. However, Luhmann notes, trust operates within the constraints of social relationships that normatively channel its expression.

From arrest to conviction by trial, decision makers extend forgiveness to many of the defendants who are believed to be worthy of trust. This is one reason why Japan has one of the lowest imprisonment rates among developed societies. Even after a prison sentence has been pronounced, the court may return the offender to the free community with or without probation. The judges' trust in granting suspensions is underscored by their reluctance to require even probationary supervision.

Japanese society has surpassed Western societies in retaining both personal and system trust in spite of massive socioeconomic changes in the last century. Rural relationships generated trust among villagers, partly in defense against Tokugawa authoritarianism. Villagers were held accountable for the crimes of their family members and nonrelatives. These traditions linger in community associations of more recent decades, but community ties have also been constructed in opposition to government, when residents believe their interests are not being respected. Management of convicted offenders is not among major public issues in Japan—no surprise, given its low crime rate.

By enlisting the services of VPOs and rehabilitation aid associations, the government has shown its tendency to avoid major investment in social services when feasible, and its faith in the willingness and capacity of private citizens to deliver needed services to the community. Although there are fragmentary linkages with events in earlier Japan, modern community corrections were initiated for the most part immediately after World War II, when there were heavy demands on the public purse.

This writer—a "cynical outsider," as Frager and Rohlen (1976:266–268) would put it—is indeed tempted to describe the enthusiasm of many VPOs and hostel workers as "saccharine naivete" falling far short of the performance of professional probation and parole officers. It may well be that future developments in the social psychology of the Japanese will justify "cynicism." At this moment in the history of Japanese community corrections, however, Japanese private supervision and aftercare programs deserve a more favorable assessment than their American counterparts. The Japanese government's trust in private persons' ability to deliver programs of community correction is proper reciprocity for the Japanese people's personal and system trust which suppresses any upsurge in their country's imprisonment rate.

Notes

1. Research for this paper was conducted in Japan under a Fulbright grant and the sponsorship of the Rehabilitation Bureau and Correction Bureau of the Japanese Ministry of Justice. Study of the operations of the Rehabilitation Bureau would have been impossible without the firm support of successive

Directors-General: Keiji Kurita, Kunpei Satoh, Tsuneo Furuhata, and Hiroyasu Sugihara. A number of staff members provided extraordinary assistance and insights, especially Masaru Matumoto, Director of the Supervision Department of the Bureau.

2. For example, Blomberg (1987:219) says: "The tendency of diversion and other community programs to widen the control net produces results that are increasing rather than reducing the number of individuals coming into contact with the formal criminal justice system."

3. Data for 1989 were supplied by the Research and Training Institute, Ministry of Justice.

4. In 1959 the Social Education Act was amended to allow the government to subsidize "social education groups" (Ishida, 1983:16).

5. Spitzer (1983:317–318) argues that the *gonin-gumi* strategy is an example of the weaknesses of central government: "The fact that local elites had to be kept in place and manipulated under Tokugawa law, rather than totally destroyed, is one indication of the political and ideological weaknesses characteristic of certain types of precapitalist states."

Discussion and Review Questions

1. What are the duties of volunteer probation officers?

2. Why do the Japanese extol community corrections as a superior alternative to imprisonment?

3. Compare and contrast imprisonment rates in Japan and the United States. Discuss.

4. Compare and contrast the role of patronage societies in corrections in Japan and Brazil.

5. To what extent did the European correctional system (Belgian and

French penal laws) play a part in the Japanese penal code?

6. Why did nineteenth-century France question the usefulness of imprisonment?

7. Describe in detail community corrections in Japan under volunteer probation officers.

8. Why did the Tokugawa Shogunate forbid Japanese from having contact with Europeans from the seventeenth through the nineteenth centuries (1603–1867)?

9. What is the "principle of extraterritoriality"?

10. On what principle is the Japanese rehabilitation system based?

11. As in Nigeria, Ghana, Sierra Leone, and China, Japanese villagers are held accountable for the crimes of their village members. Is it possible to hold a community responsible for the crime or crimes of its members in the United States?

12. Why is the management of convicts not a major public issue in Japan?

13. Punishing offenders does not have much significance in offender disposal in Japan. In what aspect of the social system do the Japanese lay much emphasis in offender disposal?

14. What is protective supervision in Japanese penology and corrections?

15. Why is Japanese community corrections a paradox among modern societies?

16. When did modern probation and parole emerge in Japanese correctional methods?

17. Write a short account on the following:

    (a) Suspended sentence

    (b) Meiji Reformers

    (c) Napoleonic Code of 1810

    (d) Conditional release

18. What are the provisions of the Volunteer Probation Officer Law?

19. What are the characteristics of the Tokugawa system of rule?

20. Compare and contrast Professional Probation Officers (PPO) and Volunteer Probation Officers (VPO).

16

Development of Penal Policy in Former British West Africa

Exploring the Colonial Dimension

John A. Arthur

Introduction

The past two decades have witnessed an increase in the number of research studies focusing on crime patterns and criminal justice administration in Africa. Most of these studies have explained crime in Africa by noting the effects of social structural changes brought about by massive migration from the countryside to the cities, socioeconomic development, changes in family relationships and cultural values, economic inequality, and poverty on crime (Clifford, 1963, 1964, 1973, 1974; Clinard and Abbott, 1973; Opolot, 1976, 1979, 1980, 1981; Brillion, 1973, 1974; Ebbe, 1985, 1989; Igbinovia, 1984; Shelley, 1982; Owomero, 1987; Rogers, 1989; Arthur, 1991). Other researchers have explained crime in Africa and other developing regions of the world in terms of foreign colonization and the introduction of capitalist modes of production (Sumner, 1982; Odekunle, 1978).

While most of the studies have focused on the social processes and the structural determinants of crime in Africa, few studies have examined the social responses to crime and the cultural ideologies related to the punishment of criminal behavior. For example, there are few studies on penal culture and correctional practice in Africa, and research is sketchy on the external geopolitical forces that shaped current penal philosophies in Africa. No sustained attention has been given to how colonial systems of criminal justice affected customary African standards and social control methods. Also, little is known about how modern Africa was affected by the major penological perspectives that developed in the eighteenth and nineteenth centuries, or about how the development of penal policies shifted or remained constant, or about what factors might account for shifts.

This chapter will examine the role British colonization played in the historical development of penal practices in former British West Africa, and will focus on Ghana, Nigeria, Sierra Leone, and Gambia. The common British colonial heritage of these countries will enable us to assess how foreign colonization affected the historical development of penal ideology and correctional administration.

We must remember from the outset that there are fundamental social, cultural, and economic differences among the nations of former British West Africa. It would not be methodologically sound to regard the four nations as a cultural monolith. Where applicable, we will note both variations and similarities in their social structures.

Knowledge of penal ideology in former British West Africa is important for several reasons. First, the study of penal policy is important for its own sake. In any modern society, criminal laws are enacted to embody, preserve, and enforce essential societal values. Punishment indicates the importance of the preservation of those norms. Second, knowledge about how external geopolitical factors shaped the historical development of penal practices will help the studies of comparative criminologists, clarifying the cultural and political foundations of currently prevailing penal philosophies. An historical perspective can also help to specify crucial developments in crime, law, and justice, and give direction for future change. Third, examining the development of prisons as socioeconomic and political entities in relation to the process of nation-building in Africa, we extend the frontiers of our discipline to include definitions and responses to crime in non-Western cultures. Modern criminologists must reinvigorate the field by introducing a cross-national perspective that it currently lacks. Comparing criminal justice in Africa with other nations will force us to construct new paradigms within which to view African culture, and enable us to avoid the insularity and parochialism otherwise characteristic of scientific criminology. Moreover, the answers to the questions we raise will help us both to understand the present penal policies of West Africa and to formulate those of the future. Finally, the study of penal policy in West Africa will yield valuable insights about the cultural stresses influencing the social responses to crime, and the social structural contexts in which those stresses are produced.

The first section of this essay describes normative violations prior to British colonization, the precolonial systems of social control designed to preserve domestic tranquility. The second section will examine the effects of the introduced British penal system on West African penal practices, comparing the resulting African system with penal policies developing at the same time in Europe, and especially in Britain. The last section will highlight the major conclusions of this essay and indicate potential areas for further research.

Crime, Deviance, and Social Control Prior to Colonization

Traditional societies in precolonial West Africa, like other societies, developed mechanisms for dealing with the problems of crime and deviance. Sanctions were imposed for normative violations such as witchcraft, sorcery, cattle raiding, theft, any sexual behavior outside the context of marriage, incest, murder, assault, and wounding.

As in other parts of Africa, social responses to violations of mores and acts of deviancy in West Africa were strongly anchored in the religions that permeated the entire fabric of traditional African society. Breaches of institutionalized norms were generally viewed as abominations requiring collective purification of the community, including the offender. As in other traditional societies, social sanctions were used to ensure domestic security and tranquility.

A chieftain system based on legitimate order was the social institution primarily responsible for enforcing law among indigenous African ethnic groups. Under this system, the social regulation of normative violations came under the authority of chiefs, elders, a council of elders, and religious leaders, all operating within extended family and kinship authority systems. Political authorities settled personal disputes and conflicts within and between groups through authoritative allocation of legal rights and obligations. Thus, institutionalized mechanisms existed to ensure that individuals complied with the law. Social control depended on self-sanctioning, and on agents acting on behalf of the ruling local councils or political authorities.

Traditional African dispute settlement procedures included bilateral negotiations, binding mediation by persons mutually recognized by the disputants, and family arbitration. Thus, many violations of shared norms were settled within a communal context. In some cases, the victim(s) and the offender(s) would avoid one another until the bitterness ended. Occasionally, both might resort to more drastic punitive measures such as self-exile, suicide, or self-help. Self-help, as a punitive measure, occurs when an offender suspects that his problem with the society's norms is a result of his previous wrongs to the gods and to his ancestors. He then offers sacrifices to appease the gods and his ancestors. In conflicts where there was resort to community intervention, the whole community became actively involved in the settlement. Members of the community would assess the evidence, express opinions as to the rights and wrongs, and exhort the parties to resolve their differences (Kercher, 1981).

Imposed punishments were intended to protect the interests of the victim and the community at large, to regularize social exchanges, and to preserve important cultural elements. Punishments took several forms. Deviants were often subjected to informal sanctions such as gossip, ridicule, or public humiliation. Property violations, including theft of agricultural produce and livestock, entailed restitutive compensations. Precolonial African society especially needed compensatory sanctions that would minimize offenses against its vital agrarian mode of economic production (Kercher, 1981). Precolonial African economics lacked the material conditions that would allow for the imposition of fines, so restitutive compensation was used as the social response to theft of agricultural produce and livestock.

For offenses of witchcraft and sorcery, the penal sanctions included outlawry,

public humiliation, torture, ostracism or dedication to a holy shrine, and bodily mutilation. For habitual offenders, death by stoning or hanging was not uncommon. Witchcraft and sorcery were punished severely and swiftly for two main reasons. First, these violations went against established religious and political authority, and a failure to punish such violations was thought to prompt curses from ancestors and spirits. Second, these violations threatened social harmony and cohesiveness, and familial solidarity.

For serious violations such as wounding, sex-related norms, and theft or robbery, the common penal sanctions were equitable restitution to the victim, family, and the community at large. Sometimes severe or harsh punishments were used to bring an offender to normative compliance, but the main thrust of traditional methods in dealing with norm violators included restoring the basic harmony and solidarity that had existed within and between the concerned individuals and groups before the offense. The offender regained the graces of his or her community by making appropriate recompense for injuries sustained (Kercher, 1981).

Usually punishments were administered collectively by the agents of social control, the offender's family, and the community at large in order to ensure that the offender did not become alienated from the community. The focus was on the individual, not on the act that was committed. A punished offender had to be reintegrated into conforming society after the punishment was served.

In the predominantly Islamic areas of West Africa, the influence of Islam has had a profound effect on law and order. Islam means total surrender or submission to the will of Allah (God), and one's duties are defined in terms of the rules that believers must follow. Islamic influence is strong in northern Nigeria, Ghana, and to a lesser extent, in Gambia. In these areas, Muslim law and authority used severe punishments for offenses such as adultery, sodomy, intoxication, forcible rape, insults to the modesty of women, and thefts of agricultural tools and products.

Islamic judges maintained legal and extralegal control over the exercise of social regulation based on historical consensus. Thus, sanctions pronounced by these judges had firm roots in precedents, and the arbitrary or capricious use of judicial discretion by an individual judge could be challenged.

The most common forms of punishment in the traditional Islamic areas were death, torture, public humiliation, branding, and the forfeiture of one's property. These forms of punishment and their numerous variations have always been considered retribution for crimes. Flogging was common in Islamic West Africa, and was used primarily to preserve discipline and to punish crimes involving public disorder. For more serious offenses such as robbery and thievery, bodily mutilation and branding were common. For violation of adultery laws, proof of guilt or innocence was established from the testimonies of at least four witnesses or from an outright confession. If guilt was established and the offender happened to be married, the usual penalty was death by stoning.

The custodial confinement of offenders was therefore not an institutional feature of African penology and social structure. The idea of prisons and the use of incarceration was an imported phenomenon. The tribal systems of punishment found by the early colonizers used punishment to achieve social reintegration and restoration of the offender; that is, they practiced reparative rather than retributive justice. The indigenous African systems of law and order were adequate to the task of minimizing lawlessness and keeping disorderly conduct in check. Mechanisms of solidarity minimized crime and social deviance, families were held accountable for wrongful acts of individual members, and collective punishment solidified the sentiments and values of the law-abiding population. Both the offender and the vic-

tim were encouraged to settle their disputes within the context of family or communal relationships, or within the traditional, local, political and adjudicatory systems; in the case of bilateral negotiations, dispute settlement focused on getting to the root of the problem rather than on dealing with symptomatic behavior.

Offenders found guilty in criminal cases faced penal sanctions ranging from torture, death, and bodily mutilation to restitution, ostracism, banishment, and outlawry. But whatever the penalty, its main thrust was to restore solidarity, to promote order and stability, and to assist in future reintegration of the offender.

The arrival of Europeans in West Africa, and the subsequent colonization of the area, had a manifold impact on the traditional forms of social control, dispute settlements, and penal practices. New adjudicatory and punitive systems were introduced giving powers to legislate, punish, and imprison to external civil authorities—the British colonial administrators. These new forms left a legacy of social and cultural dislocation in West Africa. Let us now examine in detail the dynamics and processes of British colonial intervention in West Africa, and the subsequent replacement of indigenous West African penal practices with incarceration.

Adoption of Incarceration and De-Africanization of Social Control

The development of modern penal systems in British West Africa must be examined within the nexus of British colonization and the political modernization of Ghana, Nigeria, Sierra Leone, and Gambia. British colonization and political control of these countries led to the replacement of the indigenous community-based systems of social control with a penal system alien to the region. Even though the British colonial administration claimed that they wished to keep African institutions intact and to allow them to function alongside those introduced from England, the powers of the chiefs and religious leaders eroded as the British succeeded in implementing their colonial domination. In cases where traditional laws addressed acts also considered criminal by the modern courts, the traditional laws gradually gave way.

The British colonial administration recognized the institutional effectiveness of the traditional African systems of social control and used them to shore up and legitimize their political and economic power bases. Traditional local authority councils were formed to assist in maintaining social and political order. Working through district commissioners (DCs) appointed by the colonial governor, Britain was able to maintain a dual system of shared political governance composed of Africans on the one hand and appointees of the colonial administration on the other. In this way, traditional African patterns of social control were preserved, while matters with greater geopolitical implications were resolved by the British colonial district commissioners.

Agitation for political enfranchisement and national independence weakened this dual political and social structure. Ghana, for example, attained political independence on March 6, 1957: political power fell back into the hands of the traditional local councils at the local community level, while Dr. Kwame Nkrumah, the president, assumed control over the central administration.

However, during the early years of independence, Ghana (and the other three countries as well) continued wholesale adoption of British law with only minimal changes. Ghana's criminal code after independence was essentially the same as it had been when under colonial status as the Gold Coast. The only major modifications occurred in laws pertaining to economic and political crimes such as smuggling of cocoa, profiteering, hoarding, illegal assembly, sedition, and subversion.

The postindependence penal code of Ghana establishes three broad types of offenses and punishment for each type. For capital offenses such as murder, treason, and piracy, death by hanging is sanctioned. Offenses falling under first degree felony (manslaughter, forcible rape, and abetment of mutiny) are punishable by a term of life imprisonment. Second degree felonies (bodily woundings or inflicting intentional harms, robbery, and perjury) are punishable by a period of incarceration of up to 10 years (Marenin, 1989:146–151). Variable terms of incarceration may be imposed for misdemeanors such as assault, theft, unlawful assembly, corruption, and public nuisances.

The criminal law of Sierra Leone is not contained in a comprehensive code like that of Ghana, but is made up of a series of local ordinances (the Criminal Ordinance and the Criminal Law Adoption Ordinance) substantially similar to English statutes (Kurian, 1989). The criminal code of Nigeria during the colonial era was structured on uncodified principles of English criminal law, with offenses classified as misdemeanors and felonies. The latter were punishable by death or institutional incarceration for a minimum of 3 years, whereas misdemeanors attracted sentences ranging from 180 days to 3 years of incarceration.

The British colonial administration permitted northern Nigeria to keep its distinct penal code, which was compatible with Islamic culture. The Islamic legal code, which deviates markedly from English legal codes, punishes such traditional Muslim offenses as adultery, drinking alcohol, and insults to the modesty of women. The northern penal code does not mention treason, sedition, customs violations, or counterfeiting. Statutory laws dealing with such activities have been enacted separately and appear as an addendum to the penal code.

Penal sanctions under both the criminal code in southern Nigeria and the penal code in northern Nigeria are usually harsh and calculated to achieve deterrence even though the concept of rehabilitation is acknowledged. Common penal sanctions include death, imprisonment, whipping, fines, and forfeiture of property. A death sentence cannot be passed on any offender in Nigeria under 17 years of age or on a pregnant woman. Before 1966, death sentences were carried out by hanging; since that time, the method has been public execution by a military firing squad.

By the end of the nineteenth century, a formal system of criminal justice in West Africa based on English jurisprudence had been successfully superimposed on indigenous systems and sanctions of the precolonial African societies (Kercher, 1981). The British legal systems not only redefined and reclassified crimes in West Africa, but also changed social perceptions of crime and deviance, arrest procedures, processing, adjudicating, and punishing of the offender.

As Korn and McCorkle (1959) aptly have described, the colonial system of punishment and traditional African methods of punishment differ fundamentally in their psychological consequences. Under the traditional method, great care was taken to ensure that punishment would not alienate the offender from the rest of society. Instead, the offender was made accessible to group influence and correction. Banishment, exile, or outlawry would be used only after the failure of repeated attempts at making the offender become law abiding. This contrasts sharply with the colonial legal system, which emphasized the isolation and alienation of the offender from the rest of society. This way of punishing offenders assumed that society was best protected only when the offender was physically confined and isolated from the law-abiding public. It also used punishment to achieve specific and general deterrence.

The colonial criminal justice system essentially operated as an instrument of political and social control and was de-

signed to maintain law and order among diverse cultural groups and to punish law violators with little or no regard for the victim. Criminal acts were viewed as wrongs against the sovereign state. For most West Africans, these new forms of social control and penal philosophy required some adjustments.

English legal definitions shifted the West African understanding of crime and perception of the criminal. Crime was no longer viewed as an act that offended ancestors and the religious establishment, requiring purification for the entire community. Rather, the classical approach was taken: behavior is purposive and is based on hedonism, on the pleasure–pain principle, on free will and rationality. Punishment should therefore be assigned to crimes in order to make criminal behavior result in more pain than pleasure for those who break the law. The traditional African system of punishment had relied on the extended family of the offender and was designed to ensure the gradual social acceptance and reintegration of the offender into the society after completing his or her punishment. However, the new legal system introduced by Britain weakened the relationship between the offender and his or her family by deemphasizing the family's role in the punishment process. For the first time, the criminal faced social alienation from extended family and a stigmatization that became permanent, making rehabilitation and future reintegration difficult. This was the effect of shifting criminal responsibility from the family to the offender. Furthermore, although the family was no longer held responsible for the misdeeds of its individual members, crime still brought shame to the offender's family.

Let us now examine the economic process by which the British colonial administration succeeded in virtually replacing the precolonial African legal institutions with British legal institutions.

Industrial Production and the Development of Prisons

Two primary colonial objectives of the British in West Africa were to have unlimited and unchallenged access to abundant African natural resources and to gain protected markets for British manufactured goods. A secondary objective was to obtain cheap labor for processing exportable raw materials at West African factories and industries. The British largely succeeded in achieving these goals, realizing them by implementing a low wage labor economic system and taxation of labor.

When the British introduced their commodity and wage economy to West Africa, the subsequent takeover of peasant land holdings forced peasants to seek employment in the foreign-owned agricultural plantations and industries and broke their ties with traditional modes of production. Wage labor, as a system where the laborer depends entirely on wages for subsistence, hardly existed in precolonial Africa (Shivji, 1982:41). The wage economy and the imposition of the poll and hut taxes in West Africa caused thousands of rural peasants to migrate to the urban industrial and manufacturing sectors to look for employment. Thus commenced one of the most notable and universal features of Third World economic development—the massive rural-to-urban migration of labor. Peasants had to migrate to the urban centers to find employment, so that they could pay the new taxes levied on them and at the same time earn enough money to buy imported consumer items (Todaro, 1969; Harris and Todaro, 1970; Amin, 1974; Caldwell, 1969; Todaro and Stilkind, 1981).

The concentration of population in the urban areas of West Africa and the establishment of agricultural plantations called for a new formalized system of social control by the colonizers to ensure maintenance of law and order. This was achieved through the application of English penal sanctions. As Humpheries and Greenberg

(1981:213) have noted in their discussion of the dialectics of crime control, criminalization is one tactic among many that an exploiting class will attempt to use in controlling the exploited class, defining as illegal, and trying to punish, actions that threaten their interests. New catalogues of offenses were established, ranging from minor infractions such as misuse of employers' property, using employers' property without permission, theft, intoxication, failure to commence work at the time agreed, and giving false address, to more serious violations such as desertion, willful neglect, destruction of property, and tax evasion. These offenses indicated British conceptions of the specific relationship between the owners of the means of production and wage earners. The punishment for minor offenses was a fine equivalent to half a month's wage, and for default of payment of the fine, one received imprisonment with or without hard labor for a term not exceeding 1 month (Kercher, 1981). For major violations, imprisonment and fines were used. Most British West Africans found these new laws and the penal sanctions that they attracted a new form of social control very much alien to African ideals of law and order.

These criminal definitions were put in place primarily for the benefit of the colonial administrators. Their application was a politically motivated attempt by England to redefine social relations, to establish mechanisms for protecting their political and economic interests, and to fend off French and German economic encroachment on their possessions in West Africa.

In matters of civil or tort liability, the British colonial administration allowed traditional West African legal systems to operate as institutions for dispute resolution. In northern Nigeria, under the colonial administration of Lord Lugard, this system became known as "indirect rule," a system whereby the British allowed northern Nigerian traditional rulers (Emirs) autonomy in matters of law and government. Three motives lay behind the

British decision to allow African civil and customary laws to govern interpersonal relationships and thus coexist alongside British legal norms. First, the British found in the African chiefs, elders, and Emirs a well-developed and centralized system of order maintenance that could help them achieve the goal of promoting and establishing social order and national integration, and simultaneously save them money and manpower in administrating the West African colonies. Second, the use of African legal norms in matters of civil and tort issues helped maintain good relations with the traditional chiefs and elders by giving them a sense of legitimacy and participatory governance. Third, West African legal institutions for resolving civil matters could be allowed to operate because they did not threaten the interests of Great Britain. The administration of laws dealing with economic activities such as production, marketing, and sale of goods was regulated by the British colonial administrators.

The new penal sanctions, then, clearly benefited and protected the economic interests of the British colonial administration. The new offenses and corresponding penal responses were not mere curbs for increasing crime rates and lawlessness; rather, they reflected British need to control the collective resistance of British West African labor and to ensure undisrupted economic activities. The new systems of social control basically protected Britain's economic control of its colonies. By the beginning of World War II, British West Africa had achieved immense industrial and economic development. Accumulation of capital brought about by global marketing of natural resources such as cocoa, gold, diamonds, cotton, hides and skin, and palm oil meant that funds could be appropriated for infrastructural development of railways, roads, and expansion of ports. To protect the free movement of goods and services, Britain established the West African colonial police force, a paramilitary force whose dominant role included the collection of the poll, hut, and land taxes for the colonial treasury. The perceived threats to social stability and British economic interests (emanating from mass revolts against British invasion, such as the Akasa raid in Nigeria and the Nigerian women's riot of 1929 against requiring women to pay taxes) demanded new strategies for social control. In effect, the colonial masters had to set up forces to wedge the perceived future riots. The establishment of the Ports Authority police, the Post Office police, the Maritime police, and the Railways police was intended to achieve this goal. These formal agencies of social control were charged with providing protection to the local subsidiaries of the British mercantile companies in West Africa such as the United Africa Trading Company of the Gold Coast, the Royal Niger Company, the British South African Company, and the British East African Company.

When modern policing was introduced to British West Africa, it was intended for four important functions. First, it was an instrument of state power for the regulation of social conflict: the colonial police enforced the sovereign power of the state over the individual citizen. Second, it provided protection for the elites who worked for and represented the economic interests of Britain. Third, it formed a group of paramilitary organizations that could assist in the turbulent transition caused by the replacement of African institutions with British institutions. Finally, colonial police were not only useful for preserving the internal security of British West Africa, but could be deployed—as the forces in Nigeria and the Gold Coast (Ghana) actually were—to protect British interests in such places as Burma, the Congo (Kinshasa), Egypt, South Africa, and Sri Lanka (Tamuno, 1970).

The exigencies of trade (the need to have a steady supply of cheap raw material, and the need to secure a monopoly of market outlets for industrial products) were clearly the primary considerations that influenced the introduction and development of English systems of law enforcement and penal policy in British West Africa. The custodial confinement of law breakers in prisons became the new mode of offender disposal and replaced religion as the basis of social control. In former British West Africa, as in Europe and North America, penal policies began with the onset of capitalism and later provided social and legal legitimacy to the institution of incarceration. The change from the peasant, agrarian economy to a semi-industrial manufacturing economy provided the legal context for the establishment of incarceration, a mode of punishment characteristic of capitalist societies. In turn, the changes in law gave Britain the legitimacy to control undesirable acts of labor, no matter how trivial. Social order had to be maintained to promote industrialization. Similar changes in the mode of economic production, the use of capital, and the rise of the factory system in Europe and North America also led to the emergence of the prison system (Melossi and Pavarini; 1981: Foucault, 1977). As Foucault (1977) pointed out, the development of capitalism provided another structural nexus between the prison and the economic mode of production. The capitalist mode of production is based on exploitation of the working class. Institutionalization of offenders (the prisoners) became a means of supply of cheap labor for the state and the statutory corporations. Thus, there is a structural connection between the prison system and capitalism. The development of the penitentiary system in colonial West Africa occurred along similar lines to those being developed in Europe: the driving force was the emergence of capitalism, which generated forms of criminality and systems of punishment akin to its own treatment of workers—that is, temporary deprivation of liberty or incapacitation of the offender.

Impact of Major Penal Philosophies on Corrections in West Africa

English rule and hegemony in the West African colonies was firmly established prior to the outbreak of World War II. The main objective of the British colonists was to reduce political agitation for self-determination to a minimum, and at the same time establish a stable political and economic base that would ensure the integration of West Africa into the world polity.

Criminal law, as introduced from England, became the instrument for maintaining law and order, with incarceration replacing the community-based punishments common in traditional African society. The penal system in British West Africa operated on a retributive philosophy, depriving offenders of their liberties and committing them to incarceration with hard labor.

In Ghana, the Ussher Fort and Nsawan maximum security prisons became the models and primary exemplars of British penal philosophy. Both resembled the late sixteenth-century Bridewell workhouses and houses of correction, providing for solitary confinement and labor, and neither classifying nor separating prisoners. Inmates were kept in filthy and unsanitary conditions, and men and women were held together in the same complex where they were neglected and brutalized.

In the case of Nigeria, the arrival of the English legal system in 1861 was followed by the establishment of the Broad Street Prison in the capital city of Lagos in 1872. According to Alemika (1983), the organization of the prison system in Nigeria lacks a clear-cut correctional philosophy to guide its operators, and this makes it difficult to fund improvements on the infrastructure of the prisons or to provide rehabilitation or vocational training for inmates. As Awe (1968) pointed out, prison policies and programs designed to improve the conditions of incarceration are not considered; furthermore, quality educational training for the custodial staff has been neglected consistently.

During the tenure of R. E. Dolan as director of British colonial prisons in Sierra Leone, Ghana, and Nigeria (including those of other colonies as far away as Trinidad and Tanzania), some efforts were made to deemphasize retribution in favor of rehabilitation by counseling and vocational–technical education. However, the colonial administration did not support Dolan's short-lived efforts.

To minimize inmate idleness, the newly established colonial prisons introduced work and religious instruction for inmate socialization. In all colonial prisons in both West and East Africa, the British colonial administration justified inmate work on grounds that it strengthened the work ethic and industry of the inmate and provided skills that might be useful on release; that the work component of punishment allowed the inmate to repay part of the expense of his or her upkeep; and that inmate labor and the prison industry allowed prisons to produce and market for profit items manufactured with inmate labor (Kercher, 1981).

Today, penal institutions in West Africa have retained the work component as part of penal philosophy. Inmates' handicrafts are marketed for profit, and government agencies are allowed to lease and use convict labor on penal farms or in government-approved projects. Since the attainment of political independence, all four former British West African colonies have continued this tradition.

In 1895, the Gladstone Report on the condition of British prisons was released. This report provided direction and credibility for reforms aimed at social reintegration of inmates (Kercher, 1981), but it did not affect prisons in West Africa, which continued to employ a retributive rationale for punishment and a custodial model that emphasized security, discipline, and order. The principal goals of prisons under the custodial philosophy were incapacitation,

retribution, and deterrence (general and specific). As a result, the prison system in the four countries completely encapsulated the lives of both the inmates and their keepers. Both the keeper and the kept were alienated by society, with the keeper controlling all aspects of the lives of the kept.

The major penological developments that occurred in Europe and North America in the nineteenth century were felt only slowly in the colonies. There have been four main reasons for the tardiness of the colonies in adopting modern penal reforms, as Kercher (1981), Clifford (1963), Awe (1968), and others have pointed out. First, Africa lacked well-organized philanthropic movements devoted to improving the conditions of prisoners and to remodeling penal institutions on humane and individualistic lines. Second, scientific research into prison conditions, causes of crime, and the study of criminal justice institutions in West Africa were and continue to be overshadowed by more pressing socioeconomic problems such as population growth and family planning, housing, food production, and health care. Third, the penal system and its problems have not yet acquired political legitimacy, perhaps because African societies still believe that the task of administering and caring for convicts should be a family responsibility rather than the responsibility of the state. Finally, there was disagreement in West African society about the goals of punishment. This disagreement was highlighted by the inability of the prison systems in West Africa to present to the public any credible equation between the heinousness of crime and just punishment. In 1952, half a century after the Gladstone Report, Ghana, Nigeria, Sierra Leone, and Gambia embraced the rehabilitative and reintegrative models of punishment. Nonetheless, reformatory penal policy had minimal impact on punishment in British West Africa. Although the Gladstone Report provided philosophical impetus for the introduction of innovations such as parole, probation, and the increasing use of alternatives to incarceration such as fines and restitutive compensation, these modified punishments were applied only to economic and property-related offenses. For violent offenders, the penal policy remained retributive and bound to an inefficient, overcrowded, and poorly administered prison system featuring bad food, a lack of adequate medical attention for the inmates, and poor training and compensation for custodial staffs. Commenting on the appalling state of prison conditions, the Nigerian Law Reform Commission (1983:2) stated:

Nigerian prisons are too congested, and poor ventilation is one of their glaring features; prisoners and detainees are cramped together in cells with no adequate accom-modation provided. Hardened crim-inals are made to live together with first offenders and the type of treatment meted out to the latter by the former is unimaginable. Prisoners sleep in double decker beds with no mattresses and pillows provided. In these congested cells, not all prisoners are fortunate to be provided with beds. The unlucky ones are made to sleep on dirty, bare floors. The cells stink with hot, uninviting air oozing out at intervals from the cells to the immediate environment.

The prison system completely lacks social services support. As Alemika and Kayode (1981) and Kayode and Alemika (1984) have pointed out, reliable diagnostic information concerning the social history of offenders, their family background, and their prior criminal records are not readily available to assist judges during the sentencing stage. The prisons also lack treatment and counseling facilities. Under these conditions, recidivism rates have increased over time. The Nigerian Law Reform Commission (1983:2) further stated that:

From all indications, the Nigerian prison system, as at present, is not geared toward the reformation of prisoners to enable them to live a more useful life. Instead our prison system appears more punitive and retributive, and therefore, is not in a position to help reform prisoners. Perhaps, this is why the rate of those returning to prison for the second, third, and even fourth term im-prisonment continues to be on the increase.

Innovative ideas in punishment, such as those formulated in Cincinnati in 1870 and in the Gladstone Report of 1895, have lacked the institutional support of post-colonial prisons in West Africa. In effect, the major penal reforms of this century have had little or no significant impact on penal practices in former British West African countries. No pragmatic measures have yet been undertaken to assist the offender in acquiring skills that could lead to gainful employment upon release. Also, West African prisons lack adequate equipment and employ poorly educated, poorly trained, and poorly compensated personnel. Unable to meet the challenges posed by these problems, and hampered by the lack of a community-based system of corrections, the governments of the former British West Africa have had to continue using a retributive penal policy.

The English Penal Servitude Act of 1853, the Irish System of Ticket of Leave, and the Elmira Reformatory System mandated conditional release of inmates and accumulation of "good time credit" for good behavior. British colonial rule, however, never implemented conditional release of offenders, and, because of this lack of groundwork, parole and supervision of offenders within a community setting currently have not been instituted in former British West Africa.

The penal policy has helped to redefine West African social relationships to allow for capitalist economic production and ownership of property. But for West African society as a whole, the colonial intrusion on traditional forms of penal sanctions dislocated the social definitions, classifications, and perceptions, both of crime and of the criminal. Innovative correctional ideologies have not ameliorated the problems, despite a theoretical acceptance of rehabilitation, probation, parole, and community corrections; in fact, no concerted efforts have been made to incorporate these into the existing penal frameworks. Substantial developments and reforms in penal and correctional systems did occur in England during the eighteenth and nineteenth centuries, but the British failed to support full introduction and implementation of prison reforms in the West African colonies.

Shifts in Penal Policy in Postindependence West Africa

Since their attainment of political independence, the former British dependencies in West Africa have all undergone significant socioeconomic and cultural transformations. These changes in social structure have also brought changes in definition, classification, social perception, and response to crime. Describing postcolonial changes in penal policy will help to show how the newly independent West African nations adapted foreign colonial institutions to the reality of African traditional social structure and organization.

The types and rates of crimes have changed significantly in West Africa since independence. Given moderate levels of industrialization and increases in economic production in West Africa, property-related offenses have increased. The most common form of crime in West Africa today is minor larceny or petty theft (Shelley, 1982; Clinard and Abbott, 1973; Opolot, 1981). The social perception is that minor property offenses are not as socially and economically disruptive as elite crimes such as political corruption and white-collar crimes. While minor larceny brought penal sanctions of incarceration during the colonial era, sanctions for minor larceny in postindependence West

Africa have shifted to fines, probation, restitution, forfeiture of property, public flogging, and community service. Law enforcement agents often are reluctant to enforce theft and economic malpractice laws, because they consider petty larceny necessary for the economic survival of a large segment of the urban underclass. For major crimes such as robbery, burglary, armed robbery, and murder, there has not been any major shift in penal sanctions since colonial times, except that sanctions for robbery and burglary have become more severe. In both Ghana and Nigeria, penal sanctions for strong-arm robbery and unarmed burglary range from a minimum of 7 years imprisonment with hard labor to life imprisonment, and armed robbery or armed burglary brings the death penalty by firing squad.

Political instability and weak economies have caused the four nations under study to create new categories of crimes to maintain control over their increasingly disgruntled citizens. Although the problems that confronted the fragile economies of these countries were economic and structural in nature, both Ghana and Nigeria (for example) attempted to ameliorate these problems by passing laws that proscribed offenses ranging from political crimes such as treason, sedition, unlawful assembly, and plotting to stage a coup to economic and business-related crimes such as smuggling across international borders, foreign currency trafficking, hoarding, profiteering, and refusal to sell. However, the society at large does not perceive economic "criminals" as a threat to social stability. Rather, West African society considers these offenses inevitable and even necessary for survival in an economy characterized by frequent shortages of essential consumer goods. The legislative reaction to offenses such as hoarding, profiteering, smuggling, and the illegal exchange of foreign currencies has been less severe than the reaction to violent offenses. Punishments for economic offenses range from fines, loss of property, or community service, to imprisonment for a maximum of 2 years.

Shifts in penal policy have reflected the type of government or political administration in power. Military regimes or juntas have increased use of incarceration for minor offenses and the use of the death penalty for very serious offenses such as armed robbery, treason, or plotting to overthrow the government. In Ghana and Nigeria, military governments increasingly have used house arrest, imprisonment without trial, and preventive detention to curb the activities of political activists who challenge the political legitimacy of military rule. Military regimes in both Ghana and Nigeria enforce law and order through the use of coercive and illegitimate power that does not recognize due process, constitutional or parliamentary provisions, social democracy, or equal protection. Punishments for criminal violations under the military regimes, especially for armed robbery, have tended to be very harsh, sometimes resulting in the burning to death of offenders by citizen vigilante groups before any intervention by law enforcement agents. However, in the midst of their attempts to administer severe justice, the military governments systematically overlook the massive corruption of appointed government officials who enrich themselves at the expense of ordinary citizens. In most cases, these military appointees have not been brought to justice, because they have the political backing of the ruling armed forces.

Civilian administrations have not provided ordinary citizens with much better fare. Under the guise of ensuring social democracy, fairness, and standards of equity, civilian regimes have also relied on the use of the police and army to administer social control. Like their military counterparts, the civilian regimes have used incarceration to achieve deterrence, rehabilitation, protection of society, and retribution.

Summary and Conclusion

Our primary goal has been to provide a concise sociological account of penology in colonial British West Africa, and to discuss the role of external geopolitical forces in the development of modern penology in the region. We now will highlight the major findings of this essay and suggest directions for future research.

First, one can conclude that precolonial West Africa had a well-developed system to ensure law and order and promote social stability prior to contact with Britain. This system of law and justice recognized the disruptive nature of crime and deviance, and therefore took specific steps to minimize them. The social response to law violations was based on the recognition that punishment must be used as a rehabilitative and reintegrative tool designed to ensure that the punished offender would still be regarded as a contributing member of society. Therefore, the punishment, no matter how severe, was collectively administered within the community. Only after repeated attempts at resocialization had failed did precolonial West African society resort to extreme forms of punishment such as exile, ostracism, death, bodily mutilation, and outlawry. Unlike the system of penal philosophy introduced to the region from England, which alienates the offender from society by custodial confinement and social stigmatization, precolonial West African society affirmed and stressed religion and the extended family network in the punishment process.

Second, the British penal policy of custodial incapacitation was new and alien to West Africans. The traditional system of social control became weakened as Britain took over administration of justice in her former colonies. Retributive justice replaced the traditional forms of punishment, which were based on reparation. Incarceration brought a shift in social perceptions about crime and the criminal. Crime came to be perceived as a wrongful act against the state or a sovereign entity, and only the state was allowed to decide the form and measure of punishment. The role of the extended family network, as a partner in the collective punishment of the offender, was diminished, thereby making it more difficult than ever for an offender to reenter society.

Third, the British introduced their legal system to West Africa to protect companies doing business in West Africa, to ensure uninterrupted export and import trade in the region, and finally to promote a social climate of order and stability that would ensure access to and monopoly of West Africa's natural resources. Western styles of law and order entered West Africa not in response to any waves of crime encountered by the British, but because they served to suppress mass revolt, maintain systematic exploitation of the people, and protect the economic, religious, and political interests of the colonial masters.

Fourth, the use of incarceration as the basic form of punishment during the colonial era in British West Africa manifested the gradual replacement of the traditional subsistence mode of economic production with a capitalist mode of production. The penal policy of imprisonment was incompatible with the traditional subsistence economy and the communal system of land tenure that the British found in West Africa. But economic entrenchment under capitalism changed the relationship between capital and labor. This also led to a new formalized system of social control and regulation, with the state maintaining the right to define and punish crime.

Fifth, the major penological innovations that developed in Europe and America during the past two centuries have not had any major impact on penal policy in postcolonial West Africa. Although rehabilitation, parole, probation, and community correction are recognized as part of penal policy in the former British West African nations, no concerted efforts have been made to incorporate elements of the European models into postcolonial penal policies; nor have the systems inherited from England undergone any major and coherent transformation that is distinctively African. Penal institutions in the former British West Africa are poorly staffed, and their prisoners are poorly fed and lack adequate medical care. Policies and standards do not ensure that inmates have the basic necessities of life, and the penal system is still structured on the retributive model. West Africa currently has an antiquated penal system with no articulated philosophy.

Moreover, shifts in penal ideologies in postindependence British West Africa have been influenced by political and economic considerations rather than following a coherent and systematic penal policy more rooted in African social structure. Whether under military juntas or civilian regimes, penal ideologies have been retributive and have totally disregarded the rights of inmates.

Finally, more scholarship needs to address how external geopolitical factors have influenced the development of penal policy throughout Africa. In West Africa specifically, the impact of French colonization on the development of penal policies could be assessed, especially in the former French colonies of Senegal, the Ivory Coast, Guinea, Benin, Burkina Faso, and Togo. Differences and similarities could be posed between British and French approaches to penal policy in West Africa, and the influence of Islam on current penal orientation could also be surveyed. Attention to these issues will clarify the important role played by criminal justice systems in nation-building and political modernization in Africa.

Discussion and Review Questions

1. What are the main reasons why we try to understand penal ideology in former British West Africa?

2. What were serious offenses in former British West African countries in precolonial times?

3. What are the essential features of traditional African dispute settlement?

4. Why were witchcraft and sorcery severely punished in precolonial Africa and Puritan New England?

5. Both Denmark and traditional African societies believe in a reintegrative model of offender disposal. Discuss. Compare and contrast each culture's approaches.

6. Criminal codes and imprisonment of offenders are colonial legacies to British West Africa. Discuss.

7. What was "indirect rule"?

8. What were the four purposes of colonial policing in former British West Africa?

9. What were the justifications for prison inmate labor in colonial Africa?

10. Compare and contrast punishment for violent crimes in West Africa and the United States.

11. What were the roles of traditional African religions in control of deviance in pre-colonial West Africa?

12. What were the informal methods of crime control in traditional West Africa?

13. What is the place of mediation in West African countries' criminal justice system?

14. What methods of offender disposal were meted out to witches and sorcerers in traditional West Africa?

15. In Islamic states of West Africa, what were the common methods of offender disposal in the traditional times?

16. Incarceration of an offender was un-African. Why?

17. Describe briefly the colonial system of criminal justice in West Africa.

18. Why did the British colonial administration allow African Customary Law to operate side by side with the English law?

19. What are the functions of modern system of policing in contemporary West Africa?

20. What are the problems of correctional institutions in former British West African countries today?

17

Treatment of Offenders in Denmark and Brazil

Zelma W. Henriques

Certain forces shape the posture of a given society, influencing the philosophy and policies which that society embraces. This paper identifies and examines the forces which have shaped two very different societies, those of Denmark and Brazil. Further, it provides a descriptive analysis of the organization of the prisons and treatment of offenders in each of these societies. Because of the significant differences between these societies, we will focus on contrasts rather than comparisons.

Among the benefits of a contrasting approach are the following:

1. It enables us to learn about other systems, and in so doing, we broaden our perspective

2. We gain a greater understanding of the approaches used in other societies to address our own problems

3. It helps us to deal with international crime problems (Fairchild, 1993)

Denmark: An Overview

The Kingdom of Denmark is situated in Northern Europe between the North Sea on the west, the Baltic sea on the east, Norway on the north, and Germany on the south. Denmark's only land frontier is with the Federal Republic of Germany. The Faroe Islands (18 islands, 16 of which are inhabited) are Danish external territories.

Denmark is ethnically a Scandinavian, and occupies an area of 16,638 square miles. Its capital is Copenhagen, and its population is 5,129,778 (1990), making it the most densely populated of the Scandinavian countries (Hoffman, 1991).

Denmark is a constitutional monarchy. Under its 1953 constitutional charter, the hereditary monarch and the unicameral parliament (called folketing) jointly hold legislative power. For several decades, Denmark has ranked among those countries of the world that enjoy the highest standard of living.

The small size of Denmark and its excellent system of identifying and tracking citizens make it an ideal setting for sociological and criminological research. A personal code number is assigned to every individual domiciled in Denmark (Hornum, 1986:3).

During World War II, Denmark was under German occupation. This fact is significant, because the events of the war have helped to shape policies in Denmark and have influenced the philosophy of the country in the important area of citizens' rights.

During the period of German occupation, many innocent Danish citizens were imprisoned, their only crime being resistance and opposition to the German presence. The civil rights of these confined citizens were extremely restricted. Danish citizens found the experience intolerable and have not forgotten it. As a result, when they later addressed the issue of restricting the rights of their own citizens, they carefully designed and implemented a system in which individual rights were emphasized.

Today, Denmark stresses protection of civil rights and humane treatment. Although the Danes imprison their convicted offenders, they are careful to ensure that the rights of all citizens are protected. Parliament appoints an ombudsman who is assigned the responsibility of monitoring Danish law and ensuring that any defects in the law are corrected. The ombudsman also has the power to take action against public officials on behalf of the citizens. In criminal justice matters, the ombudsman may lodge complaints with the Department of Corrections or with the Ministry of Justice, regarding procedures or conditions in prison (Jepsen, 1991:132).

Philosophy of the Social Welfare State

A most important feature of Danish society is the idea of collective responsibility: all citizens are considered responsible for each other in all areas of life. For those experiencing hardship, there are social welfare programs that cover family allowance, rent subsidies, health care, unemployment benefits, accident, maternity benefits, institutional care, and retirement pensions. This ideology is particularly suited to countries with little structural or cultural diversity, and Denmark is racially, ethnically, and religiously homogeneous. Danish is the official language and English is taught in schools as a second language. There is almost no illiteracy in Denmark because of its free and compulsory education from age 7 to 16. A large majority of the Danish population lives in cities and towns.

Criminal Justice Policy in Denmark

Criminal justice policy in Denmark must be viewed in the context of social and cultural homogeneity. The Danish penal system results from a process of reform which began under the First Danish Criminal Code of 1866. The present criminal code was introduced in 1930 and has been revised several times. Important changes include the abolition of capital punishment and corporal punishment, the abolition of imprisonment with hard labor, the introduction of youth prisons in a form that reflects the English Borstal system, and the introduction of special forms of detention for professional and habitual offenders.

These changes led to a need for open institutions and overall changes in the penal system. The criminal justice system of Denmark reflects a high degree of centralization, cohesion, and consistency. The country has low rates of interpersonal victimizations and crimes of violence, with most crimes being property crimes. The prison system policies supported by parliament and the government are very liberal: capital punishment was abolished over 100 years ago. However, pretrial detention continues to be very restrictive. For example, Denmark currently uses lengthy pretrial detention, with total isolation of the defendant to keep evidence "pure" (Umbreit, 1980: 27).

Organization of Prisons and Penal Sanctions

The Danish Prison and Probation Service (Direktoratet for Kriminalforsorgen) is organized in a directorate under the Ministry of Justice with the director responsible to the Minister of Justice. The directorate has a hierarchical structure including two departments: an administrative department, and a department concerned with the treatment of inmates, probationers, and parolees (Greve et al., 1984:3).

The department responsible for the treatment of inmates deals with use of prison and probation service, treatment programs, research, statistics, and international cooperation in the field of criminal policy. Within this department, there are the following six special sections:

1. A section in charge of cases concerning inmate release on parole, complaints, and furloughs

2. A section for the formulation of general rules governing the treatment of inmates

3. A social service and welfare unit

4. An inmate education unit

5. A prison factories unit which handles orders for their factory products from other government agencies and organizes work for inmates

6. A section for total economic management of the institution (directorate)

The Department of Prison and Probation is the agency responsible for the enforcement of all criminal sanctions in Denmark. Consequently, it is responsible for probation and aftercare as well as for prisons and local jails. As of July 1993, the total staff of prisons and probation offices was 3,800.

There are 14 prisons and 36 local jails. Of the 14 prisons, 5 are closed prisons, equivalent to maximum security prisons in the United States, and 9 (mostly older structures) are open prisons, that is, minimum-security. Most of the prisons in Denmark are small, with the largest accommodating 230 inmates. A population of 90 inmates in a prison is considered normal in size. Small prisons are maintained in order for staff to get to know inmates and to work with them toward a better understanding of their problems.

The total prison capacity is approximately 3,597 spaces, allocated as follows:

8	Open state prisons	1,299
5	Closed state prisons	1,305
	Local jails	993
Total prison capacity		3,597

The prison at Copenhagen (a closed institution for remand prisoners) has a capacity for 570 inmates. Total present prison population in 1993 was 3,516. There are 68 inmates per 100,000 population. The average length of sentence is 6.2 months of imprisonment; 4.9 months for ordinary imprisonment; and 18 days for lenient imprisonment. The staff–inmate ratio is 83.4 per 100 inmates, and the total prisons staff and probation officers are 3,800.

Ordinary imprisonment and lenient imprisonment are the most common incarcerative sanctions used in Denmark. To the Danes, the penal feature of a sentence of imprisonment is the deprivation of liberty to move about in society. Therefore, when the Danes imprison, their major concern is with humane treatment (Umbreit, 1980: 25). According to Erik Andersen (former Danish prisons administrator), "prisons are used in Denmark because we do not have a better solution. The goal is to abolish prisons." The Danes view imprisonment as a brutally negative experience, because it separates the individual from family and community and leads to disintegration of social ties. Hence, in every case, incarceration is used only when inevitable, and in such cases, every attempt is made to keep the offender in or near his or her local community.

Furthermore, the policy is to impose the shortest sentence possible. Most of the inmates are sentenced to open prisons, but are transferred to closed prisons if they violate the rules. Convicted offenders can receive sentences from 1 month to life. Lenient imprisonment is the most common of all incarcerative sanctions used in Denmark. Eighty-five percent of persons sentenced to lenient imprisonment are drunken drivers. Violations of the penal code, especially various offenses against property, are the most common crimes leading to sentences of imprisonment.

Two percent of all sentences are for 2 years or longer. Most sanctions are fines and suspended sentences, sometimes combined with probation, lenient imprisonment, ordinary imprisonment, day fines (related to the individual's income and assets), and restitution.

Rather than emphasizing punishment for offenders, the Danes believe that it is in the interest of society to provide for inmate education and rehabilitative treatment. Standard officers, the equivalent of correction officers in the United States, are assigned to duty in each wing of the prison and work closely with each inmate. They are assisted by professional officers such as welfare officers who act as consultants to provide special services. This staff enables a single group of officers with professional skills in a variety of areas to perform all duties related to prison services. These include security work, instructing of inmates at work, and service as guards and as welfare officers.

During her numerous visits to prisons in Denmark, this researcher observed inmates engaging in a range of activities, many of which related to their interests and/or abilities. The prison industries include furniture making, boat building and repair, and construction of a solar power system.

Treatment of Inmates

The rights of Danish inmates while incarcerated are determined by rehabilitative goals. Inmates have the right to vote, to own private property, to be accommodated, to have free time activities, and to have contact with the outside world. They wear their own personal clothes, have personal possessions, plan their free time, receive money, make unlimited telephone calls, and have the keys to their own rooms. These privileges provide the in-

mates with a sense of responsibility and allow them considerable personal influence in their daily routine.

At Ringe, a closed prison, male and female inmates live next to each other and are free to interact. Here inmates cook their daily meals in a kitchen where they live, using their meal payment to buy the food items in a shop in the prison complex operated by a local store owner. Once a week, inmates receive cash as wages for work and to pay for meals. They are responsible for budgeting their funds, and a local bank operates a prison "bank room" where payments are made.

Leave policies for prisoners are quite liberal; however, prisoners cannot go on leave whenever they want and for any reason whatsoever. Instead, certain time conditions must be fulfilled, and there must be special reasons for each inmate's wish to go on leave of absence (Greve et al., 1984:115). One can go on leave after serving 4 weeks of one's sentence. There are also "day leaves" which are granted for employment or vocational training whenever such a job or training is not available in the institution. All inmates are required to work and be productive in prison, as established in Section 35 of the Danish Penal Code (Jepsen, 1991:132). Prisoners may fulfill their work requirement by participating in basic and advanced vocational training courses which are designed to help the inmate even after release.

It is not difficult to understand why Danish prisons are highly esteemed internationally and represent the fond dreams of prison reformers everywhere (Serrill, 1977).

Brazil: An Overview

The Federal Republic of Brazil is in South America and is bounded by Venezuela, Guyana, Suriname, French Guiana, and the Atlantic Ocean on the north; by the Atlantic Ocean on the east; by Uruguay on the south; and by Argentina, Paraguay, Bolivia, Peru, and Colombia on the west. The capital is Brasilia. Brazil occupies a total area of 3,286,488 square miles, and its population is approximately 150 million (The World Almanac, 1991). Sixty percent of the population are of European descent, 25% are mulattoes and mestizos, 10% are of African descent, 3% are Asians, and 2% are native Indians (Info Please Almanac, 1981).

Brazil operated under a military dictatorship for 21 years (1964–1985). A new constitution was prepared in 1988 which provided for the election of a president every 5 years. In 1989, Fernando Collor De Mello became the first democratically elected president in 30 years. He resigned in 1992 following his conviction on charges of corruption (Heikers, 1993). Brazil's National Congress maintains a bicameral structure, and the country is moving slowly toward civilian democracy.

Portuguese is the official Brazilian language, but many speak German and Italian, especially in the southern cities. For years, Brazil glossed over its racial divisions with the concept of a "racial democracy," which is based on the idea that the black Brazilian man or woman knows his or her "place" (Santos Rodrigues, 1993), i.e., that black people know their role in Brazil is not leadership in government and business but a concentration in service and nonintellectual employment. They know that they are not supposed to aspire beyond blue-collar and janitorial careers.

A Legacy of Authoritarianism and Violence

Many believe that violence became a way of life in Brazil during its period of military dictatorship. Some, however, question this explanation, contending that violence was present even before military rule, and that the popular classes, including petty criminals, were victimized in order to enforce social hierarchies. The recently installed democratic government was not able to modify the situation coercively lest it risk its popularity in future elections: as one critic has noted, the democratization of government does not lead, automatically, to victory of the principles over repressive apparatus (Pinheiro, 1992). In the case of Brazil, illegal practices strengthened during the move toward democracy.

In Brazil the law has never served the interest of the poor, the miserable, the indigent, the black, or the mulatto, and in practice there is little difference between arbitrary extralegal power and the rule of law. Brazilian values include violence as a legitimate, imperative, and effective behavior in many sectors of social life (Pinheiro, 1992). The middle and ruling classes have established uses of force as a means to subordinate the poor.

Violent death is common. A substantial proportion of these deaths continued even after the end of the military regime and were attributed to death squads, to vigilante groups, and to *justiceiros* (gunmen). On the peripheries of big cities, there are approximately two hundred extermination groups. In most cases, they are financed by local communities and business owners (Brooke, 1992b).

In Brazil, the fight against crime follows the illegal lines of the period before democracy, although there are some innovative practices such as the militarization of the police patrol approved by the democratic constitution of 1988. Brazil currently leads the democratic countries of the world in number of deaths in police conflicts with the masses (Brooke, 1992a). Clearly, the legacy of authoritarianism continues to influence Brazilian society, and this includes the functioning of its prisons.

Criminal Justice Policy in Brazil

The penal system of Brazil is based on the Penal Code of 1940, which has two sections, the first of which addresses general principles, distinctions among various types of crimes, and specification of various kinds of punishments.

Capital punishment (in the form of execution by firing squad) was revoked by the constitutions of 1946, 1964, and 1967, but was reintroduced by a constitutional amendment in 1969. At the present time, the Constitution of Brazil prohibits capital punishment; however, there has been talk of reintroducing the death penalty because of increasing rates of violence (Kowalski, 1993).

Decree number 898 stipulates a maximum of 30 years in prison as equivalent to life imprisonment for serious felonious offenses. First offenders may be paroled after serving half of their sentences. The prison population in Brazil is 110,000 inmates (Luiz, 1993), with the overall prisoner-to-population ratio being 82 per 100,000 (Weschler, 1993:132).

There are approximately 5,000 penal institutions in Brazil, including 51 correctional institutions, 27 penitentiaries, 6 houses of custody and treatment, 12 agricultural colonies, and 6 houses of correction. There are 12 military prisons, 1,580 regular adult prisons (*cadeias*), 2,803 jails (*xadrezes*), and 5 institutions for minors. Fourteen of these institutions have a capacity of over 500.

A shortage of prison space has caused extensive overcrowding, with prisons in Brazil holding more than twice the number of prisoners they were designed to accommodate (Weschler, 1993:132). The states of São Paulo and Minas Gerias have begun a major building program to construct medium and maximum security regional prisons. First-time offenders are often housed with those convicted of the most serious crimes, resulting in homosexual rape of younger prisoners. Young people are sold by guards who then place them in the same cells as the buyers (Americas Watch, 1989). Brazil has been cited frequently for human rights violation in its treatment of inmates (Pinheiro, 1992).

A system of murder by lottery is operated by inmates in some prisons as a means of relieving overcrowding. In Belo Horizonte, 17 inmates were ritually murdered over a 2-month period by fellow inmates in a so-called "death lottery" designed to protest prison conditions. Prison riots in Brazil claim lives of many inmates. The São Paulo prison riot of October 1992 ended with the deaths of 111 inmates at the hands of the police. Human rights workers said the prison killings manifested a "shoot to kill" policy (Brooke, 1992b). Among the 111 known fatalities of the 1992 São Paulo prison riot, 84 were pretrial detainees, while the rest were serving sentences ranging from 2 to 30 years. All were housed together (Americas Watch, 1989:15–16).

Penal institutions for women are somewhat different. They are operated by religious orders and are not called prisons. Conjugal visitation is allowed, and children are accommodated with their mothers. Clothing for both inmate and family member(s) and a family allowance are provided by the state.

Penal Conditions

Because of overcrowding, prison conditions are poor. Sanitation is primitive: the toilet is a pan on the floor, and water for drinking and washing runs through a pipe that drips. Cells are poorly ventilated, and most of them have bare concrete floors with no bed or mattress; others have beds without mattresses. Inmates are fed one meal a day and are often beaten. Many spend their time in semidarkness, never being allowed outside their cells to exercise or to breathe fresh air. Inmates complain that cells are hot and stuffy in summer, and cold and damp in winter (Americas Watch, 1989:7). Medical care is poor or nonexistent, and AIDS-infected inmates are mixed with the noninfected inmate population. Traditional prison industries include manufacture of clothing and straw mattresses, carpentry shops, and machine and welding shops; but because the system is overcrowded, it is not unusual for inmates to be idle.

Treatment of Inmates

Inmates are controlled by violent beatings brutally meted out by prison guards. Such beatings are an "extra-official punishment for disciplinary infractions—ranging from arguing with a guard to attempted escape—as well as a means of intimidating and controlling prisoners" (Weschler, 1993:133). Inmates have no rights and may expect to serve longer sentences than determined by the court or the penal code, especially those in police lock-ups. Bureaucratic chaos reigns throughout the system.

São Paulo's House of Detention (DEIC) is designed to hold prisoners for a few days, but many of its 214 inmates serve out their entire lengthy sentences in this facility. Since such facilities are meant for short-term stay, the needs of inmates are poorly addressed. The DEIC also happens to have a reputation as a torture center. Police routinely extract confessions from criminal suspects with beatings, electric shock, water torture, and the infamous "parrot's perch," on which a tied person is suspended on a cross-bar by the knees and then abused. The screams of those so abused are unbearable. Generally, inmates are treated in brutal fashion and have no legal recourse to address these human rights violations.

Brazilian Penal Policy in Contrast with Danish Penal Methods

We will now contrast Brazil's system with Denmark's. With its high standard of living and its social welfare philosophy and programs, Denmark operates on a model based on inclusion and responsibility for all citizens. This model functions effectively because the population is both small and homogeneous. Brazil, on the other hand, with a distinctly different popula-

tion in terms of both composition and size, is faced with the problems of inequality, poverty, and inhumane treatment. In reaction to the restriction of its citizens' rights during World War II, Denmark designed a humane and liberal system for the treatment of all citizens including inmates. These policies have the support of both the Danish government and its populace. Brazil, on the other hand, having experienced strict militarism and harsh controls for a period of 30 years, has become accustomed to the use of force and violence, resulting in disregard for the rights of a significant portion of its citizens, particularly the rights of political offenders and members of the lower socioeconomic classes.

There is support in Brazil for the killing of criminal suspects, especially in São Paulo's impoverished working-class periphery. Very often, it appears that the police have been given a license to kill poor people, or those considered marginal in Brazilian society. The level of force used by police in the São Paulo prison riot was extremely high: 5,000 bullets were fired in a space of 1 hour, resulting in the death of 111 inmates (Brooke, 1992a), but São Paulo's military police commander described the police operation as "perfect." Brazilian prisons, furthermore, are poorly maintained and managed and need overall improvement in organization, administration, quality of training for personnel, and respect for human dignity. Denmark honors human rights with its institutional ombudsman; Brazil, on the other hand, casually violates human rights, and there is no internal agency charged with monitoring such violations. This has resulted in a lack of concern over human rights, especially for those who are disenfranchised. As Chevigny (1990) has noted, the elites and the polity as a whole in societies marked by extreme economic inequality may perceive a need for a show of violent force to discourage civil disturbances.

External organizations such as Americas Watch are monitoring human rights violations in Brazil, and it is hoped that pressure for change can be brought on those who regard violent response to deviants as a primary mechanism to induce conformity in society.

Discussion and Review Questions

1. What are the major benefits of contrasting criminal justice systems?
2. What is a constitutional monarchy?
3. Compare and contrast unicameral and bicameral parliaments.
4. Why is protection of individual rights very significant in Denmark? What events led to emphasis on individual citizens' rights over societal rights?
5. The ombudsman in Denmark occupies a pivotal position in the maintenance of social order. Discuss.
6. Despite the fact that Denmark has a liberal prison system in the treatment of offenders, pretrial detention continues to be very restrictive. Why?
7. Compare and contrast the organization and administration of prisons in the United States and Denmark.
8. Prisons in Denmark are designed to be small in inmate population. What are the administrative reasons for this approach?
9. What types of factories are found in Danish prisons?
10. Compare and contrast the rights of prison inmates in Denmark and the United States.
11. Compare and contrast women's prisons in the United States and Brazil.
12. What are the contrasting features of organization and administration of prisons in Denmark and Brazil?
13. What is the "Parrot's Perch" as used in Brazil?
14. Discuss in detail the rights of prison inmates in Brazil and in Denmark.
15. What do you understand by the term "death lottery" to mean as applied in Brazilian prisons?
16. Discuss and comment on the social conditions in Brazilian prisons.
17. The Brazilian penal policy is a shock to "Americas Watch." Discuss.

Part VI

Synthesis of the Criminal Justice Systems

18

The Unique and Comparative Features of the Criminal Justice Systems—Policing, Judiciary, and Corrections

A Synthesis

Obi N. I. Ebbe

Introduction

This book has presented the dynamics in the criminal justice systems and criminal justice agencies of twelve countries located in Africa, Asia, Europe, the Middle East, and North and South America. We have seen the similarities and dissimilarities in the policing, judicial, and correctional philosophies, structures, and approaches of various nations. Also, we have seen some of the factors mentioned in Chapter 1 that cause the similarities and dissimilarities: nations' historical experiences such as civil war, ethnic or racial conflicts, economic structure, political organization, religious beliefs, and custom and tradition. Now let us look at these similarities and dissimilarities between and among nations in depth.

Political Experiences and the Laws of Nations

In all of the countries studied, their political experiences mainly played a significant role in shaping their laws, the nature of crimes, and their systems of justice. For instance, the English common law tradition came from the conquest of England by the Normans under William the Conqueror in 1066 A.D. At that time each borough (municipal corporation or county) in England had its own laws and a legislative council. Consequently, the laws varied from borough to borough, and the court judges' decisions varied from borough to borough as well, because they applied different laws to the same offenses in different boroughs. The Norman king of England had to send representatives to each borough to bring him the decisions of the judges in each case. In the process of time, the king got fed up with the different decisions of the judges on the same offenses. As a result, the king ordered that any judgment passed by a court judge in one borough be upheld and applied by other court judges in similar offenses in other boroughs. The laws must be common to all boroughs and so should all court decisions in the boroughs be. Thus, we have the birth of the common law of England (*stare decisis et non quieta mov-*

ere, which means "adhere to precedents and do not unsettle things established").

It stands to reason that when England went into the wars of colonization in the eighteenth and nineteenth centuries, it introduced the common law tradition to all of its colonies and protectorates. Among the former English colonies covered in this book are the United States of America, Hong Kong, Sierra Leone, Ireland, and Nigeria. Although Israel was not a British colony, some of its laws came from British mandate laws with their common law tradition. Unmistakably, of the twelve countries studied in this book, six of them are common law countries. Every one of the six countries attributed the source its laws to English law.

As the Normans imposed their laws on England, similarly, when England conquered and colonized other nations, it imposed English law upon them. Take note of bigamy law in Nigeria (Chapter 12) and the British rule in Ireland (Chapter 3).

In China, its imperial history ended in 1911 when the Qing dynasty was overthrown. Thereafter, postimperial China was engulfed in warlordism, civil wars, and corruption under the tutelage of the Kuomintang (Chinese Nationalist) regime which overthrew the Qing dynasty. When the Communist Party, under the leadership of Chairman Mao Tse-Tung, overthrew the Kuomintang in 1949, they abolished all the laws of the Kuomintang regime. The Communists believe that the Kuomintang laws represented only the interests of the capitalist ruling class, the landlords, and the feudal estates (Chapter 8). They replaced the Kuomintang laws with Communist Party laws that protected their own interests.

Similarly, in colonial America, Hong Kong, Ireland, Nigeria, Sierra Leone, and other British West African nations, England introduced laws that represented their cultural values and protected their own economic, religious, and political interests.

Undeniably, law is dynamic, because human behaviors are dynamic and not static. When Chairman Mao died in 1976, thereby ending Maoism in China, the emerging communist party leaders abolished Maoism (the Communist theories and policies of Mao Tse-Tung). They replaced Maoist laws and policies with more democratic and liberal laws and policies than the Maoist regime. Of course, the post-Mao laws represent the values and interests of the new Communist regime. Similarly, in postcolonial nations from the United States of America (1776) to Hong Kong (1997), the English colonial, repressive laws were quickly revoked, and some new laws that represented the interests of the postindependence governments were promulgated (Ebbe, 1985b, 1996). In the United States, internal conflicts emanating from the American Civil War (1861–1865), the Aboriginal American (Indian) insurrections, the slaves' rebellion, hysteria over Jim Crow laws, and civil rights campaigns played significant roles in shaping the nature and structure of American criminal law.

In other former British colonial dependencies such as Nigeria, Sierra Leone, Ireland, and other British West African nations (Ghana and Gambia), the end of the colonial hegemony brought temporary democracy. Shortly after independence, some political parties in these countries engaged themselves in political coup d'etat. This was done by annihilating other opposing political parties and creating a one-party system of government. The party leaders formed the government and threw leaders of the opposition into jail for very insignificant reasons or for no reasons at all or get them assassinated. At the same time, they set aside colonial laws and made their own laws to protect their own interests (Nigeria, under Tafawa Balewa [1960–1966]), Kenya, under Jomo Kenyatta [1964–1978], Ghana, under Kwame Nkruma [1957–1966], and Sierra Leone, under Siaka Stevens [1968–1985]). The one-party system of government consequently created totalitarian regimes with their concomitant nullification of the rule of law.

The one-party system of government or government policies that weakened opposition parties spurred the emergence of military coup d'etat in Ghana, Nigeria, Sierra Leone, Gambia, Uganda, etc. When the military took over government, they ruled by decrees, thereby making laws that served the interests of the military regime. The military junta, like the civilian totalitarian regime before it, suspended the rule of law. Consequently, the military junta became a new totalitarian regime.

From the brief history of each of the countries discussed in this book, we have seen the role political, economic, and religious powers played in the shaping of the criminal laws of nations. The data presented here attest to the fact that although norms, values, beliefs, customs, traditions, and standards may represent the sources of traditional laws, modern laws, in the main, are "ideological constructions of those who are in positions of power to protect their own interests through legislation" (Ebbe, 1985b). We see this argument as a truism not only on the basis of data presented in this book: in the first term of President Bill Clinton's administration, when the Democrats had a majority in the House, a law was passed requiring a waiting period from the time one applies to buy an assault weapon to the time of purchase. The Republicans opposed the bill. But because they did not have a majority in the House, they lost their attempt to block it from becoming a law. However, in 1994 when Mr. Newt Gingrich moved his "contract with America" hysteria and got a Republican majority in both houses of Congress, he moved to revoke the law on assault weapons. What does that tell us? It tells us that most modern legislators represent the interests of the most powerful in politics, government, and business in the countries involved.

The Judiciary and Criminal Procedures of Nations

In the judiciary and criminal procedure, the role of the powerful in the countries studied is unequivocal in the appointments of court judges, prosecutors, and directors of strategic law enforcement agencies. In virtually all countries studied, court judges are appointed by the head of government or head of state (the United States, Nigeria, Argentina, etc.). Such a head of state will not appoint a person who does not agree with him or who will not protect his interests or political ideology. Look at what happened when Spiro Agnew, former governor of the state of Maryland (1967–1968) and former vice president to Richard Nixon, was indicted in 1973 for receiving kickbacks from contractors when he was governor of Maryland and for tax evasion. In court, when the FBI presented irrefutable evidence against him, he stated "nolo contendere" (no contest). What was his penalty? The penalty for his heinous crime was 5-year unsupervised probation, and a $10,000 fine (McCaghy, 1980). That is what we call the role of power in criminal justice. Unmistakably, the United States has too many laws, too many lawyers, and very little justice.

The practice of prosecutors and criminal court judges letting the powerful walk away with their crimes is more widespread in developing countries than in more advanced nations such as the United States and the United Kingdom. For instance, in every military regime in Nigeria, there was a political–criminal nexus, and every one of the regimes from 1966 to 1979 and from 1983 to 1998 was a predatory state (the government operating like a Mafia family) (Ebbe, 1997, 1999a). The military regimes passed decrees, then turned around and violated those decrees with impunity (Chapter 12) because they had already nullified law enforcement by appointing their cronies to be judges of the high courts and Supreme Court, and to be directors of strategic law enforcement agencies (Ebbe, 1996:120). In fact, the powerful in some of the countries studied, such as Nigeria, Ghana (in the West African region), and Sierra Leone, use the law enforcement agencies to commit various property and personal crimes. It has been recorded that the late President Abacha of Nigeria (1993–1998) used law enforcement agents to loot the Nigerian Treasury (Central Bank) and to assassinate some of his political opponents; others were thrown into detention and poisoned there by his agents (Ebbe, 1997; Onyema, 1984, 1996).

In all of the countries studied, the criminal justice system is in a state of legitimation crisis. This is because the rich can use their money or their political or economic positions to prevent being arrested for their crimes. When they are arrested they are less likely to be indicted. If indicted, they are less likely to be convicted and less likely to be imprisoned, if convicted. The few who get jail terms are out on parole in 1 or 2 years after their incarceration. But a poor man who breaks a bank and steals $5,000 does not say "nolo contendere" and receive a 5-year unsupervised probation. No, he gets 10 to 25 years in prison. Two different persons committed the same type of crime; one was sentenced to 15–25 years, and the other was sentenced to 5–10 years, because his father is a naval officer and his mother a professor (Attica prison, 1996). This is an example of what a traditionalist Nigerian titled man, "Echie" Osita Obieke, calls "criminal injustice" and not "criminal justice." This situation is found in almost all countries studied, and that is why the criminal justice system in these countries are viewed as unreliable, especially in developing countries. This "criminal injustice" is what Jeffrey Reiman (1998) meant when he titled his book *The Rich Get Richer and the Poor Get Prison: Ideology, Class, and Criminal Justice.*

Every one of the countries studied has a supreme court as its final court of appeal. In some cases, the supreme court is given a name that represents the language of the people in form of a final arbiter of the constitution or the laws of the land. Jury trial is found only in five of the countries: the United States, United Kingdom, Ireland, Israel, and Hong Kong. Jury trial, however, is not required in the lower courts in Israel, Ireland, and Hong Kong. China has lower courts that operate like a jury, but they are committees of lay judges. For instance, the people's courts in China are made up of an integrated, hierarchical system of four courts: (1) the basic people's court, which has other subordinate courts such as criminal tribunals, civil tribunals, and economic tribunals that are committees of lay judges; (2) intermediate people's courts, which also have criminal tribunals, civil tribunals, and economic tribunals; (3) the higher people's courts, which also have the three tribunals as the above two in addition to setting up other tribunals as the situation arises; and (4) the supreme people's courts, which also have the three tribunals that are set up as the situation warrants. In all of the courts, there is no court where only a single judge sits in a case as one would find in some criminal courts in the United States, Great Britain, Sierra Leone, Nigeria, Ghana, Ireland, or Israel.

Furthermore, the formal and informal court systems of China are found in Nigeria, Ghana, Sierra Leone and other West African countries. As in China the informal courts in West African countries are courts of lay judges. In the West African nations studied, the police and lawyers are not part of the formal and informal customary court sessions. The laws applied are customary laws that emanated from traditional religious beliefs, immemorial customs, traditions, and practices of the people (Ebbe, 1999b:72, 1999c:122).

The Chinese informal justice system is called mediation, and mediation is the *idea* of the formal and informal customary court systems in Nigeria and in other West African countries (Ebbe, 1999c:122). Whereas dual and tripartite systems of criminal justice are typical of former African, Asian, and Middle Eastern colonial countries, the Chinese dual system of criminal justice is a product of Confucianism, immemorial customs, and modernization. For both the Chinese and Japanese, the informal system of justice is far better than the technocratic, formalized system. The informal approach in criminal justice in both China and Japan is sustained by the two countries' emphasis on social cohesion. In both China and Japan, unlike the United States, Great Britain, and the other western European countries, society's rights precede individual rights (Ozaki, 1978:183; (See Chapter 14.)) In effect, a whole country operates and relates to one another like members of the same family.

The use of lay judges in criminal cases, however, is not the practice in Ireland, the United States, and Israel. However, status offenses are found only in the United States. Also, whereas the United States requires unanimous vote in a jury trial in order to get a conviction or find a defendant guilty of an offense, Hong Kong requires 5:2 or 7:2 votes. And the jury composition is 7 or 9 as against 12 in the United States. The former British West African countries abolished trial by jury immediately after their independence. In most of the countries studied only a single judge, who must be a certified member of the bar association of the country, sits at the district courts, magistrates' courts, and the high courts. In some situations, a high court session may require more than one judge. In all of the countries' supreme courts, there are multiple judges presided over by a chief justice.

As mentioned in Chapter 1, some countries may have many criminals in its population because of the way it handles its offenders. The area of prosecution itself can be criminogenic, if the position of the prosecutor is an elected one. When the position of a prosecutor is an elected one as in some states of the United States (New York, California, Michigan, etc.), very of-

ten innocent persons are convicted and incarcerated for crimes they did not commit because the district attorney wants to be reelected. When a district attorney is campaigning to be reelected, he proclaims to voters the number of indictments he made in the county and the percentage of convictions he got. He could have gotten the high percentage of convictions by hiding some of the evidence and manipulating police records of the cases. The county will only learn what actually happened some years after he has left office (Democrat and Chronicle, May 22, 1999, Monroe County, NY; Brown, 1990). This is a serious problem in the U.S. criminal justice system. In the United States, there are many cases of innocent persons serving 20 to 26 years in prison for a crime they did not commit, such as Betty Tyson in Rochester, New York (Democrat and Chronicle, June 3, 1999:1B). When some investigative journalist reveals the truth about the miscarriage of justice, the state involved often must pay millions of dollars in damages. In some cases, the state denies any wrongdoing (Champion, 1991).

Many countries are aware of the possible manipulation of evidence in order to get a conviction, if the position of the prosecutor is an elected one. Of the twelve countries studied in this book, only the United States has an electoral system for prosecutors generally called district attorneys (DAs). In the eleven other countries, including the United Kingdom, the state or national prosecutor is a member of the state's or nation's civil service and is called the director of public prosecution (DPP). In China, he or she is called the procurator general. In the United States, the district attorney appoints some lawyers to serve as assistant district attorneys. They prosecute cases for the DA, and they work at the DA's pleasure and only during the term of his or her office. Therefore, these assistant district attorneys prosecute cases according to the interests of the district attorney.

In contrast, the director of public prosecution in Israel, Ireland, Argentina, Brazil, Hong Kong, the United Kingdom, Japan, Nigeria, Denmark, Sierra Leone, and Ghana assigns cases to other lawyers fully employed by the state to serve under the DPP as prosecutors. This is also the case in the procuratorate in China. The procurator general has procurators who are employed by the government to serve under him or her. In some cases in United Kingdom, Nigeria, Ghana, Sierra Leone, etc., the DPP may ask a senior police officer to serve as a prosecutor. In effect, in China and all of the other countries that use the DPP, prosecuting a criminal case is not a "do or die" situation as in the United States. There is no pressure on the DPP or the procurator general and their teams of prosecutors to get a conviction by any means. Consequently, in DPP and procuratorate general countries, persons are not charged with criminal violations until the office is about 95% sure of the evidence against the accused. This is the way it should be in the United States, if we are going to reduce the rate of incarceration of innocent citizens.

Furthermore, China's insurance against misdirection of justice is demonstrated in their control of the nation's bar association. There is no private practice of law in China. There are law firms controlled by the government. With the negation of solo practice of law or private practice, defense of an accused is not to "get the suspect free from conviction" by all means, as is the case in some countries of the world. This is a unique aspect of the comparative criminal justice systems. In fact, in China, it is a crime for a defense attorney to knowingly hide the guilt of his client from the court. The rich in China have little chance of using their money to direct the course of justice.

Crime Rate

It is very hard to measure crime rate across cultures. In fact, it is unreliable. But one fact is clear. In all of the countries studied, property crimes are committed more frequently than personal crimes, even in the Communist country of China. However, the rate of property crime is higher in all of the other countries studied than in China, even with its large population.

Undeniably, economic conditions in a capitalist system coupled with malintegration can explain higher crime rates in the United States and other capitalist economies than in China. However, an industrialized country, Japan, records lower crime rates than some nonindustrialized countries such as Nigeria, Argentina, and Brazil because of the Japanese emphasis on social integration.

Another factor in crime rates of these countries is the minimum age of criminal responsibility: 7 in Ireland, 7 in Hong Kong, 10 in China, 10 in England and Wales (UK), 8 in Scotland (UK), and 7 in Nigeria (Newman, 1999:263–264). These figures appear reasonable given that in 1994, a 10-year-old shot and killed Jeremy Bullock, an 11-year-old, in Butte, Montana; a 12-year-old boy and a 14-year-old girl were convicted of murder in the second degree in Monroe County (New York) and Livingston County (New York) in 1997 and 1999, respectively. Consider also the high school murders in Littleton, Colorado, in April 1999; shootings in Jonesboro, Arkansas, and Mississippi and Kentucky high schools; and a 15-year old sophomore, Thomas J. "T.J." Solomon, shooting and wounding six high school students at Conyers, Georgia, in May, 1999. The United States is recorded as having 17 years as its minimum age of criminal responsibility (Newman, 1999:264). Crime rates are far lower in Ireland, Hong Kong, Nigeria, China, Japan, and the United Kingdom than they are in the United States. But these six countries realized that it is necessary to let today's youngsters know *ahead of time* that they will be tried as adults when they commit felonious crimes. The United States should be in company of these six countries, given that crime rates are far higher in the United States than in every one of the other eleven countries studied. Take, for instance, the homicide rate per million population in 1994 recorded by the United Nations Office for Drug Control and Crime Prevention (Newman, 1999: 285-286) shown as follows:

Denmark	51
Hong Kong	16
Israel	72
Japan	3
United Kingdom (England and Wales)	14
United Kingdom (Scotland)	22
USA	90

Murder rates for Ireland, Brazil, Argentina, China, Nigeria, and Sierra Leone are not reported. However, based on previous studies, homicide rates are lower in all of the countries studied than in the United States. For instance, in 1992 Ireland recorded twelve homicides per million and the United States ninety-eight homicides per million (FBI: UCR, 1992).

Policing

Every one of the countries studied lays emphasis on community policing. But community policing is more developed in some countries than in others. China appears to be a leader in community policing, followed by Israel, Japan, the United Kingdom, Hong Kong, Denmark, Ireland, and the United States. Community policing countries are countries where the police and the members of each community or district cooperate harmonious in solving criminal and noncriminal problems aimed at maintaining social order and social cohesion. In such countries, the police and the community try to identify sources of problems in advance. In such countries, the police see the members of the community as partners in crime prevention efforts and offender apprehension.

In countries such as Nigeria, Sierra Leone, Argentina, Brazil, and other areas of West Africa, the police are still seen as colonial instruments of repression, and the police in those countries, in fact, tend to act as oppressive instruments. This is because true democracy has been very hard to come by in those countries. Those countries have endured, and some still endure, totalitarian regimes. Undeniably, totalitarian regimes or dictatorships are more oppressive than colonial regimes. In both regimes, the police are antagonistic to the communities and are estranged from the communities. In effect, modern community policing approach is very hard to introduce in those countries today.

With the exception of the United States, the United Kingdom, and Argentina, all of the countries studied have a centralized system of policing. That means every policeman and policewoman in the country is a member of the national police force. For instance, the Israeli National Police (INP), the Nigerian Police Force, the Chinese Ministry of Public Security (MPS) as the most important of the People's Police Agencies, and other centralized systems of policing have one thing in common: the national police organization is under a single director called the inspector-general of police, the director general of police, or any other name. The national police organization may have many other subunits, but all of the subunits are under the control and administration of the national police headquarters.

In most of these centralized police organizations, the inspector-general or the director-general rose from the ranks of police officers.

There is a serious problem in a centralized system of policing in a country where there no single language is spoken by all the citizens, and where there are multiple ethnic groups with distinct languages of their own—such as Nigeria, Sierra Leone, and Ghana. Such countries should have regional police forces designed to suit the environment of each particular region. It is foolhardy to expect a police officer who does not speak the language of a community or region of a country to effectively enforce the law in the area. But in Nigeria, with more than 250 ethnic and language groups, there are no regional or state police forces. Each of Nigeria's thirty-six states should have its own police force just as in the United States. The problem is that military dictators are afraid of such decentralization in policing. Unmistakably, of all of the twelve countries studied in this book, Nigeria has the poorest law enforcement record. The records of countries with decentralized system of policing show that the more decentralized the policing strategy, the more effective the law enforcement efforts.

In the United Kingdom, there are three branches of the police organization. The England and Wales Police Force is controlled through forty-three constabularies; Scotland is administered and controlled through eight regional forces; and Northern Ireland has a single national police force—the Royal Ulster Constabulary (RUC). The Scotland Yard, like the FBI, stands as a strategic law enforcement agency for all of the regions of the country.

Argentina, like United Kingdom and the United States, has a decentralized system of policing. It has a national police as well as provincial police forces. Unlike the inspector-generals of police in Nigeria, Sierra Leone, Hong Kong, Ireland, and Israel, the chief of police in Argentina is not a member of the police force. He is a civilian appointed by the president of Argentina to administer the police at the pleasure of the president. In other words, the Argentine chief of police is not a trained police officer. He did not rise from the ranks.

In the United States, there are many police forces. A state in the United States may have as many as two hundred police forces or more, depending on the number of metropolitan cities and counties in the state. Every city or town in the United States with a population over 10,000 people has a police force in addition to the county and state police organizations. Every county in the United States has its own police force operating side-by-side with the state police. Furthermore, universities and colleges in the United States have security forces, and in some states such as New York, the state university security forces are accorded full police powers. Top businesses, service companies, and manufacturing companies in the United States have armed security units. On top of all these law enforcement forces are at least sixty-three federal law enforcement agencies in the United States. Topmost among U.S. federal law enforcement agencies are the Federal Bureau of Investigation (FBI), the United States Marshals, the Bureau of Alcohol, Tobacco, and Firearms (ATF), the Drug Enforcement Agency (DEA), and the Secret Service (SS). No other country among the twelve countries studied has a multifarious network of law enforcement agencies like that of the United States.

And yet the United States has a higher crime rate than the other eleven countries. Why? Because American society is criminogenic (breeds crime). There are many contradictions in our values, in our laws, and in our interpretation of freedom. Besides, we have a culture of violence. We cherish it in many ways (Hollywood movies, sports, and toys we manufacture). We have a right to bear arms, and we don't want to leave handguns and assault weapons for the law enforcement officers and the military. Then we turn around and complain about violence in society. Parents have no right to discipline their children. We teach our children from kindergarten to dial 911 to report parental correctional disciplines as child abuse. Worst of all, the teachers cannot severely discipline their students for wrongful acts at school. The student and his/her parents could take the teacher to court for disciplining their child. The kids celebrate their unfettered freedom by shooting other students when their girlfriends dump them (Heritage High School, Conyers, Georgia, May 1999); or drive their cars and run down and crush to death another 14-year old girl who snatched their boyfriends from them (Livingston County, New York, 1998); or shoot and kill fellow students who surpass them in academics and sports or who happen to be African Americans (Littleton, Colorado, 1999). And we turn around and complain about the youth violence. Beyond controversy, those who make our laws deserve eighty percent of the blame. As stated earlier, America has too many laws, too many lawyers, and very little justice. In fact, all of the agencies of child socialization in the United States share the blame on youth violence. A society portrays its moral values in the behavior of its youth.

All of these violent youth incidents happened in the United States. Of all the countries studied, no other permits private citizens to possess handguns and assault weapons. In the other eleven countries, parents and school teachers can still discipline their students without fear of a lawsuit or police intervention. In those countries, school is not a place for violent crimes. In most of those other countries, a simple assault against another student leads to a suspension without prior warning, and in some high schools, the student may be expelled indefinitely.

Even some U.S. youths have no respect for the police. On May 8, 1999, "a twenty year old male was arrested for disorderly conduct after he approached a police officer and repeatedly yelled obscenities. Brockport, New York police issued appearance ticket" (*Hamlin-Clarkson Herald*, May 24, 1999:8). In Nigeria, Sierra Leone, Brazil, Argentina, and elsewhere, this Brockport incident is the type of behavior that leads to police brutality.

Common to all of the countries studied are complaints of police brutality. But the police brutality is less in developed countries than in developing countries. Also common to all of the countries is the presence of fewer women than men in the police forces. In all of the countries, women police officers are struggling for acceptance both within the police force and among the members of the public. It is not a phenomenon of developing countries. It is a traditional attitude that women are not meant for forceful careers, and that attitude is what causes the problem of nonchalance toward female police officers worldwide. When the first woman was recruited into the Nigerian Police Force in 1960, it made headlines. As a small boy, I watched some adults saying: "God forbid, my daughter will never be a police officer." And this occurred at the tail-end of colonial administration in Nigeria, when public perception of the Nigerian Police Force as a colonial instrument of repression was still fresh in people's minds. Although there are many female police officers today in the Nigerian Police Force, as in many of the other countries studied, they are not assigned to SWAT teams or rigorous investigative operations. In Nigeria, Sierra Leone, Ghana, and other West African countries, you find them mostly in offices and city traffic control posts.

Correctional Perspectives

The best way to deal with a law-breaker is a problem in all of the countries studied. Some of them still have the death penalty: Nigeria, Sierra Leone, China, Brazil, Argentina, and thirty-eight states in the United States. Hong Kong abolished the death penalty in 1993. The United Kingdom abolished it in 1966, other than for treason. Israel has the death penalty only for treason, terrorism, and crimes against humanity, and Ireland abolished the death penalty in 1964, but left it for killing a law enforcement officer until 1990, when it was entirely abolished.

Some of the countries have minimum and maximum life sentences. In Ireland, the minimum life sentence is 40 years. Compare this with some states in the

United States where we have 25 years to life. That means the individual with 25 years to life can go for parole 13 years later. Nigeria has a life imprisonment statute, but Nigeria's life imprisonment statute does not allow the possibility of parole. Israel, like Nigeria, has life imprisonment without parole. In 1980, the average life sentence in Ireland was 10 years. And in Ireland an offender serving a life sentence can be released on a license. Why is the sentence called a life sentence when the offender has a possibility of parole or can be released on a license? Life imprisonment connotes the offender spending the rest of his life in prison. That is what it is in Sierra Leone, Ghana, Kenya, Nigeria, Israel and some other countries. Some states in the United States, such as Texas, avoid releasing depraved murderers on parole by giving such offenders 200 years of imprisonment, so that there will be no chance of paroling him/her.

Interestingly, China, Ireland, and Hong Kong have community sentences as a form of offender disposal. This is not the same as a judge in Nigeria, the United Kingdom, the United States, Israel, or Sierra Leone ordering a convicted offender to do some community service for misdemeanors or less serious felonious offenses. Instead, a community sentence in China or a community service order in Hong Kong and Ireland is a formalized system of minimum-security sentence short of imprisonment. But unlike the minimum-security prison, in a community sentence or community service order, the convicted offender lives in his house while he does some service to the community at specified times and days, and holds his subsistent employment (job). In the case of a Chinese community sentence, the offender may not be required to do any service to the community, but he is restricted to live in his present residence without changing to another location for a certain period, usually not more than 5 years. It is a form of probation in "which the offender is strictly monitored by the whole community."

All of the countries studied have maximum-security prisons. But some countries are more humane in their prison system than others. Japan and China would like to do away with the prison system, if they could find a better alternative. This perception is understandable given their Confucian philosophies. Prisoners are treated more nicely in Japan, China, and Denmark than in other countries studied. Prisons and prisoners are neglected in Brazil, Argentina, Nigeria, and Sierra Leone. Ireland, Israel, and Hong Kong give mild, tolerable treatments to incarcerated offenders. The United Kingdom and the United States have prisons as industries for contractors. *They throw too many persons in prison and deny them rehabilitation.* The building construction companies who build new prisons; textile manufacturing companies who supply uniforms for the inmates; contractors who supply all kinds of food for the inmates; pharmaceutical companies who supply medicines for the hundreds of thousands of prison inmates; hundreds of thousands of service personnel, prison wardens, wardresses, and superintendents; the supply of color television to the inmates; and the provision of legal services for already convicted and incarcerated offenders—all these absorb millions of taxpayer dollars annually. This makes the prison systems of the United Kingdom and the United States lucrative industries for the political and business ruling classes. In effect, rehabilitation of the offender becomes a taboo, because rehabilitation of the offender would lead to less recidivism and reduction in the amount of money spent on maintaining the prison system.

This ruling class idea of the prison industry is relevant to maintaining the capitalist system. Capitalism cannot survive without surplus population (a large population of semiemployed and unemployed persons) (Quinney, 1975).

When Republicans gained control of both houses of Congress in 1994, they cut off "Pell grants" for prison inmates' education. In the same year, in the state of New York, the newly elected Republican governor, Mr. Pataki, cut state prison Pell grants for the education of state prison inmates. That means no rehabilitation for inmates. Inmates should have been allowed to continue to use the Pell grant and be required to pay the grant money back to the government after they complete their terms of sentence; inmates with no possibility of parole should not be allowed to use the Pell grant. Instead, the Pell grant was totally abolished for prison inmates. We know, beyond controversy, that there is an inverse correlation between level of education and criminal involvement (Ebbe, 1982, 1985a). Besides, an unpublished study by New York State Department of Corrections of recidivism rate among former prison inmates 5 years after their release showed a far higher recidivism rate among inmates who did not receive a college degree or an associate's diploma prior to their release than among those who did do so.

Part of the reason for high recidivism rate in the United States is relative deprivation. When incarcerated offenders are released after their terms of incarceration with an empty grocery bag to carry all of their life possessions and $30 to take a bus back to the same environment that caused their incarceration, what keeps them from becoming involved in crime again and returning to prison? In developing countries such as Nigeria, rural populations of Hispanics in Brazil and Argentina, Sierra Leone, and developed countries such as Japan and China, informal relationships are still prevalent. Previously incarcerated relatives are received with open arms back into the community and given help to stand on their feet again. Thus, those countries do not have very high recidivism rates. In West Africa, in particular, the prison system was a colonial idea. It was imported. Africans believe that an offender is a member of the community and should be corrected in the community and not outside it. The community insists on the

offender paying a fine coupled with a communion feast and sacrifices to propitiate the gods, depending on the gravity of the offense. Undeniably, in Africa south of the Sahara, public offenses such as incest, patricide, fratricide, matricide, or desecration of a holy shrine would demand a sacrifice to appease the gods in addition to a communion feast and other communal penalties. This is why most criminal cases do not reach the attention of formalized, English-based courts in the West African countries, and the offender remains in the community. Offenders are tried and disposed at the formal customary courts (Ebbe, 1999b:72) or at the informal customary courts (Ebbe, 1999c:122). This is because these customary courts do not sentence an offender to a prison term. Incarceration of the offender had never been a system of offender disposal in Africa south of the Sahara.

Japan, China, Denmark, and other Scandinavian countries have the lowest recidivism rates among their criminal populations. This is because of the humane way they treat their incarcerated offenders (though violent criminals and murderers have no freedom in those countries). For instance, in Japan, on the day a prison inmate is released from incarceration, his community members come and stand on both sides of the prison exit door and clap their hands as the inmate trots out of the prison, and they take him home in joy and jubilation. He is still a member of the community whether he is inside or outside of the prison walls. But take note that Japan punishes women more severely than men for the same offense. This is because Japan sees women as producers and nurturers of future generation, so women should set good examples. Similarly, in Nigeria, Sierra Leone, and other West African nations, the sight of a female criminal offender in police handcuffs provokes greater outrage among the masses than a sight of male criminal. This differential perception of male and female offenders in Japan and in West African countries is still sustained because sex roles are still maintained. They do not suffer gender distortion as in the United States.

In Denmark prison inmates hold keys to their cells and receive a salary to feed themselves, so that they learn how to manage their incomes. If any inmate uses up his salary, he goes hungry (Chapter 17). Unmistakably, when prison inmates are rejected by society, the inmates, in turn, reject the society. In effect, when they come out of their state of imprisonment, they join their own kind and fight against the society. They may be caught and thrown in prison again. That is the revolving door of poor and ineffective penal policy. We should learn the truth from Japan, China, and Denmark.

Conclusion

Criminal justice systems vary from culture to culture because of differential values and historical experiences of the various countries. The nature of criminal law is demonstrated in this book and better understood through the analysis of the historical and political developments in the various countries. Criminal law is not a divine construct, and it does not wholly and entirely emanate from or represent the norms, beliefs, values, and standards of the people as consensus theorists claimed (Dunkhiem, 1933; Parsons, 1951). Instead, modern criminal law, in may cases, represents the efforts of those who are in power to protect their own interests through legislation (Quinney, 1975; Chambliss and Mankoff, 1976; Ebbe, 1985b).

The police are an instrument of the government in all countries to control the masses. However, military regimes and other totalitarian regimes use the police to achieve their illegal ends. Policing the masses today is a universal problem, but community policing is proving to be the solution in many countries. There is a need to control the police use of excessive force while enforcing the law in all countries. In Israel, the Kremnitzer Committee was set up to investigate the excessive use of force by police. This is an attempt to maintain good police–community relations. In Hong Kong, a measure to check police brutality involves the establishment of an Independent Complainant Council, which handles complaints against police officers and carries out internal investigation of police officers. This Hong Kong approach is needed in every police department or national police force of every country.

As with their police systems, most of the countries have a centralized prison system. But prison reform should be geared toward inmate rehabilitation in order to reduce the recidivism rate.

Finally, data show that the masses have lost faith in the criminal justice system, because in some countries those who have power nullify effective law-enforcement policies by motivating differential law enforcement and using their money to get undeserved justice in court. The solution to the loss of faith in the criminal justice system is establishment and stringent enforcement of checks and balances within each law enforcement agency and among the network of law enforcement agencies in each country, coupled with accountability within each law enforcement agency and among the politicians.

Discussion and Review Questions

1. Compare and contrast adversarial and inquisitorial approaches in criminal justice.

2. What are the advantages and disadvantages of state-employed prosecutorial systems of justice, district attorneys versus directors of public prosecution?

3. What is the role of the procuratorate general in the Chinese criminal justice system?

4. What do you understand by veto power?

5. What are the merits and demerits of the discretionary power of the police?

6. What do you understand by "court of first instance"?

7. In what ways can politics influence community policing in Argentina?

8. What legislative problems are there relating to the Islas Malvinas with regard to the Argentine claim to territorial integrity of the area?

9. The author described the prison system in the United States and Britain as industries for the political and business ruling class. What is your position in this argument?

10. Rehabilitation ideology is marooned in the United States prison system. Discuss.

11. In Japan in 1989, only 4.72% of all felonious offenders were sentenced to prison terms and a little over 92% of them were fined. What is the relevance of this Japanese offender disposal approach?

12. While the use of the death penalty as an offender disposal mechanism is declining in the Western world, it is increasing in the United States. Why? What do you think the United States should do to reduce the high incidence of capital offenses?

13. The Hong Kong criminal justice system is a British system in China. Explain and comment.

14. What is the future of the present system of criminal justice in Hong Kong?

15. Bigamy law is a cultural universal. Do you agree? Compare and contrast bigamy and adultery.

16. What factors led to the existence of paramilitary police in Ireland and Israel?

17. Should juveniles who committed murder be tried as adults? What steps should be taken to ensure the absence of guns at U.S. elementary and high schools?

18. Why is it that in other parts of the world, especially developing countries, high school students shooting other students is unthinkable?

19. Why is it that Nigeria uses special tribunals to try currency and narcotics drug offenders?

20. What is a predatory state?

21. What is meant by "political–criminal nexus"?

22. Can some government officials be involved in organized crime?

23. Who corrupts the police?

24. In the United Kingdom, why is it that the police could maintain law and order without carrying firearms?

25. Write a short essay on the following:

    (a) Informal customary criminal justice in Nigeria

    (b) Formal customary justice in Nigeria

    (c) Informal courts in China

    (d) Mediation in China

    (e) CAPIC in Japan

Glossary

Actus reus A wrongful deed that renders the actor criminally liable if combined with mens rea, a guilty intention.

Addendum A thing added or to be added.

Advocate A person who pleads or speaks in favor of another person in a matter or case.

Alkhali court The lowest Muslim court in Northern Nigeria, where cases involving Muslims are tried. The judge is versed in Islamic law.

Allotment Share, portion, something set apart for a purpose.

APC All People's Congress. This was a political party that ruled Sierra Leone from 1968 through April 29, 1992, when it was overthrown in a coup d'etat by the present (1995) military regime.

Appellant The person who challenges the correctness of a court order or judgment by seeking a review and relief in a higher court having appellate jurisdiction, or the person in whose behalf this is done.

Appellate court A court which has the primary function of reviewing the judgments of lower courts in a country or state. It may not act as a trial court or court of first instance.

Arcane Secret; hidden; intended only for the initiated.

Assessor An expert in customary law who helped colonial court judges in interpreting the law of the land. In China, a lay member of the court as a juror, but (unlike a juror in the United States) having equal power with the court judge in adjudication of a case. An advisory assistant.

Bicameral Literally, two-chambered, referring to a parliament or congress divided into a lower house and an upper house—for example, the senate and the national assembly or the senate and the parliament.

Bona fide In good faith; legally valid; genuine; sincere.

Buraku-kai Rural traditional communities in Japan.

Certiorari A writ issued from an appellate court for the purpose of obtaining from a lower court the record of its proceedings in a particular case.

Chonai-kai In Japanese, district or block associations of 400 to 600 households.

Criminal code Written substantive criminal law specifying acts that are crimes and punishments for violations.

Cultural genocide A program of action deliberately designed to destroy the values, standards, beliefs, and norms of a whole country, race, or ethnic group by replacing the indigenous cultural values with alien values, through alien based education. The result is total disorganization of the indigenous society.

Customary court A court where rules and regulations (laws) emanating from the immemorial customs and traditions of the people are enforced by a chief, or an elder, or a council of elders. Such courts are found throughout sub-Saharan Africa.

Daimyo (daimio) During the Japanese feudal era, a hereditary Japanese nobleman.

Danwei A Chinese work unit which assigns income and housing to its members.

Day leave A type of leave granted to a Danish prisoner for the purpose of employment or job training outside of the prison. It can be granted if such employment or job training is not available in the prison institution.

De novo Anew; from the beginning.

Denunciation An act of public condemnation or accusation.

Depraved heart One morally bad, corrupt and perverted. In murder, the offender has no regard for the value of human life; thus, depraved heart murder.

Disparate treatment case A case involving a charge against an employer for basing a decision not to hire or promote a person on unjustifiable or discriminatory grounds.

Double jeopardy The danger of being tried, and perhaps convicted and punished, twice for the same offense.

DPP Director of Public Prosecution. This is an individual who heads the prosecution department of the Ministry of Justice in such countries as England, Nigeria, Kenya, Ghana, and Sierra Leone. He or she decides whether an accused in a felonious offense should be indicted or not. The DPP is a civil service position, but is not elected like a prosecutor in the United States.

Due process of law The due course of legal proceedings according to the rules and forms which have been established for the protection of private rights. These are rights guaranteed by the Fifth, Sixth, and Fourteenth Amendments of the U.S. Constitution.

Duress Unlawful threats of harm or other pressure used to force someone to act against his or her will. Duress may also mean illegal imprisonment, or legal imprisonment for an illegal purpose.

Enza (Japanese) relatives; opposite of renza.

Exclusionary rule In law of evidence, this is the principle applicable in both state and federal courts in the United States, that evidence illegally obtained may not properly be received at the trial.

Ex parte One-sided; on, or in the interest of, one side only.

Felony murder rule or Felony murder doctrine At common law, one who, without intent, killed another in an intent to commit another felony was guilty of murder. Although some states in the United States still follow the common law rule, today the law of felony murder varies substantially throughout the country.

Fief An inheritable piece of land in the feudal period held from an overlord in return for service. The right to possess such land.

Fudai (Japanese) Allies of the Tokugawa regime (Shogunate).

Gaikaku (Japanese) A public corporation.

Gaikaku dantai (Japanese) Public corporations or extradepartmental groups.

Gemeinschaft A German concept invented by Ferdinand Tonnis (1855–1936) referring to a small community characterized by personalized, face-to-face relationships such as those found in the family, rural villages, and very small towns where everyone knows everyone else. Interpersonal relationships are informal.

Gesellschaft Ferdinand Tonnis's concept for societies, usually urban, where interpersonal relationships are formal and contractual.

Gonin-gumi (Japanese) Household groups, usually five households together.

Grand Khadi The judge of an Alkhali court in Northern Nigeria (see Alkhali court).

Habeas corpus (Latin: You have the body) The name given to a variety of writs having as their object to bring a party before a court or judge. The primary function of the writ is to release a person from unlawful imprisonment, or to determine whether a person in the custody of legal authorities is being lawfully detained.

Hogoshi (Japanese) Representatives of the government.

Importunate Urgent or persistent in demanding or asking for something.

Indictable offense A relatively serious offense that may be tried on indictment, that is, before a grand jury.

Interlocutory Provisional; temporary; not final.

Interlocutory appeal An appeal that does not resolve the controversy, but that is essential for a later adjudication of the case on its merits.

Interlocutory decree A preliminary or provisional order. It is a decree made during a lawsuit to ascertain a matter of law or fact in preparation for a final decree.

Interlocutory judgment A judgment of the court that does not determine all the issues relating to all the parties, but instead leaves something further to be adjudicated at a later proceeding.

Junta A group of political intriguers, especially such a group of military men in power after a coup d'etat.

Knesset The Israeli Parliament.

Mutatis mutandis The necessary changes having been made. With the necessary changes in detail to be made in compliance with one major change.

Naira The name given to Nigeria's money in 1973, a change from the country's original "pound" medium of exchange. In 1985, one Naira (N1.00) was equal to $1.80. In March 1995, the official rate was $1.00 = N100.00.

Nolle prosequi (Latin: To be unwilling to prosecute) A mechanism by which the prosecution service terminates criminal proceedings on indictment. The decision is made on grounds such as lack of sufficient evident or that prosecution is not in the public interest. Unlike an acquittal, a nolle prosequi does not bar further prosecution.

Opprobrium Shame; or anything that brings shame or disgrace.

Ordinary imprisonment An imprisonment from 1 month to life in Denmark.

Organic solidarity Emile Durkheim's term for an urban society where interpersonal relationships are contractual and formalized. Cities exemplify Durkheim's organic solidarity type of collectivity.

Lenient imprisonment In Denmark, imprisonment for not more than 18 days.

Maliki law The source of Islamic law in Africa.

Mandamus (Latin: We command) A writ or order issued by courts to a public official or corporation, commanding the performance of some public duty required by statute.

Mechanical solidarity Emile Durkheim's concept describing a community with personalized, face-to-face interaction such as is found in more traditional societies. There is mutual obligation among the members of the community, and peace and harmony prevail.

Jinrikisha A small, two-wheeled carriage with a hood, pulled by one or two men in Japan or in other Far Eastern societies.

Jurisdiction Authority by which courts and judicial officers hear and determine cases. The geographical delimitation of a given court's power to hear and determine cases.

Justice of the peace A judicial officer of lesser rank who has jurisdiction over minor criminal and civil cases. A person who judges less serious cases in a local court of law; a magistrate.

Kabun (Japanese) Persons of subordinate rank; opposite of oyabun.

Lay advocate One versed in the customary law of his land who pleads or speaks on behalf of another in Chinese courts or African customary courts.

Ostracize To exclude somebody from a community, group, or society as a form of punishment for crime or a breach of norms. The group refuses to meet or talk to the individual.

Oyabun (Japanese) Persons of superior rank; opposite of kabun.

Parrot's perch A type of punishment in which an offender is tied up and suspended on a cross-bar by the knees, and then abused; commonly practiced in Brazilian prisons.

Penal code A body of law dealing with the punishments for various crimes or offenses.

PPO Professional probation officer; to be contrasted with "volunteer probation officer" (VPO) in Japanese corrections.

Prefecture The office, authority, territory, or residence of a prefect or administrative official.

Preposterous Ridiculous; so contrary to nature, reason, or common sense as to be laughable; absurd.

Presumption of innocence An important principle of criminal law in the United States holding that the state (government) has the burden of proving every element of a crime beyond a reasonable doubt, and that the accused has no burden to prove his or her innocence.

Prima facie (Latin: On its face) Describing a fact convincing on first examination, without any further proof of validity.

Prima facie case A case in which the plaintiff has presented sufficient evidence to entitle him to a decision by the judge or jury; a case that compels a favorable decision when no contrary or rebutting evidence is presented.

Procurator In China, a person who manages the prosecution division (procuratorate) of the Chinese criminal justice system. He or she resembles the DPP in England or Nigeria (but has more power), represents the government in all criminal matters, and is not an elected official. (In general terms, a procurator is one employed to manage the affairs of another, an agent.)

Procuratorate The office and powers of a procurator.

Prohibition An act or law making some thing or behavior illegal; especially, the prohibition of the manufacture, sale, or transportation of intoxicating liquors except for medicinal purposes by the Eighteenth Amendment to the United States Constitution (1920). (This prohibition amendment was repealed by the Twenty-first Amendment in 1933.)

Proportional representation A system aimed at giving political parties a representation in parliament as proportional as possible to their voting strength. For example, in Ireland, there is a transferable vote and the second and subsequent choice votes of candidates come into play once the candidate is eliminated or is elected with surplus votes above a calculated quota.

Raison d'etre Reason for being; justification for existence.

Recidivism Repeated criminal involvements and penalties by an individual.

Referendum The practice of submitting a question directly to the electorate or the people of a country or state to decide a national or constitutional issue by a vote, as in Ireland where the constitution can only be amended if the majority of the voters agree.

Renza (Japanese) Unrelated persons; opposite of enza.

Samurai The aristocrats of the pre-Tokugawa era who became the bureaucrats of the Tokugawa regime in Japan.

Self-incrimination Any action or admission made by a person, either before trial or at trial, that implicates him/her in the commission of a crime.

Sharia court In Northern Nigeria and Middle Eastern nations, a court where only Islamic laws are applied.

Sharia law Synonymous with Maliki law or Islamic law.

Shogun Any of the feudal military governors of Japan who made up a quasi dynasty, exercised absolute power, and relegated the emperors to a titular head of state.

Shogunate The powers, territories, and reign of a Shogun.

Summary offense A minor offense that cannot be tried before a jury but is dealt with directly by a magistrate or a judge in the lower court.

Stare decisis (Latin) To stand by decided cases; to follow precedent.

Taisei-gai (Japanese) Within the system.

Taisei-nai (Japanese) Outside the system.

Tozama Those samurai who submitted to the Tokugawa regime in Japan only after the Tokugawa gained control over Japanese affairs.

Ultra vires (Latin) Beyond granted powers. Conduct that exceeds the powers given to an officeholder such as a prime minister, president, or CEO of a corporation.

VPO Volunteer probation officer (used in Japanese corrections).

Waku (Japanese) The social control system in which group interest is superior to self-interest.

Bibliography

Achebe, Chinua. 1959. *Things fall apart.* New York: McDowell Obolensky.

Adewoye, Omoniyi. 1977. *The judicial system in southern Nigeria, 1854–1954: Law and justice in a dependency.* Atlantic Highlands, NJ: Humanities Press.

Adler, F. 1983. *Nations not obsessed with crime.* Littleton, CO: Fred B. Rothman.

Aguda, Akinola T. 1974. *The law of evidence in Nigeria.* London: Sweet and Maxwell.

_____. 1980. *The law and practice relating to evidence in Nigeria.* London: Sweet and Maxwell.

Ai, Xue. 1989. New "People's Mediation Committee's Organic Rules" promulgated in China. *Outlook Weekly* 42:10.

Alemika, E., and O. Kayode. 1981. Some attributes of recidivism: A study of the inmates of a Nigerian prison. *International Journal of Comparative and Applied Criminal Justice* 5 (2):187–195.

Alemika, Etannibi E. O. 1983. The smoke screen: Rhetoric and reality of penal incarceration in Nigeria. *International Journal of Comparative and Applied Criminal Justice* 1:137–149.

Allen, G. Frederick. 1987a. Reforming criminals in China: Implications for corrections in the West. *International Journal of Comparative and Applied Criminal Justice* 11 (1):77–86.

_____. 1987b. Where are we going in criminal justice? Some insights from the Chinese criminal justice system. *International Journal of Offender Therapy and Comparative Criminology* 31:101–109.

Allison, Gary D. 1975. *Japanese urbanism: Industry and politics in Kariya, 1872–1972.* Berkeley: University of California Press.

Allott, A. N. 1963. *The future of law in Nigeria.* London: Sweet and Maxwell.

Americas Watch. 1989. *Prison conditions in Brazil.* New York: Human Rights Watch.

Amin, S. 1974. *Modern migrations in West Africa.* London: Oxford University Press.

Amir, M. 1998. Organized crime in Israel. In *Crime and justice in Israel*, edited by R. Friedmann, 121–138. Albany, NY: State University of New York Press.

Anagata, Shizuo. 1990. Some aspects of volunteer probation officer (hogoshi) system in Japan. Paper delivered at the United Nations Asia and Far East Institute for the Prevention of Crime and the Treatment of Offenders (UNAFEI), Tokyo.

Ancel, Marc. 1971. *Suspended sentence.* London: Heinemann Educational Books.

Annual statistical digest. 1970. Sierra Leone Government, Freetown: Central Statistics Office.

_____. 1971. Sierra Leone Government, Freetown: Central Statistics Office.

_____. 1984. Sierra Leone Government, Freetown: Central Statistics Office.

_____. 1989. Sierra Leone Government, Freetown: Central Statistics Office.

_____. 1990. Sierra Leone Government, Freetown: Central Statistics Office.

Anonymous. 1856. Irish crime and prison statistics. *Irish Quarterly Review* 4:559–568.

Anonymous. 1858. Irish convict prisons. *Dublin University Magazine* 51:166–172.

Anthony, R. 1992. An investigation of the requirement for the Metropolitan Police Service to include the words "sexual orientation" in its statement of equal opportunities policy. Master's dissertation: University of Exeter, England.

Aoyagi, Kiyotaka. 1983. Viable traditions in urban Japan: Matsuri and chonaikai. In *Town-talk: The dynamics of urban anthropology*, edited by Haus Ansari and Peter J. M. Haus, 96–107. Leiden, Denmark: E. J. Brill.

Archer, D., and R. Gartner. 1984. *Violence and crime in cross-national perspective.* New Haven, CT: Yale University Press.

Argentine Penal Code 1853 and 1994.

Arikpo, Okoi. 1967. *The development of modern Nigeria.* Baltimore: Penguin Books, Inc.

Arthur, J. 1991. Development and crime in Africa: A test of modernization theory. *Journal of Criminal Justice* 19:499–513.

Association of Chief Police Officers (ACPO). 1990. *Statement of common purpose and values.* London: Scotland Yard.

Austern, David. 1987. *The crime victim's handbook.* Harrisonburg, VA: R. R. Donnelley and Sons Company.

Awe, B. 1968. History of the prison system in Nigeria. In *The prison system in Nigeria*, edited by T. O. Elias, 28–36. Lagos, Nigeria: Faculty of Law, University of Lagos.

Balkin, J. 1988. Why policemen do not like police women. *Journal of Police Science and Administration* 16: 29–38.

Bandura, A. 1977. *Social learning theory.* Englewood, NJ.: Prentice-Hall.

Barnes, Harry Elmer. 1942. *Social institutions in an era of world upheaval.* New York: Prentice-Hall.

Bartolomei, Maria L. 1994. Gross and massive violations of human rights in Argentina. Ed. Juristforlaget i Lund, Sweeden. p.300.

Bayley, D. 1992. A Fresh Perspectives Paper: The best defence. Washington, D.C.: Police Executive Research Forum.

Beasley, William G. 1972. *The Meiji Restoration.* Stanford, CA: Stanford University Press.

_____. 1990. *The rise of modern Japan.* Tokyo: Charles E. Tuttle.

Bensinger, G. J. 1998. Criminal justice in Israel. In *Crime and justice in Israel*, edited by R. Friedmann, 43–64. Albany, NY: State University of New York Press.

Bentham, Jeremy. 1843. A view of the Hard-Labor Bill. In *Works of Jeremy Bentham*, Vol. 4, edited in 1962 by John Bowring. New York: Russell Sage Foundation.

Benyon, J. 1987. Interpretations of civil disorder. In *The roots of urban unrest*, edited by Benyon and Solomos. London: Pergamon Press.

Bestor, Theodore C. 1985. Tradition and Japanese social organization: Institutional development in a Tokyo neighborhood. *Ethnology* 24:121–135.

Bevins, A. 1992. Labour MP says police are sexist. *Independent*, 18 July.

Binchy, D. 1978. Ancient Irish law extracts. Dublin: Institute of Advanced Studies.

Bindzus, D. 1991. Criminal justice in Hong Kong. *Hong Kong Law Journal* 21(2):181–199.

Birch, R. 1990. *Operational policing review*. Surbiton: Sierra Leone Joint Consultative Committee.

Black, Henry Campbell. 1979. *Black's law dictionary*, 5th edition. St. Paul: West Publishing Company.

Blomberg, Thomas G. 1987. Criminal justice reform and social control: Are we becoming a minimum security society? In *Transcarceration: Essays in the sociology of social control*, edited by John Lowman, Robert J. Menzies, and T. S. Polys, 218–226. Alderholt, England: Gower.

Bossard, A. 1990. *Transnational crime and criminal law*. Chicago: The Office of International Criminal Justice (OICJ).

Bracey, Dorothy H. 1989a. Corrections in the People's Republic of China. In *Social control in the People's Republic of China*, edited by Ronald Troyer, John Clark, and Dean Rojek, 159–168. New York: Praeger Publishers.

_____. 1989b. Policing the People's Republic. In *Social control in the People's Republic of China*, edited by Ronald Troyer, John Clark, and Dean Rojek, 130–140. New York: Praeger Publishers.

Brady, C. 1974. *Guardians of the peace*. Dublin: Gill and MacMillan.

Brady, James P. 1982. *Justice and politics in People's China: Legal order or continuing revolution?* New York: Academic Press.

Braibanti, Ralph J. D. 1948. Neighborhood associations in Japan and their democratic potentialities. *Far Eastern Quarterly* 7 (2):136–164.

Brecher, E.M., and the editors of *Consumer Reports*. 1972. *Licit and illicit drugs*. Boston: Little, Brown.

Brett, Sir Lionel, and Ian McLean. 1963. *The criminal law and procedure of Lagos, eastern Nigeria and western Nigeria*. London: Sweet and Maxwell.

Brewer, John D., Adrian Guelke, Ian Hume, Edward Maxon-Browne, and Rick Wilford. 1988. *The police, public order and the state policing in Great Britain, Northern Ireland, the Irish Republic, the USA, Israel, South Africa, and China*. New York: St. Martin's Press.

_____. 1973. Evolution of crime in the Ivory Coast. In *Urban and rural crime and its control in West Africa*, edited by Young Brillion, 112–124. Montreal: University of Montreal Center for International Criminology.

Brillion, Y. 1974. Crime prevention and sentencing in the Ivory Coast. Paper presented at the 4th West African conference on comparative criminology, April 25–27, Abidjan, Ivory Coast.

Brogden, M. 1987. The emergence of the police: the colonial dimension. *British Journal of Criminology* 27: 1.

Brook, L. 1992. Exit Collor, enter confidence. *Newsweek*, October 12:48.

Brooke, J. 1992a. Brazil's police enforce a law: Death. *New York Times*, November 4:A22.

_____. 1992b. Looting Brazil. *New York Times*, November 8:31–33, 42, 45, 70.

Brown, Joyce Ann. 1990. *Joyce Ann Brown: Justice Denied*. Chicago: The Noble Press, Inc.

Brown, L., and M. Wycoff. 1986. Policing Houston: Reducing fear and improving service. *Crime and Delinquency*, January.

Brown, M. 1988. *Working the street: Police discretion and dilemmas of reform*. New York: Russell Sage Foundation.

Brownson, Anna. 1994. *Judicial staff directory, 1995*. Mt. Vernon, VA: Staff Directories Ltd.

Bureau of Justice Statistics (BJS). 1991. *Sourcebook of criminal justice statistics*. Washington, D.C.: U.S. Department of Justice.

BJS. 1992a. *Criminal victimization in the United States, 1991*. Washington, D.C.: U.S. Department of Justice.

BJS. 1992b. *Census of State and Federal correctional facilities, 1990*. Washington, D.C.: U.S. Department of Justice.

BJS. 1993. *Census of State and local law enforcement agencies, 1992*. Washington, D.C.: Department of Justice.

BJS. 1994a. *Prisoners in 1993*. Washington, D.C.: U.S. Department of Justice.

BJS. 1994b. *Comparing Federal and State prison inmates, 1991*. Washington, D.C.: U.S. Department of Justice.

BJS. 1994c. *Pretrial release of felony defendants, 1992*. Washington, D.C.: Department of Justice.

BJS. 1994d. *Capital punishment, 1993*. Washington, D.C.: U.S. Department of Justice.

BJS. 1994e. *Criminal victimization in the United States, 1992*. Washington, D.C.: Department of Justice.

Buddle, Cliff. 1999. Influx fears after victory on abode. *South China Morning Post*, 30 (January).

Burns, Alan. 1929. *History of Nigeria*. London: George Allen & Unwin Limited.

Butler, R. F., and M. Garsia, eds. 1966. *Archbold pleading, evidence and practice in criminal cases*, 36th ed. London: Sweet and Maxwell.

Byrne, R., and P. McCutcheon. 1996. *The Irish legal system*. Dublin: Butterworths.

Caldwell, J. C. 1969. *African rural–urban migration*. Canberra: Australia National University.

Campbell, John Creighton. 1977. *Contemporary Japanese budget politics*. Berkeley: University of California Press.

_____. 1985. Governmental responses to budget scarcity: Japan. *Policy Studies Journal* 13:506–516.

Carter, D., A. Sapp, and D. Stephens. 1989. *The state of police education*. Washington, D.C.: Police Executive Research Forum.

Central Bureau of Statistics. 1998. *Israel's annual statistical almanac*. Jerusalem, Israel.

Centre for Police Studies (CPS). 1989. *The effect of the Sex Discrimination Act on the Scottish police service*. University of Strathclyde, UK: Centre for Police Studies.

Chambliss, William, and Milton Mankoff. 1976. *Whose Law? What Order?: A Conflict Approach to Criminology*. New York: John Wiley & Sons.

Champion, Dean. 1991. Jail inmate litigation in the 1990s. In *American jails: Public policy issues*, edited by Joel A. Thompson and G. Larry Mays, 197–215. Chicago: Nelson-Hall Publishers.

Chan, W. T. 1998. Victims of crime and related programmes: An introduction to the victim's charter in Hong Kong. *Journal of Youth Studies* 1(2):59–66.

Chang, D. H., ed. 1976. *Criminology: A cross-cultural perspective*, Vol. 1. Durham, NC: Carolina Academic Press.

Chang, David W. 1984. Government and crime control in China: Its relevance to U.S. criminal justice. *International Journal of Comparative and Applied Criminal Justice* 2:94–111.

Chapin, Bradley. 1983. *Criminal justice in colonial America, 1606–1660*. Athens, GA: University of Georgia Press.

Chen, Dahao. 1993. Inmates' human rights in China. *Outlook Weekly* 9:8.

Ch'en, Paul Heng-Chao. 1981. *The formation of the early Meiji legal order*. Oxford: University Press.

Chen, Phillip M. 1973. *Law and justice: The legal system in China—2400 B.C. to 1960 A.D.* New York: Dunellen Publishing Company.

Chevigny, P. 1990. Police use deadly force as social control: Jamaica, Argentina and Brazil. *Criminal Law Forum* 1:3.

Children and Young Persons Act. 1945. Cap. 44 of the Law of Sierra Leone. Freetown: Government Printer.

Chubb, B. 1970. *The government and politics in Ireland.* Oxford: Oxford University Press.

Clark, John P. 1989. Conflict management outside the courtrooms of China. In *Social control in the People's Republic of China*, edited by Ronald Troyer, John Clark, and Dean Rojek. New York: Praeger Publishers.

Clifford, W. 1963. The evaluation of methods for the prevention and treatment of juvenile delinquents in Africa south of the Sahara. *International Review of Criminal Policy (UN)* 21:11–17.

_____. 1964. The African view of crime. *British Journal of Criminology* 4:477–486.

_____. 1973. *Development and crime.* Chichester, England: Rose.

_____. 1974. *Introduction to African criminology.* Nairobi: Oxford University Press.

Clifford, William. 1977. White collar and corporate crime: The modern challenges to Commonwealth criminal justice systems. *Commonwealth Law Bulletin* 3(4):679–689.

Clinard, Marshall B., and Daniel J. Abbott. 1973. *Crime in developing countries: A comparative perspective.* New York: John Wiley and Sons.

Coffee, S., J. Brown, and S. Savage. 1992. Policewomen's career aspirations: Some reflections on the role and capabilities of women in policing in Britain. *Police Studies* 15:13–19.

Cohen, Jerome A. 1968. *The criminal process in the People's Republic of China: 1949–1963.* Cambridge: Harvard University Press.

Cole, George F. 1986. *The American system of criminal justice.* Monterey, CA: Brooks/Cole Publishing.

_____, ed. 1989. *Major criminal justice systems: A comparative survey.* Beverly Hills, CA: Sage Publications.

_____. 1981. The United States of America. In *Major criminal justice systems*, edited by George F. Cole, Stanislaw J. Fankowski, and Marc G. Gertz, 3–27. Beverly Hills, CA: Sage.

Collick, Martin. 1988. Social policy: Pressures and responses. In *Dynamics and immobilist politics in Japan*, edited by J. A. A. Stockwin, 205–236. Honolulu: University of Hawaii Press.

Committee for the Prevention of Torture and Inhuman or Degrading Treatment or Punishment (CPT). 1995. *Report on Irish places of detention.* Strasbourg: Council of Europe.

Constitution of Argentina 1853 and 1994. Buenos Aires: Government Printing Press.

Constitution of the Federal Republic of Nigeria. 1963. Sec. III, 2 and Sec. I, 1. Lagos: Government Printing Press.

Constitution of the People's Republic of China. 1986. Beijing: Foreign Languages Press.

Constitution of Sierra Leone. 1961. Order-in-Council, Public Notice No. 78. Government of Sierra Leone. Freetown: Government Printer.

_____. 1971. Act No. 6. Government of Sierra Leone. Freetown: Government Printer.

_____. 1978. Act No. 12. Government of Sierra Leone. Freetown: Government Printer.

_____. 1991. Act No. 6. Government of Sierra Leone. Freetown: Government Printer.

Council of Europe. 1989. *Prison Information Bulletin* 13 and 14:16.

Council of Europe. 1992. *Penological Information Bulletin*, No. 17. Strasbourg: Council of Europe.

Court of ResolutionLaw, Cap. 28. Law of Northern Nigeria, 1963. Revision Section 3, 1. Lagos: Government Printing Press.

Courts Act, No. 31. 1965. Government of Sierra Leone. Freetown: Government Printer.

Courts Law (consolidated version). 1984. Jerusalem, Israel.

Coyle, Andrew. 1977. Prisons in Africa. *West Africa*, November 1–7.

Craig, Albert M. 1961. *Chosu in the Meiji Restoration*. Cambridge: Harvard University Press.

Criminal law and the criminal procedure law of China. 1984. Beijing: Foreign Language Press.

Criminal Procedure Act, No. 32. 1965. Government of Sierra Leone. Freetown: Government Printer.

Criminal procedures ordinance. 1960. Lagos, Nigeria: Government Printing Press.

Crosby, P. 1990. *Leading*. London: McGraw-Hill.

Cross, Sir Geoffrey, and G. D. G. Hall. 1964. *The English legal system*. London: Butterworths.

Cullen, L. 1976. *An economic history of Ireland since 1660*. London: Batsford.

Cullop, Floyd G. 1984. *The Constitution of the United States: An introduction*. New York: Penguin Books.

Customary courts edict, no. 2. 1966. Lagos, Nigeria: Government Printing Press.

Daiichi, Ito. 1988. Policy implications of administrative reform. In *Dynamics and immobilist politics in Japan*, edited by J.A.A. Stockwin et al., 77–105. Honolulu: University of Hawaii Press.

Danish statistical abstract. 1995. Copenhagen: Government Publications Office.

David, Rene, and John E. C. Brierly. 1989. *Major legal systems in the world today*. New York: The Free Press.

Day, F. D. 1964. *Criminal law and society*. Springfield, IL: C.C. Thomas.

Denham Commission on the Courts. 1996–1998 *First to Sixth Reports*. Dublin: Stationery Office.

Department of Foreign Affairs. 1995. *Facts about Ireland*. Dublin. The Stationery Office.

Department of Justice. 1997. *Tackling crime: A discussion paper*. Dublin: The Stationery Office.

Dike, Kenneth O. 1959. *Trade and politics in the Niger Delta, 1830–1891*. Oxford: Oxford University Press.

Dobinson, I. 1997. What impact has the return to Chinese sovereignty had on Hong Kong criminal justice system? *Current Issues in Criminal Justice* 9(2):180–183.

Doolan, B. 1991. *Principles of Irish law*. Dublin: Gill and MacMillan.

Dooley, Edna. 1995. Homicide in Ireland 1972–1991. Dublin: Department of Justice.

Doorley, B. 1987. Newgate Prison. In *The gorgeous mask: Dublin 1700–1850*, edited by David Dickson, 121–131. Dublin: Trinity History Workshop.

Dore, Ronald P. 1958. *City life in Japan: A study of a Tokyo ward*. Berkeley: University of California Press.

Dore, Ronald. 1987. *Taking Japan seriously: A Confucian perspective on leading economic issues*. London: Athlone Press.

Downey, B. 1976. Combating corruption: The Hong Kong solution. *Hong Kong Law Journal* 6(1):27–66.

Drug Enforcement Administration (DEA). 1985. *Drugs of abuse*. Washington, D.C.: U.S. Department of Justice.

Du, Xichuan, and Linyuan Zhang. 1990. *China legal system: A general survey*. Beijing: New World Press.

Duke, Benjamin. 1986. *The Japanese school: Lessons for industrial America.* New York: Praeger.

Durkheim, Emile. 1933, reprinted 1964. *The division of labor in society.* New York: Free Press.

Duus, Peter. 1967. *Feudalism in Japan.* New York: Alfred A. Knopf.

Ebbe, Obi N. I. 1977. The seriousness of selected criminal offenses: A cross-cultural inquiry. Master's thesis, Western Michigan University, Kalamazoo.

_____. 1982. *Crime in Nigeria: An analysis of characteristics of offenders incarcerated in Nigerian prisons.* Ann Arbor: University Microfilms International.

_____. 1985a. The correlates of female criminality in Nigeria. *International Journal of Comparative and Applied Criminal Justice* 7:171–192.

_____. 1985b. Power and criminal law: Criminalizing conduct norms in a colonial regime. *International Journal of Comparative and Applied Criminal Justice* 9 (2):113–122.

_____. 1988. Juvenile justice system in southern Nigeria. *International Journal of Comparative and Applied Criminal Justice* 12 (2):191–204.

_____. 1989. Crime and delinquency in metropolitan Lagos: A study of crime and delinquency area theory. *Social Forces* 67:751–765.

_____.1996. The judiciary and criminal procedure in Nigeria. In *Comparative and international criminal justice systems: policing, judiciary, and corrections,* 1st edition, edited by Obi N. I. Ebbe, 103–122. Boston: Butterworth–Heinemann.

_____. 1997. Political–criminal nexus in Nigeria: An excerpt. *Trends in Organized Crime* 3(1):73–77.

_____ .1999a. The Political–criminal nexus "Slicing Nigeria's National Cake":

The Nigerian Case. *Trends in Organized Crime* 4(3):29-59.

_____ .1999b. Customary justice: a day in an informal court of justice in Nigeria. In *Global report on crime and justice (United Nations Office for Drug Control and Crime Prevention),* edited by Graeme Newman, 72. New York: Oxford University Press.

_____ .1999c. Informal customary justice in Nigeria. In *Global report on crime and justice (United Nations Office for Drug Control and Crime Prevention),* edited by Graeme Newman, 122. New York: Oxford University Press.

Edgeworth, Linda, et al. 1991. *Sierra Leone: A pre-election assessment report.* Washington, D.C.: International Foundation for Electoral Systems.

Edwards, Terry. 1995. University of Louisville, Justice Administration. Phone conversation with author, April 7.

Elias, Oluwale Taslim. 1954. *The groundwork of Nigerian law.* London: Routledge & Kegan Paul, Ltd.

_____. 1963. *The Nigerian legal system.* London: Routledge & Kegan Paul, Ltd.

_____. 1967. *The British Commonwealth: The development of its law and Constitution—Nigeria,* Vol. 4. London: Steven & Sons, Limited.

_____. 1972a. *The Nigerian magistrate and the offender.* Benin City: Ethiope Publishing Company.

_____, ed. 1972b. *Law and social change in Nigeria.* Lagos, Nigeria: Evans Brothers Ltd.

Encyclopaedia Britannica. 1983. *Prisons and penology,* 15th edition 14: 1097–1104.

Encyclopaedia Britannica.1998. *Book of the year 1998.* Chicago: Encyclopaedia Britannica, Inc.

Encyclopedia of new China. 1907. Beijing. Foreign Language Press.

Extradition Law. 1954. Jerusalem, Israel.

Fairchild, E. 1993. *Comparative criminal justice systems*. Belmont, CA: Wadsworth Publishing Company.

Fairmanner, S. 1992. Equal opportunities in two countries. Master's dissertation, University of Exeter, England.

Fang, Y. 1988. Public Security Organization. In *Analyzing informal mechanisms of crime control: A cross-cultural perspective*, edited by Mark Findlay and Ugljesa Zvekic. Rome: United Nations Research Institute for Social Development (UNRISD).

Federal Bureau of Investigation. 1992. *Crime in the United States 1991*. Washington, D.C.: U.S. Government Printing Office.

Federal Bureau of Investigation. 1994. *Uniform crime reports for the United States—1993*. Washington, D.C.: U.S. Department of Justice.

Felkenes, George T. 1989. Courts, sentencing, and the death penalty in the PRC. In *Social control in the People's Republic of China*, edited by Ronald Troyer, John Clark, and Dean Rojek, 141–158. New York: Praeger Publishers.

Fennell, C. 1993. *Crime and crisis in Ireland: justice by illusion*. Cork: Cork University Press.

Fishman, G., V. Kraus, and H. Lever. 1982. Factors affecting juvenile court decisions in Israel: a multivariate approach. *Sociological Inquiry* 52(4): 292–305.

Fishman, G., and A. Ratner .1997. The Israeli criminal justice system in action—is justice administered differentially. *Journal of Quantitative Criminology* 13(1): 7–28.

Flanagan, Timothy J., and Kathleen Maguire. 1991. *Sourcebook of criminal justice statistics—1990*. Washington, D.C.: Bureau of Justice Statistics, U.S. Department of Justice.

Flynn, Frank T. 1951. Employment and Labor. In *Contemporary corrections*, edited by Paul W. Tappan, 238–253. New York: McGraw-Hill.

Forde, M. 1987. *Constitutional law of Ireland*. Cork: Mercier Press.

Foucault, Michael. 1977. *Discipline and punish: The birth of the prison*. Translated by Alan Sheridan. New York: Pantheon Books.

Fox, Vernon B., and Jeanne B. Stinchcomb. 1994. *Introduction to corrections*. Englewood Cliffs, NJ: Prentice Hall.

Frager, Robert, and Thomas P. Rohlen. 1976. The future of a tradition: Japanese spirit in the 1980s. In *Japan: The paradox of progress*, edited by Lewis Austin, 255–278. New Haven, CT: Yale University Press.

Friedmann, R. R. 1998. Assessing the knowledge-base toward the twenty-first century. In *Crime and criminal justice in Israel*, edited by R. Friedmann, 391–418. Albany, NY: State University of New York Press.

Fu, Hualing. 1991b. Police accountability: The case of the People's Republic of China. *Police Studies* 14:40–49.

Fukui, Haruhiro. 1977. Studies in policy-making: A review of the literature. In *Policymaking in contemporary Japan*, edited by T. J. Pempel, 22–59. Ithaca, NY: Cornell University Press.

Funke, Gail S., Billy L. Wayson, and Neal Miller. 1982. *Assets and liabilities of correctional industries*. Lexington, MA: Lexington Books.

Fyfe, Christopher, and Eldred Jones. 1968. *Freetown: A symposium*. Freetown: Sierra Leone University Press.

Gallagher, G. P. 1992. *Risk management behind the blue curtain: A primer on law enforcement liability*. Arlington, VA: Public Risk Management Association.

Gates, D. F., and D. K. Shah. 1992. *Chief: My life in the LAPD*. New York: Bantam Books.

Geary, R. 1985. *Policing industrial disputes 1893–1985*. London: Methuen.

Gelatt, Timothy A. 1982. The People's Republic of China and the presumption of innocence. *The Journal of Criminal Law and Criminology* 73:259–316.

Geller, William A. 1992. *Deadly force: what we know, a practitioner's desk reference on police involved shooting*. Washington, D.C.: Police Executive Research Forum.

George, Aurell A. 1988. Japanese interest group behaviour: An institutional approach. In *Dynamic and immobilist politics in Japan*, edited by J. A. A. Stockwin et al., 106–137. Honolulu: University of Hawaii Press.

Geva, R. 1998. Community policing in Israel: planning, implementation and organizational change. *The Police Chief* LXV (12):77–81.

Gifford, Lord. 1986. *Independent enquiry into the disturbances at Broadwater Farm Estate—Tottenham*. London: Broadwater Farm Enquiry.

Gill, Howard B. 1931. The prison labor problem. *Annals of the American Academy of Political and Social Science* 157:83–101.

Glensor, R. 1990. Community oriented policing—plus. Report for the Reno Police Department, August.

Goldstein, H. 1977. *Policing a free society*. New York: Ballinger.

_____. 1990. *Problem oriented policing*. New York: McGraw-Hill.

Gong, Jian-guo. 1989. Interpretation of the constitution and statutes of the People's Republic of China. *Criminal Justice Review* 14:166–175.

Gottfredson, Stephen D., and Sean McConville. 1987. *America's correctional crisis: Prison populations and public policy*. Westport, CT: Greenwood Press.

Grassi, A. 1989. Combating organized crime: The Maxi trials in Sicily. In *Transnational crime: Investigative responses*, edited by Harold Smith, 37–46. Chicago: OICJ.

Gray, P. 1991. Juvenile crime and disciplinary welfare. In *Crime and justice in Hong Kong*, edited by H. Traver and J. Vagg. 25–41. Hong Kong: Oxford University Press.

_____. 1998. Sovereignty and juvenile justice in Hong Kong. *Journal of Youth Studies* 1(2):23–34.

Greve, V., O. Ingstrup, S. V. G. Jensen, and M. Spencer. 1984. The Danish system of criminal justice: An outline." Paper delivered at the Fourth Colloquy on the Use of Computers in the Administration of Justice and Computers in Correctional Administration and Links with Criminal Justice, sponsored by the Council of Europe, Copenhagen.

Griffiths, Arthur. n.d. *Oriental prisons: Prisons and crime in India, the Andman Islands, Burmah, China, Japan, Egypt, Turkey*. London: Grolier Society.

Gutteridge, H. C. 1949. *Comparative law: An introduction to the comparative methods of legal study and research*, 2nd ed. Cambridge: Cambridge University Press.

Haberfeld, M., S. Kutnjak Ivkovich, and C. B. Klockars. 1998. The measurement of police integrity in Israel. Unpublished paper presented at the 50th annual meeting of the American Society of Criminology, Washington, D.C.

Hagan, F. E. 1987. *Introduction to criminology*. Chicago: Nelson-Hall.

Halford, A. 1987. Until the twelfth of never. *Police Review* 18:2013–2019.

Hane, Mikiso. 1982. *Peasants, rebels, and outcastes*. New York: Pantheon Books.

Harrell-Bond, B., and Ulrica Rijinsdrop. 1974. *Family law in Sierra Leone: A research report*. Leuiden: Sierra Leone. Africa Studicentrum.

Harris, J., and M. Todaro. 1970. Migration, unemployment and development: A two sector analysis. *American Economic Review* 3:126–142.

Hashimoto, Noboru. 1983. Japan's use of volunteers in community-based treatment. In *Proceedings of 12th Annual Congress of Correction*, 183–189. College Park, MD: American Correctional Association.

Hassin, Y., and M. Horovitz. 1998. Juvenile and adult probation in Israel. In *Crime and criminal justice in Israel*, edited by R. Friedmann, 316–336. Albany, NY: State University of New York Press.

Hayashi, Shuji. 1988. *Culture and management in Japan*. Translated by Frank Baldwin. Tokyo: University of Tokyo Press.

Hazou, Winnie. 1990. *The social and legal status of women: A global perspective*. New York: Praeger Publications.

Heikers, D. 1993. Fernando Collor De Mello. *U.S. News and World Report* 114 (January 11):12.

Heilbronn, Gray N. 1990. *Criminal procedure in Hong Kong*. Hong Kong: Longman Group (Far East) Ltd.

Henderson, Dwight. 1985. *Congress, courts, and criminals: The development of federal criminal law, 1801–1829*. Westport, CT: Greenwood Press.

Herzog, S. 1998a. Police violence in Israel: the complaints against police officers. Unpublished doctoral dissertation. The Hebrew University of Jerusalem, Israel.

_____. 1998b. Police violence in Israel: evaluating the civilian police board. Unpublished paper presented at the 50th annual meeting of the American Society of Criminology, Washington, D.C.

High court of justice. 935/89. Ganon against the Attorney General.

High court of justice. 3846/91. Maoz against the Attorney General.

Hiromatsu, Yashiro. 1972. *History of penal theory and practice of penalties* (in Japanese). Tokyo: Sobunsha.

_____. 1973. History of penal institutions in Japan. *Law in Japan* 6:1–48.

Hirst, M. 1990. *The ACPO statement of common purpose and values—New Scotland Yard*. London: HMSO.

Hoffman, Mark S., ed. 1991. *Info Please*. New York: The World Almanac.

Holdaway, S. 1990. *Recruiting a multi racial police force*. London: HMSO.

Home Office. 1982. *Report of a study group: Recruitment into the police service of members of ethnic minorities*. London: HMSO.

Home Office. 1989a. *Equal opportunities policies for the police service*. Home Office Circular 87/89. London: HMSO.

Home Office. 1989b. *Review of police consultancy arrangements*. Home Office Circular 62/1989. London: Home Office.

Home Office. 1995. *Digest 3: Information on the criminal justice system in England and Wales*. London: HMSO.

Hong Kong Federation of Youth Groups. 1998. *A study on the age of criminal responsibility in Hong Kong*. Hong Kong: Author.

Hornum. F. 1986. The criminal justice system of Denmark. In *International criminal justice system*, edited by Dorothy H. Bracey and Charles R. Fenwic, 2–14. Omaha, NE: The Academy of Criminal Justice Sciences.

Houlihan, M. 1986. *The relevance of the courts in anti-social behavior*. Limerick: Mid-West Regional Development Authority.

Hubbard, Sally. 1992. The Halford Case . . . *The Independent*, July 26, 38.

Humpheries, D., and D. Greenberg. 1981. The dialectics of crime control. In *Crime and capitalism*, edited by David Greenberg, 205–254. Palo Alto, CA: Mayfield.

ICAC Review Committee. 1994. *Report of the ICAC Review Committee*. Hong Kong: Government Printing Department.

Igbinovia, P. 1984. A comparative and analytical appraisal of crime and criminality in Nigeria. *International Journal of Offender Therapy and Comparative Criminology* 3:11–19.

Ignatief, M. 1978. *A just measure of pain*. London: Penguin Books.

The important documents of the First Plenary Session of The People's Political Consultative Conference. 1949. Beijing: Foreign Languages Press.

Inciardi, James A. 1984. *Criminal justice*. New York: Academic Press.

Ingraham, Barton L. 1987. *The structure of criminal procedure laws and practice of France, the Soviet Union, China, and the United States*. New York: Greenwood Press.

Ishida, Takeshi. 1983. *Japanese political culture: Change and continuity*. New Brunswick, NJ: Transaction Books.

Ishii, Ryosuke. 1980. *A history of political institutions in Japan*. Tokyo: University of Tokyo Press.

Israel National Police. 1996. *Community policing in Israel*. Jerusalem, Israel.

_____.1998. *Annual report 1998*. Jerusalem, Israel: Ministry of Internal Affairs.

Israel Prison Service. 1998. *Annual report 1998*. Jerusalem, Israel: Ministry of Internal Affairs.

Jackson, R. M. 1953. *The machinery of justice in England*. Cambridge: University Press.

Japanese Correctional Association. n.d. *A guide to CAPIC*. Tokyo: Correctional Association Prison Industry Cooperative.

Jasanoff, Sheila. 1989. *Science on the witness stand. Issues in Science and Technology*, 80–87. New York: Russell Sage Foundation.

Jepsen, J. 1991. Denmark. In *Imprisonment today and tomorrow: International perspective on prisoners' rights and prison conditions*, edited by Dirk van Zyl Smit and Freider Dunkel, 99–160. Boston: Kluwer Law and Taxation.

Jiang, Bo, and Yisheng Dai. 1990. Mobilize all possible social forces to strengthen public security—a must for crime prevention. *Police Studies: The International Review Of Police Development* 2:1–9.

Johnson, Chalmers. 1978. *Japan's public policy companies*. Washington, D.C.: American Enterprises Institute for Public Policy Research.

Johnson, Elmer H. 1983. Neighborhood and the police: The People's Republic of China. *International Journal of Comparative and Applied Criminal Justice* 7:209–215.

Jones, Kenneth, Louis Shainberg, and Curtin Byer. 1979. *Drugs and alcohol*. New York: Harper and Row.

Jones, S. 1987. *Policewomen and equality*. London: MacMillan.

Jones, T., J. Young, and B. MacClean. 1982. *Islington crime survey: Crime, victimization, and policing in inner-city London*. Brookfield, VT: Gower.

Juran, J. M. 1989. *Juran on leadership for quality*. London: Free Press.

Kaplan, Irving, et al. 1976. *Area handbook of Sierra Leone*. Washington, D.C.: U.S. Government Press.

Karibi-Whyte, A. G. 1964. Some recent amendments to the criminal code (Nigeria). *Nigerian Law Journal* 10:156–164.

Kasumu, A. B. 1978. *The Supreme Court of Nigeria*. London: Heinemann.

Kayode, O., and E. Alemika. 1984. An examination of some socioeconomic characteristics of inmates of a Nigerian prison. *International Journal of Comparative and Applied Criminal Justice* 8 (1):85–91.

Keay, E. A., and S. S. Richardson. 1966. *The nature of customary courts in Nigeria*. London: Sweet & Maxwell.

Keefe, William J., William H. Flanigan, Morris S. Ogul, Henry J. Abraham, Charles O. Jones, and John W. Spanier. 1990. *American democracy: Institutions, politics, and policies*, 3rd ed. New York: Harper and Row.

Keogh, E. 1997. *Illicit drug use and related criminal activity in the Dublin metropolitan area*. Dublin: Garda Headquarters.

Kercher, L. C. 1981. *The Kenya penal system*. Washington, D.C.: University Press of America.

Kinsey, R., J. Lea, and J. Young. 1986. *Losing the fight against crime*. London: Basil Blackwell.

Kiralfy, A. K. R. 1967. *The English legal system*. London: Sweet and Maxwell.

Kolasa, Blair, and Bernadine Meyer. 1987. *The American legal system*, 2nd ed. Englewood Cliffs, NJ: Prentice-Hall.

Korn, Richard, and Lloyd McCorkle. 1959. *The Highfields story: An experimental treatment project for youthful offenders*. New York: Holt.

Kosai, Yutaka, and Yoshitaro Ogino. 1984. *The contemporary Japanese economy*. Translated by Ralph Thompson. London: Macmillan.

Kouhashi, Hiroshi. 1985. Courts' selection of offenders to be placed under probationary supervision. Paper delivered at UNAFEI, Tokyo.

Kowalski, B. J. 1993. Death-penalty debate. *World Press Review* 40(4):28.

Krase, Jerome, and Edward Sagarin. 1980. Formal and informal social control in cross-cultural perspective. In *Crime and deviance: A comparative perspective*,

edited by Graeme R. Newman. Beverly Hills, CA: Sage Publications.

Kube, E. 1989. Technological research and international crime. In *Transnational Crime: Investigative responses*, edited by Harold Smith, 125–132. Chicago: OICJ.

Kuhn, A. 1998. "Overview of the differences in prison population around the world." Unpublished paper presented at the 12th International Congress on Criminology, Seoul, Korea.

Kurian, G. T. 1989. *World encyclopedia of police forces and penal systems*. New York: Oxford University Press.

Kyokai, Keimu. 1943. *Manuscript for history of Japanese prison administration in modern age* (in Japanese). 2 vols. Tokyo: Keimu Kyokai.

Landau, S. F. 1999. Personal communication, e-mail: January 1999.

Landau, S. F., and L. Sebba. 1998. Victimological research in Israel: past and current perspectives. In *Crime and criminal justice in Israel*, edited by R. Friedmann, 359–387. Albany, NY: State University of New York Press.

Langworthy, Robert H., and Lawrence Travis, III. 1994. *Policing in America: A balance of forces*. New York: Macmillan Publishing Company.

Law of Criminal Procedure (consolidated version). 1982. Jerusalem, Israel.

Law of Criminal Procedure—Enforcement Powers and Arrests. 1996. Jerusalem, Israel.

Law of northern Nigeria. 1963. Lagos: Government Printing Press.

Law Reform Commission. 1993. *Consultation paper on sentencing*. Dublin: The Stationery Office.

Law yearbook of China. 1992. Beijing: China's Law Press.

Lee, F. W. L. 1998. The police role in the prevention of juvenile crimes. *Journal of Youth Studies* 1(2):35–41.

Lee, J. 1989. *Ireland 1912–1985: Politics and society*. Cambridge: Cambridge University Press.

Legum, Colin, ed. 1961. *Africa: A handbook*. London: Anthony Blood.

Leiserson, Michael. 1966. Political opposition and political development in Japan. In *Regimes and oppositions*, edited by Robert Dahl, 341–398. New Haven, CT: Yale University Press.

Leng, Shao-Chuan. 1982. Criminal justice in post-Mao China: Some preliminary observations. *The Journal of Criminal Law and Criminology* 73:204–237.

Lethbridge, H. J. 1985. *Hard graft in Hong Kong*. Hong Kong: Oxford University Press.

Leung, Sharon S. K. 1998. The effectiveness of rehabilitation programmes for young offenders in Hong Kong. *Journal of Youth Studies* 1(2):11–22.

Levene, Ricardo. 1937. *A history of Argentina* (translated by William Spence Robertson). New York: Russell and Russell.

Lewis, Orlando F. 1922. *The development of American prisons and prison customs, 1776–1845*. Montclair, NJ: Patterson Smith.

Lindquist, John H. 1988. *Misdemeanor crime: Trivial criminal pursuit*. Newbury Park, CA: Sage.

Lo, T. W. 1993. *Corruption and politics in Hong Kong and China*. Buckingham: Open University Press.

_____. 1998. Juvenile justice system in Hong Kong. *Journal of Youth Studies* 1(2):115–126.

Lo, T. W. , S. W. Wong, W. T. Chan, S. K. Leung, and C. K. Chan. 1997. *Research on the effectiveness of rehabilitation programmes for young offenders: Full report*. Hong Kong: Government Printing Department.

Local Courts Act, No. 20.1963. Government of Sierra Leone. Freetown: Government Printer.

Lock, J. 1987. How long must she wait. *Police Review* 95:1810–1811.

Lombardo, Lucien X. 1989. *Guards imprisoned: Correctional officers at work*. Cincinnati, OH: Anderson Publishing Company.

Lubman, Stanley B. 1983. Emerging functions of formal legal institutions in China's modernization. *China Law Reporter* 4:196–266.

Lugard, Frederick. 1913. *Sir Frederick Lugard: Political memorandum*. Ibadan, Nigeria: National Archives Library, University of Ibadan.

Luhmann, Niklas. 1979. *Trust and power*. New York: John Wiley.

Luiz, A. F. 1993. Penal philosophy: A perspective from Brazil. *American Jails* 6:70–71.

Luthra, M. 1986. *Increasing the black in the blue line: Some key questions on recruitment of black officers and equal opportunities in the police*. London: HMSO.

Ma, Stephen K. 1986. Reform corruption: A discussion on China's recent development. *Pacific Affairs* 58 (4):129–136.

Manning, P. K. 1989. The occupational culture of the police. In *The encyclopedia of police science*, edited by L. Hoover, et al. Dallas: Garland Press.

Mao, Tse-tung. 1966. *Four essays on philosophy*. Peking: Foreign Language Press.

Marcussen, E. 1981. *Social welfare in Denmark*, 4th rev. ed. Copenhagen: Det Danske Selska.

Marenin, O. 1989. Ghana. In *World encyclopedia of police forces and penal systems*, edited by G. T. Kurian, 146–151. New York: Oxford University Press.

Martin, J. M., and A. T. Romano. 1992. *Multinational crime: Terrorism, espionage, drug and arms trafficking*. Beverly Hills, CA: Sage Publications.

Martin, S. E. 1979. Policemen and police-women: Occupational role dilemmas and choices of female officers. *Journal of Police Science and Administration* 7:314–323.

Martin, Steve J., and Sheldon Ekland-Olson. 1985. *Texas prisons: The walls came tumbling down.* Austin: Texas Monthly Press.

Masland, John W. 1946. Neighborhood associations in Japan. *Far Eastern Survey* 15 (23):355–358.

Maurice, J. F. 1981. *Politics in Denmark.* London: St. Martin's Press.

McAuley, F. 1993. *Insanity, psychiatry and criminal responsibility.* Dublin: Round Hall.

McCabe, Edward J. 1989. Structural elements of contemporary criminal justice in the People's Republic of China. In *Social control in the People's Republic of China,* edited by Ronald J. Troyer et al., 115–129. New York: Praeger Publishers.

McCabe, Sarah. 1988. *The police, public order, and civil liberties: Legacies of the miners' strike.* New York: Routledge and Paul.

McCaghy, Charles H. 1980. *Crime in American society.* New York: MacMillan.

McCullagh, C. 1996. *Crime in Ireland: A sociological introduction.* Cork: Cork University Press.

McKenzie, I. K., and Gallagher, G. P. 1989. *Behind the uniform: Policing in Britain and America.* New York: St. Martins Press.

Melossi, Dario, and Massimo Pavarini. 1981. *The prison and the factory: Origins of the penitentiary system.* Translated by Glynis Cousin. London: Macmillan.

Merton, Robert. 1968. *Social Theory and Social Structure.* NY: Free Press.

Mesch, G., and G. Fishman. 1998. Entering the system: Ethnic differences in closing juvenile criminal files in Israel. Unpublished paper presented at the 50th annual meeting of the American Society of Criminology, Washington, D.C.

Metcalf, Dac. 1990. *Report into the Trafalgar Square Riots of 30 March 1990.* London: Metropolitan Police.

Michael, Jerome, and Mortimer Adler. 1971. *Crime, law and social science.* Montclair, NJ: Patterson Smith.

Ministry of Justice. 1990a. *Community-based treatment of offenders in Japan.* Tokyo: Rehabilitation Bureau.

Ministry of Justice. 1990b. *Correctional institutions in Japan.* Tokyo: Correction Bureau.

Ministry of Justice. 1991. *Annual report of statistics on corrections for 1990,* Vol. 1. Tokyo: Correction Bureau.

Ministry of Justice. 1993. *Annual Report of Statistics on rehabilitation for 1992.* Tokyo: Rehabilitation Institute.

Moeran, Brian. 1984. *Last innocence: Folk craft patterns of Onta Japan.* Berkeley: University of California Press.

Munro, Donald J. 1977. *The concept of man in contemporary China.* Ann Arbor: University of Michigan Press.

Munyard, T. 1988. Homophobia at work and how to manage it. *Personnel Management,* June, 48.

Nagel, Stuart S. 1972. The rights of the accused: Overview, effects, causes. In *The rights of the accused,* edited by S. Nagel. Beverly Hills, CA: Sage.

Nakamura, Hachiro. 1968. A re-examination of Chonaikai (Urban Ward Association). In *Readings in urban sociology,* edited by R. E. Pahl, 190–207. Oxford: Pergamon Press.

Nakamura, Takafusa. 1981. *The postwar Japanese economy.* Tokyo: University of Tokyo Press.

Nakane, Chie. 1981. *Japanese society.* Tokyo: Charles E. Tuttle.

Narinam, Fali S. 1993. La Universalidad de los derechos humanos. *Rev. de difusion de la Corte Internacional de Justicia*, No. 50, Suiza (Julio), 21.

National Institute of Justice (NIJ). 1993. *Videotaping interrogations and confessions*. Washington, D.C.: Department of Justice.

NIJ. 1995. *NIJ research plan: 1995–1996*. Washington, D.C.: U.S. Department of Justice.

Newcombe, Tod. 1993. High-tech tools for war on crime. *Governing*, August, 20–21.

Newman, Graeme (ed.) 1999. *Global report on crime and justice (United Nations Office for Drug Control and Crime Prevention)*. New York: Oxford University Press.

Newton, Ronald C. 1977. *German Buenos Aires 1900–1933: Social change and cultural crisis*. Austin, TX: University of Texas Press.

Nigerian Constitution Order-in-Council. 1960. Lagos, Nigeria: Government Printing Press.

Nigerian Law Reform Commission. 1983. *Report and draft bills for the reform of prisons in Nigeria*. Lagos: N.L.R.C.

Niven, C. R. 1957. *A short history of Nigeria*. London: Longmans, Green & Co., Ltd.

Noda, Tosiyuki. 1976. *Introduction to Japanese law*. Translated by Anthony H. Angelo. Tokyo: University of Tokyo Press.

Northern region law report, 94. 1960. Lagos: Nigerian Law Reform Commission.

Nwabueze, Boniface B. 1963. *The machinery of justice in Nigeria*. London: Butterworths.

O'Brien, Patricia. 1982. *The promise of punishment: Prisons in nineteenth-century France*. Princeton, NJ: Princeton University Press.

Obilade, A. O. 1969. Reform of customary law court systems in Nigeria under the military government. *Nigerian Law Journal* 3:29–36.

_____. 1979. *The Nigerian legal system*. London: Sweet and Maxwell.

Odekunle, F. 1978. Capitalist economy and the crime problem in Nigeria. *Contemporary Crises* 2:83–96.

Ogawa, Taro. 1976. Japan. In *Criminology: A cross-cultural perspective*, Vol. 2, edited by Dae Chang, 586–656. Durham, NC: Carolina Academic Press.

Okonkwo, Cyprain O., and Michael Naish. 1964. *Criminal law in Nigeria (excluding the North)*. London: Sweet and Maxwell.

Oloyede, E. O. 1972. The present scope of the Nigerian criminal law." In *Law and social change in Nigeria*, edited by Taslim O. Elias. Lagos, Nigeria: Evans Brothers, Ltd.

O'Mahony, Paul D. 1992. The Kerry babies case: Towards a social psychological analysis. *Irish Journal of Psychology* 13(2):223–238.

_____. 1994. The Irish psyche imprisoned. In *The Irish psyche*, special commemorative edition of the *Irish Journal of Psychology* 13(2):456–468.

_____. 1996. *Criminal chaos: seven crises in Irish criminal justice*. Dublin: Round Hall Sweet and Maxwell.

_____. 1997. *Mountjoy prisoners: A sociological and criminological profile*. Dublin: Stationery Office.

_____. 1998. The Constitution and criminal justice. In *The evolving Irish Constitution*, edited by T. Murphy and P. Twomey, 183–197. Oxford: Hart.

Onyema, Ugochukwu. 1984. The return of the military. *West Africa* (9 January):53–56.

_____.1996. Fraud in Nigeria. NaijaNews at the University of Michigan (Internet news).

Opolot, J. 1976. *Criminal justice and nation building in Africa.* Washington, D.C.: University Press of America.

———. 1979. Organized crime in Africa. *International Journal of Comparative and Applied Criminal Justice* 4:177–183.

———. 1980. Analysis of crime in Africa by the mass media in the 1960s and 1970s. *International Journal of Comparative and Applied Criminal Justice* 4:43–48.

———. 1981. *Crime in the new states of Africa.* Washington, D.C.: American University Press.

Ossorio, M. 1992. *Diccionario de ciencias juridicas, politicas y sociales,* de. Heliasta, 20 edic. act., corregida y aumentada por cabanellas de las cuevas, G., Arg.

Ostrom, E., R. Parks, and G. Whitaker. 1978. *Patterns of metropolitan policing.* Cambridge, MA: Ballinger.

Owomero, B. 1987. Crime rates and development in Africa: Empirical analysis of data from Nigeria, Kenya and Tanzania. *Indian Journal of Criminology* 2:107–120.

Ozaki, Robert S. 1978. *The Japanese: A cultural portrait.* Tokyo: Charles E. Tuttles.

Palmer, John W. 1973. *Constitutional rights of prisoners.* Cincinnati, OH: Anderson.

Parker, H., M. Casburn, and D. Turnbull. 1981. *Receiving juvenile justice.* Oxford: Blackwell.

Parsons, Talcott. 1951. *The social system.* New York, New York: The Free Press.

Perkins, Rollin M., and Ronald N. Boyce. 1984. *Criminal law and procedure.* Mineota, NY: The Foundation Press.

Pettigrew, T. F. 1989. Police and ethnic minorities. Paper read at a conference on Police Organizations and Minority Groups. Noordwijk, Netherlands, January.

Pharr, Susan J. 1990. *Losing face: Status politics in Japan.* Berkeley: University of California Press.

Pinheiro, P. S. 1992. The legacy of authoritarianism in democratic Brazil. Paper presented at the Fifth University Seminar on Human Rights, Columbia University, New York.

Plath, David W. 1964. *The after hours: Modern Japan and search for enjoyment.* Berkeley: University of California Press.

Police Act, No. 7. 1964. Government of Sierra Leone. Freetown: Government Printer.

Public Committee (headed by Or). 1997. *The public committee for the revision of the courts' structure: report.* Jerusalem, Israel: Ministry of Justice.

Questions and answers on the professional work of the procuratorate. 1986. Beijing: Law Publishing House.

Quinney, Richard. 1975. *Class, state, and crime: On the theory and practice of criminal justice.* New York: David McKay Company.

Raffell, A. 1994. The Prosecutions Division of the legal department. In *Introduction to the Hong Kong criminal justice system,* edited by M. S. Gaylord and H. Traver. 55–108. Hong Kong: Hong Kong University Press.

Rahav, G. 1998a. Criminal statistics. In *Crime and criminal justice in Israel,* edited by R. Friedmann. 65–78. Albany, NY: State University of New York Press.

——— .1998b. Juvenile delinquency. In *Crime and criminal justice in Israel,* edited by R. Friedmann. 76–96. Albany, NY: State University of New York Press.

Raphey, D.M. 1979. Racial discrimination in urban police departments. Cited in Winship, P.J. 1982. *Towards a multiracial police service.* 19th Senior Command Course, Police Staff College: Bramshill, Hants.

Reid, Sue Titus. 1992. *Crime and criminology*. New York: Holt, Rinehart and Winston.

_____. 1994. *Crime and criminology*. Orlando, FL: Harcourt Brace and Co.

Reiman, Jeffrey. 1998. *The Rich get Richer and the Poor get Prison: Ideology, Class, and Criminal Justice*. Boston: Allyn & Bacon.

Reiner, R. 1992. Fin de siecle: The police face the millennium. *Political Quarterly* 63 (1):37–49.

_____.1994. Policing and the police. In *The Oxford Handbook of Criminology*, 705–772. Oxford: Clarendon Press.

Reiss, A. 1992. Police organization in the twentieth century. In *Modern policing*, edited by M. Tonry and N. Morris,. Chicago: University of Chicago Press.

Ren, Jianxin. 1993. Stop smuggling illegal immigrants into foreign countries. *People's Daily*, Aug. 7.

Report of the conference on the safety of women. 1993. Dublin: Stationery Office.

Report into restrictive practices in the legal profession. 1990. Dublin: Stationery Office.

Richelson, Jeffrey T. 1988. *Foreign intelligence organization*. Cambridge, MA: Ballinger Press Company.

Roberts-Wray, Sir Kenneth. 1959. The need for study of native law. *Journal of African Law* 1:82.

Rodriquez, M. 1989. Strategy and reality. In *International drug trafficking*, edited by Dennis Rowe, 135–152. Chicago: OICJ.

Rogers, J. 1989. Theories of crime and development: An historical analysis. *Journal of Development Studies* 25:314–328.

Rojek, Dean G. 1985. The criminal process in the People's Republic of China. *Justice Quarterly* 2:117–125.

Rottman, D. 1984. *The criminal justice system: Policy and performance*. Dublin: N.E.S.C.

Rottman, D., and P. Tormey. 1985. Criminal justice system: An overview. In *The report of the committee of inquiry into the penal system*. Dublin: Stationery Office.

Samaha, Joel. 1993. *Criminal law*, 4th ed. Minneapolis: West Publishing.

Santos Rodrigues, J. J. 1993. The new beat of black Brazil sets the pace for self-affirmation. *New York Times*, April 1.

Satchell, M. 1988. The just war that never ends. *U.S. News & World Report*, December 19.

Sato, Tsuneo. 1990. Tokugawa villages and agriculture. In *Tokugawa Japan: The social and economic antecedents of modern Japan*, edited by Chie Nakane and Shinzaburo Oishi, 37–80. Tokyo: University of Tokyo Press.

Satoh, Kunpei. 1989. Rehabilitation services in Japan: Present situation and problems. Paper delivered at UNAFEI, Tokyo.

Scarman, L. J. 1981. *The Brixton disorders: 10–12 April 1981*. (Cmnd, 8427). London: HMSO.

Schafer, S. 1976. *Introduction to criminology*. Reston, VA: Reston Publishing Co.

Sellin, Thorsten. 1938. *Culture, conflict and crime*. New York: Social Science Research.

Serrill, M. S. 1977. Profile Denmark. *Corrections Magazine* 3:23–29, 34–43.

Sessions, William E. 1992. Image technology: Enhancing investigative capability. *Vital Speeches of the Day* (unpublished essay collection), 624–626.

Seymour, James D. 1987. Cadres accountability and law. *Australia Journal of Chinese Affairs* 3:95–107.

Shacher, L. 1994. Criminal procedure. In *Yearbook on Israeli law 1992–1993*, edited by A. Rozen-Tzvi. Tel-Aviv, Israel: Faculty of Law of the Tel-Aviv University.

Shadmi, E. 1998. Police and police reform in Israel: The formative role of the state. In *Crime and criminal justice in Israel*, edited by R. Friedmann, 207–241. Albany, NY: State University of New York Press.

Shavitt, G. 1998. The Israeli prison system. In *Crime and criminal justice in Israel*, edited by R. Friedmann. 275–314. Albany, NY: State University of New York Press.

Sheleff, L. 1998. Punishment, prisoner's rights and pardons. In *Crime and criminal justice in Israel*, edited by R. Friedmann. 245–274. Albany, NY: State University of New York Press.

Sheley, Joseph F. 1995. *Criminology: A contemporary handbook*, 2nd ed. Belmont, CA: Wadsworth Publishing Company.

Shelley, L. 1982. *Crime and modernization*. Carbondale: Southern Illinois University Press.

Shihgetoh, Hozumi. 1943. The Tonari-Gumi of Japan. *Contemporary Japan* 12:984–990.

Shikita, Minoru. 1972. The rehabilitative programmes in the adult prison of Japan. *International Review of Criminal Policy* 30:11–19.

Shikita, Minoru, and Shinichi Tsuchiya. 1990. *Crime and criminal policy in Japan from 1926 to 1988*. Tokyo: Japan Criminal Policy Society.

Shivji, I. G. 1982. Semi-proletarian labor and the use of penal sanctions in the labor law of colonial Tanganyika. In *Crime, justice and underdevelopment*, edited by Colin Sumner, 40–60. London: Heinemann.

Si, Wen. 1989. The forging system of people's mediation. *Outlook Weekly* 42:9.

Siegel, Larry J. 1989. *Criminology*. St. Paul: West Publishing.

––––––––. 1992. *Criminology: Theories, patterns, and typologies*, 4th edition. St. Paul: West Publishing.

Skitt, B. 1991. The implementation of equal opportunities in the police service. Unpublished papers, The Police Staff College, Bramshill, Hampshire, England.

Skolnick, J., and D. Bayley. 1986. *The new blue line: Police innovations in six American cities*. New York: Free Press.

Skolnick, Jerome H., and James Fyfe. 1993. *Above the law: Police and the excessive use of force*. New York: Macmillan.

Smith, D. J. 1982. *Police and people in London: A survey of Londoners*. Report No. 618. London: Policy Studies Institute.

Smith, J. 1988. *Psychology, homosexuality and homophobia*. New York: Haworth Press.

Smith, J. C., and B. Hogan. 1978. *Criminal law*. London: Butterworths.

Smith, Robert J. 1961. The Japanese rural community: Norms, sanctions, and ostracism. *American Anthropologist*. 63:522–533.

Sobel, Lester A. *Argentina and Peron 1970–75*. 1975. New York: Facts on File, Inc.

Sparrow, M., M. Moore, and D. Kennedy. 1990. *Beyond 911: A new era for policing*. Basic Books: New York.

Spitzer, Steven. 1983. The rationalization of crime control in capitalist society. In *Social control and the state: Historical and comparative studies*, edited by Stanley Cohen and Andrew Scull, 321–333. Oxford: Martin Robertson.

Steiner, Kurt. 1965. *Local government in Japan*. Stanford, CA: Stanford University Press.

Stephens, Gene. 1990. High-tech crime: Fighting the threat to civil liberties. *Futurist*, July/August, 20–25.

Stewart, J. K. 1989. International research and the federal role. In *Transnational crime: Investigative responses*, edited by Harold Smith. Chicago: OICJ.

Stucky, G. 1986. *Procedures in the criminal justice system*. Columbus, OH: Charles E. Merrill.

Sumner, C., ed. 1982. *Crime, justice and underdevelopment*. London: Heineman.

Sykes, Gresham M. 1958. *The society of captives: A study of a maximum security prison*. Princeton, NJ: Princeton University Press.

Tadao, Kiyonari. 1979. Small businesses. In *Politics and economics in contemporary Japan*, edited by Murakani Hyoe and Johannes Hirschmeier, 157–182. Tokyo: Japan Culture Institute.

Takigawa, Seijiro. 1972. *A history of prison administration in Japan* (in Japanese). Tokyo: Seikeibou.

Talarico, S.M. 1987. Social control in the People's Republic of China. *Criminal Justice Review* 15:137–139.

Tamuno, T. 1970. *The police in modern Nigeria*. Ibadan, Nigeria: Ibadan University Press.

Taylor-Cooke, R. Whately. 1886. *Introduction to a history of the factory system*. London: Bentley and Son.

Taylor, O. P. 1975. The position of women under Sierra Leone customary law. In *African indigenous law*, edited by T. O. Elias, S. N. Nwabara,, and C. O. Akpamgbo. Nigeria: University of Nsukka.

Taylor, S., N. Ainsworth, and P. Gallan. 1990. *The Metropolitan Police seminars on recruiting and retention of black and Asian officers: Analysis of data from seminar, July 1990*. London: Metropolitan Police.

Terrill, Richard T. 1984. *World criminal justice systems*. Cincinnati, OH: Anderson Publishing Company.

_____. 1987. *World criminal justice systems: A survey*. Cincinnati, OH: Anderson Publishing Company.

Thames Valley Police. 1990. *Making quality contact*. London: Report of Thames Valley Police.

The criminal law and the criminal procedure law of China. 1984. Beijing: Foreign Languages Press.

The criminal procedure law of the People's Republic of China. 1982. *The Journal of Criminal Law and Criminology* 1:171–203.

The Prison Ordinance. 1971. Jerusalem, Israel.

Thomas, Charles. 1987. *Corrections in America: Problems of the past and the present*. Newbury Park, CA: Sage.

Thompson, Bankole. 1991. Child abuse in Sierra Leone: Normative disparities. *International Journal of Law and the Family* 5:13–23.

_____. 1992. Constitutionalism in Sierra Leone: Prospects—the proposal 1991 Multi-Party Constitution. *Commonwealth Law Bulletin* 18:338–346.

Todaro, M. 1969. A model of labor migration and urban unemployment in less developed countries. *American Economic Review* 16:138–148.

_____, and J. Stilkind. 1981. *City bias and rural neglect: The dilemma of urban development*. New York: Population Council.

Tonomura, Hitomi. 1992. *Community and commerce in late medieval Japan: The corporate villages of Tokuchin-ho*. Stanford, CA: Stanford University Press.

Tournier, P., and M. Barre. 1990. A statistical comparison of European prison systems. In *Prison information bulletin*, 10, edited by Council of Europe. Strasbourg: Council of Europe.

Townsend, Deborah E. 1987. The concept of law in post-Mao China: A case study of economic crime. *Stanford Journal of International Law* 23:78–92.

Traver, H. (ed.). 1994. *Introduction to the Hong Kong criminal justice system*, 95–108. Hong Kong: Hong Kong University Press.

_____. 1994. The Royal Hong Kong police. In *Introduction to Hong Kong criminal justice system*, edited by M. S. Gaylord and H. Traver. 29–50. Hong Kong: Hong Kong University Press.

Traver, H., and M. S. Gaylord. 1991. The Royal Hong Kong police. In *Crime and justice in Hong Kong*, edited by H. Traver and J. Vagg. 98–110. Hong Kong: Oxford University Press.

Treason and State Offences Act, No. 10. 1963. Government of Sierra Leone. Freetown: Government Printer.

Udo, Goro. 1990. Rehabilitation aid hostels in Japan. Paper delivered at UNAFEI, Tokyo.

Umbreit, M. 1980. Danish use of prisons and community alternatives. *Federal Probation* 44 (2):24–28.

Vagg, Jon. 1991. Corrections. In *Crime and justice in Hong Kong*, edited by H. Traver and J. Vagg. 139–152. Hong Kong: Oxford University Press.

Van Wolferen, Karel. 1989. *The enigma of Japanese power*. London: Macmillan.

Vito, Gennaro, and Ronald Holmes. 1994. *Criminology: Theory, research and policy*. Belmont, CA: Wadsworth.

Wagatsuma, Hiroshi, and George A. DeVos. 1984. *Heritage of endurance: Family patterns and delinquency formation in urban Japan*. Berkeley: University of California Press.

Walsh, William F. 1932. *A history of Anglo-American law*, 2nd ed. Indianapolis: Bobbs-Merrill.

Wang, Zheng. 1993. Some new crime trends in China: Their impact on the United States. *Police Studies: The International Review of Police Development* 17:12–23.

Ward, Richard H. 1985. The Police in China. *Justice Quarterly* 2:111–115.

Weschler, J. 1993. *The Human Rights Watch global report*. New York: Human Rights Watch.

West Africa annual. 1971. Lagos, Nigeria: John West Publications.

West, Nancy. 1992. New Hampshire Police defend use of high-tech snooping to find marijuana growers. *New Hampshire News*, 11 October.

Westney, D. Eleanor. 1987. *Imitation and innovation: The transfer of Western organizational patterns in Meiji Japan*. Cambridge: Harvard University Press.

Weston, Paul B., and Kenneth M. Wells. 1987. *The administration of justice*, 5th ed. Englewood Cliffs, NJ: Prentice-Hall.

Whitaker, Arthur P. 1956. *Argentina upheaval: Peron's fall and the new regime*. New York: Praeger.

Whittacker, B. 1979. *The police in society*. London: Methuen.

Wong, R. 1998. Sentencing options for young offenders in Hong Kong. *Journal of Youth Studies* 1(2):52–58.

Working Group on Review of the Superintendent's Discretion Scheme. 1994. *Report on review of the Superintendent's Discretion Scheme*. Hong Kong: Government Printing Department.

Woronoff, Jon. 1986. *Politics the Japanese way*. Tokyo: Lotus Press.

Wozner, Y. 1998. Rehabilitation efforts in the state prison service. In *Crime and criminal justice in Israel*, edited by R. Friedmann. 337–355. Albany, NY: State University of New York Press.

Xu, Qingzhang. 1992. "Enterprise crime and public order." In *Enterprise crime: Asian and globe perspectives*, edited by Ann Lodl. Chicago: The University of Illinois at Chicago Press.

Yanigimoto, Masaharu. 1970. Some features of the Japanese prison system. *British Journal of Criminology* 10:209–244.

Yett, C. E. 1989. Employment law for peace officers and other government employees. Unpublished paper, Austin, TX: Attorney General's Office.

Yokoyama, Minoru. 1982. How have prisons been used in Japan? Unpublished paper delivered at the World Congress of the International Sociological Association, Mexico City.

Yoshino, Michael Y. 1968. *Japan's managerial system: Tradition and innovation.* Cambridge: The MIT Press.

Zhang, Min, and Shan Changzong. 1990. Inside China's court system. *Beijing Review* 45:15–20.

Zhang, Xiufu. 1993. Illegal financial institutions are not protected by law. *People's Daily*, July 22.

Zhou, J. 1987. An introduction to the present legal system of the People's Republic of China. *North Carolina Criminal Justice Today* 5:8–15.

Index